Columbus, Shakespeare and
the Interpretation of the New World ∾

Columbus, Shakespeare and the Interpretation of the New World ∿

Jonathan Hart

palgrave
macmillan

First published 2003 by
PALGRAVE MACMILLAN™
175 Fifth Avenue, New York, N.Y. 10010 and
Houndmills, Basingstoke, Hampshire, England RG21 6XS.
Companies and representatives throughout the world.

PALGRAVE MACMILLAN is the global academic imprint of the Palgrave Macmillan
division of St. Martin's Press, LLC and of Palgrave Macmillan Ltd. Macmillan® is a
registered trademark in the United States, United Kingdom and other countries. Palgrave
is a registered trademark in the European Union and other countries.

ISBN 0–312–29615–0

Library of Congress Cataloging-in-Publication Data
Hart, Jonathan Locke, 1956-
Columbus, Shakespeare, and the interpretation of the New World / by Jonathan Hart.
    p.   cm.
  Includes bibliographical references and index.
  ISBN 0–312–29615–0
  1. Shakespeare, William, 1564–1616—Knowledge—Geography.   2. Shakespeare,
William, 1564–1616—Knowledge—America.   3. America—Discovery and
exploration—Historiography.   4. English literature—History and criticism.
5. Geographical discoveries in literature.   6. Columbus, Christopher—In literature.
7. America—In literature.   8. Geography in literature.   9. Explorers in literature.
10. Indians in literature.   11. Islands in literature.   I. Title.

PR3014.H37 2003
—dc21

                                                                        2002074937

A catalogue record for this book is available from the British Library.

Design by Letra Libre, Inc.

First edition: January 2003
10 9 8 7 6 5 4 3 2 1

Printed in the United States of America

For Mary, Julia and James

. . . comme le guy sur vn arbre mort.

Michel de Montaigne,
Sur des vers de Virgile

Contents

Y luego que legué á las Indias, en la primera isla que hallé tomé por-fuerça algunos d'ellos, para que deprendiesen y me diesen noticia de lo que avía en aquellas partes, é así fué que luego entendieron, y nos á ellos, quando por lengua ó señas; y estos han aprovechado mucho.

And as soon as I arrived in the Indies, in the first Island which I found, I took by force some of them, in order that they might learn and give me information of that which there is in those parts, and so it was that they understood us, and we them, either by speech or signs, and they have been very serviceable.

—*Columbus, "Letter of Columbus"*

Preface and Acknowledgements

The first idea for this book, which until recently was called *By Speech or Signs: Columbus, Shakespeare and the Interpretation of the New World,* began at Harvard in 1986–87, but it was not ready to go until 1989–90, when I was completing a research proposal for the Social Sciences and Humanities Council (SSHRC), which along with the British Council, the Fulbright Commission, funded me for this and other projects during the 1990s. My thanks to the directors, trustees, academic committees and staff of those organizations, without whose support I would have had difficulty completing this and other research. The original proposed research for SSHRC was on rhetoric and seduction and focused on America as a woman and the questions of gender boundaries in the colonization of the New World. As I work slowly and had qualms of turning the exception into the rule, a few exceptional tropes, paragraphs and images among a multitude, I put this work aside and decided that, rightly or wrongly, this research on the gendering of the New World in the early modern period was better set in context. Having been a student of irony for some time, it did not surprise me how slow and halting the labor, and that work soon appeared in the area. It was not the first time that my penchant for multiple plots and hesitation led to such a conclusion.

My thanks to these agencies mentioned above and to the faculty, staff and students of the following institutions for having me as an academic visitor, resident scholar, visiting fellow, visiting scholar or researcher in their midst: the School of Criticism and Theory; the Department of English and American Language and Literature, the Department of Comparative Literature, and Kirkland House (Harvard); Clare Hall and the Faculty of History (Cambridge); and to the following institutions for invitations to give talks and seminar papers on this and related topics: the Renaissance Society of America, the Shakespeare Association of America, the Pacific Northwest Renaissance Conference, the International Comparative Literature Association, the Canadian Comparative Literature Association, and the Centre d'Études et de Recherches sur la Renaissance Anglaise de l'Université Paul-Valéry, Montpellier III. As usual, but something not taken for granted, the University of Alberta has shown support, understanding and scope. At Alberta, years ago now, Peter Meekison, Linda Woodbridge and James Forrest helped me to settle in and to explore research opportunities, and present administrators and colleagues have continued in this vein. My thanks also to my students at Alberta and elsewhere, whose perspectives always enriched mine.

The idea for this volume started at Harvard, then began to develop at the School of Criticism and Theory (SCT) in 1988 (then at Dartmouth), then took shape at Harvard in 1992–93, although most of it was completed subsequently at the University of Cambridge and when I was a Fulbright Faculty Fellow at Harvard in 1996–97. Since then I have done some supplementary research to fill in the gaps. My thanks also to Lionel Gossman, Stephen Greenblatt, Geoffrey Hartman, Michael Riffaterre and Hayden

White for getting me involved with SCT at its inaugural conference in 1986 and for lively debate and discussions they provided there. At SCT in 1988, seminars with Thomas Greene and Edward Said, as well as briefer seminars with Roberto González-Echevarría and Robert Stepto and a talk on gender, academic and political geography in New York by Nancy Miller helped me to think anew about questions of colonialism that were in my early schoolbooks and beyond and my times (1976–78) at Sainte Marie-among-the Hurons, where the French Jesuits settled among the Ouendat or Huron from 1639–49. To all my friends and colleagues at Sainte-Marie, who discussed French-European contact among one another and with visiting historians and the public, I give my thanks. At Harvard, my particular thanks to Daniel Aaron, Alfred and Sally Alcorn, Diane Barrios, W. Jackson Bate, G. Blakemore Evans, Bette Anne Farmer, Marjorie Garber, Barbara Johnson, Elena Levin, Donald and Cathleen Pfister and Jan Ziolkowski. The Departments of English and Comparative Literature, as well as Kirkland House, welcomed me with the greatest generosity during three separate years as this book began to take root and unfold in my mind. I have expressed thanks elsewhere so I will briefly add here to what I have said before. With gratitude I remember Harry Levin, mentor and friend. At Cambridge, I would especially like to give thanks to Anthony Pagden (now at Johns Hopkins), who stretched my thinking about Europe and the New World while reminding me of focus. In the Faculty of English and at Trinity College, Cambridge, Anne Barton and Jeremy Maule have been good and generous friends who also welcomed me into their seminars on the Renaissance and on manuscripts respectively. Stephanie Palmer (Faculty of Law) and Philip Ford, at Clare College and the Faculty of Modern Languages, also showed their generosity to my family and me. The President, Fellows, Visiting Fellows and students of Clare Hall and with members of the Faculty of History and at the University of Cambridge, most notably with Maria Athanasopoulou, James Binns, Peter Burke, Philip Charier, Marjorie Chibnall, Stefan Collini, Philip Ford, John Garrod and Mark Kaplanoff, Edward Jarron, Anthony and Belle Low, Sarah Morgan and Diana Smith showed support and intellectual generosity.

Thanks also to my hosts at Harvard, Oxford (Terence Cave, Nigel Smith), Wales (Catherine Belsey, Terence Hawkes, Jane Moore, Christopher Norris), Southampton (Ken Hirshkop), Hull (Tom McAlindon, Rowland Wymer), British Columbia (Daniela Boccassini), Samyung Women's University [Korea] (Dong-Ho Kim, Ker-Yong Park), Nanjing Normal (Yang-qui Gui, Fu Jun), Nanjing (Hai-ping Liu), Hong Kong (Mimi Chan, Q. S. Tong), Montpellier III (Jean-Marie and Angela Maguin, Charles Whitworth), Cambridge, Deakin (Brian Edwards, Robyn Gardner), Melbourne (Ken Ruthven), Madeira (Maria-Alzira Seixo, Maria Luisa Leal), Salford (Peter Buse) and elsewhere since 1992 who heard me give various papers in the field and provided me with stimulating suggestions and questions. More generally, over the years, Ron Ayling, Catherine Belsey, E. D. Blodgett, Nicholas Canny, Ross Chambers, Patricia Demers, Olive Dickason, Milan Dimić, Margaret Ferguson, Peter Hulme, Roxanne Gentilcore, John Greszczuk, Nicole Mallet, Paul Morrison, Christopher Norris, John Orrell, R. B. Parker, Patricia Parker, Mireille Rosello, Gordon Teskey, John Herd Thompson, Robert Wilson, Michael Worton have been supportive and have enriched the field with their own diverse work. I have had too many wonderful teachers at all levels to mention here, but it has been a pleasure to return to questions in *Representing the New World* and here that relate to those my Roman law professor, E. J. Weinrib, introduced me to so brilliantly all those years ago. To my parents, family and teachers, I owe a debt for being examples of those who found pleasure and knowledge in history and literature.

More thanks to the librarians, curators and archivists at Widener, Houghton and the other libraries at Harvard, the John Carter Brown, the Firestone (Princeton), the Rutherford and Special Collections (Alberta), Robarts and Thomas Fischer (Toronto), the Baldwin Room (Metropolitan Toronto), the Royal Ontario Museum (Toronto), Museum London (Ontario), the Glenbow Museum (Calgary), the Provincial Museum of Alberta, the National Gallery (London), the Fitzwilliam and the University Library (Cambridge), the Bodleian (Oxford), the British Library, the Bibliothèque Nationale (Paris), the Archive National in Paris, the Archive d'Outre Mer (Aix), the Bermuda Archives (Hamilton), and too many museums and galleries to note here in Bath, Bristol, Durham, Coggeshall, Bury St-Edmunds, Tetbury, Wells, Cornwall, Paris, Montpellier, Arles, Pezenas, Aix, Leiden, Amsterdam, Vienna, Rome, Florence, Venice, New York, Princeton, Boston, Cambridge, Mass., Denver, Montreal, Ottawa, Toronto, Jasper, Rocky Mountain House, Banff, Waterton, Vancouver, Victoria, Sooke, and so on.

Thanks to the editors who encouraged earlier versions of some of the research that appears here (and which are acknowledged in the notes): Victor Ramraj at *Ariel;* Milan Dimić at the *Canadian Review of Comparative Literature/Revue Canadienne de la Littérature Comparée;* Jean-Marie Maguin at *Cahiers Élisabéthains* and Bruce Ziff and Pratima Rao, editors of *Borrowed Powers* (Rutgers University Press). Editors like these make it much better to write. To the Photography Department at the Fitzwilliam Museum for permission to use the portrait for the cover (M.64 Philip of Spain), my gratitude. Anthony Pagden encouraged my work on the promotion of empire; Ross Chambers enabled me to think about mediation in different ways; Katy Emck helped to widen my perspective on gendered representations of America; Pratima Rao was particularly helpful in suggesting ways to think about appropriation.

Although this study began a long time ago, it would have taken longer still and been far less pleasant to complete without the encouragement of my editor at Palgrave, Kristi Long, and her colleagues, Donna Cherry, Roee Raz, and Rick Delaney; the help of Irene Sywenky; a Camargo Fellowship in France in 2001; and a Visiting Professor and Fellow at Princeton beginning in 2000. Thanks also to François Moreau for his invitation to visit his innovative Le Centre de Recherche sur la Littérature des Voyages at the Sorbonne (Paris IV) and for his hospitality and to Jean Bessière in Comparative Literature (who, as usual, gave me sage advice) and Jean-Michel Lacroix in Canadian Studies and Président de l'Université at the Sorbonne-Nouvelle (Paris III). These scholars made my visits to Paris an even greater pleasure. These opportunities let me put the finishing touches on this manuscript. At Camargo, my thanks to the Trustees, the academic committee, Michael Pretina and his staff for their hospitality and support and to the other fellows who taught me a good deal and with whom I had many memorable conversations: for instance, Robert Duplessis and I explored the Centre des Archives d'Outre-Mer (merci à Jacques Dion et ces collègues là) and he shared his great knowledge of colonial history, and Eric Marty showed a wonderful combination of creating music with the understanding of computers and provided generous support for this and other projects. The British Library and the Archives d'Outre-Mer have kindly given permission to quote from or helpful directives for the use of archival materials. My particular thanks to Dale Miller, the Chair of the Committee for Canadian Studies and his colleagues and staff, for inviting me to Princeton and for their wonderful hospitality, support and intellectual generosity. Dale Miller and Carol Porter were always gracious, kind and engaging hosts to my family and me. Thanks also to Philip Nord, Chair of the Department of History and his colleagues and staff, for having me as a visiting fellow in their midst and for being such splendid and generous hosts in every way. The Davis Center, the Program in Latin American Studies, the fellows talks at Wilson College and the program of the Committee for Canadian Studies helped to provide a stimulating intellectual environment while I filled in the gaps and completed the finishing touches on the book. My thanks also to Sandra Bermann and the Department of Comparative Literature for making me so welcome. Thanks also to Miguel Centeno, Master of Wilson College, and the fellows, students and staff there for being so gracious. The Presidents of Princeton during my stay, Harold Shapiro and Shirley Tilghman, also showed great personal and institutional support for the library and the research area I was working in at Princeton: my gratitude to them. To the administrators who have made my life at Princeton much better, Judith Hanson, Kari Hoover, Margaret Reilly, Randy Setlock, Marcia Snowden, Carol Szymanski, Charlotte Cooney Zanidakis, among others, many thanks. Among the many people at Princeton I wish to thank are Jeremy Adelman, Christine Cheng, Howard Dobin, Robert Fagles, Stephen Ferguson, John Fleming, Anthony Grafton, Emmanuel Kreike, Michèle Lamont, John Logan, Michael Mahoney, Kenneth Mills, Lara Moore, Annalee Pauls, Don Skemer, Karin Trainer, Sarah-Jane Mathieu, Meg Sherry Rich, Robert Tignor and Julia Zarankin. At the Institute for Advanced Study, my particular thanks to Jonathan Israel, Karin Schüller and Liana Vardi; and my gratitude to Lloyd Moote, who so kindly invited me to his early modern group that brought scholars together from well beyond Princeton.

Along the way some others, like Peter Sinclair and Shelagh Heffernan, Steven Mobbs and Pauline Thomas, Philip Ford and Lenore Muskett, have been friends to me, my family and this book. As Montaigne said about friendship, "En l'amitié, c'est vne chaleur generale & vniuerselle, temperée au demeurant & égale, vne chaleur constante & rassize, toute douceur & pollissure, qui n'a rien d'aspre & de poigna[n]t." While I send this book out more generally with thanks to all those who have been there along the way, I particularly dedicate it to my wife, Mary, and our children James and Julia, *merci encore.*

Introduction

Coming to terms with the New World was a matter of interpretation of some places and some people radically different from Europe and Europeans. Although this turning point in history—Columbus' landfall in the Caribbean— was existential, the traces of that moment and its consequences were left to contemporaries and posterity in the form of verbal and visual signs. Columbus' speech and actions soon became written or visual signs to be recorded, interpreted and debated. Representations, already interpretations, begot more interpretations. What Columbus thought he saw and heard soon yielded to what others thought he had said and done. This problem of interpretation haunted his successors and writers like Shakespeare, whose *Tempest* has become a controversial text and performance in debates on colonialism and post-colonialism, and haunts us still. The interpretative paradox, already evident in the syllogism in logic long before Columbus sailed west or Shakespeare wrote his last plays, is that in part a premise is a conclusion and a conclusion a premise. An argument has a pretext and its end begets more arguments. Before Columbus and Shakespeare there were travel and ethnological texts, and both figures, as well as their predecessors, contemporaries and successors, found themselves within, and breaking, the bounds of representational strategies found in the realm of argument and rhetoric that non-fiction and fiction share along some long, shifting and notional boundary. Factual and interpretative realms overlap and presented, and continue to present, difficulties that are not readily resolved.

Understanding involves a vexed problem: where does fact end and interpretation begin? Other related questions arise as part of an inquiry into the nature of people and things: What is this world that appears before me? What is the relation between I and others and is there a possibility of speaking about an "us"? What are these signs before me or us and are they constant or changing or is there a constancy beneath the change or a change beneath the constancy? Can the strangeness of other cultures or the past be understood through interpretation, or is difference or change such that the gap in understanding and communication from culture to culture or across time is insurmountable or at least ever-widening? The problem and difficulty of knowing is at the nub of discussing the meeting of Europeans and Natives in the western Atlantic in 1492 and after. Although the Vikings were in Greenland and northern America centuries before, their stay, while important, was not as influential, widespread and enduring as that of the Spaniards and other Europeans that Columbus inaugurated. The Spanish came for good and affected the lives of all of Europe and, directly and indirectly, all of the Americas or New World. Columbus, for better or for worse or for both, was and is, in Hegel's terms, a world historical figure. His ships left an intellectual and cultural, as well as a commercial wake, that Europeans were, for a while, sometimes slow to identify and comprehend. The lives of Europeans, and of the Natives of the islands and mainland of America, or the Indies, or the Americas, or the New World, as the new lands variously came to be known in Europe, were altered significantly and the meetings, some violent and some peaceful, of these peoples created such a sea-change in both larger cultural groups (Native and European), but especially of those who had had their lands invaded, that it is tempting to talk about Columbus' landfall as one of the key moments in "modernity" if not in human history more generally. Regional, linguistic, religious and political differences qualify the terms "Native" and "European," which are used even if they can sometimes occlude distinctions on both sides of the Atlantic in the centuries this study discusses.

It is no wonder that the Europeans talked of "discovery" as much as about "conquest" because for them, as the Mediterranean island far from Milan was for Shakespeare's Miranda, these lands in the western Atlantic were a place of newness, wonder and, some hoped, uncovering and recognition. By erasing or eliding this term, "discovery," a kind of peripetetic anagnorisis for explorers like Columbus, we lose as much as we gain. It is important to remember the pain, death and disruption that landfall caused for the Natives of the New World, so that to make "discovery" a problematic word is helpful. The Europeans had a tradition of travel-writing that could be as mythographic as proto-ethnographic. From their reading of Herodotus, Pliny, John de Mandeville and others and from oral traditions, Europeans especially brought with them to the New World a set of expectations, gleaned from their tradition, of fantastic natural phenomena, such as pygmies, satyrs, cannibals and Amazons.[1] Europeans were sometimes prone to recognize or hope to discover something that was not actually there. Discovery was not always a triumph of knowledge and God in search of spices and riches, but it could also be a misreading of new lands and peoples. The cautionary function of throwing the term "discovery" into question has been salutary because there was, for so many centuries, a tendency toward a kind of triumphalism that could creep in to the European discovery of America. This tendency was, however, tempered with some idealized views of Natives as wiser and more noble than Europeans, something found in Bartolomé de Las Casas, Michel de Montaigne, John Dryden and Jean-Jacques Rousseau as well as in parts of Columbus' texts as well. The rhetoric of these texts had mixed motives and often a typological function, where America was used to read the signs of Europe or as a kind of ethnological critique or, to use Bertolt Brecht's phrase, an estrangement effect. In "discovering" the New World, the authors and readers would discover their own Old World anew. Recognition was as much about knowledge as about travel. The otherness of travel and the alienation of different cultures or the past was not simply linear or binary but occurred simultaneously on many levels. In an example I will use below, the traditional division between Aztec and Spaniard in the battle for Mexico, while clearing the way for an epic struggle or a tragic fall and permitting the clarity of genre, obscures the alliances between the Spanish forces and other cities in the area of Mexico against the dominant empire of the Mexica (Aztecs). The Spaniards, examples for the Portuguese, French, English, Dutch and other Europeans in the settlement of the New World, were themselves divided and created a body of images and texts that represented their intricate and mixed response to the New World. The English and the French displayed ambivalent and contradictory attitudes toward the Spanish—their power and their precedence in the colonization of the lands in the western Atlantic.[2]

Time, history and human behavior are too complex for a straightforward narrative of the meeting or clash of cultures in the New World. The Natives, although they suffered terribly and unfairly and could appeal to the development of the discourse and laws of human rights that Europe and its colonies developed, did not live in paradise. Wars and disease were known in these lands between the Atlantic and the Pacific oceans, but it was the sheer scale that European organization and writing brought that made this "encounter" sometimes so tragic. While I appeal to various Native perspectives to disrupt the European interpretation of signs they found or made in the New World, because that disruption is important to remember and try to understand, I am here discussing how the Europeans brought their hermeneutical repertoire in representing and interpreting signs in the New World. It is valuable to turn the ethnographical lens back on the Europe, where ethnography was developed, to regard other cultures like those in the western Atlantic. The ethnological urge is something of increasing importance in historical studies.[3] To say that earlier writers displayed this urge is not to say that they are anthropologists in terms of a discipline that developed in the nineteenth century. This shift in points of view has something to do with my own perspective, which attempts to achieve critical distance in order to overcome limitations that time and culture help to create, an urge to the paradoxical situation that an acceptance that my understanding is limited might lead to more understanding of the subject at hand.[4] Just as the Europeans were contradictory and conflicted about reading the signs about the past, even and perhaps mostly when they were certain of what they saw and how they interpreted those signs, so too are all of us who look back at those Europeans and the Natives of the Americas. The well-known idea that in the face of the Spanish invasion Montezuma (Motecuhzoma) also had a divided mind—Bernal Díaz decades later remembered the leader this way and centuries later others, like Tzvetan Todorov, developed this view—also suggests that indigenous responses to the arrival of the Europeans, although often showing different stresses, were as fractured as that of the European account of the meeting of Natives in the western Atlantic.[5] The Aztec (Mexican or Nahua) account, while sharing this view of their leader feeling divided to some extent, provides another perspective. Here, Montezuma is a leader concerned with omens who consults magicians and seers to read the signs of the omens; he sends messengers to find out who the strangers are, sends them gifts, feels terror and apathy because of the new arrivals, considers fleeing, experiences despair before he even encounters Cortés.[6] In this version of the fall of the capital of the Mexica, Motecuhzuma welcomes Cortés like a god who had come back to earth: "Our lord, you are weary. The journey has tired you, but now you have arrived on the earth. You have come to your city, Mexico. You have come here to sit on your throne, to sit under its canopy."[7] Such a description suggests the European claim that the Natives thought them spirits or gods, and I have long been skeptical of such assertions. Can this really be a Native point of view or have Spanish mediations put words in the mouths of the Aztec or at least reoriented them? Miguel Leon-Portilla thinks that the Aztec considered the Spaniards to be Quetzalcoatl and other deities coming back from overseas while the Spaniards, as much as they admired Tenochtitlan (later Mexico City), thought the Aztec barbarians and sought to seize their wealth, convert them, to make them Spanish subjects.[8] It is a constant challenge for ethnologists, historians and others to come to terms with different kinds of historical evidence and notions of individuality in various cultures over time: notions of authorship as well as the textual transmission of early modern works intensify that refractoriness.

One of the cruxes of my book is that textual origins and transmission are problematic and in turn make interpretation refractory. Columbus' text is unstable and is the originary text of an enduring exploration and colonization of the western Atlantic. The complex web of editing, including ideological editing (selection and ordering texts according to propaganda, familial, career or personal concerns, and religious and political myth), translation and primary interpretation (prefatory matter, notes and commentary, introductions) of texts of this European "scramble for America" makes the foundation of the European and Native encounter a sign that is hard to fathom.[9] This double irony, of the blindness of Columbus and that of the later interpreters to the New World, even if often with different blind-spots that might well be owing to changes in historical circumstances and in culture, lies at the heart of my study. This blindness extends to Natives as well. A kind of incommensurability of cultures was partly in operation when various groups of Europeans and Natives met in the western Atlantic. Peoples from distinct cultures have a difficult time seeing the other for what it is. The Aztec were not immune to such blindness, and the historical transmission of their texts, some of which were already full of myth and historical revisionism, complicates the ways of seeing that those of us in later times have in reading the evidence they have left behind. Spanish and other European and European-American mediations have also intervened to make the story more intricate. The "Native" account of the fall of the Aztec, compiled—adapted and translated first as *Visión de los vencidos* (1959), whose title translates literally as "Vision of the Vanquished" but in English appeared as *The Broken Spears* (1962)—has textual problems in provenance and transmission, like some of the other texts I will discuss in this study. The crux, like that in Díaz's account of this invasion, is that this indigenous version appears to have been written decades after the fact. Other problems derive from it being in alphabetic Nahuatl (writing in Latin script, something Spanish missionaries taught the Nahua). This system of written signs already incorporates European thought translating for the Native population their image-based language. The translated account, *Broken Spears,* also involved editing (deleting and modification of the text) and came to include later permutations or interpretations from the eighteenth and twentieth centuries of the earlier texts, presumably from the 1550s.[10] The Spaniards destroyed many Aztec writings, although some missionaries, like Bernardino de Sahagún and Diego de Duran, collected a few codices, saved many songs and narratives and worked out a way of writing Native languages in the Latin alphabet.[11] The textual ambivalence—the Spanish repugnance from, and attraction to, these Nahua cultural and religious works—also created a means of extending, translating and promulgating Nahuatl but in doing so bringing it into the sphere of Latin and romance languages, like Spanish, from an indigenous system of writing that combined "pictographic, ideographic and partially phonetic characters or glyphs, representing numerals, calendar signs, names of persons, place names" and so on.[12] There were many more participants in the battle for Mexico: for instance, the Spanish were divided as Cortés ignored authority to make his march and the Huexotzincas and the Tlaxcalans joined the Spaniards in defeating the Mexica.

One of the principal aims of this comparative study of key cultural and literary texts is to place canonical figures like Columbus and Shakespeare, who hold central places in European if not global culture, in context, both in relation to each other but also in connection with other figures, some well known and others not, involved in exploration, education, writing, and the production of images. The further key context for this goal is to discuss this topic of interpreting the New World, the making sense of speech or signs in the meeting of European and Native cultures actually, as in Columbus' text or in allegories and typologies, such as in Shakespeare's. Despite there being fiction in the archive, as Natalie Zemon Davis, Robert Darnton and other historians have argued, there is also the archive in fiction.[13] The boundaries blur between story and history and sometimes between imagery and image, that is between visual and written representations. There seems to be, as I have suggested, a paradox in that while there is historical change, something in the way we write and interpret remains relatively constant or at least intelligible. Put another way, there is communication across the changing times. This relation between writer and reader, speaker and listener, or painter and viewer is as intricate as it is vital. Rather than seek out an arcane and technical version of semiotics (the science of signs) or rhetoric, I will here adopt a general rhetoric of text and image as one way into this paradox. I do so even though there are drawbacks to such an approach (a word I use because interpretation, like other forms of writing, seem asymptotal) but because this general rhetoric is something, especially as concerns written texts, that was part of education in the early modern period and now. In fact, rhetoric has been a significant element of education in Europe, despite disruptions and geographical shifts in the centers of learning, from early classical times on.[14] This art of oratory and, to use Aristotle's terse definition, of persuasion was part of the education of the ruling classes and by the period under study had percolated down to the schools. Figures such as Erasmus became associated with the importance of rhetoric in the Renaissance, as part of reinterpretation and reaffirmation of classical learning, but the Middle Ages had also made rhetoric one of the cornerstones of instruction. More informally, the relation between speaker and audience and writer and reader would, at least in one of the forms, impact on all people then as it does now. The illiterate, who in a study of representation or mimesis, do not have a great place, would also hear speeches and enter the art of conversation as much as any other group. The relation between speaker/writer/image-maker and audience is the focus of much of my book: problems of authorship, editorial intervention, reproduction and transmission sometimes trouble this connection. What we are looking at is a vital question in this book. Verbal and visual rhetoric are its main concerns. Is the writer or artist trying to persuade the reader or viewer or is there a free artistic space that can, however momentarily, move beyond persuasion, motivation, ideology and political theater? The emphasis here is to read texts and observe images closely from the highly motivated nonfictional texts like Columbus to fictional works like Shakespeare's *The Tempest* and images from woodcuts accompanying the work of Columbus to paintings that might be freer of as direct or motivated patronage. These verbal and visual signs will come to tell an intricate story that breaks up stereotypes—sometimes with stereotypes—and will modify any one-eyed theory of colonialism and postcolonialism.

Historical contexts should connect "postcolonialism" with "colonialism," and this is one of the movements of this book. It is a temptation to see the postcolonial as solely a utopian enterprise freed from history and as an academic study independent of its social contexts. The colonial needs to be in the postcolonial because there is a certain reality principle in the past. While a vision of the future need not be tied entirely to the past, it cannot be ahistorical. Land, property and appropriation are central to the European arrival in the western Atlantic, and this will be the focus of my discussion in the last chapter, partly because the topic needs to be addressed in terms of the colonial and postcolonial and partly because I do not wish to repeat what I have stated elsewhere.[15] Cultural appropriation is something that is an issue in Columbus' texts, both in the ways he appropriates and expropriates Native lands and culture, sometimes literally and with the force of canon and civil law behind him, as well as in those successors who would make Columbus their cultural capital through myth-making and editing his works in the wake of his landfall in the New World. Cultural appropriation is still a central struggle in societies with a history of colonization, such as Australia, where in the Mabo case during the early 1990s the courts overthrew the ancient legal doctrine of *terra nullius*—that lands not possessed in ways the Europeans defined as civil may be settled—which the Portuguese had used in their expansion into Africa over five centuries before. Appropriation extends beyond colonialism into other aspects of the past and present such as trade, cultural and intellectual property, and human rights.

One of the key aspects of my argument is that Columbus, Shakespeare and others who wrote about travel, exploration and the meeting of cultures suggest imagery that relates closely to the visual representations of such themes. The cover of this book is a portrait of Philip of Spain in the Fitzwilliam Museum in Cambridge, while the book jacket of my last study of the New World was a woodcut from the 1493 edition of Columbus' Letter, entitled "Insula hyspana," from the Princeton University copy. Both covers stress the dominance of the Spaniards in the New World over other Europeans and the Natives and slaves for at least the first hundred years after Columbus. A manuscript from the sixteenth century describes the fear and envy of the power of Philip II of Spain, an image that especially dominated English discourse about the New World: it tells of "Kinge Philip of Spayne vncharitably maligning other Christyans" and keeping his markets to himself.[16] Philip as a monarch of the great power of the sixteenth century— Spain—and, from 1552 to 1558, a monarch of England is a dominant figure in the early modern period. For a while, it seemed, at least to Richard Eden, that the union of Spain and England might create a great imperial power. Eden, like Richard Hakluyt, Samuel Purchas and Melchisédech Thévenot, was an editor and collector of materials concerning European travel and exploration.[17] Collections in publication and in museums, libraries and galleries have become widespread and more systematic than they were in the Renaissance. The collection of art and books, Columbus at Princeton and Philip in Cambridge, reminds us that the translation of empire is closely connected with the translation of art and study. Early modern verbal and visual representations suggest that much of Europe was coming to terms with Spain, with Columbus' landfall and the apogee of power under Philip II. The weekend edition of *Financial Times* in London on August 22–23, 1998, ran an article on Philip that showed him in a drawing signed by Ferguson as a giant bureaucrat armed with quill presiding over the Escorial above the title in extra-large letters, "Right Royal Enigma."[18] The drawing has this king-scribe in armor, and as he writes at this desk in the shape of his castle, the viewer can see to the king's left a large stack of papers in an inbox with titles such as "Protestantism," "Inquisition," "France," "Turks," and "Low Countries." The last few letters of the word that should be "Lutherans" is shuffled sideways in the pile. In the outbox the last six letters of "America" are part of the only visible title on the papers. In the waste basket there are papers with titles like "England," "Armada," "Juan de Escobedo" (one of Philip's functionaries murdered in 1578) and "Don Carlos" (Philip's unsettled son, who was murdered and is the subject of Verdi's opera). The reach of Philip, the drawing implies, is not just global in the sixteenth century but extends into the present. Adam Hopkins' accompanying article about an "exhibition celebrating his [Philip II's] quatercentenary" uses a circular technique, asking at the end of the second paragraph, "Are we dealing with a man or a monster?" and returns at the end of the article to the question "whether he was indeed a monster or just a misunderstood man." The center of the article features in a large bold print the phrase "Philip's greatest significance for today is that he set up Spain as the world's first policemen" and it is not surprising to find a comparison to Bill Clinton's United States in the first column in a series of parallels between Philip's century and the twentieth century. In general terms, Hopkins focuses on what he thinks most significant about Philip II:

> Philip was the world's first super-bureaucrat, battling to rule an empire via papers, reports and written instructions, complaining endlessly in marginal notes of his weariness and the impossibility of his self-appointed task.
>
> His greatest significance for today is that he set his country as the world's first police-man, in this role embroiling himself in the most bitter controversies. He still has an impact on Spanish politics.[19]

Hopkins' Philip is an ambivalent figure, the subject of William the Silent, Prince of Orange's *Apologia,* a key text in the Black Legend of Spain, and a person who admired Titian and owned 33 paintings by Hieronymous Bosch by 1574. That Philip II can still evoke so much interest in an exhibition and in a leading article in a key London news-paper 400 years after his death indicates how much the past haunts the present and how history goes underground. In a general history I read in school, *Europe Divided: 1559–1598,* J. H. Elliott begins his ninth chapter, "The Growth of Spanish Power," with a section, "The Problems of Philip II," which examines the mid-1570s as a par-ticularly difficult time for the king as he faced war in the Netherlands and in the Mediterranean; had low tax revenues in the Italian viceroyalties that was increasing the tax burden for his vassals in Castile; he was dependent on Genose bankers, who were masters of the American bullion, to provide bridge financing (making up for revenue shortfalls) for the wars; his possible complicity in, or direction of, the murder of Es-cobedo, and so on.[20] Spain is not as easy to forget today as people might have thought, and certainly at the height of its power, it was the subject of much writing and many images.

How central the example of Spain is, may be occluded because new empires do not like to give much credit to old empires even as they imitate them or are indebted to them. In some ways Philip II moderates between Columbus and Shakespeare. He in-herited the lands that Columbus and others claimed for Spain; was married to Mary I of England in the decade before Shakespeare's birth; and ruled Spain until the play-wright was about 35, including the time of the Spanish Armada, which coincided with the flourishing of the English public theater. Spain was something to be superseded in English texts, first as a hope and then as an actuality. The model of Spain, both positive and negative, in the colonization of the Americas was something that came to be oc-cluded by other European imperial powers in their accounts of their own influence in the region. While I wish to bring Columbus and Shakespeare together in the interpre-tation of the New World, I would also like to call attention to images and paintings and to lesser known artists and writers who represented the Americas. The ghosts of Philip, Columbus and others haunted those who came in their wake, not to mention the Na-tives who had to live with their legacy. The Spanish, contrary to the Black Legend of Spain, also sent some remarkable people to the colonies and had writers who criticized Spain in its colonization there. Stereotypes are not enough even as they persist and per-meate cultures over time. It is the surprising juxtapositions that make the terrain that this book "covers" suggestive.

The dialogue between verbal and visual images, between renowned explorers and writers and those known mainly to specialists, complicates the usual discussion of verbal *mimesis* in philosophy, poetry and history that Plato and Aristotle set out, most notably in *Republic* and *Poetics* respectively. Although my analysis of the visual will be most concentrated in chapters 3 and 4, it will, Osiris-like, scatter itself in fragments throughout the book and thus serve as a reminder that, were there space and time enough, the study would develop its visual dimension. These images can move, not like traditional stereotypes, so that a motion picture, like *The Conquest of Paradise,* combines a narrative movement, dialogue and a sequence of images of Columbus and the Natives. This film, rather than the heroic epic of earlier times, had as its protagonist a French actor playing Columbus speaking English, an image in itself that shows the European and European-American interest in the "original" moment of contact, the great originator and the translation of this event and this figure (once a hero now a hero-villain or just another complex modern person caught in the ambiguity of cultural contact and modernity). The opposition or alternative from within Western culture becomes enacted in a film that was part of a movement in the 1990s (particularly leading up to, and the denouement from, 1992) from a celebration of Columbus' discovery of America to a commemoration and italicizing of that discovery. This is a film that sets out, among many other things, the will to build in the heat and challenges of an unfamiliar nature and the languid corruption of some of Columbus' fellow Spaniards. In this film, Columbus is a grand mixture of contradictions, embodying good and evil but not quite getting beyond it, a flawed visionary who has not quite figured out what Zarathustra has in mind. This and other Columbuses, a figure so interpreted and mythologized, can also overwhelm, particularly in the realm of popular culture and the media, the textual Columbus, the author or figurehead of the *Letter* and the seminal writings attributed to him. This textual Columbus is like a fire-fly over the swamp, disappearing and beckoning over the horizon at once. This less familiar Columbus, although typologically linked to all the other Columbuses and particularly to those in our own time like Gérard Dépardieu playing a Hollywood Columbus with a critical edge, deserves to be better known outside the world of specialists and historians of early modern Europe and the Atlantic world. I shall begin the body of my study with Columbus and his representations of the land and the Natives.

The main part of the book I will almost end with Shakespeare, another illustrious and complex figure. *Shakespeare in Love* is another film about a leading icon, who, like Columbus, is controversial. Shakespeare is many things to many people in the English-speaking world and, like Columbus, has been translated beyond the gates of language. Once the great aesthetic genius, and still that way to many, Shakespeare has become, outside the world of blockbuster films, where he is still witty and in love, a figure appropriated by the Establishment as all things good about England or the English-speaking world and its mission in the world or by radicals or writers from former European colonies who would either talk back to Shakespeare and the imperial center or cast his work as something that rebels against tyranny and false order. There are many Shakespeares between and beyond these, but the aesthetic and political allegories in *The Tempest* have been perhaps the most enduring and pressing issues in Shakespearean studies over the past few decades. This crux is the tension between these two allegorical Shakespeares—the aesthetic and political writer. His New World is an island in the Mediterranean that is and is not Bermuda.

Chapters 2 and 6 are almost bookends, but they will modify and be modified by the other chapters, forging a new context for each figure, so that some chapters focus most on figures that have little currency in general or popular culture. In Chapter 3, "After Columbus," I discuss some of the many written and visual representations of Columbus in the decades and centuries following his landfall. This chapter emphasizes the ambivalent attitude to Columbus, as the originary figure of Spain as a colonizer in the New World: Europeans and others not from Spain could show praise and blame, adulation and envy and other motives in the representation of the "discoverer" of America. As I discuss the example of Spain more widely in the other two books in this series, *Representing the New World* and *Comparing Empires,* I have decided to limit my discussion of it here and to concentrate mostly on Columbus. There is a dance of coming after Columbus, especially among those who discuss him in their writings, that is making a later appearance and taking aim at the great explorer.

In "Sexing America," chapter 4, I shall discuss the gendering of America in erotic terms, in the representation of the New World and its peoples. Sex is one sign in this cultural exchange: interpreting it can be difficult, partly because the rhetoric of seduction was not the only dimension of the representing of sex and gender. Anxiety, voyeurism, attraction, repulsion are important factors in the texts and images of this early contact between European and Native. Although this type of language may have helped to attract readers by appealing to travel as romance and ethnology, it is hard to gauge its significance in the promotion of empire. Recurring types occurred in the texts in this chapter: cannibals, sodomites, Amazons, and other kinds of aboriginal women all appeared in texts that mixed desire, fear and hope. America as a woman is not simply a woman waiting to succumb to desire or rape, which could be construed by over-stressing parts of Walter Ralegh's description of Guiana in 1596. By beginning with Columbus and the Spanish and also discussing the French, I hope to provide a wider context that will show how exceptional are the remarks so well known in English that Ralegh made about Guiana as a woman ready to be taken by force. The myth of the Amazons, which Ralegh made much of, derived from classical and medieval sources. It is possible that some of the representations of sex in the texts and images under discussion are types, but this stock nature does not prevent them from having social, physical or psychological dimensions.

"Between Cultures," chapter 5, will suggest that contact between Natives and Europeans in the New World was many-sided. Mediation through kidnapping, interpretation, translation, trade and marriage—the mixing of cultures—helped to make up variable and intricate cultural practices. The Natives had a great deal of cultural influence, especially on the French and English in the first years of contact. This was a varied exchange. Ambivalent and resistant voices in the documents find expression in all sorts of mediation. Images of the Native in European texts involve translation, ventriloquy, refraction and occlusion. Kidnapping, mediation and *métissage* inform this chapter, which is a coming to terms with some key instances of hostages, go-betweens and the mixing of cultures. The various European and Native groups qualify a unified cultural identity on both "sides" in such an exchange. Go-betweens served as translators, peacemakers, negotiators, so they could evoke hope or provoke suspicion and anxiety in the different cultures. These mediators or go-betweens disturb boundaries, which is a fascinating prospect that will be one of the main concerns of the chapter. Theory and examples qualify each other. Rather than use a theory of the other without instances, I am trying to see what those examples yield. Rhetoric is mediation and persuasion: it can communicate and overpower. Those writing about the past address history: Aristotle and Brecht are suggestive guides as they show the lure and estrangement of *mimesis,* something that pertains to considering the problems of representations of or in the past. Go-betweens or mediators can be scapegoated and excluded in any cultural negotiation. After Columbus, interpreters, that is Europeans, Natives, or others of mixed backgrounds who interpreted signs and languages in negotiations and other cultural mediations, played key roles. The problem of stereotyping becomes a key factor in the representation and interpretation of European and Native mediators of various cultures. These mediators suggest the possibility of a dialogue or community between two different cultures, but they also show their difficult position historically.

Columbus and Shakespeare, although most prominent in chapters 2, 3 and 6, will also be suggestive figures in and for the other chapters. While they will "haunt" the rest of the book, they will have particular importance in chapter 7, "Cultural Appropriation." Both are great cultural icons, not just for Italy and Spain for Columbus or for England or Britain for Shakespeare, but in the wider world as well. In popular culture and in the West, Columbus is the great explorer generally and of America particularly and Shakespeare is an extraordinary exemplar of literature. Both Columbus and Shakespeare are cultural symbols who appropriated knowledge and mythology, stories and history into their worldviews and representations. In turn, they became figures of appropriation, especially to the interpreters and editors of posterity. They became parts of national and imperial pride, Columbus first for Spain and Shakespeare then for England/Britain. The United States came to appropriate both of them in its own myths and in its education: Shakespeare was from the mother country and spoke the same language and Columbus became an honorary American. Apparently, the first public monument to Columbus in the Americas was erected in 1792 in Baltimore and the tercentennial of his landfall was celebrated in New York and Boston.[21] In 1792, for instance, speaking at Harvard, Jeremy Belknap made Columbus into a champion of reason, commerce and science and a man of the Enlightenment:

About the middle of the fifteenth century, when the Portuguese under the conduct of Prince Henry, and afterward of King John II, were pushing their discoveries along the western shore of Africa, to find a passage by the south to India; a genius arose, whose memory has been preserved with veneration in the pages of history, as the instrument of enlarging the region of science and commerce, beyond any of his predecessors. CHRISTOPHER COLUMBUS, a native of the Republic of Genoa, was born in the year 1447, and at the age of fourteen entered on a seafaring life, as the proper sphere, in which his vigorous mind was destined to perform exploits which should astonish mankind.* [Life of Columbus by his son Ferdinand—Chap. 4. See Vol. II. of Churchill's Collection of Voyages.] He was educated in the sciences of Geometry and Astronomy, which form the basis of navigation ; and he was well versed in Cosmography, History and Philosophy. His active and enterprising genius, though it enabled him to comprehend the old systems, yet would not suffer him to rest in their decisions, however sanctified by time or by venerable names; but, determined to examine them by actual experiment, he first visited the seas within the polar circle, and afterward those parts of Africa, which the Portuguese had discovered, as far as the coast of Guiana; and by the time that he had attained the age of thirty-seven, he had from his own experience received the fullest conviction, that the opinion of the ancients respecting the torrid and frigid zones was void of any just foundation.

When an old system is found erroneous in one point, it is natural to suspect it of farther imperfections; and when one difficulty is overcome, others appear less formidable. Such was the case of Columbus.[22]

Belknap's Columbus broke up the old regime and ushered in a new world, which we have come to think of as modernity. He helped, as Belknap mentioned just before this passage, to go beyond the dream of Scipio, Thulé and the pillars of Hercules. This Columbus transformed a world of ideas—geographical, mythological, technical, philosophical and economic.[23] From the old the new system transformed what was to what had been. Winifred Sackville Stoner, Jr.'s "The History of the United States" (1919) appropriated Columbus: "In fourteen hundred and ninety-two/Columbus sailed the Ocean Blue."[24] Shakespeare became part of the school curriculum, was filmed in Hollywood, and spawned festivals in the United States. Shakespeare and Columbus were part of the myth-making and the translation of study that was associated with the translation of empire.

Chapter 7, "Cultural Appropriation: Colonialism and Postcolonialism," will discuss changes in the translation of empire and focus on exploring what cultural appropriation is and its part in imperialism, colonialism, and postcolonialism while suggesting ways in which colonialism relates to cultural property and resistance to it. This chapter will stress that postcolonialism needs to be placed in its context. Imperialism is about the expansion of political property that continues to have repercussions. Cultural appropriation, a question of cultural rights and difference, raises problems of fairness, reciprocity and community. Do postmodernism and postcolonialism help to provide such hope? Possibly, the controversy over cultural appropriation reflects or refracts fault lines in contemporary multicultural societies. In keeping with the framework of the study as a whole, this chapter explores some dilemmas and paradoxes that arise from the topic and the evidence. Colonialism and postcolonialism, then, can also be viewed productively in the context of cultural appropriation, something that needed to be done.

The texts and images of the New World are their own language and signs that we long after try to decipher and understand. The gulf between Columbus and us is vast, just as it was between him and Charlemagne, and Charlemagne and Constantine, and so on. Commercial, technical and technological revolutions, as well as the very "discoveries" that Columbus and others made in exploration, have made that gap perhaps even larger. Shifts in time, place and language make the very act of interpretation vexed, but despite that vexation the attempt to understand and communicate between periods and cultures is ever-pressing.

Some of these shifts occur in the figuration itself. For instance, De La Warre, the only English Lord to come to the New World and to settle early on, seems to have been shifting to keep his name and to try not to be defeated by the experience. His words in the early seventeenth century, written about the time of Shakespeare's *The Tempest,* contained analogous shifts to those found in Columbus' *Letter* and were meant to advertise and justify himself to his associates and nation:

I am so farre from shrinking or giuing ouer this honourable enterprise, as that I am vvilling and ready to lay all I am worth vpon the aduenture of the Action, rather then so Honourable a worke should faile, and to returne vvith all the conuenient expedition I may, beseeching your Lordships, and the rest, not onely to excuse my former wants, happened by the almighty hand: but to second my resolutions vvith your friendly indeauours: that both the State may receiue Honour, your selues Profit, and future Comfort, by being imployed (though but as a weake Instrument) in so great an Action.

And thus hauing plainely, truly, and briefely, deliuered the cause of my returne, vvith the state of our affayres, as we now stand, I hope euery vvorthy and indifferent hearer, will by comparing my present resolution of returne, with the necessitie of my coming home, rest satisfied with this true and short Declaration.[25]

De La Warre was blaming his ill-fortune on his health. He balanced between profit and honor, downplaying his own desire for riches and power and appealing to his readers, people he has promised much to in the enterprise of Virginia, visions of wealth flowing from his own integrity and vindication. He bowed to his audience and appealed with his words, plain, brief and true, to justify his actions. Columbus, while writing over a hundred years before and transforming the European navigational knowledge and worldview, had to justify himself to his backers and protect his reputation and interests in as high terms as possible in the official texts or the accounts sent out for consumption. Columbus is the first in a long line of explorers and leaders of settlements who have to promote themselves and their colonies, to justify the ways of men to men, and De La Warre, trying to break new ground for England, is caught in the predicament of a bold precariousness. The settlements were tentative beginnings but the leaders had to use high astounding terms of paradise, bounty and promise to convince those at home to back them and their colonies. De La Warre, too, could describe a paradise:

> The Countrey is wonderfull fertile and very rich, and makes good whatsoeuer heretofore hath beene reported of it, the Cattell already there, are much encreased, and thriue exceedingly with the pasture of that Countrey: The Kine all this last Vvinter, though the ground was couered most vvith Snow, and the season sharpe, liued without other seeding then the grasse they found, vvith which they prospered well, and many of them readie to fall with Calue: Milke being a great nourishment and refreshment to our people, seruing also (in occasion) as well for Physicke as for food.[26]

This description is more bucolic and pastoral than that in Columbus' tropical paradise. The problem was, too, that De La Warre had become ill in such a land and used that to defend himself against his critics. Columbus, De La Warre and many others had to answer to many critics within their own association, company, court and country, so the expansion to the New World could not be intended as a univocal policy. The Europeans stumbled on imperialism in the West through images of a great and profitable trade with Asia. America got in the way and changed the world and America, too, was changed ineluctably.

The great visions Columbus described did not find full expression in the visual reproductions that accompanied his texts. The woodcuts in the different editions of Columbus' *Letter* were basic types. The illustration for the Basel edition (1493), the "Letter to Sánchez," depicts a dressed Columbus trading with naked Natives under the heading, "Insula hyspana" or "Spanish Island," so that the image was possessing the land for Spain as Columbus' text was. Even the Natives in this woodcut were ambivalent: some are moving away from Columbus while others in fairly equal numbers are approaching him. Columbus is trying to trade or exchange gifts in what might be construed, owing to the nakedeness of the inhabitants, as an Edenic setting. The Florentine edition of the *Letter, La lettera dellisole che ha trouato nuouamente il Re dispagna,* places the King of Spain in the foreground, where he seems to be directing Columbus, who is in a ship across the water.[27] There is no mistaking who is giving direction here, whereas the king did not appear in the Basel woodcut. The naked figures may be giants here. Apparently, as is well known, to save money and time, the printers used woodcuts that represented motifs like the virgin land from books not about the New World or Colum-bus.[28] Both the texts and the images of Columbus' landfall carry with them European myths and preconceptions and in their own ways blur the association with Columbus.

It is to this mythologizing and uncertain blurring of the individuality and distinc-tiveness of Columbus as an author that we now turn. The great original moment of "au-thorship" is, as can still be the case today, caught in the web of illustration, editing and various imprints. Columbus and the Natives, in their first encounter, was a scene revis-ited, but even from the first, it was a problematic moment, something so monumental that Columbus could not be left to be his own publicity. A Columbus workshop would develop as a Shakespeare industry later would. The signs were public from the start, and at the heart lay "misplaced" pictures and displaced manuscripts. There is a gap and an erasure that makes it hard to know, a ghost in the making.

Chapter 2 ~

Columbus and the Natives

I n Jonathan Swift's *Gulliver's Travels*, after his journey to Brobdingnag, Gulliver reports on how Captain Thomas Wilcocks, who has rescued him, receives Gulliver's report of the land of the giants:

> The Captain was very well satisfied with this plain Relation I had given him; and said, he hoped when we returned to *England*, I would oblige the World by putting it in Paper, and making it publick. My Answer was, that I thought we were already overstocked with Books of Travels: That nothing could now pass which was not extraordinary; wherein I doubted, some Authors less consulted Truth than their own Vanity or Interest, or the Diversion of ignorant Readers. That my Story could contain little besides common Events, without those ornamental Descriptions of strange Plants, Trees, Birds, and other Animals; or the barbarous Customs and Idolatry of savage People, with which most Writers abound. However, I thanked him for his good Opinion, and promised to take the Matter into my Thoughts.[1]

The relation that Swift gives to Gulliver in the 1720s is anything but plain. If by the early eighteenth century Swift could satirize the proliferation of travel literature, by the 1990s, especially in the wake of the commemoration of Columbus' first voyage, and in light of a new millennium, people often felt even more saturation, perhaps in particular regard to commentary about the European voyages and their records and narratives. Caution, skepticism and humility are therefore advisable in facing this topic, realizing that, like Gulliver, it is easy to deny vanity vainly. The events that Gulliver represents are anything but common.

Nor have we caught Swift and Gulliver when we read the jarring phrase, "the barbarous Customs and Idolatry of savage People," because in the 1735 edition Swift attaches the prefatory "*Letter from Capt. Gulliver to His Cousin Sympson*," in which Gulliver admits, even before the reader witnesses the four voyages, that he has given up on reforming humanity or the Yahoos, as they are so corrupt as to make such a project absurd.[2] In facing his Yahoo critics Gulliver criticizes them:

> Do these miserable Animals presume to think that I am so far degenerated as to defend my Veracity; *Yahoo* as I am, it is well known through all *Houyhnhnmland*, that by the Instructions and Example of my illustrious Master, I was able in the Compass of two Years (although I confess with the utmost Difficulty) to remove that Infernal Habit of Lying, Shuffling, Deceiving, and Equivocating, so deeply rooted in the very Souls of all my Species; especially the *Europeans*.[3]

It is a commonplace that Swift uses irony and shifts in perspective in service of his satire, so that his reader is off-balance and cannot assume a position for Gulliver and his creator. While Gulliver has called the Amerindians barbarians, he has turned his savage indignation against all of humanity but especially the Europeans. As in *A Modest Proposal,* here Swift is satirizing the blindness of the imperial center. Nor is this an isolated critique of Europe. The King of Brobdingnag, at least in Gulliver's report, hopes that owing to his life of travels Gulliver has escaped the vices of England, which he extols chauvinistically. Nonetheless, the king does not mince words about the English: "But, by what I have gathered from your own Relation, and the Answers I have with much pains wringed and extorted from you; I cannot but conclude the bulk of your Natives, to be the most pernicious Race of little odious Vermin that Nature ever suffered to crawl upon the Surface of the Earth."[4] Not even Gulliver's obstruction and imperial chauvinism can prevent the king from piercing English ideology.

Nor is Swift the first to offer resistance, ambivalence and indignation in the face of European imperialism. In light of the Spanish contact with the Amerindians, Thomas More made his Utopians disdain the gold that the Spaniards so valued and so motivated them to make war on and enslave the Natives. Bartolomé de Las Casas described the Spanish abuse of the Natives and sides with the Indians, saying that the Spaniards dashed the heads of Native babies against the rocks and burned Indians alive for the greater glory of Christ and the twelve apostles.[5] Very soon after Columbus' landfall in 1492, ambivalence over the American enterprise and horror over its excesses occurred within Europe itself. It was difficult for Columbus to convince others to launch his project, but, ever since, the results of the encounter with America have been contested.

As we do not as yet have nearly as many records of what Natives of the Americas thought about Europeans in their encounter during the Renaissance than European views of aboriginal inhabitants (although an increasing number are coming to light), it is difficult to find a balanced view of the Natives. With such an imbalance in evidence, it is important to be as skeptical as possible about European representations of the indigenous peoples. It is also a historical and logical problem to speak about pure indigenous and European cultures and about originary reactions to their first encounters. First indigenous reactions were most often retrospective and involved translation into European languages or Christian idioms. First European reactions to the encounters with Amerindians, though more plentiful, relied on rumor, reports and ex post facto reconstructions of Columbus' first contact, which itself is reconstructed. We do not have "pure," unmediated accounts of the encounter. By definition, any account of the other culture on either side before the encounter would be speculation and legend. This chapter will provide an attempt to find ambivalence and resistance within the European encounter narratives, concentrating on the "Letter of Columbus."

I

The question of the European representation of the Native also relates to the Amerindian representation of the European arrival in, and colonization of, America. One of the difficulties for pre-conquest Native documents, as James Lockhart mentions in relation to the Nahuas of central Mexico, is that even the most informative among them were mostly redone under Spanish influence during the 1540s and after.[6] The Europeans and their American settlers frequently wrote about the Natives from the vantage of conquest and triumph.[7] Gordon Brotherston has attempted to examine the European

myth that the Amerindians had no writing: "when the Europeans did encounter unde-
niable evidence of writing, of literacy equivalent to their own, they did their best to erad-
icate it, because it posed a threat to the Scripture (the Bible) they brought with them."[8]
During the first three decades of the conquest (1492–1519), owing in part perhaps to
the quick decimation of the Natives, there was no Amerindian chronicler of the encounter. It was Bartolomé de Las Casas who rose to write a defense of the Native population.[9] Las Casas also defended the Natives at Valladolid—where in 1550–51, King
Charles of Spain convened theologians and philosophers—against Juan Ginés de
Sepúlveda. The debate centered on whether the Indians were human beings with culture or brutes, as Aristotle defined them, who could become servants to the civilized nations. More generally, since the conquest or encounter in 1492, the Europeans had
viewed the Natives from a theological perspective in which they were identified with the
lost peoples of the Old Testament or as brutes who originated in the "Americas."[10] Las
Casas insisted on a place for the Amerindians as members of a human civil society.[11]

But the represented also represent. Although Native images of the Europeans have
not been widely disseminated, Gordon Brotherston describes a number of important
cases, such as the annals of the Valley of Mexico (1516–25), a Tupi taunt of French missionaries in Brazil (1612) and an Algonkin account of Europeans entering North America (seventeenth century). These three examples represent but a small fraction of the
Native texts that describe the encounter with the Europeans in the first two centuries of
contact. The first instance involves an account of Cortés' invasion of the Aztec empire
that is copied from a screenfold that recorded the history of metropolitan Tenochtitlan
from the twelfth to sixteenth centuries. The annal notes the presence of the Europeans
(*popoloca*) in the calendar when they intervene directly in affairs of national importance.
The Tupi taunt of the French missionaries involves a "carbet" or the form used by braves
to taunt rivals through examples of the braves' own prowess. The account of Europeans
arriving in the late sixteenth century on the mid-Atlantic shore of North America occurs near the end of the second part of the Walum Olum of the Lenape-Algonkin, which
describes in chronicle form the list of successive Lenape *sachems* (chiefs) over a few centuries.[12] The representation of the Natives and the Amerindian representation of the Europeans have left evidence only in the wake of Columbus' encounter with the world of
the western Atlantic. If only briefly, it is important to record this cultural meeting in representation, even if I am focusing here mainly on Columbus' writings about this encounter and how these writings also represent a corporate or collective account subject
to the vicissitudes of production and transmission in the early modern period.

Finding ambivalent and resistant voices in the documents surrounding Columbus'
four voyages to America reminds us that these doubts and oppositions in the text involve
all kinds of mediation. The image of the Native is translated as well as ventriloquized.
Although much has been said about Columbus and his relation to Natives or Amerindians at first contact, we have no documents in his hand describing this momentous event.

Instead, we have Columbus' *Journal* and *Letter,* which, in Cecil Jane's view, he did
not compose, and if he did, it has appeared after much textual and cultural mediation.[13]
It is possible that Columbus, who may have come to literacy late, could not write at this
time, but Jane, who argues this position, has not found incontrovertible evidence to justify the claim. Whether he even recorded the daily occurrences of the first voyage is
based on the reports of Hernando Columbus and Las Casas, who were not with him on
the voyage. This son and this friend are, in Jane's view, liable to idealize Columbus. Possibly, Columbus had a clerk record his thoughts in writing. Clerks and copyists often

edited at this time, so that mistakes and misrepresentations of Columbus are possible, if not probable. The clerk might give to Columbus' words their literary form. When Columbus is speaking in these documents, who actually is speaking?[14] The *Letter* is preserved in edited form and the extent of editing cannot be determined. Las Casas' précis of the *Journal* is not complete and it is difficult to know how vital the omissions are. It is possible to think that these mediations magnify the glory of the voyage and play down the disappointment it caused Columbus. The image of the Native in these voyages involves a high degree of mediation and textual uncertainty, so that when we say that "Columbus" said this or that about the Natives, it should be stated with much care and skepticism and even more than usual with a suspicion of the "author" as an individual agent. Furthermore, there are more recent contentions concerning the nature of Columbus' text and role as colonizer, the one inextricably linked to the other. Text and context are more complex and contradictory than they first appear.

II

Centuries before Swift, then, others in Europe offered resistance, ambivalence and indignation in the face of European imperialism. In fact the ambivalence, if not reluctance, with which the monarchs of Europe, even Ferdinand and Isabella, received Columbus' proposal to sail westward does not present Columbus as a triumphant visionary who had unalloyed and prompt royal backing. Columbus worked hard in seeking a trade route that would bring riches but did not seem to have intended some imperial scheme. Columbus as a site of contesting powers, as an interpretative venture or controversy, is something of which we can speak more readily. The reception of Columbus becomes even more important than it is for Shakespeare and others, as his first and most important "text" is of more uncertain provenance and involves even more textual problems. Like Shakespeare, Columbus has been a cultural icon for centuries and has often been made to sing the imperial theme of European expansion, so that in this age of the global village and of apparent decolonization, the traditional European iconography of Shakespeare and Columbus has been called into question.[15] Like Shakespeare after him, Columbus has been the subject of dozens of biographies (the first of which was by his son Hernando shortly after Columbus' death in Valladolid on May 20, 1506) and many portraits, engravings and other likenesses.[16] Theodor de Bry's engraving of a serious-looking, clean-shaven, long- and wavy-haired and learned Columbus in robes and surrounded by the solemnity of Latin inscriptions proclaiming Columbus as the first person to the Indies; Anthony More's Englished portrait of Columbus as a bearded gentleman with closely cropped hair; Guiseppe Banchero's copy of Antonio del Rincón's portrait of a youthful, long- and straight-haired Columbus; Lorenzo Lotto's striking Columbus, his right hand on a stack of books, his left holding an unfurled scroll of paper, which is more akin to Banchero's copy, but with the head turned to the viewers right rather than left; Leopold Flameng's nineteenth-century Romantic Columbus, with a beard well-cut and with billowing sleeves and a plumed hat, whose work is hinted at by the instrument in his left hand at the bottom right hand of the portrait; Egide Charles Gustave Wappers' almost Lear-like Columbus, the subject of ingratitude and injustice, with rough beard and in chains, staring squarely at the viewer; all show one sample of the variety of Columbuses near the time of his death and in centuries following.[17] In chapter 3 I will discuss other images of Columbus, including a "postcolonial" portrait. Ambivalent and contradictory interpretations of Columbus in print and in images began early. Shakespeare's ambivalence is also well known: Prospero and Caliban are

complex characters in the history of Shakespearean criticism, that is in the oscillation between aesthetic and political hermeneutics. But the ambivalence of Columbus' texts, his
Journal and *Letter,* is often forgotten or elided outside the sphere of specialists in the field
(editors, bibliographers and historians). He was a sailor, a practical man who made history as event and, to some unverifiable extent, history as story. History is both event and
the discourse about event. There is myth in history and history in myth. Experience and
imagination become overlapping parts of the same whole, and so the question of the pri-
ority of mythology or ideology continues to nag at the historian, literary theorist and
philosopher alike. Columbus' *Journal* is a good example of the contested relation between narrative and argument. Its production and textual history show the tangle of
story in dialectic. The *Journal* is supposed to be a description of what Columbus saw, a
ship's log, but it is used to tell a story and has been much argued over.[18] Whether discourse structures material reality or the converse is probably impossible to say and is now
a debate between materialism and constructivism as it once was between materialists and
idealists. Whatever the first cause or provenance, the relation between material events
and the representation of events in writing seems to be reciprocal. History as event and
story are inextricably entwined.

Although I am most concerned with Columbus' *Letter,* I have been taking and will
take a brief detour into the textual life of the *Journal* in order to provide a context for
the controversy over the Columbian canon. While I am not suggesting that we disinte-
grate Columbus as an author into his son Hernando or his editor Bartolomé de Las
Casas—as this would be at its extremes as ill-advised as making Shakespeare into Francis Bacon, the Earl of Oxford or his editors, Heminges and Condell—it is important to
avoid a kind of literalism and naïveté that makes Columbus into a modern author who
is, apparently, master of his own intentions. In *Colonial Encounters* (1986) Peter Hulme
gives a good summary of the difficult and uncertain transmission of Columbus' *Journal:*
"the actual text . . . disappeared, along with its only known copy, in the middle of the
sixteenth century. The only version we have . . . is a handwritten abstract made by Bartolomé de Las Casas, probably in 1552, and probably from the copy of Columbus' original then held in the monastery of San Pablo in Seville. There have subsequently been
various transcriptions of Las Casas's manuscript."[19] The state of textual uncertainty in
Columbus' *Journal* or diario leads David Henige into even more radical bibliographical
skepticism in *In Search Of Columbus* (1991):

> it became routine to treat the diario as if it were almost entirely an undefiled version of the
> shipboard log that Columbus presumably kept. It is true that one-fifth of the diario's text
> purports to be in Columbus's own words. It is also true that by the time Las Casas, in
> whose hand the diario is written, came into possession of whatever text he copied and para-
> phrased, it had undergone an unknown number of transmissions, with all the corruption
> this necessarily entails. To treat the diario as the product of Columbus is simply to banish
> caution and substitute for it a species of credulity that can have little hope of withstanding
> serious scrutiny. Little enough seems certain about the diario, but one thing that should be
> beyond cavil is that its principal author is not Christopher Columbus but Bartolomé de las
> Casas, aided and abetted by Columbus and any number of intermediate scribes. [20]

This kind of textual disintegration has been part of biblical textual scholarship since the
humanists and was especially strong in nineteenth-century Germany. The same kind of disintegration, multiplication and splintering of the text has occurred in Shakespearean editing, most recently in the *Oxford Shakespeare.* Although these textual questions are

interesting, I think they are a means to an end and that we have to shift from conflating the author function with the historical individual. It is probably better to think also of "Shakespeare" or "Columbus" as collective productions depending on writing, editing, printing and reception, and not simply as ground-breaking individuals. The Romantic myth of the individual—of the great man—is still with us despite the great changes in thinking about class and self that have occurred since Marx and Freud and have intensified in conjunction with explorations of questions of race, class and gender since the Second World War. Do we really need to name that author? Is that aspect of Carlyle, Nietzsche and Shaw still with us? Great disputed texts, like the Bible, are received into culture, and while questions of authorship fascinate us and are not without significance, to negate a text because its authorship is uncertain or different constitutes a partial, if not misguided, move. The warnings about Columbus as author need to be considered and, if convincing, heeded, but the "Columbian" texts of which we speak should not be relegated to curious and unread works of doubtful authorship or apocrypha. Paradoxically, it may be that Columbus' texts become even more fascinating cultural documents, though viewed from a new vantage, if the complexities of production, transmission and reception are taken into consideration.

The main focus of this chapter is the relation between world and text. It argues that the writing of Columbus, like Shakespeare's works and the Bible, is full of textual problems and that so much unacknowledged and unknowable editing and transmission have occurred in the texts that to speak of Columbus is to speak about subsequent exchange as much as about the man himself. In this sense, the texts of the encounter move beyond the intentions of the individual author and constitute a collective cultural production.

The mediation between the European observer and the Native that Columbus is representing becomes problematic. The historical document, such as the *Letter* of Columbus, is like a fiction whereby the authority and intention of the author find their complication in the transmission and reception of the document. It is difficult to say who is making Columbus speak in the *Letter*, but out of shorthand, we say Columbus, who is as much an embodiment of the Spanish collective enterprise of the Indies as the captain who convinced the monarchs to back his venture and set sail for the western Atlantic. Except for whatever historians have verified, Columbus' account of his voyages does not differ much from classical travel tales and dozens of other encounter narratives that Richard Hakluyt later brings together in the last decade or so of the sixteenth century. There are wonders, monsters, obstacles, abundant lands and plants and peoples whose local customs need elaborating. Columbus brought the myths of Pliny's natural history with him as much as the descriptions of exotic peoples in Herodotus' history. Discourse attempts to structure the material world, that is the Spanish captain would have liked the new lands to be Marco Polo's Cathay, but Columbus also discovered that America was neither Africa nor Asia. To some extent, the desire that discourse is the world itself, a fantasy today among some postmodern travelers to hyperreality, took hold of Columbus and his successors. The rhetoric of classical travel and historical writing was used as a means of promoting the newfound lands at court at home in Europe, but it was also a block to understanding the Natives and their environment. It may be that the very use of representing the present New World as if it were the China of the European past enabled Columbus and the Spaniards to take possession of those lands without having to come to terms with the rights of the inhabitants.

All this is to say that when we meet once again with the famous opening of what is said to be the *Letter* of Columbus ("Carta de Colón," written, it appears, to Luis de Sant'

Angel) about the first voyage, it is difficult to know just what we are hearing and from whom. The letter proclaims:

> SIR, As I know that you will be pleased at the great victory with which Our Lord has crowned my voyage, I write this to you, from which you will learn how in thirty-three days, I passed from the Canary Islands to the Indies with the fleet which the most illustrious king and queen, our sovereigns, gave to me. And there I found very many islands filled with people innumerable, and of them all I have taken possession for their highnesses, by proclamation made and with the royal standard unfurled, and no opposition was offered to me. To the first island which I found, I gave the name *San Salvador,* in remembrance of the Divine Majesty, Who has marvellously bestowed all this; the Indians call it 'Guanahani'.[21]

There is no original of this letter, which has been reconstructed from four Spanish versions as well as three Italian versions and one Latin version. The report of first contact between Columbus and the Indians is contained in a lost document. This situation is not unusual in the early modern period. After all, we have only a few signatures and perhaps some lines in Shakespeare's hand from the *Thomas More* fragment, but few Shakespearean scholars or editors would suggest this fact as evidence that there never had been originals and that Shakespeare never wrote his plays. Nevertheless, we have to entrust ourselves to intermediaries, to the Heminges and Condells, and hope that with materials as ideologically charged as Columbus' letter and, for that matter, all his writings, that the clerks, printers, historians and others were not tempted, like those whom Gulliver rails against, to change the record. One small example, which has been discovered, might serve as a reminder that there may be more undiscovered instances of ideological editing. In the passage I have just quoted the first Latin translation of the letter of Columbus does not mention the queen and credits only the king for having sent Columbus on his voyage. Did Leandro Costco, the translator, want to credit Columbus' "discovery" for Aragon alone, as Henry Harrisse suggested in 1872, or was it a printing error or a sign of the inability of Castilians, no matter how loyal, to admit the equality of Isabella with Ferdinand, as Cecil Jane speculates in the early 1930s? Columbus' possession of the Amerindians, which had such devastating material consequences for the indigenous populations of the Americas, rests with the editors, whether they be clerks, scribes, notaries, civil servants, lawyers, historians and others, because they have helped to make and reconstruct Columbus' writings and the Columbian legacy. The image of the Native at first contact as a possession becomes closely related to the question: Who is in possession of the text? If Columbus is supposed to have met with no opposition from the Natives, as the letter says, we have to take his word for it or his word reconstructed through editors. Whether by accident or design, Columbus becomes a corporate enterprise based on the legal interests of Spain. The rules and laws of the Pope and the Spanish sovereigns do not consider those of the Natives. In this passage Spanish names, in the name of Christianity and Spanish secular power, replace the Indian names.

III

The letter of Columbus recorded his great expectations. Columbus, as we have him here, clearly wanted to find evidence of a great civilization to convince his sovereigns of the importance of his voyage and the wisdom of their investment:

> I sent two men inland to learn if there were a king or great cities. They travelled three days' journey and found an infinity of small hamlets and people without number, but nothing of importance. For this reason, they returned.
>
> I understood sufficiently from other Indians, whom I had already taken, that this land was nothing but an island.[22]

For Columbus, the many Indians were in his possession, but they were not yet marvelous enough for his ambitions. The lands became the marvelous ("maravilla") while Columbus grew lyrical about its grandeur and, for the moment, seems to forget the people who inhabit it. In summary he proclaims "Española is a marvel" (6; "la Española es maravilla" [7]). In his paean to this world that was new to him he had already introduced cattle and built towns and villages, partly as a means of suggesting Spanish settlement to the court (6).

Columbus' motivation is difficult to interpret, but it seems that he was emphasizing the abundance of the land and the timidity of the people in order to show the potential of this land for settlement, conversion and material exploitation:

> The people of this island, and of the other islands which I have found and of which I have information, all go naked, men and women, as their mothers bore them, although some women cover a single place with the leaf of a plant or with a net of cotton which they make for the purpose. They have no iron and steel or weapons, nor are they fitted to use them, not because they are not well built men and of handsome stature, but because they are marvellously timorous. They have no other arms than weapons made of canes cut in seeding time, to the ends of which they fix a small sharpened stick. And they do not dare to make use of these.[23]

This prelapsarian nakedness did not prevent Columbus from speculating on the Natives' desire and ability to make war. They fled the Spaniards, but later came to give them whatever possessions the Spaniards desired—primarily gold. Columbus said that he soon prevented his men from trading worthless things for gold, and he himself gave the Indians "a thousand handsome good things" ("mill cosas buenas") so they "might become Christians and be inclined to the love and service of their highnesses and of the whole Castilian nation, and strive to aid us and to give us of the things which they have in abundance and which are necessary to us."[24] Whether gold is as necessary as food is left unsaid.

Columbus then emphasized their religion and intelligent explanations. He also represented the Natives as not having a creed and as not worshipping idols. In his image they were a blank slate ready for conversion and did not have any bad religious habits that might prejudice Columbus' opponents in Spain against the Indians and, ultimately, against Columbus' enterprise. These Indians, Columbus said, thought that he and his men were from heaven not because the Natives were unintelligent but because they had never seen people with clothes and such ships. Columbus admired their ability as navigators and, once again, marveled "how good an account they give of everything" (10; "que es maravilla la buena cuenta qu'ellos dan de toto" [11]).[25] His praise of the Indians' powers to give proper account later allowed Columbus to accept an apparent mixture of story and explanation without differentiation.

In the *Letter* of Columbus there are contradictions. Later, Díaz spoke of Montezuma's (Mutezuma's) divided mind, which became a trope in the Spanish view of the fall of the Mexican empire, but Columbus' letter suggested a division in his own mind (or perhaps in the corporate Spanish editorial project on Columbus and the encounter). After having said how timid the Natives were, Columbus admitted that he had taken some of them by force: "And as soon as I arrived in the Indies, in the first Island which I found, I took by force some of them, in order that they might learn and give me information of that which there is in those parts, and so it was that they soon understood us, and we them, either by speech or signs, and they have been very serviceable."[26] Columbus then reiterated that the Natives still treated him like a god and said that they inclined to Christianity, but what he did not emphasize is why he had thought it necessary to use force to capture Indians as interpreters. Was it his ignorance of their timidity or was it a feeling that they were his property because they were, in his eyes at least, subjects and possessions of the crown? Almost like Swift or Borges, Columbus, perhaps with a certain credulity and perhaps not, mixed with fantastic descriptions precise measurements and details of the land. For instance, after having given the measurements of the island Juana, which he said is larger than England and Scotland, Columbus stated that one of its provinces, Avan, contained people that were born with tails.[27]

The possession of gold and the notion of force reassert themselves when Columbus promised Ferdinand and Isabella gold mines and great riches and when he spoke about his fortification of the town, which Columbus names La Navidad. He mentioned that he had left men to fortify it, so that at the time of writing they would have already had completed it. Columbus' anxiety contradicted or conflicted with his earlier claim that the Natives were timid because he had left "sufficient men" ("gente que abasta") for the building and with arms, artillery and provisions for more than a year. The anxious Columbus claimed that he had left them a ship and a master to build others, perhaps in case they had to leave or escape, and added that the king of that land was such a good friend "that he was proud to call me, and to treat me as, a brother" (Jane 14; "que se preciava de me llamar y tener por hermano" [15]). Then Columbus' anxiety became explicit: "And even if he were to change his attitude to one of hostility towards these men, he and his do not know what arms are and they go naked, as I have already said, and are the most timorous people that there are in the world, so that the men whom I have left there alone would suffice to destroy all that land, and the island is without danger for their persons, if they know how to govern themselves."[28] If Columbus' men might not "know how to govern themselves" ("sabiéndose regir") and if the Indians might rebel against Spanish possession, why then is Columbus leaving them there? After this extreme moment of vulnerability and self-justification, Columbus switched the topic.

In a very small space he compressed the topics of women, private property, monsters, race and climate. Men, except the king, seemed content to be with one woman; the Indians shared and did not seem to value property as a private possession. Columbus admitted that he had not come across any "human monstrosities, as many expected."[29] But Columbus proceeded to report at length danger in paradise, a kind of menace that he had heard about but not witnessed, a human monstrosity, that is the coming together of cannibals and Amazons, those that eat men and those who can do without them:

As I have found no monsters, so that I have had no report of any, except in an island "Quaris," the second at the coming into the Indies, which is inhabited by a people who are regarded in all the islands as very fierce and who eat human flesh. They have many canoes with which they range through all the islands of India and pillage and take as much as they can. They are no more malformed than the others, except that they have the custom of wearing their hair long like women, and they use bows and arrows of the same cane stems, with a small piece of wood at the end, owing to lack of iron which they do not possess. They are ferocious among these other people who are cowardly to an excessive degree, but I make no more account of them than of the rest. These are those who have intercourse with the women of "Matinino," which is the first island met on the way from Spain to the Indies, in which there is not a man. These women engage in no feminine occupation, but use bows and arrows of cane, like those already mentioned, and they arm and protect themselves with plates of copper, of which they have much.[30]

Here are monstrous humans who threaten the boundaries of gender roles, men with hair like women and women who fight like men. Columbus' annotations to *Imago Mundi* show that he was aware of these stories of human monstrosities and may have led him to expect them on his voyage: his notes to *Historia Rerum Ubique Gesterum* demonstrate his acquaintance with stories of lands wholly inhabited by women and may have prepared him to expect or be receptive to stories of such women in the lands he encountered.[31] These Native women were fated to be "Amazons," perhaps against all fact and out of the need for such a legend to sustain the European, or at least "Columbus'" worldview. It becomes difficult to know whether the myths and stories of Europe helped to determine the image of the Native. Does history imitate story here or does history as event derive from, or find its form in, history as story? Some of these issues surrounding Amazons and the imputing of Amazonian characteristics to Native women will come up again in the discussion of the "sexing" of America in chapter 4.

The mediation of writing and reading seems to affect the images of the Native in the first contact in Columbus' reading. Perhaps it also has an effect on the transmission and editing of his account as well as on the rhetorical relation between speaker or writer and audience, between Columbus and the sovereigns (whom he had in mind and whom he addressed). And this relation has a very material dimension. Columbus proceeded to promise Isabella and Ferdinand vast riches and slaves in return for their "very slight assistance" (16; "muy poquita ayuda" [17]). In this possible contract, in this quid pro quo, the Natives got lost, were transformed into slaves. These slaves, as many as sovereigns shall order to be shipped, would be chosen from the idolaters, so that Columbus could have a clear conscience and could, with a highly imperfect knowledge of the language and culture of the Natives, decide who practiced idolatry and who did not. Slavery was fine for those Columbus thought worshiped idols instead of Christ. In fact, like Las Casas (i. 46), I do not think that Columbus' forcible possession of the Natives as interpreters was justifiable and I suspect that it marked the beginning of the Spanish maltreatment of the Indians. Columbus took several Natives with him on the voyage home, and only seven survived the journey. One of these survivors acted as an interpreter on the second voyage. As we do not have the Natives' account, we can wonder whether they went on Columbus' ship of their own accord or whether they were forced. Just after having said he would have done much more, if his ships had served him "as reason demanded" (16; "como razón demandava" [17]), perhaps trying to get the sovereigns to outfit him better, Columbus returned to the men he left at Navidad. Here perhaps were the men he had abandoned or pawned as evidence of the success and commitment of Columbus' voyage: they were pawns to his ambition. As he had begun the letter, he ended it—with an appeal to God, "Who gives to all those who walk in His way triumph over things which appear to be impossible" ("el qual da á todos aquellos que andan su camino victoria de cosas que parecen imposibles") like Columbus, who had "ocular evidence" ("vista") rather than the conjectural talk and fables about these lands (18; [19]).[32] The Redeemer had given the king and queen of Spain a great religious and temporal victory. Columbus wished for Spain and Christendom to hold "great feasts" ("grandes fiestas") and give "solemn thanks" ("oraciones solemnes") to the Holy Trinity for "the turning of so many peoples to our holy faith" (18; "en tornándose tantos pueblos á nuestra sancta fe" [19]). He spoke of the conversion as a fait accompli. The ultimate image of the Natives is of two kinds, the devout Christian, and the idolatrous slave. The disturbing implication is that the Natives will not have a choice in the image that the Europeans make for them, and that this image will materially affect their lives beyond recognition.

IV

Columbus had expected to find Asia and great wealth, but his encounter with the Natives without vast and opulent cities came as a surprise to him. He had labored for years to convince a monarch that his way to Asia was the most effective route. A great investment he must have had in his enterprise of the Indies. The admiral arrived in the western Atlantic with great expectations, and the hopes, desires and fears of the Spaniards, who had much invested in the success of this venture, was refracted in the "Columbus" texts.

Whatever the relation of fact to fiction here, as in the case of Columbus' accounts, religious and secular narratives about the New World did not allow Europeans enough wonder and openness to see the world entirely anew. They brought expectations with them that helped to judge the Natives before the actual encounter. History as writing brought with it an encounter before the encounter became a historical event. The image of the Native seems to have preceded the Native, and the Natives soon suffered when they didn't comply to the image and when they did. The image could degrade them as much as idealize them: the price the Natives paid for this "imaging" and "imagining" was material. The Europeans made them into texts the Europeans alone could interpret, and often with ready-made interpretations. This colonial and postcolonial hermeneutic will be the focus of the next chapter and beyond.

In what follows we shall observe that the opposition that Columbus faced in setting up his enterprise was not isolated. Even those who might regard expansion as something positive were not always supportive of the consequences. The abuses by the Spaniards of the Natives became, even among the Spanish themselves, a matter for debate. While focusing on a few important instances, I hope to make more intricate European views of expansion to the Americas. Sometimes in the past decade or so, there has been a tendency to read back later ideas of empire and a kind of triumphalism among Europeans. Some Europeans shared *avant la lettre* some of the indignation and satire of Swift's narrator. The great originary moment of Columbus turns out to be more complex textually and contextually than it is often given credit. It is harder to praise or blame the refractory and elusive. The "moment" is no less significant for being an enigma: the code requires more care and is more elaborate a story than the myths might suggest.

In the following chapters, I will emphasize close textual and visual analysis and examples from colonial texts that will suggest that without such an anchoring of the modern in the early modern or the postcolonial in the colonial, they can become unmoored. The coming to terms with the New World is intricate and I will suggest some problematics of the stereotyping of Columbus, women or the Natives, Shakespeare and his characters, or some writers, readers and theorists of our time. Just as Columbus failed to interpret the fullness of the speech and signs of the Natives he encountered, so too is it equally tempting for us to ignore our blind-spots. Examples will open up preconceptions and suggest some complex and intriguing aspects of the coming of Europeans to the New World.

Chapter 3 ～

After Columbus

The meeting of Columbus and the Natives is a narrative of events that no matter how filtered and problematic is difficult to forget. This defining history as narrative and event has challenged those who have come after Columbus in both senses of that phrase. The uncertain textual provenance of Columbus' work makes the origin of the Spanish and European claims to the New World complex and indeterminate. This problem of authorship, transmission and reception in the late Middle Ages and Renaissance is not uncommon. Columbus became much more than his text, and his image, life and actions were represented in writing and paintings long after his death. The mythology of Columbus, like that of Shakespeare, grew into something well beyond the person and his putative words and signs. The interpretive urge would not leave Columbus alone as a figure either in art, writing, scholarship or the popular and public domain. Unlike Shakespeare, who came to be known for his poetry and theater and in print, even if many of those texts were probably published in circumstances beyond authorial control (about half the plays were printed for the first time after the playwright's death), Columbus was known for his principal action—the "discovery" of the New World.[1] His writing, or at least those texts associated with this landfall and his subsequent voyages, has taken on the properties of a fetish or talisman, as have Shakespeare's dramatic and non-dramatic poetry. Festivals and anniversaries have long celebrated both of these historical figures and both have in the past decades become increasingly associated with the controversies surrounding European expansion and imperialism. Shakespeare never seems to have taken Natives captive or advocated slavery for the indigenous peoples of the New World, but his representation of Caliban, as we shall see later in this study, has become part of the representations of liberation from imperialism and the discourse of colonialism and postcolonialism. The tension between Caliban and Miranda has come to be read as sexual and racial, so that those who come after Shakespeare, as well as those who are after Columbus, have pursued him as well as having read him in the context of their own times. Shakespeare has been imitated in adulation, envy, anger, desire for displacement, as a source of power turned back on itself: Columbus has also generated such contradictory and mixed motives. Some of these mixed responses have arisen over questions of gender: for instance, there is a violent "sexual" side to the Columbian voyages, as in the case of Michele de Cuneo, who whipped a Carib woman whom Columbus had given him during the second voyage until she submitted to him.[2] The representation of sexuality is something that I will discuss more in chapter 4.

No one, not even or perhaps especially figures as significant as Columbus or Shakespeare, can control his or her reputation. Even the most able of representers cannot govern their representation: no matter how carefully the rhetorical contract is managed between writer and reader, it is subject to change over time. The aesthetic power of Shakespeare is seductive for readers and audiences and, while not of the same magnitude in this regard, Columbus' texts hold a great fascination. Some of the common draw that the Shakespearean and Columbian texts share is their narrative and dramatic power. Shakespeare's history plays represent events that are central to the story of England and, as history unfolded, therefore Europe and the world. His more fictional plays—comedies (including the romances at the time of the First Folio) and tragedies—rely respectively on the structure of a movement to a new order in a society and of the fall of a great individual or two remarkable individuals. Columbus' texts combine a fondness for myth and romance with actual historical events. The fascination with interpretation is at the heart of the matter: Columbus provoked disparate views before he sailed for the New World and this difference intensified after his landfall in the New World and his subsequent attempts to claim his rights in the western Atlantic and to win favor with court and country in Spain.

Columbus, like Shakespeare after him, came to be known to such an extent that would have been hard to imagine in his lifetime. This explorer, for instance, in V. E. Fuchs' view, "was difficult, contrary and imaginative; his tendency to support his proposals with inaccurate statements demanded increasing dissemblance to maintain his credibility, and it was this which ultimately led to disgrace in his time. Yet he had the strength to overcome obstacles, and his achievements are honoured in history to a much greater extent than either he or his contemporaries could have thought possible."[3] Columbus is a world historical figure but is not always honored: he helped usher in great changes in the Western hemisphere and in the world at large, the very changes that have helped to make the world we inhabit, yet his means and methods have drawn criticism from the start and have become more part of public and official discourse in schools and government. The view of Columbus, as a man of accomplishment but also of masks and subterfuge, is something that is interesting to contemplate: he may have sought what came to be unreal—a direct western passage by sea from Europe to Asia. He could not admit that he had come upon a new world but adhered to his claim, at least rhetorically, that he had reached Asia.[4] It is easier to look back and see folly or error, but sometimes even the greatest visionaries, thinkers or soldiers cannot take in the magnitude of the events in which they have participated or helped to form.

Columbus is in images and texts, not simply in his time or in 1592, 1692, 1792, 1892 and 1992, but his body and the memorial monuments to him have moved in time as well. For example, there is a memorial tablet to Columbus in the Cathedral of Havana, to which his bones were removed after Spain ceded Hispaniola to France near the end of the seventeenth century; in Seville Cathedral, Arturo Melida sculpted a great tomb of Columbus before a great mural; at the Palazzo Tursi in Genoa, an urn, decorated with the Genoese coat of arms, contains the ashes of Columbus.[5] In Stratford Shakespeare's grave—Oxonian and Baconian claims aside—has a curse on anyone who might move his bones. Even in the deaths of Columbus and Shakespeare, there are different claims. The New World, Spain and Genoa claim Columbus: in the West Indies his memorial changed places according to wars and other vicissitudes just as his reputation has been subject to shifting grounds after "decolonization" and independence. In what follows, I will set out some of the ways Columbus and the "Columbian" are represented, what happens after the explorer's landfall and later death, both in images and words. This chapter, which is selective because if it were not radically so the topic would fill up many volumes in a long line of books about Columbus, should help to provide another context for this figure that supplements that in the previous chapter and gives more particulars that should be a groundwork to the later parts of the study.

I

It is well known that Columbus (Cristoforo Colombo) was an Italian in the service of Spain, but that is easily elided when considering him in the context of the Spanish expansion into the western Atlantic. Columbus, like Shakespeare, has not come down to us in any realistic likeness during his lifetime that can be proven to be of the man himself.[6] The bust of Shakespeare in Holy Trinity Church in Stratford-upon-Avon seems to be the only contemporary image and, although commissioned by the Shakespeare family, is not like the more mysterious image of the posthumous portraits but more that of a burgher. Vanishing origins pertain as much to images of Columbus and Shakespeare as to their manuscripts and unedited texts. The image of Columbus, like that of Shakespeare later on, became a mixture of mythology, iconography and national, imperial or European ideology. These figures have belonged to a cultural symbology.

One of the first images of Spain in the New World was the figure of Columbus and the Natives, a woodcut that includes the heading *Insula hyspana,* in *De Insulis inventis Epsitola,* or the Columbus *Letter,* that J. Wolff printed in Basel in 1493. Chapter 2 discussed the textual and verbal dimensions of Columbus and the Natives, but there was also an important visual aspect to this encounter. Although I discuss the figure from the *Letter* elsewhere, I wish to mention here the nakedness of the Natives, who in this woodcut approach and flee Columbus, who is clothed and in a ship and, being outnumbered as he is with a single confrere, appears to be offering a gift. The Spanish ship in the foreground seems to dwarf any other single person or object in the picture.[7] Another image of Columbus, which depicts Columbus on Hispaniola, this one over 100 years later, can be found in one of the purveyors of the Black Legend of Spain, Girolamo Benzoni, an Italian compatriot, whose *Americae Pars Quarta* was published in Frankfurt in 1594. This Columbus stands square in the front of the picture, with two soldiers behind him, facing a group of almost naked Natives bearing gifts. Behind these soldiers and in the middle ground of the image, three Spaniards have almost erected a cross while others a little back and above the right side of Columbus' head are armed and are guarding the largest of three ships, where other Spaniards are disembarking and beside which, on the land, five naked Natives seem to be involved in dance or some exercise in which they are stretching their limbs. The focus is clearly on Columbus, his staff or spear jutting into the largest ship. In another image from this book, Columbus parts from Ferdinand and Isabella at Palos, a fictional event in the actual place from which he departed to the New World, a kind of interpretation about 100 years after the landfall, something akin in visual terms to Ralegh's invocation of Columbus near the end of *Discoverie of Guiana* in 1596.[8]

There are many visual representations of Columbus, but I will mention only a few here. For instance, Jean François de Troy's painting of Columbus landing in America, painted some time before 1718 and now found in the collection of the Musée des Arts Décoratifs, appears to have been part of a commission from the senate of Genoa, along with work by Francesco Solimena, to decorate the main room in the Palazzo Ducale. In this picture Columbus stands in a central place and has a commanding presence. The Natives adore the cross, which the Spaniards are setting up on the other side of the ship that lies in the background between that point and Columbus. This is an example of a Baroque allegory of the evangelization of the New World found in art and literature of the time, for instance, in Madame du Boccage's epic, *La Colombiade, ou la foi portée au Nouveau Monde* (Paris 1758). The magnitude of Columbus, like that of Shakespeare afterwards, was not recognized fully until two or three generations after his death. Not until 1571 was the biography by Columbus' son, Hernando, published in Venice; in 1581 Torquata Tasso praised him in *Gerusalemme Liberata* (Canto XV, stanzas 30–32); in 1614 Lope de Vega's play, *El Nueuo Mundo descubierto por Cristóbal Colón*, was the first work of Spanish literature that focused on the explorer; other plays, like Cardinal Pietro Ottobani's *Colombo ovvero L'India scoperta* in the versions of 1691, 1710 and 1730 and Pietro Chiari's *Colombo nell'America* (1754), and operas like Fabrizi's *Colombo e la scoperta delle Indie* (1788) and others by Morlacchi (1828), Mela (1857) and Franchetti (1892) and a ballet by Monplaisir (1892) suggested the increasing popularity and recognition of Columbus. It was in his native Genoa that Columbus was remembered mostly as the propagator of the Catholic faith in the New World, for instance in Lazzaro Tavarone's paintings in the Palazzo Negrotto Cambiaso about 1615 and Giovanni Battista Carlone's frescoes of the discovery of the New World in the chapel at the Palazzo Ducale. It took 300 years to set up a statue to Columbus.[9]

Various events of Columbus' life became the subject of paintings among Romantic artists and painters. In 1838 Eugène Delacroix depicted Columbus and his Son, Diego, at the monastery at La Rábida in 1484, where the prior, Juan Peres de Machena, a learned man, befriended them and helped them in their enterprise to find a western route to Asia. In this painting, which is in the National Gallery in Washington, a figure, perhaps the prior, speaks with a fellow monk, who seems to point to Columbus, who looks at a map: this is the explorer who will affect many maps for years to come. A companion piece of 1839, which portrays the return of Columbus from the New World, also by Delacroix, is in the collection of the Toledo Museum of Art. This painting represents Columbus with Natives and riches before Ferninand and Isabella, the rulers who backed his enterprise, who stand high in the right corner at the top of stairs and in front of a throne.[10] The New World has come to the Old, which will never be the same. Hermann Freihold Plüddemann, a German painter, produced a series from circa 1836 about Columbus, but these have been lost. In the Museum Folkwang in Essen a pencil and wash has survived that shows Columbus disputing with the scholars Isabella had assembled at Salamanca in 1486 concerning the plausibility of his western enterprise. Plüddemann's lost paintings included representations of Columbus' arrival at La Rábida, his sighting of America, his appearance before Ferdinand and Isabella in Barcelona, his return in chains after his third voyage and his death.[11] In Plüddemann's sketch of the dispute at Salamanca, Columbus, who has books under his left hand and who rests his right hand on the top of a globe, is the focus of the picture and of most of the attention of those present, who are not engaged in reading or writing. He is the lone advocate of his cause. In the nineteenth century prints also depicted the great events of Columbus' life, and the most popular of these was a set of lithographs by Nicholas Eustache Maurin between about 1835 and 1850, which represented Columbus' landfall, his reception at Barcelona, his "egg-trick" and his return in chains to Spain after the third voyage.[12] His lithograph about Columbus building a fortress shows Columbus shaking hands with a Native chief, and, behind him, there are Native women, half-clad, before Spaniards in dramatic poses: this image can now be found in the cabinet des estampes at the Biblio-thèque Nationale in Paris. In 1870 Claudius Jacquand, a member of the Lyonnais school, painted in oil an image showing Columbus in his last moments, where he, look-ing old and weary, is indicating his chains to his son and the title of the painting em-phasizes that he wants his son to bury him with chains in his coffin, something that would call attention to his humiliation in 1500 when he returned to Spain in chains and his death in obscurity and poverty in Valladolid in 1506. The seated Columbus, in mod-est dress, seems to be speaking to his son, who holds his face in anguish with his hand: both are light figures in a dark room. About this time, other painters like Plüddemann (1840), Pierre Nolasque Bergeret (1851), Joseph Nicolas Robert-Fleury (1860) and Luigi Sciallero (ca. 1870–90) represented the same scene.[13] A portrait of Columbus by Lorenzo Lotto, a Venetian painter, whom I mentioned in chapter 2, was displayed at the Columbian Exposition in Chicago in 1893.[14]

A more postcolonial portrait of Columbus may be found in Museum London, in Ontario—Carl Beam's "Christopher Columbus: The Geometry of Finding Gold" (1990), in which texts and images, in acrylic and photoemulsion on canvas, gloss the image of Columbus and interact to represent the tension of this explorer and his legacy. The portrait of Columbus in the upper lefthand corner takes up about two-fifths of the canvas but is presented in juxtaposition with images of insects and traffic lights, the world of biology and technology that have also defined modernity and the changes to the New World. From these images it is hard to know whether the flies are fruit flies and have implications for genetics and what is the lit-up color of the traffic lights (the image is not in the color as we would see it on a street) so as to give some hint at the symbol-ism of the lights. Beneath the title of the work is a maze and below this are words not always easy to read and with ellipses in which the painter speaks of "establishing a his-tory" amid "autobiographical errata" and "in an alphabet world." While this brief and almost fragmentary comment makes up part of the work, it is suggestive and is not a complete gloss on the painting itself. Here is a painter in the Americas now trying to es-tablish a personal history in terms of Columbus but who is probably well aware of the longstanding group of European and "American" painters who have expressed them-selves through a representation of the famous explorer. What I have called the trope of God and gold is played out in a late-twentieth-century Canadian painting.[15] Coming after Columbus also meant coming after Spain, which, as a consequence of the Columbian enterprise, developed colonies in the western Atlantic. Columbus is the originary figure who haunts other explorers, writers and artists representing the New World. Rather than explore this imaging and imagining of Columbus here as it is a vast topic by itself, I will place Columbus in a different context by shifting to a discussion of the more general imitation and attempts at displacing Spain. Depicting Spain in the New World was novel and ambivalent from the start.[16]

II

Columbus made Spain famous and infamous, and this ambivalent notoriety made the Spanish in the New World a negative and positive example. This doubleness occurred in images not simply of Columbus but of Spain and its colonies more generally. First the negative: the Black Legend of Spain occurred through images as well as through words. In Oppenheim in 1614, J. T. De Bry printed Bartolomé de Las Casas' *Narratio Regionem Indicarum per Hispanos quosdam devastatarum verissima*, which included one image among others, the Spanish cruelty toward Natives, in this case the burning alive of the mostly naked Natives of Hispaniola, men and women, who are hanging by their necks above the flames, while in the background Spanish soldiers, with various instruments of war, including clubs and swords, subdue some more victims not long for this world.[17] While one crouching Spaniard front and center seems with his left hand to be holding and checking the feet of a hanging and burning Native to see how well his left foot is being consumed while with his right hand increasing the flames with a torch, another Spaniard, this one standing, has a naked infant (who appears to be male) by his calves and has parted the legs of the upside-down child and appears ready to dash it against some kind of wall. This anti-Spanish propaganda, which had a strong but not exclusive Protestant element, used Las Casas, who was an advocate of the Natives within a system loyal to the Spanish crown, against Spain. They went after Spain with one of its great patriots who criticized excesses in order to make the Spanish colonies in the Indies stronger: their strength would gather from fairness to the Natives who would prove devout and devoted subjects of the monarchs of Spain. Theodor De Bry, who sometimes created images after Jacques Le Moyne and John White, could also show Native retaliation for Spanish cruelty as he had in an image, "Indi Hispanis aurum sitientibus," in *Grand Voyages,* Part IV, a Latin version published in Frankfurt in 1594, in which the "Indians," male and female, seem, in the background, to be sizing up, cooking, cutting and eating the limbs from Spaniards: in the middle one Spaniard lies naked and bleeding to death from the leg that one Native male seems to be bringing over for cooking and, in the middle ground, another naked Spaniard is about to lose his arm to the coordinated effort of three Native males. In the foreground center, five Natives are attending to yet another bound Spaniard down whose throat they are pouring molten gold as a reward for the violent greed that gold has engendered in the Spaniards. Even though this image has a certain poetic justice to it, for the Natives have suffered at the hands of the Spaniards, it also shows—even if the primary aim is not to do so—that there could be excesses on the Native side as well. De Bry, in an image, *Indianer können der Spanier,* Part IV of the German version of this work (Frankfurt 1594), depicted men, women and children among the Natives of the New World committing suicide in quiet and violent ways rather than submitting to slavery at the hands of the Spaniards. In Part IV, De Bry also portrayed a Spanish attack on the Natives that included all kinds of violence. Moreover, in Part V, De Bry represented the mistreatment of fugitive African slaves in the New World: here, in plate 4, several soldiers even lance one from the height of their horses, not to mention the variety of violent deaths set out in this catalogue of horrors. In Part VI, the sixth volume in De Bry's collection of travel accounts to America and the third volume of three devoted to *Historia del mondo nuouo* by Girolamo Benzoni, there are engravings that show the cruelty of the Spaniards in the conquest of Peru and, in plate 10, how the Natives brought Pizarro great amounts of gold to ransom Atahualpa (Attabaliba here).[18] Even Samuel de Champlain, an apparently staunch Catholic, could discuss in his text, *Brief Discours* (c. 1599–1600), the ways in which the Inquisition made the Natives flee to the hills and the pursuing Spaniards were eaten; but one of the images shows two brightly dressed Spaniards on either side of barely clad Natives, who look fairly European as they are being consumed in the flames.

Sometimes images could show Spanish power from the vantage of the Native. The conquest, portrayed in "A West Indian Scene" or "West Indian Landscape" (ca. 1540–1550), probably the earliest known painting of the Americas and that now resides in the Frans Hal Museum in Haarlem, by Jan Mostaert, was first mentioned in *Het*

Schilder-boeck (Alkmaar, 1604) by Carel van Mander, a painter and art historian. This painting placed the Natives in the foreground and pushed the Spanish off to one side (the right hand). The viewer observes the naked Natives fighting with the armed Spanish in full armor. It is quite possible, as Hugh Honour suggests, that Mostaert is using similar techniques to stress the pastoral as he did in his painting of Adam and Eve and that there are parallels here between the Spanish advance in the New World and that in the Netherlands.[19] Quite possibly, the painting encourages the viewer to take sides with the Natives and, if there is a typology, with the Netherlands against Spain. Timing and the dating would be important in this potential allegory, for at the height of the Dutch Revolt, such typological renderings found intense expression. Margaret of Austria, the aunt of Charles V who ruled over New Spain and the Netherlands, was a patron to Mostaert, but how much Las Casas' descriptions of Spanish atrocities in the New World or the behavior of Spanish troops in the Low Countries would have influenced Mostaert is hard to say and, without evidence, is speculation, no matter how interesting, so that this part of Honour's interpretation, though suggestive, requires further proof. It may be that this invasion is an intrusion into an Ovidian golden age rather than any specific event or typology. Shakespeare's *The Tempest,* as we shall see in chapter 6, embodied the qualities of nature and nurture, good and evil in Europeans and Natives. Caliban, for Prospero, showed lust and treachery, but Prospero, for Caliban, betrayed his love, gifts and hospitality, so that Caliban learned to curse this newcomer-turned-master: "Curs'd be that did so" (I.2.339). In his "I' th' commonwealth" speech (2.1.145f.), Gonzalo echoes John Florio's translation in 1603 of Montaigne's description of an ideal commonwealth in his essay "Of Cannibals."[20] Ambivalent tensions occurred between positive and negative representations of Europeans and Natives in fictional and non-fictional texts as well as in visual images concerning the New World.

The power of Spain and the homage to Spain were other themes of visual representations. Maps could also show the puissance of Spain, for instance the one apparently made for Mary Tudor that displayed the extent of the empire over which her husband, Philip II, reigned. This map derives from an atlas of nine maps: one of the maps represented the British Isles with a shield that bears the arms of Philip II impaling those of Mary I. Diogo Homem's map of the world, which contains the royal arms of England, divided overseas possessions between Spain and Portugal as they were determined by the Treaty of Tordesillas during the 1490s, a division that Spain insisted be respected long after.[21] This was the possibility of a joint Spanish and English rule at home and overseas that Richard Eden advocated in the 1550s. In Bernardo de Vargas Machuca's *Milicia y Descripcion de las Indias* (Madrid, 1599), there is an image of a conqueror who rests his left hand on his sword and his right on a compass that divides the world: at the bottom is a message "Ala espada y el compas/Mas. y mas. y mas. Y mas" (With the sword and the compass/More. And more. And more. And more)."[22] Here the expansion of Spain, at least to some Spaniards, seemed without limit—the sun never sets on imperial ambitions. Conquests, as the lesson of *translatio imperii* teaches, have their end. This was true for Spain and its rivals and successors. Columbus' "conquest of paradise" had its own forms of fall and exile.

The "God and gold" motive for the expansion of Europe to the Americas shows a clash between feudal obligations and commercial desire. This was, as we saw in chapter 2, the major tension in Columbus' coming to terms with the Natives in the western Atlantic islands. By 1511, on the Continent, there already were versions of Columbus' *Letter* in six countries, Italian, Latin and German editions of Vespucci, and newsletters about the Portuguese in India from German and Italian presses, while nothing had appeared in English. Apparently, the printing of travel narratives in English was not then viable.[23] During the middle decades of the sixteenth century, the English and French continued to see Columbus and Spain as a model for colonization in the Americas. In 1555, Richard Eden, who in an earlier passage had proclaimed that "The Spanyardes haue shewed a good exemple to all Chrystian nations to folowe," justified the gold before, but along with, God.[24] André Thevet's *Universal Cosmography* (1575), which derived from his experience with Villegagnon in Brazil, represented Spain in a positive light.[25] The Spaniards were the first to discover Peru and to see "the way of life of these poor barbarians and Savages, cruel through and through, and without civility, not more than beasts."[26] He had more derogatory views of the Natives, which contrasted with his praise for explorers like Columbus, Magellan and Cartier.[27] The first part of Martin Fumée's French translation of Gómara's *La Historia* in 1578 described Columbus, his enterprise and Hispaniola ("l'isle Espagnole").[28] Urbain Chauveton was also critical of Spanish abuses in the New World. In the "Avertissement" of the *Histoire Novvelle dv Novveav Monde* (1579) Chauveton seemed to be using the work of Le Challeux, and in the "Summary of the first book" he stressed Benzoni's critique of the cruelty of the Spanish in the West Indies—how, for instance, they hunted slaves—as well as asserting that some Spanish historian had taken away the honor of the discovery of the New World by Columbus.[29] Chauveton's summary described Benzoni's account of how the lands were found, how the Spanish abused such a singular gift from God, how they brought with them avarice, ambition, cruelty, war and other vices leading in Hispaniola to troubles, "that is to say judgements of God on the head of those who have oppressed this poor people."[30] In 1589 Richard Hakluyt's *The Principall Navigations* included a map between the "To the Reader" and the dedicatory poems in Greek and Latin, which has inscribed on what is now western Canada that America was first detected by Columbus in 1492 in the name of the king of Castile.[31] John Smith, although fashioning himself on the heroic model of Cortés and commending Columbus and Queen Isabella for having the vision to back him, could proclaim: "And though I can promise no Mines of gold, yet the warlike Hollanders let vs imitate, but not hate, whose wealth and strength are good testimonies of their treasure gotten by fishing."[32] Gabriel Sagard's *Histoire dv Canada et voyages qve les freres mineurs Recollets y ont faicts pour la conuersion des Infidelles* (1636), which concentrated on conversion but in his history from 1615 to the fall of Québec to the English in 1629, noted that America was named after Vespucci but reminded his reader that the honor was due to Columbus, who discovered the New World five years before.[33] This rehashing of the origins of America and the first European contact with it occurred, almost as an obsession, in French and English writing from the sixteenth century onward. While the figure of Columbus, and later Las Casas, became part of the lexicon and imagery of the French and English archive of the Americas, the revisitation of origins to the right to settle the New World was something that the French and English felt compelled to repeat, perhaps because the Spanish and Portuguese continued to insist on the legitimacy of the papal bulls of the 1490s and first decade of the 1500s and the treaties between Spain and Portugal at that time. Certain traumatic events—Columbus' discovery of the New World, the papal donation of the new lands to Spain and Portugal, the first meetings of Natives and Europeans, the death of the Huguenots in Florida, the Revolt in the Netherlands, the Spanish Armada—recurred in the French and English writings about the New World.[34] The seizing of Natives is something that Columbus, Cabot, de Gonneville and others from each European country seemed to have practiced.[35] No matter how much others tried to forget Columbus, even in the wider context of the famous adventurers, writers and rulers who followed him, he was hard to suppress, dismiss or put aside for those who came after him, in praise and blame, not simply in Spain but throughout western Europe.

III

Even while trying to circumvent Columbus with the trope of the translation of empire, tailored to a certain national interest, there was also no denying that the Columbian voyage of 1492 also marked, for other Europeans, a new beginning and a radical break with the past. The New World changed the Old World. In the 1590s, about 100 years after Columbus' landfall, Walter Ralegh, who, in his *Discoverie of Guiana* (1596), suggested that England emulate, rival and displace Spain in parts of South America, represented the explorer in a cameo role. Near the end, when Ralegh attempted to make a final rhetorical appeal to Elizabeth I to back a conquest, he brought back the ancient lost opportunity that Henry VII had to employ Columbus in his enterprise:

> The West Indies were first offered to her Maiesties Grandfather by Columbus, a straunger, in whome there might be doubt of deceit, and besides it was then thought incredible that there were such and so many lands & regions neuer written of before. This Empire is made knowen to her Majesty by her own vassal, & by him that oweth to her more duty than an ordinary subiect, so that it shall ill sort with the many graces and benefites which I haue receaued to abuse her hignes, wither with fables or imaginations. The countrey is alreadie discouered, many nations won to her Maiesties loue & obedience, & those Spanyards which haue latest and longest labored about the conquest, beaten out, discouraged and disgraced, which among these nations were thought inuincible.[36]

This is a diplomatic and positive reshaping of what I have called the wound of Columbus, Henry's lost chance to have backed the enterprise of the Indies and the "discovery" of America. Ralegh showed some understanding of Henry's reluctance by imputing it to a suspicion of strangers, something that the king seems to have gotten over quickly as Giovanni Caboto, or John Cabot, although familiar in Bristol, was Italian. It is quite possible that Henry never held this kind of xenophobic view as his historian, Polydore Vergil, was an Italian humanist. Ralegh, while excusing Henry, needs Columbus as the putative deceitful stranger as an opposite to himself, a home-grown, reliable vassal. Implied in all this is the positive comparison between Columbus, who discovered a New World in which the Spaniards came to find gold and riches, and Ralegh, who would do the same. Elizabeth, the implication goes, should not make the same mistake as Henry VII because she can trust in Ralegh. Thus, Ralegh brings out Columbus to help cinch his argument, and, although as understandable as Ralegh makes Henry VII's decision, he is hoping to create a nagging doubt in Elizabeth that, if she does not back Ralegh, she will make a grievous mistake. Ralegh's book spends most of its argument on the power and riches the Spaniards have reaped in the New World and what that has done to the balance of power in Europe. In other words, if England were not to emulate Spain and try to rival it in South America, it would continue to be aversely affected, subject to Spanish might. It was time for an English Columbus: and he was Ralegh.

    This passage also makes it sound as though Columbus knew he was going to come across many lands and regions not represented in writing when he was in search of

Cathay and Cipango, regions that Marco Polo and others had described. Although Ralegh identifies himself with Columbus, he also distinguishes himself from him when he wants to minimize the risk for Elizabeth. Whereas Columbus discovered new lands, Ralegh was in a region already discovered, so that Ralegh had already "beaten out" the Spaniards, who in the wake of Columbus had performed a conquest there, thereby showing the Natives that the apparently invincible Spanish could be defeated. Whereas Columbus is necessary for a comparison to flatter Ralegh flattering the queen, Ralegh separates him from those Spaniards who followed Columbus. Ralegh purports to bring Elizabeth the truth of a country already explored rather than something concocted "with fables and imaginations." Elsewhere, however, as we shall see in "Sexing America," Ralegh has already presented Guiana as a virgin land that, in a twist, the Virgin queen is to enter. Coming after Columbus is coming after Spain, although writers sometimes tried to divide him from the country for which he sailed on his enterprise. Like the English, the French could plan to divest Spain of the lands Columbus had claimed for them and those they conquered as a result of his voyages. What this French equivalent of Cromwell's enterprise of the Indies in 1655 was leading up to was a sense that if the French took the two key Spanish islands in the Antilles, including Cuba, then they could hold in "subjection all the main land of New Spain and the rest of Mexico."[37] The author of a memorandum in the Antilles in 1669 used a similar argument to that which Ralegh had employed in his work on Guiana in 1596, except here the case is extended to all the people, including descendants of the conquerors, and not just the Natives: the inhabitants of the Spanish colonies in the western Atlantic will welcome a change because "the inhabitants are much maltreated by the viceroys" and other officials "sent from Spain to govern them that they have little affection for the government."[38] The challenge to Spain, from France and England, was remarkably persistent and the Spanish empire in America endured far longer than the French and English had hoped or expected.

About 100 years after Ralegh's plan, England was still challenging Spain and producing texts that mentioned or meditated on Columbus as an example. As R. B. put it in *The English Empire* (1685), the figure of Columbus was an instance to be followed: "Columbus at length returning into Spain, he there died in 1506, and was buried at Sevil; after whose example several others made further Discoveries, till at last this New World, is almost wholly come to the knowledge of the Old."[39] Almost 200 years after Columbus' arrival in the western Atlantic, a book on English imperialism paid homage in typological terms of Old World and New to the great Italian explorer who sailed for Spain. The ambivalence toward Spain occurred in R. B.'s work, something that can be observed in a later passage: in 1572, by the Sound of Darien, Drake "found a certain People called Symerons, which are for the most part Negro's, and such as having been Slaves to the Spaniards, by reason of their cruelty and hard usage run away from them, and live in woods and other wild places of the Countrey in great companies together like other Savages, hating the Spaniards deadly, and doing them what mischief they can upon all occasions."[40] R. B. decoupled Columbus from Spain, which is framed in terms of cruelty, a central part of the Black Legend of Spain. Slaves and Natives, those Spain oppressed, become examples for other Nations of groups to be liberated. England, even before the full development of Whig views of English liberty, becomes a liberator who comes after feudal and futile Spain. This myth becomes a spur to and rationalization of the translation of empire in the New World from Spain to England.

The origins of English colonization, like those of French expansion, in the Americas were more halting than the colonies of the 1680s when R. B. was writing. Despite the promising beginnings with the voyages of John Cabot, the English soon fell behind the French in their challenge of Spain, which had established permanent colonies as a result of Columbus' voyages. The anxiety over Spanish hegemony led to new ideologies and mythologies that the French and English used to combat the power of Spain. These powers needed to imitate Spain but to deny its precedence and ascendancy in the New World: they wanted rights to it as well. This assertion of legitimization and reinterpretation of the "discovery" of America by the rival country, and not Spain, persisted for centuries as an attempt to justify competition with, and displacement of, the leading and first great colonial power in the Americas.

It was quite apparent that by the end of the sixteenth and the beginning of the seventeenth century the Spanish, English and French, not to mention the Dutch and the Portuguese, all contended in trade and war in the New World. By the eighteenth century the rivalries continued and the English still seemed to rejoice in having Spain as an enemy, so that the War of Jenkins's Ear (1739–48) was like old times. For instance, the opening paragraph of the Anonymous *The British Sailor's Discovery: or the Spaniards Pretensions Confuted* (1739) began by distinguishing among titles, conquest and actual possession. Beside the title in the margin, "Spain's Pretensions vain and boundless," the anonymous author challenged Spain's right to America and its questioning of British rights there; Spain "by an arbitrary, and unwarrantable Authority, pretends too set Limits and Boundaries in the greatest of Oceans, whereby to exclude all others from sailing past the same."[41] The author then presented an "Introduction towards a Review of the Discovery by Columbus," the source of this pretense, wherein he compared the "Iniquity" of Spanish discoveries with the "Equity" of English ones and concluded "that the much boasted Right of Spain, here taken notice of, is founded upon Possession obtained by unjust Conquests, which were attended with most execrable Murders, Cruelties, Devastations, and other Acts of Inhumanity, unbecoming one fellow Creature to act towards another; much less for those who professed Christianity."[42]

Even as British America was splitting apart during the War of Independence, an interest in Columbus and Spain persisted. David Ramsey's *The History of the American Revolution* (1789) is a case in point, but so too is Jeremy Belknap's meditation on the 400th anniversary of Columbus' landfall, both a little over 100 years after R. B.'s work.[43] Belknap was ambivalent about the Spanish. In describing Columbus, he declared:

> It is not pretended that Columbus was the only person of his age who had acquired these ideas of the form, dimensions and balancing of the globe; but he was one of the few who had begun to think for themselves, and he had a genius of that kind, which makes use of speculation and reasoning only as excitements to action. He was not a closet projector, but an enterprising adventurer; and having established his theory on principles, he was determined to exert himself to the utmost, to demonstrate its truth by experiment.[44]

Belknap's Columbus combined knowledge, principled theory, action and experimental method. He was a scientist who could sail. For Belknap, then, the explorer was part of a move toward the application of new learning or science. In a context that includes Daniel's prophecy, in a form of enlightened religion, Belknap provides in a transition a wider context still for Columbus and exploration in science: "Having thus traced the steps by which the discovery of America was made to the Europeans; let us take the view of its connexion with the advancement of science."[45] This was a Whig view of history, but the shift began from England to America as the promised land and Columbus started to be a figure for this new country, the United States, to form its identity and mission in history.

The role of America, which Columbus first brought to light, was growing in the context of the American Revolution and, although it was unspoken in this passage, with the French Revolution. Liberty, according to Belknap, was the legacy of America at home and in Europe:

> The discovery of America has also opened an important page in the history of man. We find our brethren of the human race scattered over all parts of the continent, and the adjacent islands. We see mankind in their several varieties of colour, form and habit, and we learn to consider ourselves as one great family, sent into the world to make various experiments for happiness.
>
> One of the grandest of these experiments has been made in our own part of this continent. Freedom, that noble gift of heaven, had here fixed her standard, and invited the distressed of all countries to take refuge under it. Our virtuous ancestors fled from the imposition and persecutions to which they were subjected in England, and found in this wilderness an asylum from that tyranny. Their example was followed by others, and in North America, the oppressed of Europe have always found safety and relief. But we were designed by Providence for a nobler experiment still: Not only to open a door of safety to our European brethren here; but to show them that they are entitled to the same rights in their native countries; and we have set them an example of a hazardous, but successful vindication of those rights, which are the gift of God to man.[46]

Here is an ideal or ideology that has persisted and has been a dominant one in the United States, the kind that surrounds the Statue of Liberty. In what follows this quotation Belknap also finds fault with proud notions of English liberty and also condemns the lack of tolerance in his home state: "And, even at this enlightened period, I blush to own, that, by the Constitution of the Commonwealth, the Jew, the Mohametan, the Gentoo, and the Disciple of Confucius, are excluded from our public councils, be they ever so good citizens; whilst men, who for convenience, call themselves Christians, though deeply tinged with infidelity, and destitute of moral principles, may freely be admitted."[47] Belknap lamented this state of affairs but said that improvement has been made in this regard in the United States because the federal constitution, unlike those of certain of the states, "leaves religion where all civil governments ought to leave it; to the consciences of individuals, under the control of the supreme Lord."[48] This call for the division of church and state and for tolerance is an extension of the tradition of John Locke: Belknap was part of, and helped to shape, a new legacy in the wake of Columbus.

He brought a new wrinkle to the Black Legend, which is in the context of the abolition of slavery:

> Our astonishment is further excited, by considering that the discovery of America has opened a large mart for the commerce in slaves from the opposite continent of Africa. So much has been written and spoken on the iniquity attending this detestable species of traffic, that I need not attempt again to excite the feelings of indignation and horror, which I doubt not have pervaded the breast of every person now present, when contemplating this flagrant insult on the laws of justice and humanity. I shall only observe, that the first introduction of the negro slavery into America was occasioned by the previous destruction of the native inhabitants of the West-India islands, by the cruelty of their Spanish conquerors, in exacting of them more labour than they were able to perform. The most remarkable and

unaccountable circumstance attending the beginning of this traffic, is, that it was recommended by a Spanish Bishop, one of the most benevolent friends of the Indians, whom he could not bear to see so wantonly destroyed by his countrymen.[49]

Belknap contrasts his praise for the great benevolent Spaniard, Las Casas, with the cruelty of the conquering Spaniards and in doing so lays the blame for slavery in the Americas on Spain. Never mind the role of the Portuguese early and the French, English and Dutch later or the existence of slavery, which Belknap admits as an evil, in the United States. Like Las Casas, Belknap wanted to see his compatriots do the right thing, although, for a long time, Las Casas seemed much more interested in protecting the Natives than the African slaves.[50]

The "Ode" at the end of the body of Belknap's published version, which one can imagine being sung as part of the ceremony in Boston in 1792, brought back Columbus in a circular narrative to the center of the "American" experience:

VI

Then, guided by th'Almighty Hand,
    COLUMBUS spread his daring sail;
Ocean receiv'd a new command
    And *Zephyrs* breath'd a gentle gale.

VII

The Western World appear'd to view,
    Her friendly arms extended wide;
Then FREEDOM o'er th'Atlantic flew,
    With pure RELIGION by her side.

VIII

Tyrants with mortal hate pursu'd;
    In vain their forces they employ;
In vain the Serpent pours his flood,* [Rev. XII, 15]
    Those heaven-born Exiles to destroy.

The Zephyrs, or west wind, found in Geoffrey Chaucer's General Prologue to *The Canterbury Tales,* have here blown in a "Western World," and the two words in capitals, Freedom and Religion, side by side, fight tyranny though the Providential exilic settlers who left Europe at their backs. This discussion of Belknap, who also figured at the beginning of the study, is a look ahead, but looking back, the colonies were all within the sphere of their European progenitors and the French especially had a presence in the northern part of the Americas and, with England, came to terms with Spain. The beginnings of English and French exploration, and particularly settlement, in the New World were much more halting than Belknap's study in, and ode to, liberty might suggest, so turning back from the end of the eighteenth century to the beginning of the sixteenth is instructive in realizing that retrospective prophecy is much more certain in reading history than being buffeted in the present or extrapolating from the past into the future.[51]

IV

In North America in the late eighteenth century and beyond, the figures of Columbus and "Columbia" were prevalent. British America, most notably but not exclusively the new United States, identified with Columbus. The Columbia River, once in the British Oregon territory, ceded to the United States in 1846, ran between British North America and the United States. In British North America, after the Confederation of Canada, a new province, the most westerly one, British Columbia, joined the country in 1871. As the United States expanded westward a number of towns and cities were named after Columbus: Washington, the capital, was in the District of Columbia. This Italian-born and partly Portuguese-trained explorer now became a symbol of Anglo-American progress and expansion, as if the first landfall in 1492 was meant teleologically to lead to the extension of the English-speaking peoples.

Here I can only discuss a few key instances of the "translation" of Columbus as part of this *translatio imperii*. Writers had long found Columbus a worthy subject even in brief appearances or in passing. A poet of the young American republic used Columbus as the pretext or thematic inducement for his epic. The frontispiece of the 1813 Paris edition of *The Columbiad*, an epic poem by Joel Barlow, is an image with the title "Hesper Appearing to Columbus in Prison," and the epigraph, in Italian, from canto xv of *Gierusalem Liberata*, about Columbus, Richard Fairfax translates in 1600 as follows:

> Thy ship (Columbus) shall her canuasse wing
> Spread ore that world, that yet concealed lies,
> That scant swift fame her lookes shall after bring,
> Though thousand plumes she haue, and thousand eies.
> Let her of Bacchus and Alcides sing,
> Of thee to future age let this suffies,
> > That of thine actes she some forewarning giue,
> > Which shall in verse and noble storie liue.[52]

The fame of Columbus' story, in Tasso's verse in the sixteenth century and later in Barlow's in the nineteenth, was to spread into each future age in transmutating form. This voyage was a sea-change, a kind of embedded epic within an epic. Whereas Tasso uses Columbus as a kind of ekphrasis, an inset, Barlow makes him the protagonist of his epic.

In his preface Barlow provides a gloss on the frontispiece, which is a key to the poem and embodies the classical unities that should govern an epic: "It may be added, that in no poem are the unities of time, place and action more rigidly observed: the action, in the technical sense of the word, consisting only of what takes place between Columbus and Hesper; which must be supposed to occupy but few hours, and is confined to the prison and the mount of vision."[53] Despite this allegorical image as frontispiece and as epic apparatus, as a means to classical unities through beginning in medias res, Barlow claimed, in his preface, that "The Columbiad is a patriotic poem; the subject is national and patriotic."[54] The representation of Columbus and of the republic that his actions helped to bring about are the chief aims of Barlow's epic, so that, in the second regard, Lucan, "the only republican among the ancient epic poets," serves as his model, not Virgil, who "wrote and felt like a subject, not like a citizen" and who, like Homer, encouraged "the great system of military depredation."[55] The goals of the poem is a topic that Barlow spells out in detail in the preface:

In the poem here presented to the public the objects, as in other works of the kind, are two: the fictitious object of the action and the real object of the poem. The first of these is to sooth and satisfy the desponding mind of Columbus; to show him that his labors, tho ill rewarded by his contemporaries, had not been performed in vain; that he had opened the way to the most extensive career of civilization and public happiness; and that he would one day be recognised as the author of the greatest benefits to the human race. This object I steadily kept in view; and the actions, images and sentiments are so disposed as probably to attain the end. But the real object of the poem embraces a larger scope: it is to inculcate the love of rational liberty, and to discountenance the deleterious passion for violence and war; to show that on the basis of the republican principle all good morals, as well as good government and hopes of permanent peace, must be founded; and to convince the student in political science that the theoretical question of the future advancement of human society, till states as well as individuals arrive at universal civilization, is held in dispute because we have had too little experience of organised liberty in the government of nations to have well considered its effects.[56]

Columbus is the object of the story of the poem, but the moral aim is to exalt the republic and its institutions as means to happiness and, in America, to implant in the "minds of men," through poetry, painting and other fine arts, "true and useful ideas and glory" and not "the false and destructive ones that have degraded the species in other countries."[57]

After the preface, which takes as its subject the nature of this epic and its themes, the introduction makes the life of Columbus its sole concern. The opening paragraph makes no mistake that Barlow considers Columbus to be a hero, who deserves to be better known, so that, before the poem, the poet provides a life of the explorer:

Every circumstance relating to the discovery and settlement of America is an interesting object of inquiry, especially to the great and growing nations of this hemisphere, who owe their existence to those arduous labors. Yet it is presumed that many persons, who might be entertained with a poem on this subject, are but slightly acquainted with the life and character of the hero whose extraordinary genius led him to discover the continent, and whose singular sufferings, arising from that service, ought to excite the indignation of the world.[58]

The visionary and suffering genius neglected by his society or country is a Romantic theme, but it also was to serve a moral and perhaps even satiric function of arousing indignation in the reader. Perhaps this is what made William Blake think that Milton was of the devil's party because of the eloquence and suffering that he gave to Satan in the great English and "republican" epic *Paradise Lost* (1674). Barlow explicitly disconnects Columbus from the Black Legend of Spain by wishing that the Spaniards who accompanied and followed the admiral to the New World would have behaved more like him: "Had his companions and successors of the Spanish nation possessed the wisdom and humanity of this great discoverer, the benevolent mind would have had to experience no sensations of regret in contemplating the extensive advantages arising to mankind from the discovery of America."[59] Barlow airs a grievance on Columbus' behalf: "The continent, instead of bearing his name, has been called after one of his followers, a man of no particular merit."[60] The poet also makes that distinction between Columbus as good Spanish explorer and someone who was his opposite: "And in the modern city of Mexico there is instituted and perpetuated, by order of government, an annual festival in honor of Hernando Cortez, the perfidious butcher of its ancient race; while no public honors have been decreed to Christopher Columbus, one of the wisest and best among the benefactors of mankind."[61] Barlow, who says that he owns a half-length oil portrait of Columbus copied from the original in a gallery in Florence, praises Hernando Columbus' life of his father that describes the simplicity of his grave, stating simply the explorer's name in Spanish: "CHRISTOVAL COLON."[62] This account is quite a different version from what happens subsequently to the body of, and monuments to, Columbus. His body and reputation do not rest in peace. It is as if, as an American, Barlow was defending the genius of Columbus, too much maligned or neglected in Spain and Spanish America, which was on the verge of revolution and the independence movements that entailed.

John Milton came to provide an argument for *Paradise Lost* when the request was made of him: Barlow followed this convention. The argument for the first book of Barlow's *Columbiad* is clear in setting out the action and suggesting the atmosphere:

> Subject of the Poem, and invocation to Freedom. Condition of Columbus in a Spanish prison. His monologue on the great actions of his life, and the manner in which they had been rewarded. Appearance and speech of Hesper, the guardian Genius of the western continent. They quit the dungeon and ascend the mount of vision, which arises over the western coast of Spain; Europe settling from their sight, and the Atlantic ocean spreading far beneath their feet. Continent of America draws into view, and is described by its mountains, rivers, lakes, soil and some natural productions.[63]

The image of Columbus in prison unjustly treated by Spain as well as Hesper as a classical means of expressing the later westering of empire, which also has physical embodiments in this first book and beyond, leave the reader with an epic poem, whose hero is a visionary genius who sailed under the authority of Spain, speaking in English to a primarily American audience, which has just broken its bonds with Britain and has discovered liberty.

In case there is any doubt about Barlow's emphasis, the opening lines of Book 1 amplify this theme in heroic couplets reminiscent of John Dryden and Alexander Pope but with a tone more Romantic than either of these English poets:

> I SING the Mariner who first unfurl'd
> An eastern banner o'er the western world,
> And taught mankind where future empires lay
> In these fair confines of descending day;
> Who sway'd a moment, with vicarious power,
> Iberia's sceptre on the new found shore,
> Then saw the paths his virtuous steps had trod
> Pursued by avarice and defiled with blood,
> The tribes he foster'd with paternal toil
> Snatcht from his hand, and slaughter'd for their spoil.
> Slaves, kings, adventurers, envious of his name,
> Enjoy'd his labors and purloin'd his fame,
> And gave the Viceroy, from his high seat hurl'd,
> Chains for a crown, a prison for a world.[64]

The opening lines have a Virgilian echo—despite what Barlow has said about Virgil he cannot resist playing a variation on the beginning of the *Aeneid*. Columbus leads to "future empires," which is a kind of retrospective prophecy. Barlow's mariner comes to find the Natives whom he treated with "paternal toil" taken and killed for riches by those who benefited from his labors and purloined his reputation, leaving the great explorer and representative of the king in chains in jail. This poet's interpretation of Columbus is clear and it may be that the abuse and neglect of Columbus by the Spaniards was something that British Americans, now independent, would set right through works like those of Barlow. The tenth and final book of Barlow's poem ends with a vision of progress in science and commerce and political harmony for humankind, a utopian world without envy and malice without complaint over "The loss of empire and the frown of kings."[65]

Other Columbian poems appeared and they did not always feature Columbus but became texts that celebrated Columbia, America by another name that might have been, and the science, industry, peace and prosperity that were the stuff of its progress. For instance, Richard Snowden's *The Columbiad,* which is about the American Revolution, as the title and advertisement says, and about George Washington and "Columbia," rather than about Columbus, began with these lines: "THAT chief I sing: Columbia's fav'rite son,/ His acts record, and glorious conquests won!"[66] Its thirteen cantos appear to be a celebration of the independence of the thirteen colonies. British America became transformed into Columbia and all that it is not. King's College changed its name to Columbia College when it reopened in 1784 after the American Revolution (it became Columbia University in 1912).[67] The republican Columbia, perhaps like Belknap's vision in 1792, seems to lend Columbus' name to a republic of liberty freed from British tyranny.

Harriet Munroe's *Columbian Ode* (1893) was, as its note declares, "written at the request of the Joint Committee on Ceremonies of the World's Columbian Exposition, accepted by that honorable body, and delivered on the four hundredth anniversary of the discovery of America, October 21, 1892, before an audience of more than one hundred thousand persons, during the ceremonies in the building for Manufactures and Liberal Arts."[68] The note also mentions that Professor George Chadwick of Boston set some of the more lyrical passages to music, including, "Columbia! men beheld thee rise" and, as a finale, the eight lines beginning "Lo! clan on clan, /The embattled nations gather to be one," which "were given by a chorus of five thousand voices, to the accompaniment of a great orchestra and military bands."[69] The scale of this celebration is not something lyric poetry would be accustomed to and, by its sheer magnitude, would become cultural ritual and political theater. The ode begins with "Columbia! on thy brow are dewy flowers/Plucked from wide prairies and from mighty hills."[70] Munroe does not mention Columbus by name and moves her poem to a Columbia triumphant in a kind of birth from the seas and apotheosis in the skies.

Columbia is a shifting signifier, a land, a lady, a goddess. The speaker addresses Columbia early in the poem:

> Spain, in the broidered robes of chivalry,
> Comes with slow foot and inward-brooding eyes.
> Bow to her banner! 't was the first to rise
>   Out of the dark for thee.
> And England, royal mother, whose right hand
> Molds nations, whose white feet the ocean tread,
> Lays down her sword on thy belovèd strand

> To bless thy wreathèd head;
> Hearing in thine her voice, bidding thy soul
> Fulfil her dream, the foremost at the goal.
> And France, who once thy fainting form upbore,
> Brings beauty now where strength she brought of yore.
>   France, the swift-footed, who with thee
>   Gazed in the eyes of Liberty,
>   And loved the dark no more.[71]

This movement from the medieval chivalry of Spain to the royal mother country, England, to the revolution for liberty with France makes Columbia the United States; still addressing Columbia, the speaker makes the Norse, Russia, Germany all part of "her" story; Italy "opens wide her epic soul" while the "Orient," from Palestine to Japan, "Salutes thy conquering youth."[72] Columbia, although a fair woman, is like Ralegh's Elizabeth I, whom he addresses in *Discoverie of Guiana* (1596), someone given to conquest and empire. In making his final appeal to Elizabeth I, Ralegh had ended the body of his book trusting in God of the truth he had written and that "it will suffice, and that he which is king of al kings and Lorde of Lords, will put it into her hart which is the Lady of Ladies to possesse it, if not, I wil iudge those men worthy to be kings therof, that by her grace and leaue will vndertake it to themselues."[73] Here then is another celebration of power as female form and potency, although Ralegh was trying to sway the queen while praising her and Munroe's speaker is making a public display whose intrumentality relies less on one person. At the end of the tribute that the nations pay to Columbia, the speaker in Munroe's poem proclaims, "Dead centuries, freighted with visions vast,/Blowing dim mists into the Future's eyes. Their song is all for thee, Daughter of mystery."[74] Arisen from mystery, Columbia has also been the seer of liberty: the past sings for her. Europe celebrates her while Asia yields to her, however protean and contradictory, a nation bursting with opposites in its song of itself, a kind of collective celebration of aspects of Walt Whitman's democratic America.

This Columbian ode without Columbus, which seems a genre in the United States from the American Revolution, ends with the speaker addressing Columbia and telling how men beheld her "rise/A goddess from the sea./Lady of joy, sent from the skies,/The nations worshiped thee;" she is also in each successive stanza "Lady of Love" then "Lady of hope" then Lady of beauty," the last of whom shall "win/Power and glory and length of days," kin to sun and moon, for whom the stars sing praise while the "we" the speaker expresses, "bring thee vows most sweet/To strew before thy wingèd feet./ Now onward be thy ways!"[75] Columbia is winged beyond the traditional seas and others bring her the past to transform, perhaps as much in homage as with vows. Columbia is and is not a nation, personified as a woman of beauty at the end: Columbus' name lies buried in this name, perhaps in redress for the original designation of America for the land he came upon, but he is absent as a figure or character in this poem. The 400th anniversary of his landfall is much more about the translation of power and empire to the United States in the present and future as about a celebration of the countries and cultures of the world. That intent might be buried in allegory, allusion and symbol, but this ode has some functions that gesture beyond literary translation.

Columbus becomes translated into the culture of British America and, after the Revolution, of the United States. This translation has many interpretative facets, some of which I have touched on here and will discuss in what follows. Columbus can be elided into Columbia and the Columbian, which can have even more tenuous connections with the explorer. Columbia and the Columbian, whether in the diaries and letters of women writing in English in North America or in regards to the female figure who marked and did not represent "America" at the Chicago Exposition of 1893 will be two of the topics I will discuss in the remainder of the chapter.

V

There are unexpected turns in the representations of Columbus and not all of the allusions to him are public or were published at the time. A pertinent example of this phenomenon is the appearance of Columbus in women's diaries and letters in North America, sometimes by those native born or by emigrants or "tourists," from the late eighteenth-century onward. Over more than a century and a half, Columbus took on many forms in this private writing. It is instructive to overhear these voices as they interpret Columbus in their private thoughts about identity, family, selfhood, culture, history, nation and many other contexts. Some of the themes and specific references to Columbus, his contemporaries and the Columbian World Exposition of 1893 relate closely to concerns throughout this chapter and study.

In the middle of the American Revolution, Columbus appeared in the diary of an Anglo-American woman in the North American colonies. On May 7, 1779, Louisa Aikman wrote about a chase of what she called a privateer, which had taken a schooner that had left "Charlestown" the same day her ship had but also mentioned Columbus: "I was much amused when the Gulph Stream with the Flying-Fish which abound there, and with the Gulph Weed floating about. Well poor Columbus be deceived and conjecture himself not far from land."[76] In the first part of the nineteenth century, Columbus continued to make it into the private papers of women. Another diarist, Harriet Hillard, commented in January 1830, "Commenced Irving's 'Columbus' this morning; find it very interesting."[77] Washington Irving's biography of the explorer was a detailed treatment by one of the leading early writers of the United States and something that provoked thought on the origins of European settlements in the New World and the eventual development of key British American colonies into a promising republic. Later on, we will see that Irving on Columbus was a subject for other women. On Sunday, September 2, 1832, Frances Anne Kemble, on hearing the call "Land, land!," wrote that

> I rushed on deck, and between the blue waveless sea, and the bright unclued sky, lay the wished-for line of darker element. 'Twas Long Island: through a glass I descried the undulations of the coast, and even the trees that stood relieved against the sky. Hail, strange land! My heart greets you coldly and sadly! Oh how I thought of Columbus, as with eyes strained and on tip-toe our water-weary passengers stood, after a summer's sail of thirty day's, welcoming their mother earth. The day was heavenly, though intensely hot, the sky utterly cloudless, and by the same token, I do not love a cloudless sky. They tell me that this is their American weather almost till Christmas; that's nice, for those who like frying. Commend me to dear England's soft, rich, sad, harmonious skies and foliage, commend me to the misty curtain of silver vapour that hangs over her September woods at morning, and shrouds them at night:—in short, I am home-sick before touching land.[78]

Columbus becomes here the prototypical voyager to the New World as well as a character in this romantic description with whom the author compares herself. Kemble's typology is about the shock of recognizing otherness: home or Europe becomes the beloved while America is strange and inhospitable. Even with changes in technology and in comfort 240 years after Columbus, this voyager keeps her log, as Columbus kept his, and if she feels such disorientation what would he have felt as he made the "originary" voyage? How homesick was Columbus, despite his vast experience sailing in the service of Portugal to Ireland, Iceland, Madeira and São Jorge da Mina on the Gold Coast of West Africa?

Sometimes Columbus is part of other myths or narratives of personal or national identity. On January 11, 1841, Anne Gorham Everett wrote from Florence to a cousin in which she describes high society and Greenough's statue of America, which was being made there for the rotunda in the capitol at Washington. She brings together in her description many significant elements of the making of American identity:

> Washington, of colossal size, is represented as sitting with a drapery gracefully thrown over him. One hand is raised to heaven, the other extended, holding a sword. The chair is beautifully sculptured, and the hand of it particularly, has very rich bas reliefs. At one corner of the back of the chair is Columbus, holding a globe in his hand; at the other, an Indian, leaning on his tomahawk. The statue is going to America in the spring, to be put up in the capitol. It would really be worth making a journey to Washington to see it. Mr. G. has also a group for the capitol, consisting of an early settler who surprises an Indian in the act of slaying his wife and child. The expression of the faces is very fine. This is yet only in plaster.[79]

Columbus literally takes a back seat to Washington but also props him up in the mythology of the American republic. That Washington is caught between Columbus and the Natives may be an unintended dilemma for him. The potential violence of the tomahawk is played out in the group of sculptures that would play on the anxiety over, and the ancestral fear of, being subject to Native violence. No scene of the Native helping the settlers survive and adapt is part of this sculpture.[80] In her diary entry of October 15, 1841, Anne Everett mentions temples that contain modern busts of Virgil and Tasso but that the King of Naples will not allow people to enter, and the next day, still on the topic of art, she refers to a visit with her father, who has just heard this day that he will be Minister to England, "to see a group of statuary, which Mr. Persico, an Italian sculptor, is making for the capitol at Washington. The group consists of Columbus, who is represented as having just landed in the new world, and near him an Indian girl, in a posture of wonder. The figure of Columbus is yet only sketched out in marble. We saw here a bust of papa, taken in Boston four years ago."[81] Columbus is here a figure of marvel, the girl paying homage to him, but he is also part of the writer's and sculptor's "family," as he is in the company of papa and a sculpture of papa. Columbus is part of a translation of art, study and empire in the Italy of the poets Virgil and Tasso and the sculptor Persico, and from Italy to the United States.

In 1844, Mother Theodore Guerin gives a sense in what might be called her epistolary journal or diary, her address to Louis Veuillot and Leon Aubineau, concerning the New World. On the first day of January, which was their thirty-fourth day of travel, Guerin found an unaccustomed and stifling heat: "Such a temperature in the month of January told us too plainly how far we were from our dear France."[82] On January 14, they saw land for the first time, the island of San Domingo, an incident in whose history she mentions: "We saw no inhabitants, but a thick smoke that rose out of the woods made us suppose that the negroes must be burning their trees for the purpose of cultivating the land. After the massacre of the whites in 1793, the negroes remained masters of the beautiful island." This is an aspect of the French Revolution we will touch upon in chapter 7. All was not peace in paradise, and the issue of slavery came to haunt all the imperial powers and the young republics of the Western hemisphere. Guerin's ship passed Tortuga and saw Cuba: "In this island, conquered by Valasquez without the loss of a single man to Spain, there is a catholic Church to which the remains of Christopher Columbus have been transferred."[83] Mother Guerin considers this discoverer and conqueror in relation to her:

> For us Religious, a thought more consoling than all the glory of conquests moved our hearts. Our Lord Jesus Christ dwelt in that land. Oh! How happy for us could we have gone and cast ourselves at His Feet to return thanks for His having preserved our lives which are consecrated to Him. We could thank Him only from afar. In calling to mind the labors and fatigues of the conquerors of the New World, we were humiliated by our want of courage. They conquered a hemisphere; but one soul alone is worth more than the whole world. Pray to God for us that we may become less unworthy of our beautiful vocation. To Him alone be the glory of our labors, and to you, dear friends, the recompense on account of the assistance you will give us.[84]

The notions of conquest and conversion are quite alive in this text from the mid-nineteenth century. The glory of conversion is here greater than worldly conquest, although Guerin has mentioned that not a Spaniard was lost in the taking of Cuba and that she needs, presumably, the material backing of the gentlemen to whom she is writing. As much as Mother Guerin liked to be on the upper deck, she deplored the cabin passengers, who, "although of a more elevated rank in society, rivaled in irreligion those of the lower deck," for she decried an atheist, a skeptic, a Protestant, two faithless men of the world, a freethinking woman and so on.[85] She had obviously classified the heretics and sinners in some detail. For Mother Guerin, who wondered at the sun and sky over the "tropical" waters, the lower deck of the ship included every vice and "was in truth a very antechamber of hell."[86] In the Gulf of Mexico she admired the flying fish and saw them as a metaphor and comparison, for, "were it not that God, as if to supply for their exceeding weakness, has given them wings wherewith to escape the voracity of their enemies. This, too, is our state, was my reflection; God has given us the wings of prayer to enable us to escape the snares of the devil."[87] Like the fish, whose wings cannot support themselves for long, we, as Guerin implies, fall back and "are obliged to live a good deal" among enemies.[88] This is a worldview with which Columbus himself would have been familiar—slaves who revolt, heretics, sinners, enemies. Columbus' bones had been moved or were said to have been moved amid upheaval. Mother Guerin's was not the face of tolerance and progress that was the face the Chicago Exposition of 1893 presented to the world.

Other references to Columbus occurred in diaries of the 1840s, such as Mary Wallis' observation of deaths by cholera on "the United States ship Columbus" in Manila.[89] The various centennials were not the only occasions for the federal government to invoke or use the name of Columbus. A diary, just begun by a ten-year old, Catherine Havens, places, on August 15, 1849, Columbus in a comic situation in a space between invention and truth, poetry and history: "I hate my history lessons. Ellen likes history because she knows it all and does not have to study her lesson, but one day our teacher asked her to recite the beginning of the chapter, and she had only time to see there was a big

A at the heading, and she thought it about Columbus discovering America and began to recite at a great rate, but the teacher said, 'wrong,' and it was about Andrew Marvell. Once a girl in our class asked our teacher if what we learned in history was true, or only just made up. I suppose she thought it was good for the mind, like learning poetry."[90] Rather than a lesson about Europe at Columbus' back, she finds out it is about the author who mused on time's wingèd chariot at the back. . . . Columbus is part of this school's lesson, so that he has entered education and history in the United States beside English literature. Susan Augusta Fenimore Cooper, a naturalist, likens the relations between America and Europe, Columbus and the Vikings, to rival passenger-pigeons: "it has been calculated that our passenger-pigeon might go to Europe in three days; indeed, a straggler is said to have been actually shot in Scotland. So that, whatever disputes may arise as to the rival merits of Columbus and the Northmen, it is very probable that American pigeons had discovered Europe long before the Europeans discovered them." For all its wit and dexterous use of analogy, this passage does turn on its ear discussions of origins and discoveries, especially as it pertains to European naturalists discovering the nature of the New World as if it were not part of a larger Atlantic (not to mention Pacific) ecosystem.[91] The entry that refers to Columbus in a letter of Hariet Preble (1795–1854) is undated, but as she died in the early 1850s, I have included it here. She mediated on melancholy, strangeness and exile, not to mention the passage of time: "In dwelling on the past, however, the thought that comes uppermost is not one of *regret,* that a wild and ignorant race should have been crushed and driven back towards more distant regions. When Columbus planted the standard of the Cross in the New World, it was more than the mere act of taking possession of the country. That Cross was the symbol of the religious destinies of a whole regenerated continent. The mild effulgence of Christianity, the useful sciences, fine arts, pure and moral habits,—all these were to flow from it."[92] Columbus' cross was a legal and Christian sign. Preble's description is a kind of manifest destiny of religious regeneration and scientific, artistic and moral progress amid the remembrance and melancholy of her own exile, as if the displacement of the Natives from their homes did not warrant similar feeling. Preble also mentioned that on July 4 she experienced "My first anniversary of this national festival in America; and this day made me feel more strongly than I had yet done, that I am in a *strange land.* In the midst of their rejoicings I carried the heart of an exile."[93] An exilic sadness, echoing the biblical strangers in a strange land, informs this passage in Preble's letter, but her empathy did not seem to extend to the indigenous peoples.

The references to Columbus in women's letters and diaries from 1850 to the 400th anniversary of the landfall in 1892 are varied. Allusions to, and discussions of, lectures and readings provide glimpses of the reception of Columbus in the United States leading up to the World Columbian Exposition of 1893 in Chicago. A diarist with a wonderful katascopic name, Ellen Douglas Birdseye Wheaton, gave an overview of her experience on Friday evening, December 19, 1856, when she "went to hear Rev. E. H. Chapin, lecture in the new Wieting Hall. Subject. Columbus."[94] Her description provides an idea of how Columbus was being represented at the time, just as articles surrounding the Chicago Expo do the same over thirty years later. Chapin

commenced with a description of the returning ship of the discoverer from his first voyage, as shattered & worn, it made its way into the harbor of Palos. He described his triumphal reception by the city dignitaries, and then his still grander reception by the king and queen, and their astonishment at his relation. When he had finished, they with the assembled court, prostrated, themselves upon their knees, and returned thanks, to God, for giving them such a magnificent addition to their domain. He pictured, Columbus as he at first, was seen wandering from Court to Court, seeking in vain for assistance, in his great project, ever hoping, ever trusting, still persevering—At last fortune was propitious, he was heeded and with many interruptions, and delays, he did set sail, on his mysterious voyage, thro' all the dreary, and discouraging period, and when at last success crowned his efforts, and when again, his enemies, strove to destroy his world-wide fame, and *seemed* to succeed, when his generous patroness died. He still retained that undaunted perseverance, that lofty faith, that sublime patience, which exalted him so much above other men. Amidst neglect, & ingratitude, & injustice, his character shone serene and clear, and when at last, "worn out with the toils and cares of this rough and weary world,"—as he himself said of Isabella, as his departure approached. "Into Thy hands I commit my spirit," was his invocation of the Almighty, "and with one long swell of the Eternal Sea, Columbus was again a discoverer"—He took an admirable subject and handled it, splendidly, to a full house—Came home in a storm of sleet and snow, and sat down, to write off this brief sketch.[95]

Chapin begins in medias res, with Columbus triumphant, then flashes back to Columbus unheeded and unassisted in his enterprise, and with Columbus, and Isabella, in a special relationship, serving God in the ultimate triumph in eternity from this weary world: in this metaphor the Ocean Sea leads to the Eternal Sea. This is empire in mystery with all its religious and political expansiveness without an emphasis on conflict and lasting regret and disappointment. In this heroic portrait of an indomitable spirit on earth in view of heaven, there is no mention of Columbus' personal woes, the destruction of the "Indians" or the regret writers in England seem later to have felt at Henry VII not securing the services of Columbus.

In the Civil War era, as in the period of the War of Independence, Columbus was a figure that appeared in letters and diaries. In a diary entry of March 20, 1864, Catherine Edmonston mentioned an archeological find that places Columbus in the context of Native settlement: "One thing is certain, from the vast quantity of these pieces of pottery & the area over which they are thickly distributed, this country must in former days have supported a dense Indian population. Would that one could speak & relate to us its history & tell us how many years have rolled by since it last saw the light! The only perfect pot I have ever seen is in my possession at Hascosea & was dug out by the negroes whilst excavating earth for the dams at Polentia. It was found sitting on some charcoal & half burned sticks at some depth in the earth, just as the Indian Squaw who last used it may have left it! It may be older than Columbus!"[96] The history of Natives who preceded European settlement of the area and the legacy of African slavery is something that related to the diarist and to her use of Columbus. Shards and pots, not simply words and images, became part of the historical record of the United States and the Americas. Some references to Columbus possessed a certain levity about them. If Washington and the District of Columbia could cohabit, Washington and Columbus could also coexist in a joke—Annie Adams Fields, in her diary during September 1865, after the Civil War had gone on for four years, could report: "Judge Hoar said also that he knew a man once with a prodigious memory; before dinner he could recall General Washington, after dinner he remembered Christopher Columbus!"[97] Edmundo O'Gorman has talked about the invention of America and in this chapter I have been speaking about the invention of Columbus and Columbia.[98]

The period after the Civil War produced private correspondence and journals that were concerned about the place of Columbus in private and public culture, that is in personal, family and community life as well as in American history and culture. In a letter written in January 1873, Ellen Tucker Emerson, some of whose letters to her father, Ralph Waldo Emerson, are still extant, discusses Columbus in terms of inventions, this past "discoverer" in terms of the discoveries of progress: she speaks of Pauline and wishes "she could only be by to hear Father go on about the corkscrew that is in it she would be amused. He says the man who invented it is equal to Columbus, and asks who gave it to me, where it was made, whether anyone ever had one before, and romances over it as he does about the tangerinas."[99] This humor also shows the changes in domestic life—diet, eating and drinking—that trade and invention had made to New England. Another letter of Ellen Tucker Emerson, composed in Concord, Massachusetts, and addressed again to Edith Emerson Forbes, which also mentioned Judge Hoar, spoke of her father, saying that "he came down and sent away my dear pretty child, and took me into the study and showed me a copy of Titian's Columbus by Raf. Mengs. The Chamberlaines, Lizzy Bartlett's relations, have come home and brought it, and puzzled Father well about their intentions. Sometimes they make it seem as if they brought it for him, sometimes as if they only asked his advice what to do with it. He said he had proposed that they should hang it for one year in the Town Library, and then present it to Harvard College. However last night came Mr C. & said he really desired to give it to the Town of Concord, a town whence all his light had sprung."[100] Here, the elder Emerson and the town of Concord consider what to do with Columbus, or at least this representation of his representation.

Columbus' landfall could also become a trope for the first sighting of land by ship passengers. On board *The Alcapulco,* on Tuesday afternoon, May 25, 1874, Emily McCorkle FitzGerald addressed her "Dear Mamma," proclaiming, "I am up on deck again. About half an hour ago we sighted land. Everybody has rushed to this side of the deck and they are all using their glasses. You don't know what a comfort the sight of land is. Why I feel better already. But it is land I never expected to see—the San Salvador of Columbus. I believe the one we are passing now they call Watling Island."[101] This use of the Columbian landfall as a marker or allusion in women's diaries and letters endured into the twentieth century.

Still a young child, Helen Keller, in a letter of January 8, 1890, in which she invited Dr. Everett Hale Jr. to learn braille, thanked him for the shells he sent her: "I shall always keep them, and will make me happy to think, that you found them, on that far away island, from which Columbus sailed to discover our dear country. When I am eleven years old it will be four hundred years since he started with the three small ships to cross the great strange ocean. He was very brave."[102] Later, in a letter to Caroline Derby on December 28, 1893, in which she thanks Miss Derby for the "pretty shield, " Helen Keller discussed a comparison between Columbus and herself when it seemed more explicit: "It is a very interesting souvenir of Columbus, and of the Fair of the White City; but I cannot imagine what discoveries I have made,—I mean new discoveries. We are all discoverers in one sense, being born quite ignorant of all things; but I hardly think that is what she meant. Tell her she must explain why I am a discoverer."[103] Ignorance and blindness, the difficulty of reading the signs, is something that Helen Keller, as young as she was, understood: the paradoxical recognition of being born into ignorance. But I am getting ahead of the buildup to the Chicago Exposition of 1893 with Helen Keller's reaction of a souvenir, a memento of the White City as something already past.

Columbus also became part of a list of worthies, illustrious people and monuments, so that he could find himself in different company. Fannie Miller, who took a trip east, discussed Boston, Philadelphia and other places; her visit to Philadelphia in September 1891, not long before the Columbian Exposition, recalled the Centennial of 1876 and places Columbus in a distinctly U.S. context:

> We rode over the Centennial Fair Grounds, and noted Memorial Hall, 1876, as the mon-
> ument of that great year, remaining in the park, also the superb fountain erected by the
> Maryland citizens of Philadelphia, being a gigantic figure of Moses as a centerpiece, stand-
> ing upon a firm foundation of massive rock. Around this imposing form are the handsome
> marble full-size statues of Father Matthew, the Apostle of Temperance, Charles Carroll, of
> Carrollton, the fearless Signer, Most. Rev. John Carroll, the first Archbishop of Baltimore,
> and Commodore John Barry, the illustrious Wexford man, who so ably distinguished him-
> self in the American naval service. Here, also, is a basaltic column from the Giant's Cause-
> way, Ireland, duly inscribed. A large figure of Christopher Columbus also adorns a place in
> the park, presented by the Italian citizens. A fine statue in bronze on a granite pedestal of
> General Meade is an attractive feature.[104]

She also mentioned William Penn's house, a statue of Niobe and another of Jeanne D'Arc, so Columbus, while being related to the American Revolution, the Centennial, the Italian-American community and the American military, is also given a wider part in a classical and medieval revival, in a translation of art and mythology, of prominent female figures—all on the eve of the celebrations of the 400th anniversary of Columbus' landfall. Here, perhaps consciously or not, is an eclectic, possibly pluralistic, multicul-tural display, a collection of tourist venues, of memories, ruins and monuments, to the history and ruins of America, both as the United States and the Americas.

Florence Trail's journey to, and stay in, Britain and France in 1891 is about social and artistic observations. After leaving the S. S. *Etruria* and after her time in Britain, she discusses her observations of works of art in France. Trail mentions, for instance, that the "whole character" of the museum, the Luxembourg, had changed since her last visit eight years before because it housed contemporary works only; she could be quite critical of works she thought bad, gross or meretricious.[105] Here, "The illustrations of historical events interested us most. *The Conference of Poissy 1561* painted by Robert-Fleury, who is just dead, and *Columbus Received by Isabella on his Return from the New World*, are charming."[106] Historical paintings joined biographical and religious works in this hall: Trail also spoke of her friend, Miss Parker, who lived in a tiny apartment at 13, rue Boissonade, and who had copied two landscapes at the Louvre and who was ready to choose one from the Luxembourg, with the approval of her guest, Florence Trail: "I am thoroughly satisfied with her choice of subjects."[107] Copying originals, which was not a new practice, was prevalent at this time and its prevalence may have had something to do with an intensified historical sense in the period and, along with collection, a means of the New World appropriating or assimilating the Old World. Columbus could become part of a movement to historical art but also a coming of terms of emigrants and settlers to the New World, in search of ancestral events and landscapes in Europe or how Europe begot settler America, and the growing cultural aspirations and power of that New World, still derived largely from Europe. The wealthy came back to assimilate and collect European history and aesthetics through art, documents and books. The Emersons, too, had to consider what to do with the copy of Titian's *Columbus*.

On October 18, 1892, Ellen Tucker Emerson wrote a letter to Edith Emerson Forbes about the "Columbus festival," something that would have been new to families and this town so important in the American Revolution.[108] Columbus, who had not received much notice about the time of the Salem witch hunts in the 1690s, who began with Belknap and others to be noticed at the time of U.S. independence as a means of creating a new identity, now had become part of the Puritan and non-conformist Protestant "English" Americas and the cradle of the Revolution. The first Columbus celebration in Concord was private and familial: "On Tuesday night we had a family Columbus festival. I invited Edward's family, Charley [Cabot?] & Therchi and Mrs Sanborn. To my joy every soul came. At tea we finished Mother's birthday cake."[109] The domestic scene of this family party had literary and ritual dimensions: "Everyone was lovely at my celebration and Charley read his Columbus ballad & Edward Mr Charles Ware's 'The game of Chess' about Ferdinand & Isabella, both of which were very good and were appreciated. Then we offered the incense of a bowl of marigolds before the photograph of the statue of young Columbus sitting on the dock, and each lighted a candle-end to burn before it in a ring around the bowl, and I thought it a pretty little spectacle. With much demur our children consented to stand up, as a choir, and sing their school songs, or rather a verse or two from each. Even Raymond joined in softly."[110] Columbus, who begot poetry early in the life of the United States republic, inspired more such verse about the time of the 400th anniversary. Ellen Emerson also looked ahead to public events in which the children would take part with school songs and for which they had been practicing: "You know the Town Columbus celebration is coming off this week."[111] The second, described by Ellen Emerson to Edith Forbes on October 21, was public. The town had organized a celebration with fanfare:

> I have just got home from the Columbus celebration. Each school had a banner. The Emerson school had the Stars & Stripes, with a white streamer with EMERSON SCHOOL on its gold letters. The High School had a square white banner with Concord High School emblazoned in gold on it. The Ripley School in which Raymond, dear soul!, was marching had a purple one with its name in gold, and the West Concord School a glorious cardinal red one with its name and a gold ship. Oh! My dear, the joy of this affectionate little Town Celebration was immense. Crowds of relatives drew up at Stow St. and smiled to see the banner at each school-house door, and the front rank of four files of our youth motionless behind it. At last the brass band is heard; out step the columns. 'Oh there come the infants! Oh how cunning! Little dears!' cried a voice, as the Ripley School begins to pour forth, all the babes taking hold of hands. Why, we had over five hundred children there on Stow St. sidewalk.[112]

This vast congregation of children and townspeople had helped to celebrate—with colors, songs and marches—Columbus. They continued with their English words, largely Protestant denominations and U.S. civic and military symbols:

> The military advance, solemnly led by Ashley How. One gun of the battery follows. Then the G. A. R. Post; now the schools fall in. The town rushes after, lines of wagons accompany, both sidewalks are full. The Town being at last arranged round the soldiers Monument, as on Decoration Day, Prescott Keyes addressed them and said we would raise the flag. The gun fired; every horse & every creature started, then commanded itself. The flag was raised, and suddenly Dong Dong! Cried the Orthodox bell, and the Unitarian swung wildly to & fro trying to get ahead with the Ding. A moment of great delight. "Now Three

Cheers for the Flag!" cried Prescott. Given well. Then *William* and the Schools *sang with the brass band*. Then Mr Reynolds addressed us; and it rained, but stopped very soon. Then the Town sang America with the brass band; and with much gratulation on all hands the celebration ended.[113]

Columbus had become part of an America and Americana born in the Revolution and made in the century or so thereafter. He seems to have entered the personal, family and public lives of Ellen Emerson and her fellow citizens of Concord and environs. This kind of celebration found an outlet at the Chicago World Exposition of 1893 even though this was but one of the ways Columbus was represented there.

Columbus took on many forms in 1893 and beyond. On the Wagner vestibuled train, part of the New York and Chicago Limited, Susan Hale wrote to Lucretia Hale at 10:15 in the morning of Saturday, February 4, 1893, and reported about an apparent waxworks that placed "Columbus subdued by a smile of Indian Maiden" beside "1, Bo-peep; 2, Mary had a little Lamb" and so on.[114] Columbus became part of the discourse of the World Exposition of 1893 and the social set that helped to bring it into being. In a letter of May 23, 1893, Mary Perkins Quincy mentioned a visit to Miss Gardiner at the same time "the Infanta Eulalia of Spain, and her husband Prince Antonio d'Orléans, with their suite, were arriving in New York, *en route* to the World's Fair, at Chicago, that was opened officially by President Cleveland, on May first."[115] With Miss Gardiner, Quincy caught "glimpses of the Spanish caravels at anchor in the waters of the Hudson. Does it seem possible that the armament of Christopher Columbus (as history records) 'consisted of two caravels, or light vessels without decks, and a third of larger bur-den'!"[116] She also reported that Spanish warships—perhaps those that might have been later used in the Spanish-American War of 1898, accompanied the replica ships: "the Infanta Isabella with the Santa Maria (the reproduction of Columbus' own vessel), the Nueva España with the Pinta, and the Reina Regenta towing the tiny Niña!"[117] Quincy described the ships in great detail, including the remark that "The Santa Maria, how-ever, differed from the two caravels, being larger and of greater importance, as befitted the ship of Columbus, who, in seeking the India of Marco Polo, discovered a New World. Although in October last came the true quadro-centennial of the landing at San Salvador, the appearance of the Santa Maria in American waters gave all who cared to visit the ship an opportunity of seeing the cabin of the great Genoese, 'the chair where he sat, and the chart he had used.'"[118] This event is a commemoration, a mediation on history and of a life past, although Quincy and Miss Gardiner preferred to view the ships from a distance, so her report, although informed, also has the dimension of being a mixture of an eyewitness account and a report of a report, not unlike some of the early narratives of exploration and settlement. In this description Quincy also identifies with Columbus' descendent, Duke of Veragua—she had been at Seville at Easter and had dri-ven out to see the kind of Spanish bulls on the campagna that the duke bred, and Quincy's little wooden *cassetta* or chest from Granada, while being "the same size as that of Queen Isabella from which Her Majesty's jewels were sold to aid the enterprise of Columbus," which Quincy had seen "In the sacristy of the cathedral, at Granada," was made of iron and velvet while the queen's was "a marvel of workmanship and—of gold."[119] In addition to the mythology of Columbus and Isabella, nobility also fasci-nated Quincy, for she, while mentioning the betrothal of the Duke of York and Princess May of Teck, had already remarked: "It is interesting that the Duke of Veragua, a de-scendant of Christopher Columbus, represents his distinguished ancestor at the

Columbian Exposition. The Duke, and the Duchess, and the Duke's brother, the Mar-
quis of Barboles, were present at the opening of the great Fair."[120] Here is an onlooker
as well as an eyewitness, someone who follows royalty and nobility but is not part of
their celebrations and does not know them: although there was a historical and republican aspect to the celebration of Columbus in the United States, there seems also to
have been an element of high society or the watching of the upper echelons and famous,
the kind of social voyeurism that has continued into the world of magazines, television
and elsewhere.

On February 6, 1896, at sea, Mary Quincy, speaking of history and discovery once
more, observed: "It is curious that Martinique should claim discovery by Columbus in
1502 and that its colonization by the French should have been begun in 1635, only fif-
teen years after the Pilgrims arrived in New England in the 'Mayflower'! At several
epochs England owned its fertile soil, but for generations the island has remained a possession of France."[121] Quincy's relation of Columbus to Martinique's claim and history,
also in the context of the English colony at Plymouth, also occurred in the context of
the local nobility, most notably the Empress Josephine, whose parentage and marriages,
including that to Napoleon in 1796, are outlined; "It is not surprising that the lovely
Creole should have always kept the charm of her tropical home, for once the traveller
has seen its radiance, he has lived to realize the vision of an enchanted land! The women
of Martinique are renowned for their beauty."[122] This kind of early tourist writing,
something that might well be found in a travel book even though it appears in a letter,
is the wider context for Columbus here. Quincy also mentioned Madame de Maintenon, who came to Martinique as a child, François, granddaughter of Théodore
Agrippa d'Aubigné, "'the Huguenot historian of his time, and the friend an companion
of Henri IV,'" married at sixteen to Scarron, the poet, and later to Louis XIV: even the
name of the person who married them, Louis' confessor, Père la Chaise, is brought into
the description of the marriages, which, according to Quincy, "are well known."[123] The
interest here in figures like Columbus, Josephine and Madame de Maintenon, as well as
their part in history, seems to be detailed and sincere but also bordering on an intellec-
tualization of social climbing: historical figures and the notables and nobles they represent were in the nineteenth century part of the tour and tourism.

In the early twentieth century women also kept up an interest in Columbus. Sometimes the references can be made lightly: Laurette Taylor—an actress who was part of
the patriotic star tour of "Out there" writing during the Great War—mentioned in her
diary how England valued its theater and actors while the United States did not, and,
while in Cincinnati on a tour of Ohio and beyond, played on the name of her next destination, named after the "discoverer" of the New World: "Now, on to Columbus!
Christopher! What a large country our own United States is! As an English comedian
who travelled it for the first time said, 'Why give him credit for *discovering* America?
How could he miss it?'"[124] This joke becomes part of a tour of her vast country, a way
for her and the audience to come together in a time of crisis. Other diarists wrote about
travels, for instance, Clare Sheridan, an artist, who said in a diary entry of February 22,
1921, about her exhibit of "Russian busts": "Two hundred people came to my exhibition to-day. It is very amusing, all kinds of cranks introduce themselves to me . . . some
say they are Bolsheviks, or Communists, and they hand me literature which gives me
news of Moscow! Others who tell me how they hate the Bolsheviks, the Sinn Feiners, or
the Knights of Columbus, and so on. I am always amused by people who want to kill
off all Bolsheviks, all Sinn Feiners, all Germans and all Jews. . . . It would make for a

wonderfully emptier world. Perhaps it would be more peaceful! Anyway, it is very emblematic of the Christian spirit of to-day!"[125] Hatred for the Knights of Columbus suggests that a Protestant-Catholic divide still exists and that the conflict is not simply binary between the believers and the Communists. The hatred toward Germans and Jews tells of remaining bitterness over the First World War and a lingering anti-Semitism. Tolerance is not something that Sheridan has found in Pittsburgh, New York and elsewhere, so that Christianity has not necessarily freed itself from its earlier internal and external conflicts. Sheridan, a self-described "Bolshevik, who had at first been denied a visa to Mexico on the those grounds," on Thursday, June 23, 1921, wrote about her arrival in Cuba: "The Cathedral where Columbus was buried alone stands out in my memory as a thing of beauty, but we got no further than an inner courtyard—the Cathedral itself was closed for repairs. The town seemed to have innumerable, modern marble monuments, each one more in ill taste than the other and each Cuban patriot thus commemorated had to be described at length by our unshaven guide. As for living Havanians, they seemed to me to be a people asleep."[126] Columbus is an absent presence here, someone missed but there, at least as remains, amid many other monuments, which were not to this artist's taste. Columbus becomes here part of the crowd of the living and dead, a monument among monuments, in the sleep of death among a people sleeping their lives away. Sheridan's descriptions of Havanians sleeping are on the verge of falling into stereotypes, and she is sometimes interested in national and racial descriptions elsewhere in the diary, for example, during her stay in Mexico. Another text written amid the turbulence of Mexican politics in the early 1920s is a letter from Rosalie Caden Evans to Daisy C. Pettus, from Mexico City on June 8, 1923; she opens the letter with a double representation of Columbus: "All the morning I indulged myself in Irving's *Life of Columbus*. I read it so long ago and it left a pleasing impression, as Columbus forms the center of a little group of my photographs collected in Spain and hangs in my living-room on the hacienda—perfectly in place and in harmony with his surroundings. I brought the book down with me in the hope of taking a peep, never dreaming of a disaster such as this, an attack of grippe, that I should lie down on my back and read for hours, drifting through tropical seas in search of a new world. How little the Indians have changed, scant clothing, simple credulous minds, and only brave in numbers. Of all the absurd turns of fate, this present nonsense of 'reform' being applied to Mexico!"[127] Sheridan had described "Tata-Nacho" in the Mexican Consulate in New York, "this strange looking descendent of Montezuma," so that the otherness of Natives and their stereotyping in relation to historical figures seems to have been something these two women pursued, consciously or not, as a representational strategy.[128]

A diary, written by Mary Matthews Bray, that did not note the years but was published in 1920, emphasized vision and romance in sailing the seas. Is not a clipper "an embodiment of man's far-seeing vision,—a result of his dream or desire or belief—whatsoever it may be termed—that the area which he can see with his eyes, or traverse with his limbs, is not the whole world? Was it not such a vision, that led Columbus, Ponce de Leon, Americus Vespucius, Sir Francis Drake, and other explorers, to embark upon unknown seas, trusting that the inspiration which led them on, would sooner or later be justified by realization? Is there not also in these later years romance connected with the ocean and with commerce?"[129] Columbus is part of this vision and romance, which can also be encountered when sailors seek land as well: "There, they encounter perhaps, savage tribes, and the story of their adventures may almost equal those of Marco Polo, or Baron Munchausen, even with a much greater regard for truth."[130] What Marco Polo meant for Columbus is something that is part of the enterprise and legacy that is never quite stated explicitly in the sources for Columbus' voyages. The relation between story and truth, of tall tales and fact, is a topic Bray raises here and that is key for assessing Columbus and the narratives of exploration and settlement as well as travel literature more generally. Vision, romance and truth may just coexist in complex and ironic ways that are hard to distil.

In the month of the stock market crash in October 1929, Monica Storrs, who had left Liverpool late in September, is not impressed with those on ship with her, Canadian and New York "profiteers" and their families, but her sighting of an iceberg made her consider another voyage: "First we passed quite close to a huge ice-berg, so close that I thought it must be a bit of C. P. R. scene-painting; but they all said it was real, so I photographed it from the top deck. I was surprised at the colour, having expected to be like greenish glass whereas it was really pure white and glistening in the sun like a small escaped snow mountain. I supposed it reminded everybody of the *Titanic,* but we didn't say so till today."[131] The painting of the Canadian Pacific Railway had presented something like and not like the new natural scene Storrs had come to face. The great disaster haunts the arrival of this ship and this diarist, who turned her gift for description to new thoughts about more ancient history: "Then at 3 P.M. (Wednesday, October 2) we sighted the first land, Belle Isle on the Starboard bow, and a little later the coast of Newfoundland further off on the Port bow. This meant that we were beginning to enter the St. Lawrence River and should have calm-going for the rest of the voyage. It was an extraordinary feeling—that first sight of the huge New World—and of the land where Father was born. I'm afraid it was not altogether a friendly feeling I had for it, but something very near resentment for not being the coast of England. But all the same it made me feel rather like a little Columbus. My word—what a man was Columbus! But whether a benefactor to the world is quite another question."[132] Here, once again, is a typology between the unfamiliar, alienating and exilic New World and the familiar, comforting and home-like Old World. Even in a British and Canadian context, Columbus appears; Storrs felt ambivalence for the land where her father was born, and, like Frances Anne Kemble in September 1832, she feels homesick for England and an alienation from this new land she is seeing for the first time. Storrs' ambivalence and resentment leads her to think of Columbus and to see herself a "little Columbus," but, while diminishing herself, she builds up the explorer—"what a man was Columbus!"—only to deflate him, because she asks rhetorically or at least suspends an answer about whether he benefited the world. In the Peace River country of western Canada, on February 22, 1930, Storrs describes Taylor's Flats, and "Herbie Taylor, the father of the Flats, whose Indian wife I visited across the river a fortnight ago. He is a sturdy old halfbreed, very friendly and full of talk;" when he told Storrs she would not have to see his wife as she was better, he "rewarded (or punished)" her "by the production of an immense family photograph album, containing all the halfbreeds there can ever have been since Columbus, arranged in wedding-groups, and culminating in a terrific series of old Herbie himself at all ages."[133] This reference to Taylor, Natives and people of mixed Native-European backgrounds is jocular, familiar and satiric so that the tone is never quite certain. Storrs has traveled a long way from Liverpool and she sometimes shows this kind of comic, novelistic manner in describing other people in her diary even if her quip about Columbus can seem a little off to later ears.[134]

Still during the Great Depression, Betty May Hale wrote in her diary on June 29, 1937, about Norway, where she was traveling, and a description of a church near Leda brought up the inevitable discussion of the Viking voyages to the New World: "The first king was crowned there in 1000. The church was pretty and the cemetery was too. We passed a house hidden by trees and found that it was where Leif Erickson was born. Erickson came to America originally planning to go to Greenland. He discovered America before Columbus."[135] This controversy, which was at about the time of the World Columbian Exposition in 1893, was settled later in the twentieth century, when excavations beginning in 1960 showed that there had been Viking settlements in present-day Canada.[136] Before Columbus though they were, it took centuries after Columbus for this evidence to come to light. Although Columbus remained central to the expansion of Europe, his landfall became decentered and qualified by the Norse voyages and Native accounts of their world before Columbus as well as their interpretation of the encounter.

This discussion of Columbus in women's diaries and letters in North America over about 140 years ends with a diary, which does not identify the years, published in 1939—that of Viola Chittenden White, who had a keen interest in flora. She quotes from Henry David Thoreau's *Journals: "Even the expeditions for the discovery of El Dorado and of the Fountain of Youth led to real, if not compensatory discoveries. Columbus thought he was approaching the garden of Eden, the sacred abode of our first parents—the Orinoco seemed to him one of the four rivers flowing from Paradis;"* which causes White to ask and gloss: "And how far will Miami console us for El Dorado, or the opening up of South America for the four lost rivers of Paradise?"[137] This is a question, perhaps a rhetorical question, about desire and the remoteness of impossibility of compensation between the vision and the achievement, between heaven and the earth that Columbus and all who followed him in search of El Dorado, including Walter Ralegh, tread with desires and dreams and promises. The Chicago World Exposition of 1893 might well have been an argument of a certain kind that would have vindicated Thoreau's question: the United States and progress had more than compensated. White's question, however, will remain before us even at the end of this book.

VI

Columbus had fallen on hard times just before his death, and, intermittently, his reputation was neglected after his death. In 1792, as we have seen, he became a symbol for the young republic celebrating its struggle for independence. The anniversaries did not apparently receive much attention between the three and four hundred anniversaries of the landfall. In 1882 the Knights of Columbus, a Catholic fraternity, was founded and attempted to change that and argued that he was a seer or prophet as well as an instrument of Divine Providence and that October 12 should be made into a national holiday; in 1892, New York spent five days celebrating Columbus, including the construction of Columbus Circle, which had a large statue of the explorer at the entrance to Central Park, Anton Dvorak's symphony, "From the New World," and a speech celebrating Columbus as a kind of St. Christopher, carrying salvation to the New World.[138] Chicago became the prime focus for the celebration of Columbus and what I call the "Columbian," indirect U.S. or "American" (in the larger sense) uses of Columbus as a pretext to celebrate itself, its arrival as an industrial, economic and political power, to itself and the world.

The spirit and material artifacts and replicas of Columbus and his life were also present in the Exposition: the planners from the United States took that aspect seriously. In some ways the ghost of Columbus sailed again for the Americas. Careful replicas of the *Nina, Pinta,* and *Santa Maria,* built in Spain under the supervision of the Spanish navy and government, sailed to Chicago for the World Exposition and were moored on South Pond, where the public could board them. A replica of the Monastery of La Rabida, in Palos, where Columbus stayed at a crucial time in his advocacy of a voyage to the western Atlantic housed many "Columbian" artefacts as well as a copy of his first correspondence about the New World.[139] Claims for Columbus' predecessors, which have proved to be correct according to recent digs in Canada by archeologists, were not white-washed in the White City but not given quite as prominent a place. The Government of Norway, according to Norman Bolotin and Christine Laing, "sent an exact replica of the 1,000-year-old vessel commanded by Leif Ericson for display at the exposition. The 76-foot-long vessel was patterned after the original Viking ship, which was purportedly unearthed just four years before the fair was held. The ship was moored at the Naval Pier in Lake Michigan."[140] The "purportedly" cried out for a gloss in a book on the Chicago Exposition of 1893 published during the year of the 500th anniversary of Columbus' landfall because the authors would know about the Viking settlements in North America but might have evidence that although this was a replica of a Norse ship, there was a mythical link to Leif Ericson. (If indeed that is the implication or evidence.) Discovering America is still controversial and was not simply something the organizers of the fair in the 1890s alone had to consider.

An official and authorized memorial volume concerning the Exposition has, after the letter of authorization, a portrait of Columbus facing on the opposite page photographs of his descendent, the Duke of Veruga, and his wife; on the next right-hand page, facing a blank left sheet, are other members of the family, beginning with "His Excellency, Christopher Columbus, The Duke's Son." Continuing this familial and Spanish theme, the next left-hand page, which faces a photo of the Convent La Ribida and the California State Building, also referred to here as the "Spanish Monastery," contains a letter from Columbus' descendent, the Duke:

May 1893
Chicago

The City of Chicago closes the festivities of the four hundredth anniversary of the Discovery of America with a great Exhibition.

The initiators of this idea deserve credit, for the splendid display takes place in one of the most important regions enlightened by Columbus with Gospel, source of all progress.

It must serve to unite more closely the inhabitants of both Hemispheres by way of Commerce, in that they may seek in their own efforts the legitimate means of triumphing in the struggle sustained by all Nations to increase their wealth, thus contributing to the well-being of humanity.

Cristobal Colon
Duque de Veragua[141]

This message of trade and evangelization through the gospel was a theme in the texts of, or surrounding the voyages of, the original Christopher Columbus, at the Chicago Exposition of 1893 and in this letter by the later eponymous descendent. Progress and the connection between Columbus and the United States are also themes of the exposition and this letter, which helps to introduce the memorial volume at the close of this world's fair. The rest of the book, while showing the great variety within the fair, cele-brates this point of view. For instance, the volume declares: "This is the golden age of American industry, American progress and American development. Wonders have been achieved in every branch of thought, and in every line of trade. We are at home and abroad. It is fitting that we, as the greatest nation on the continent discovered by Christopher Columbus, should lead in the celebration of the 400th anniversary of that event, and call upon the people of the civilized world to unite with us."[142] While not the only representation in the exposition, the idea of the triumph of progress and the United States as a leader under a new *Pax Americana,* was explicitly and implicitly a major official theme of the exposition.

The Columbian World Exposition of 1893, which was delayed a year, took on many forms and represented gender, race and class in ways that still hold the interest of scholars, historical societies and the public.[143] This Exposition, as well as the sec-ond such exposition in Chicago in 1933–34, made significant contributions to archi-tecture and design in the United States and beyond.[144] The celebration was as much about the arrival of the United States as Columbus' arriving in the New World. One America, by claiming that name, was becoming in this celebration a synecdoche for America or the Americas. Here, I will concentrate on aspects of a few of the many el-ements of this Exposition—praise to Columbus and Columbia; homage to the United States; the vision of progress in science, industry and commerce; the role and repre-sentation of women, Natives and black Americans. These concerns overlap and will not be treated in discrete discussions.

In their address at the exposition to President Grover Cleveland of the United States, William Boldenweck and Maier Weinchenk sounded somewhat like Belknap did in 1792, for they represented Columbus as a bearer of Enlightenment. Here, in 1893, Columbus was an agent of progress who helped to lead humankind away from super-stition, bigotry and feudalism:

> When the dark clouds of political and religious bigotry were enshrouding the sun lit heav-ens of then benighted Europe, and freedom of thought and the expression thereof was re-garded as the key-note of treachery and treason: when ambition of thought was stifled, and the spirit of progress was stayed, for fear of offending the powers of might. Our Hero, Columbus, strong in his convictions of the truth of his cause, after weary hours of waiting, finally gained royal consent and aid to the attempt of the consummation of that which seemed to the populace at large a foolhardy errand.[145]

Columbus, as in Barlow's epic, is a "Hero," an agent of freedom, truth and ambition whose thought and bold plan was stifled and misunderstood by king and people. The typology of the Old World and the New here is that Columbus was the first emigrant with a new vision of the world that America would develop and that old cultures could not abide. Moreover, for Boldenweck and Weinchenk, "the misfortunes of Columbus in quest of then hidden shores were indeed paltry and slight, when compared with the great ocean of wealth which that voyage contributed to the enlightenment and educa-tion of the world at large."[146]

Sometimes these authors, in their pursuit of the theme of progress, molded Colum-bus' life in directions he probably did not take. Columbus comes to mean America, which becomes identified with the United States here. As the authors assert:

the discovery of America may well be called the cornerstone of the great bulwark of progress, the vanguard of the march of civilization, the promoter of the spirit of education which has blessed the centuries which followed. The flag unfurled and the cross erected on the sandy banks of Florida, in 1492, were ready conquerors of the ignorance of the native tribes, who, wonderingly admired, and fearfully beheld the signs and symbols of enlightenment.[147]

This representation is a later variation on Columbus' reading of the speech and signs of Natives, and even his landfall is displaced to Florida, which became part of the United States. Columbus brought progress to America and America to the world, which begot more progress. Boldenweck and Weinchenk amplify their points on progress, and the wonder of the Natives before Columbus is something that the explorer represented in his own accounts of his voyages and that others pick up on, such as Anne Gorham Everett's description in 1841 of a statue being prepared in Italy for the U. S. Capitol in which Columbus strikes wonder in an Indian girl. This Native wonder before Columbus and the Europeans generally is a traveling trope.

Columbus is read back through the history of the United States, as if millions escaped religious persecution to Brazil or New Spain, when this does not seem to have been the case. Columbus becomes appropriated politically and culturally in a teleology of progress, as if he could have embodied or predicted the United States: "The hope of Columbus was realized, America was discovered, and the supremacy of thought and reason established over the dicta of bigotry and superstition."[148] A democratic or republican imperialism may have been the end of Columbus' journey. How much the Europeans, who themselves brought about the Enlightenment, and especially the French, who had had their own revolutions, and the British, who had passed reform bills, such as that in 1832 and had instituted general public education, would have agreed with this view is another matter. Certainly, as we shall soon see, a number of women, Natives and African Americans did not see the United States as having made progress enough toward liberty, equality and social justice. There were then contending versions of America at this Exposition, but the dominate one was that which Boldenweck and Weinchenk expressed and the architecture, monuments and inscriptions emphasized.

Like Belknap, these authors emphasize liberty but they also include a message like that which is part of the ideology of the Statue of Liberty—the United States as a place safe from the oppression and unfairness of Europe:

The new land was soon looked forward to and considered as a harbor of refuge for the down-trodden and oppressed. The systems of persecution in Europe, too bitter to be endured, drove millions of people to the shores of the promised land, and 'ere two centuries had past, in 1620 the pilgrim Fathers, of blessed memory in the history of our country, landed on our shores and by their coming added pillar and post to that structure of prosperity so auspiciously begun by Columbus' discovery. With their advent upon our soil, the spirit of prosperity and enterprise, aided and nurtured by their sturdy industry and zeal, poured forth as a beacon light to bring liberty and truth to all the world. Upwards of a century did they toil mid the pristine forests of primeval New England's waste, progressing steadfastly and earnestly to their goal of success, peace, happiness and prosperity; hemmed in and oppressed by their task-masters in the land of their nativity, they determined, as Israel of old, to throw off the shackles of slavery and oppression. Brave in the heart and firm in the conviction of the justice and right of their cause, they demanded freedom, liberty to think and liberty to act.[149]

These authors make it sound as though millions of oppressed and down-trodden Europeans left for America before the Pilgrims arrived in 1620: this does not seem to be how
Portuguese, Spanish and French writers would have described their colonial efforts in
this period. The Inquisition did not tolerate much religious plurality in the Iberian
colonies in America. It appears that Boldenweck and Weinchenk are reading the English experience, especially after 1620, and the American situation after the War of Independence back on previous times and on different cultures. The Pilgrims, in this version,
built with enterprise, industry and zeal on the prosperity that Columbus had enabled
with his discovery. They toiled to make something more of the "wastes" of the
"primeval" forests of New England, even though their English "task-masters" were hem-
ming them in, so that, in this liberation narrative, they threw off "slavery and oppression," and, seeking justice, achieved freedom. Boldenweck and Weinchenk repeat words
like "prosperity," "oppression" and "liberty," as well as synonyms to emphasize the way
that Columbus led to the Pilgrim Fathers and how they fought for their independence.

In this story of freedom it is not hard to guess what will come next. The Declaration
of Independence seems to be a direct growth from Columbus' Enterprise of the Indies.
The bravery of the Pilgrims is the bridge between the explorer and the birth of the
United States:

> Their courage and perseverance conquered, and 'ere four centuries had past the Declara-
> tion of Independence became a household word, a nursery rhyme, wherever civilization
> had found lodgement; ours became the land of freedom and enlightenment and the spirit
> of progress touched into life by the discovery of Columbus, nurtured and protected by the
> landing of the pilgrim Fathers, was broadened and expanded by the signing of the Decla-
> ration of Independence and since then has progressed steadfastly, ever broadening and
> widening in influence and encompassing art, science, and every branch of industry in its
> manifold and mysterious folds.[150]

This great new country is a land of "civilization" as well as "freedom and enlightenment"
given to the "spirit of progress" that Columbus' discovery "touched into life" and that
the Pilgrim Fathers (the women are not mentioned explicitly) and the Declaration of Independence "broadened and expanded." This movement of progress is almost like that
of the Holy Spirit, a secularized translation of empire and evangelization: this spirit
dwells—rather than in the church—in art, science and industry. These authors use a
theological language, especially in describing "its manifold and mysterious folds," somewhat like Munroe's Columbia, who, at the end of the ode, is called "Daughter of mystery." Boldenweck and Weinchenk create a climax, a kind of American Whig version of
progress, as if the United States, and not Hegel's Prussia or Germany, were the end of
history. In more practical terms, Boldenweck and Weinchenk end with a direct address
to President Cleveland: "and that the World's Columbian Exposition, this day by you
dedicated to the entire world, may be another great factor in the onward march of
progress in science, in art, and in every branch of industrial life" and maintain, in a
utopian crescendo, that "peace, plenty, and prosperity" will be the heritage in a "glorious and happy age."[151]

The Columbian Exposition paid tribute to Columbus, to America and to the United
States. Homage to Columbus also occurred in the various monuments in his honor at
the Exposition. The Rand McNally guide of 1893 is a good place to go to see how these
works were described at the time of the fair:

Fronting the Administration Building, on the verge of and facing the Main Basin, stands the finest and most artistic composition on the Exposition grounds—*the Columbian Fountain* (N 19), designed By Mr. Frederick MacMonnies, and executed by him principally in his Paris studio. Resembling closely in symbolical design a remarkable sketch alleged to have been made by Columbus himself, in part it follows the general design of the fountain at the Paris Exposition. . . . Enthroned and above all sits Columbia, majestic in dignity and pose, the personification of liberty, freedom, and power, with Father Time as steersman, "like Palinurus nodding at the helm." Assisting in the propulsion of the Ship of State, on either side are four female figures, representing the arts and sciences, gracefully pulling huge sweeps, or oars. At the bow of the barge, Fame, a beautiful female figure, with a herald's trumpet in hand, proclaims with clarion note the advent and progress of the nation. The motto *"E pluribus unum"* (out of one many) is graven on the pedestal supporting the principal figure.[152]

As in the address to Grover Cleveland, in this description, Columbus leads to the United States and the ideas of liberty and progress, but here this partly occurs through Columbia. Columbus and the Columbian are central to the exposition and gesture to themselves as well as to the march of time to the power of the United States. The guide does not mention that Time, whose scythe was attached to a rudder, which, Wim de Wit says, consisted of a bundle of fasces, was a symbol of authority in ancient Rome.[153] This detail would suggest yet another example of the traveling trope of the translation of empire.

The Rand McNally guide paid a good deal of attention to *"the Convent Santa Maria de la Rabida* (Saint Mary of the Fronier) (N 23), where Columbus found shelter in time of trouble and 'begged a pittance for his child.'"[154] The great Columbus is here praised under a picture of William E. Curtis, someone whose scrapbooks will figure in our discussion: the reproduction of this convent "cost $50,000, contains priceless relics of the great discoverer, and is guarded night and day by United States troops. The reproduction and the collection of rare relics of the Noah of our nation are in more than a measure due to the indefatigable perseverance of the Hon. William Eleroy Curtis of the Bureau of American Republics, who traversed the whole of Europe searching for traces of the great Genoese admiral and procuring relics, maps, etc. for exhibition here. It may be questioned if there are any persons on this continent who can speak with greater authority as to Columbus than this talented writer." Having read his scrapbooks, I think that Curtis, whose subjoined article is clear and elegant, drew on many sources from different countries, including the noted scholar Henry Harrisse. After telling about the monastery, Curtis sums up its significance and thus its choice to house the relics of Columbus: La Rábida was "as a famous American writer has said, 'the corner-stone of American history.'"[155] Literally nothing known about Columbus has been overlooked, so that Curtis has organized documents, maps and images from sources like the archives of the Vatican, England, France and Spain and from private collectors and the descendents of Columbus, a cannon from the *Santa Maria,* the ruins of Isabella (the first European town in the New World) brought from Santo Domingo to Chicago on "a United States man-of-war," and Frederick A. Ober's photographs and relics of places Columbus visited on the American continent, an essay in images and objects from the disputed places of his birth to the two places that "claim possession of his bones.[156] This "Noah of our nation, "as the guide, not Curtis, calls him, is also in a place of honor, "a collection that includes," in Curtis' words, "the original, or a copy, of every portrait of Columbus that was ever painted or engraven, eighty in number, and a model or a photograph of every monument or statue that was ever erected in his memory."[157] Curtis left nothing unturned and did an admirable job for the admiral. This article ends beneath a painting, "The Landing of Columbus. From the celebrated picture of John Vanderlyn, in the Rotunda of the capitol at Washington, D.C." This rotunda, which we saw was the object of discussion in a diary from the 1840s, was part of a cultural appropriation in the District of Columbia, in whose territory is the capital, Washington. The general shares his nation symbolically with the admiral. The metonymy of Columbia, that is the transplantation of Columbus symbolically to the United States, joins the synecdoche of "America" (the United States) as America (the Americas). La Rábida is a religious place, not simply a convent or Noah's ark, but a shrine to the secular aspirations of a Christian nation, whose very constitution separated church and state. Columbus as a progenitor of the United States in the way I have just described is something born in the "American" Revolution and developed thereafter, something that was reaching a climax at the World Columbian Fair in 1893 in Chicago.

Part of this Exposition was the notion of display generally, showing the world this America, a legacy of Columbus, and part of that inheritance was the indigenous peoples who were on the land thousands of years before that "discovery." Columbus, Cabot, Gonneville, Cartier and others had taken Natives back to Europe, where they had been put on display. Now the world would come to Chicago and see the show of and in America. One such pair of photographs is a kind of stereotyping as it is literally two albumen stereo cards, and, following the number 8146, is entitled "Esquimaux children and dogs, Columbian Exposition."[158] In this double presentation of the same image placed side-by-side three husky dogs are in foreground, then in the middle distance three Inuit children of varying sizes and then three male Inuit adults. All but the boy in the very middle are hooded. The photograph does not provide a context for these displaced figures but places them on a ground with a fence behind them. The accounts of Frobisher's voyage represented the Inuit in writing in the 1570s and now they were "captured" in a relatively new medium—the photograph. They were now explicitly placed in a more direct Columbian context than their ancestors, who were far from the islands where Columbus landed and were more closely related to the Norse voyages before and the English voyages in the wake of John Cabot or Giovanni Caboto like those of Frobisher, Davis and Hudson. Another image in this genre by the same B. W. Kilburn, is a pair of albumen stereo prints on a tan card—number 8306—of "California's Great Orange, State Building, Columbian Exposition," and this time in this more open scene, full of trees and light, the theme is largely bounty: a banner in the foreground of the photograph proclaims "THIS FRUIT WAS/GROWN IN SOUTHERN CALIFORNIA/THE LAND OF SUNSHINE AND FLOWERS." This is the bounty that Columbus and many who followed him spoke about in describing the islands and mainland of the New World. Hakluyt, Cartier and others had listed the commodities and natural resources of northern America and here the aspect of trade show, which builds on this trope of plenty, recurs centuries after. Before this building, this great orange, is a bear, the symbol of the state of California, so that the stuffed and tamed and exploited wildness of the land is also on display in this grove or garden of plenty. The Native and European ways on show in these two stereo images, of Inuit and California, represent an unspoken tension in this post-Columbian America.

Another image suggests some of the ideography of the Columbian World Exposition. In a lithograph by Rodolfo Morgari, Columbus stands amid American presidents, with Lincoln to Columbus' left (our right) and Washington to Lincoln's left; Columbus, in the top left-hand corner of the picture, holds a modern map of the Americas in his right hand while his left hand rests on top of a globe; his right foot disappears into a cloud while his left rests on it as if its white vapors were solid. Grover Cleveland is in a framed picture, with his name at the bottom, all the way to the right of Lincoln, who begins this line of U. S. dignitaries in the upper part of the image. The next "level" beneath this Columbian-U.S. band is, from left to right, an eagle with a wreath with a banner on which appears 1893; a woman with a robe of stars, perhaps the flag as it matches the U. S. flag she is holding in her left hand, occupies the center of the picture and to her left is what appears to be an angel with a torch, held in the right hand, with a banner with the word "Excelsior" on it. Beneath the eagle on our left is the Columbian Exposition literally from a bird's-eye view and on the other side of Columbia is a man in Western dress and beside him, perhaps Justice, with a Roman-style helmet with laurel about it; in her left hand is a tablet with a picture of the scales of justice on it and the words "Corpus Juris" and a sword before it. She looks ahead, as does the man, but the surrounding figures of the various Natives and peoples of the world look up through Liberty (the figure with the flag) and beyond to Columbus and the U.S. leaders.[159]

The Columbian Exposition of 1893 in Chicago also gave a pretext for many other interests and themes, such as education and the role of women, in the United States and the world. Columbus was not always front and center but provided an occasion for the United States, as part of and on behalf of the Americas, to display its accomplishments to the Old World and the wider world. Education was on show in Chicago: the positioning of colleges was considered carefully—the exhibit for Princeton College, for instance, being "in the gallery at the south end of the Liberal Arts Building, immediately over its main central aisle. Harvard University was located on one side of it and Columbia College on the other."[160] The Princeton exhibit included a vast array of objects, including 3,000 books; the writing of alumni and members of the faculty; the portrait of Washington by C. W. Peale in 1784, which had hung for a century in North College, draped with the flag of the United States, flanked by portraits of ten of the presidents of the college; on the side walls, crayons of Presidents McCosh and Patton and portaits of two revolutionary governors, Belcher and Patterson; models, relief maps and images of the college; Humboldt's magnetometer; an original Fahrenheit thermometer made in Amsterdam in 1632; Benjamin Franklin's electrical machine, and so on. This exhibit, which Mr. Street organized, "was intended to cover the history, the activity, and the scope of the institution."[161] This display was successful: in *The Evening Star,* V. Lansing Collins wrote on December 11, 1893, "Princeton University has been awarded four prizes for her exhibit at the world's fair. The first and most coveted prize is for the general excellence of the exhibit, the second is for her scientific apparatus; the third for her mechanical drawings and the last for her alumni library."[162] Such a celebration of knowledge, culture science, engineering, which brought the world to the United States, under the rubric of Columbus, is after him in another sense. In 1893, scientific and industrial progress were the theme with a strong echo of the liberty and enlightenment—the portrait of Washington as well as those of the revolutionary governors and the flag pay such tribute—that occurred in Belknap's celebration of Columbus but not nearly so directly tied to Columbus himself. Columbus, although a pretext in both senses, could be superseded and occluded in a celebration that invoked his name.

Women also sometimes explicitly swept Columbus aside for their own reform agenda. The timing was right. In 1893 New Zealand became the first country to grant women suffrage: it took the United States twenty-seven more years to do the same, when it became the sixteenth country to do so: as early as the World's Fair in New York in 1853 Susan B. Anthony and others had defied critics and spoken up for women and on related issues, and women at the U. S. centennial at Philadelphia had received a more welcoming reception; but that did not stop Congress from leaving women out of the planning of the celebration of Columbus in Chicago, just as they had done in planning the Centennial, which prompted Isabella Beecher Hooker to say: "A male oligarchy has called itself a republic for a hundred years, and during forty of them good men and women have patiently protested against the misnomer and asked for justice."[163] Speaking to a rare audience of both sexes at a formal event, Bertha Honoré Palmer, a Chicago socialite, art collector and reformer, ensured that her husband would donate funds for a separate Woman's Building and that the architect would be female; as the elected president of the board of lady managers, a body of 115 women that Congress had created probably in response to women's protests over the lack of say in the planning of the Chicago Exposition, Palmer stressed the part Queen Isabella had played in Columbus' voyage and declared: "even more important than the discovery of Columbus, which we are gathered to celebrate, is the fact that the General Government has just discovered woman."[164] Women also contributed to the debate on race, which was also an issue at the Chicago Exposition of 1893 as Native and African Americans felt that they did not have proper representation.

Buffalo Bill Cody's Wild West show, which attracted about 2 million visitors near but outside the Exposition grounds, showed the skill of Natives but also staged white rescues of other European settlers from Native attacks and cruelty (a long way from Las Casas' representations of the indigenous peoples); Natives took little part in the Exposition and their artifacts were displayed in what the Board of Indian Commissioners described as small and mean in the middle of grand structures; the Exposition had invited Simon Pokagon, Chief of the Potawatomi, son of the leader who deeded in 1833 the land on which the fair was being hosted, to speak on Chicago Day (October 9)—five days before Italian Day, which coincided with Columbus Day—and he criticized publicly the Chicago Exposition's disrespect for Natives.[165] The Inuit (Esquimaux or Eskimos, as they were referred to at the time) from northern Labrador came to Chicago six months before the fair to get used to the heat: they built a stockage in Jackson Park and charged an admission fee; when summer came many Inuit left as they claimed that the contractor had deceived them; one reporter said, "Had the Esquimaux settled on Midway Plaisance and held together, their remarkable ethnological character would have received earnest public attention."[166] Native Americans did protest the lack of consultation with them in the planning of the Chicago Exposition. Early in the planning of the Fair some Native Americans wrote to the U. S. Commissioner of Indian Affairs, asking for a voice: "We, American citizens of Indian blood, most earnestly petition you to grant us through the forthcoming World's Fair and anniversary of the discovery of America, some recognition of our race; some acknowledgement that we are still a part, however inferior, of America and the Great American republic."[167] The Natives had been pushed back systematically in the nineteenth century and it was difficult for them to make their cultural and political presence felt. The appeal was for self-representation: "With a Native American, or Indian exhibit in the hands of capable men of our own blood . . . a most interesting and instructive and surely successful feature will be added"; it "will show to both and all races alike, that our own advancement has been much greater than is usually supposed."[168] Some despair and frustration were expressed in this appeal: "Give us . . . some reason to be glad with you that

[America] was so discovered."[169] This term "discovery" has long been problematic for Natives in the "New World."

The situation for African Americans was also difficult. The legacy of slavery and unfair treatment still haunted Americans of African descent. Women were prominent in airing grievances on behalf of Black Americans: for instance, Fannie Barrier Williams spoke to audiences of women on the injustice of slavery and how it had marked African-Americans; the Dahomean village on the Midway was the only exhibit to include Black people, which was one of the reasons that Frederick Douglass and Ida B. Wells wrote a pamphlet about the lack of Black participation at the fair that they distributed to visitors and thereby tried to reach an audience beyond the United States. Whereas Wells did not attend the Colored People's Day, Douglass, once a part of the Centennial celebrations and the U.S. representative in Haiti, delivered a speech, "The Race Problem in America."[170]

Let me turn back from public to private images of this Exposition. In my brief account I have tried to blend various responses, public and private, in popular and high culture in the United States, to Columbus, Columbia and the Columbian. Julian Street's scrapbook, now at Princeton, provides an interesting representation of the Fair, because it includes clippings from a variety of sources, many of which would have been available to those who visited the Exposition in 1893 or read about it in magazines and newspapers.[171] One of the images, which is not affixed in this scrapbook, is a black and white photograph, entitled "The Barge of the Columbian Fountain," without attribution or bibliographical information, but which is amidst various color prints of the fair from the *Chicago Tribune Art Supplement,* from June into September, 1893. He also has the *Official Souvenir Programme of the Dedicatory Ceremonies of the World's Columbian Exposition, Chicago, Oct. 20th, 21st & 22nd 1892,* which describes the procession, which begins with the Joint Committee on Ceremonies, the Director General of the Exposition and the President of the Centennial Commission of 1876, at Philadelphia, and Director General of that commission; the President of the United States, the World's Columbian Commission and the Vice-President of the Exposition; the Vice-President of the United States; and many others including the Supreme Court, the House of Representatives and Senate, former high ranking officials of the federal government. The Government of the United States had invested a great deal of prestige and cultural capital into the World Exposition of 1893, which seems to have grown out of the Centennial celebrations of 1876 and was even connected ceremonially to it in this procession.

The dedicatory ceremonies began with "Columbus March and Hymn" and various religious hymns, the "Star Spangled Banner," "Hail Columbia" and prayers and benedictions. At the end of the *Programme* is the music of "The Hallelujah Chorus." Columbus, Columbia and the United States were given a vast ceremony and rousing beginning. One article, "Three Fairs in One," on the front page of the *Chicago Sunday Tribune World's Fair Supplement,* April 30, 1893, announced that this fair had an "area under roof equal to that of Paris in 1889, Philadelphia in 1876, and Vienna in 1873 combined." This fair was on such a scale as to outdo the Old World and the Centennial celebrations of the United States together: this identifying "America" with the legacy of Columbus seems to have gathered more investment, culturally and financially, than the great celebration of the birth of the nation in Philadelphia. The scrapbook also shows the vastness of the Liberal Arts Building and the grand monuments of the Columbian or Macmonnies Fountain and the Central Arch of the Peristyle, where Columbus welcomed visitors to the fair from high above. Many other images are in the scrapbook, from the inside of Cologne Cathedral to the inauguration of President Cleveland on March 4, 1885. Among the many pictures of people from around the world are the classical images of "The Gladiator by Pio Welouski" and a statue of Caesar Augustus from the Vatican under the rubric "RETROSPECT," is an image of the monument to Columbus in Genoa, with its large inscription at the center of the base: "A Cristoforo Colombo La Patria." Julian Street was also interested in images of ships and warships and drew some yachts with watercolors and in buildings, including those from other countries like Norway and Canada, and from various of the states of the United States, as well as the reconstruction of the monastery, La Rábida, where Columbus stayed in 1491 (two images; the Peristyle shows up more than once). The *Chicago Tribune Art Supplement*'s lithograph of "The Liberty Bell" (October 22, 1893), appears in the scrapbook: the bell is accompanied by two U.S. flags and the inscription above it, "1776: Proclaim Liberty." Columbus became part of the consumption of the world, or a representation of the world, and Julian Street includes many images and objects, souvenirs with which to remember the Fair: for instance, *the Souvenir Programme Turkish Theater: Midway Plaisance Chicago World Fair* (Pierre Antonius & Co. Managers), including "The Bethlehem Woman," whose name is Mary and whose husband's name is Joseph; a signature in Roman characters and in Chinese characters of Woo Sokwing from Canton in China, a description of "The Java Village," images of various scientific inventions, a note in perhaps Street's hand about linguistic and cultural cultures between England and the United States, different views of a variety of buildings on the site of the Exposition and monuments, such as "The Columbus Quadriga." And "The Barge of Columbia," a program of John Stoddard's lecture on Japan. This miscellany continues with Street's sketches and watercolors of various figures, including his grandfather, and places he has been; images of a nymph (Henrietta Rae's "The Nymph of the Stream"), seductive women and noble and royal women as well as *Tribune* supplement lithographs of "A Reading from Homer" and "Top of Fujisan," Bourguereau's "The Youth of Bacchus," a picture of "The Infanta Eulalie of Spain," with a note on the back, mechanically reproduced, about the kindness of those in America to her and a wish to stay longer next time; buildings, the Union Stock yards; the insides of the woman's, electricity, transportation, machinery and forestry buildings; and snapshots about the Fair. This mixing of materials and the classical motif with that of progress was not simply a feature of this scrapbook as a collection but of all collections, including the Columbian World Exposition of 1893, if regarded whole as a collection. For instance, for Norman Bolotin and Christine Laing, "The ancient state carriage of Dom Pedro, the first emperor of Brazil, for some unknown reason was displayed among the relics of American transportation."[172]

The last three items of the Street scrapbook show the miscellaneous nature and mixed and contradictory images of the World's Exposition in Chicago in 1893, in which Columbus, Columbia and the Columbian dwell: a *Tribune* lithograph, "The Struggle for Work"; an undated newspaper article, "Worked by the Hindoo Idol," with no place of publication, by Nellie Bly with diagrams and images; and a loose image, perhaps not meant in this place originally, "Durham Cathedral, From the River Bank." This scrapbook, of someone coming of age, in a place that was having its coming-out party, suggests the meanderings of collection and cultural production and reception. The lack of an ostensible plan—with no guidelines or instructions—takes this scrapbook, an important step in this person's life and something cherished enough by his family to give to Princeton Library, as a personal response that includes making Columbus part of that process. In this way it is like the allusions to Columbus in the letters and diaries of the women in North America that I have discussed. These are, in their own ways, monuments or tributes to Columbus as to the Exposition, as well as a look into an aspect of the private lives and artifacts of people without great public roles.

William Eleroy Curtis also kept scrapbooks, mainly of newspaper clippings of his writings for the *Chicago Record* from 1874 to 1911 or related articles: he was chief of the Latin American department, so his collection concerning the Chicago Exposition of 1893 is of particular interest. An article from the *Washington Star* in April 1891, "THE COLUMBUS RELICS," has a series of subtitles—"The Convent of La Rabida to Be Re-produced in Chicago," "Mr Curtis' Collection," and "The Great Discoverer Had Two Graves—Both of Them to be Shown in Replica—Many Portraits to Be Shown—A Welshman Said to Have Preceded Him." There is interest here in Columbus and his life, death and representation as well as the British claim that Madoc, Prince of Wales, sailed to America in the twelfth century. This last detail is trying to heal the wound of Columbus, that he was first, or at least to consider a circumvention of the "discoverer" of the New World, in whose name this Chicago Exposition was supposed to be launched. This is a recent example of the contradiction and ambivalence with which other nations greeted Columbus' landfall and the resultant advantage of Spain in the New World. The article begins in such a way that all the themes of this upcoming exposition were brought together under the name of Columbus:

> There will be a great many very interesting exhibits at the world's fair, but none will be more so than the collection of Columbiana now being gathered together by Mr. William E. Curtis. Visitors to the fair whose lives are closely intertwined with the mechanical arts may fail to realize the value of the treasures included in the Columbiana aggregation and the enthusiastic agriculturalist may glance listlessly at its historical wealth, but the general public will appreciate the good things which wideawake minds and busy hands are preparing for the great display of 1893. The historian will revel in the feast of fat things, and the student of American history will have an opportunity to see for himself what changes the centuries have wrought since Columbus landed on the western edge of the Atlantic. Everything connected with the name of Columbus that an enthusiastic collector can secure will be presented to the public gaze.
>
> Not the least of the many features will be the building in which all these relics and facsimiles and models will be displayed.
>
> THE CONVENT OF LA RABIDA.[173]

The article then proceeds to tell the story about how Columbus and his twelve-year-old son were returning from the failed attempt to interest the Spanish monarchs in his Enterprise of the Indies; how they stopped at this monastery, where, fortunately Prior Marchena, once the confessor to Queen Isabella, dwelt and how he helped Columbus to secure her support, which falls under another title, "HOW QUEEN ISABELLA WAS WON OVER." This building will serve as the headquarters for the Latin American department and in the convent chapel they hope to lodge a panorama that illustrates the life of Columbus. Although historians deny there is any portrait in the likeness of Columbus, Mr. Curtis has gathered together thirty-four. The article even goes through the claims of the two rival portraits with the best claims, the Yanez portrait and the Venetian Mosaic portrait. The article says that "De Bry claims that this portrait was painted from life by order of King Ferdinand." This description is perceptive and suggestive of the many splendors of the representations of Columbus:

In the collection Columbus is represented in many different postures and styles of garb. The Jovins portrait has him as a monk; De Bry engraved him at full length on the deck of a caravel and then represented him as standing the historical egg on end; in the Jomard picture, which it is claimed was painted by Titian, Columbus has a Flemish ruff, pointed beard and a great gold chain; another presentment, artist unknown, has the discoverer clad as a familiar of the Inquisition. The variety is wonderful.[174]

This understanding of the difference between myth and history, something that developed acutely in the nineteenth century, shows the sophistication of those putting together the Fair and writing about it at the time. The evidence is weighed and the artistic and imaginative rendition of Columbus is brought to bear as much as the historical figure. This unnamed author celebrates the variousness of these representations and alludes to one of the works I mentioned from the diary of Anne Everett: "Persico carved out the figure of Columbus which is on the east front of the Capitol, but historians say the result of Mr. Persico's labors is without real merit and has no claim to notice."[175] The section, "MAPS OF THAT DAY," despite some interesting historical discussions, becomes a pretext for humor: Leonardo Da Vinci, a great artist, could not pass a civil service exam today and "The Ptolemy map looks a good deal like a misshapen squash."[176] This section chronicles the first maps with "America" on them and Mastea Cesarea's map, which shows the coast from Labrador to the Strait of Magellan. The practice of museum exhibits and library research, which intensified in the nineteenth century, is evident here. The theme of evangelization and the translation of religion and culture are embodied in a reproduction: "Another fac simile will be that of the famous map drawn in 1500 by Juan de la Cosa, who was a pilot on Columbus' vessel. Cosa, in this map, represents Columbus as St. Christopher bearing the infant Christ to the new world." A generalization of this theme occurred in the Columbian World Exposition, in its opening ceremonies and its construction.

From this discussion, including remarks on Columbus' marginalia in Pierre D'Ailly and the appearance of the word "America" in 1507, the author moves to the mythical under the heading, "A WELSHMAN WHO PRECEDED COLUMBUS." This section begins with an attempt to separate opinion from historical fact: "It is extremely probable that the great majority of those who dwell within the limits of the United States are of the opinion that Columbus was the first white man to set foot on this continent. This opinion, according to historians, is decidedly incorrect, but there is more than a little diversity of opinion as to the original nationality on this side of the Atlantic."[177] This tale of Madoc, a Welsh prince who sailed in 1170 for what is now America, was current in Renaissance England in authors like Richard Hakluyt the Younger and was in some way, even as they acknowledged Columbus and the power of Spain in the New World, a means of circumventing the Spanish right and claim to America and of giving their own nation precedence. Some Anglo-Americans, like the author of this article, picked up on this move, which would give their own British ancestors the earliest claim. This move would provide a certain continuity in the translation of culture and empire to the United States with, at this time, a large population of British descent. The Norse claim, which was far stronger, was selectively ignored here. To subvert Spanish claims further, and this may be a strategy that helps to contribute to the ideology that led up to the Spanish-American War of 1898, this author cites an authority, David Powell's *History of Cambria*, which was supposed in 1384 to have been translated from a Welsh text that was 200 years old, that would place Madoc's destination in the sphere of Spanish America: "this land to which Madoc came must needs be some part of Nova Hispania or Florida. Whereupon it is manifest that that countrie was long before by Brytaines discovered afore either Columbus or Americus Vesputius led anie Spaniardes thither."[178] The quoted authority, Powell, also says: "I am of opinion that the land, whereunto he came, was some part of Mexico: the causes what make me thinke so be these," and he continues with two points, the Aztec tradition of strangers from over the seas having ruled them and Montezuma's oration to this effect in submitting to the king of Castile; and the British words and place-names used in Mexico.[179] The trouble is that the dates do not add up: How can Powell's book, at least as reported by the author of this article, be written in 1384 and speak about New Spain and Montezuma? There is the usual contradiction or at least problem here that if the Mexica were descended from Britons, why would they pay homage and submit to Spain? Most of the material under this heading is a quotation from this historical text. Here, then, perhaps in the name of ethnic nationalism, for Britain and the United States, do we have a mixture of the sophistication of historical research, which intensified so much in the nineteenth century, and the mythography that was long an element in Anglo-American and other cultures. The Enlightenment seems to have been inconsistent in its methods and aims in the context of this article at least.

This was to be a Columbian Fair, and the title of this piece is about the Columbus relics. And so the article ends with a section, "Two Tomes in the Field." The author maintains that there is no competition about the house in which Columbus was born, so such a replica will cause no difficulties. There have been many books that do unto Columbus what others later did unto Shakespeare, and that is to explore myths of origin and various possible identities. If Shakespeare has been Irish or a member of the nobility; Columbus has been Jewish and has been given various places of birth in Italy. What the author concentrates on here is the rival claims of burial places for Columbus—San Domingo and Havana—and in a diplomatic move, the Exposition will have two models of the rival tombs. One thing is a matter of agreement: "When Don Diego Columbus, son of the discoverer, was governor of Santo Domingo he removed the remains of his father to Santo Domingo from Seville. The bones, everyone concedes, remained in their second resting place until Spain turned San Domingo over to the French."[180] The contestation is whether the wrong bones, perhaps those of Columbus' brother, Bartholomew, were moved to Havana. Shakespeare may have been prescient to curse anyone who might move his bones. Columbus, as a result of the movement of bones and history, has many shrines. For both Columbus and Shakespeare, there came to be no shortage of critics.

This Curtis scrapbook is largely about free trade, protectionism and reciprocity between the United States and Latin America, so that the article on the Chicago Exposition is in a suggestive context. Trade, finance and progress are, for William Curtis, consciously or not, the wider realm for culture. The Columbus "memorabilia" and portraits also occasion other articles.[181] Curtis himself played a role in Latin America and the Chicago Exposition in 1893, as one article, "South America and the World's Fair," described: "Mr. W. E. Curtis, the energetic chief of the Bureau of American Republics of the State Department, has just granted me another interesting interview, which gives many new facts concerning the participation of the South American Republics in the World's Fair of 1893."[182] This private scrapbook is full of the clippings of a public person, a key figure in the organization of the Fair. Curtis' interest was wide-ranging and was as much a matter of details as negotiation and vision. In his search for a proper exhibition of Columbus, drawing on Latin America, he cast his net widely. Columbus and origins were important to him and the fair for which he worked: for instance, one article, "A Famous Papal Bull Wanted," began: "William E. Curtis is, in the interest of the World's fair, hunting for a copy of the famous bull of Alexander VI. (1493) dividing the new world between the Spaniards and Portuguese. The particular copy he is after was bought at auction in London 37 years ago for some as yet unidentified New York collector. The only other known copy of the original pamphlet is in the Royal library in Munich."[183] This was the bull made in response to Columbus' landfall in the western Atlantic. The portraits of Columbus were another keen interest of Curtis and his contemporaries. An article in *The New York Times* on May 31, 1891, "*COLUMBIAN MADNESS,*" begins by focusing on this "mania":

> The nearness of 1892 and the stimulus of the World's Fair have affected the market for portraits of CHRISTOPHER COLUMBUS in a way that must be deeply gratifying to the few thousands of persons who own them. Mr. WILLIAM E. CURTIS of Pan-American memories has rushed into the fray with all the Christian simplicity of a Western person, and begun to form a collection of portraits of COLUMBUS. At last accounts he had thirty-five; but a vein of caution seems to run athwart his sanguine mind, for he remarked to a reporter that of these none could be proved genuine. This collection is for the World's Fair. When the returns are all in Mr. WILLIAM E. CURTIS will wish that he had never stirred the topic, particularly in the present conjuncture, for Columbus portrait collecting is a madness that has blasted many lives otherwise innocent and devoted to human good.[184]

Thus, the market forces are at work in the melodramatic rhetoric of this piece. Besides the stereotypical caricature of Curtis, the article does point to the pressures of supply and demand in collecting and also notes that Thomas Jefferson, in 1784, had requested a copy of a portrait of Columbus in Florence and, in 1814, Israel Thorndike had presented it to the Massachusetts Historical Society. It is apparent that the interest in Columbus in the period just after the independence of the United States building up to the three hundredth anniversary of Columbus' landfall, of which David Ramsey and Jeremy Belknap were a part, has connections to the period leading to another Columbian event in 1892–93. The interest in Columbus never goes away but concentrates on those 100s as intensive markers of the encounter, something that annual Columbus Day celebrations of the last century or so cannot achieve. "Columbus at the fair," a note by J. B. Thacker of Albany in Curtis' scrapbook, looks ahead: "This is the first time our Nation has celebrated the Columbian Discovery. It is safe to predict that for all time this event will be observed with appropriate ceremonies on the ninety-second year of each century, perhaps more frequently. It therefore becomes important in establishing a precedent, that we should be correct as to our dates. We want to impress the people who come after us in the next century and who will celebrate the Columbian Discovery in 1991, that we knew enough to correct a false date." Looking back in 1992 and beyond shows, as 2092 will, that prophecies are best read backward then forward, as the books of the New Testament and Shakespeare's histories suggest, because to peer into the future and predict as this writer did in the 1890s is one of the hardest tasks people can try to perform. People can be as accurate as possible, as this writer is saying, but some dates can also be controversial and their interpretation and reception even more so.

The Columbian World Exposition of 1893 is a topic that has been the subject of much interest and interpretation. In the context of the theme of after Columbus, it both celebrates and displaces him—he becomes the honored founder or pretext who is surpassed. In 1893 Ben Truman's *History of the World's Fair* put on display the variety and vastness of the Exposition. Columbus appears here in context, and I can refer to just a few examples. Truman devoted Part VI and five chapters (including one on children) to "The Women of the Exposition and Woman's Work," which included child-rearing as a main component. But stereotypes are misleading. The headings of the first chapter in Part VI, "The Woman's Building and Its Purposes," include two that proclaim: "Women the Originators of Most of the Industrial Arts—The Woman's Building an Inspiration of Woman's Genius."[185] This chapter begins: "In no previous exposition has woman essayed so important and conspicuous a part as she has been called upon to perform at the great Columbian Exposition of 1893. At no time in her history has she been accorded such a place as she now occupies as an integral part of the mammoth display of the achievements of mankind. It seems fitting that contemporaneously with her advanced position as part of the world's force she should display the benefits which her emancipation has worked, and that side by side with the products of man's brain and energy, woman's should be placed for comparison."[186] This emancipatory rhetoric is positive, although it helps to celebrate the beneficence of the Exposition and Congress, which had not paid enough attention until women forced the issue and the possible undertow of comparisons with men, which could be odious. Still, a chapter that reports the portraits of Sappho and Hypatia, Matilda of Flander's Bayeux tapestry, reproductions of Sabina von Steinbach's statues for Strasbourg Cathedral in the Woman's Building is not suppressing evidence of the accomplishment of women for over two thousand years.[187]

In the chapter on "The Department of Liberal Arts," Truman shows his own ability to choose topics and the scope of his interpretation. He decides to discuss an exhibit on education, which he had announced in the chapter headings, from Québec: "As one among half a million unique and interesting exhibits that came from Québec, under charge of Canon Bruchesi, D. D., appointed by the government, assisted by brother Pelerinus, is entitled to special mention. The collection comes from 200 convents and academies, and the McGill University, Protestant, of Montreal. The exhibit of the latter is not as extensive as the merit of the university warrants, but the space could not be obtained. The work represented shows the system of education of the convents and academies by grades, from the first step to the graduating course. There are compositions in English, French, German, and Spanish by pupils of the various schools, and some of these are illustrated with pen drawing by the student."[188] Truman's openness here to different languages, cultures and religions suggests his volume is something more than a mere triumph of the English-speaking Protestant elite of the United States.

In the chapter "Department of Ethnology," Truman begins with: "There is a certain structure that is not so often visited as many of the others; and yet it is one whose contents challenge the admiration of students of antiques and others of scholarly attainments. Over the portal of this building are the words "Anthropology—Man and his Works."[189] Truman mentions that this Ethnology Building resulted from the overcrowding of the Manufactures and Liberal Arts Building, which, as vast as it was, was too small to house everything it was intended to, so, "at the eleventh hour it was decided that ethnology must go."[190] Other disciplines joined it, so ethnology was not alone in being punted. It looked back while industry looked forward. Despite this spirit of progress and a vision of the future, Truman found something interesting in each building. His favorite here was a display of the Coastal Indians: "What strikes the attention first and excites the greatest interest is the model of the Indian village of Skedegats, on Queen Charlotte's Island, in British Columbia. This collection was secured by Chief Putnam, and is charge of James Deans, an aged Scotchman, for thirty years a resident of the islands."[191] Whether this display had Native consent and participation is left unsaid but I am assuming that the reference to F. W. Putnam, who brought together the American collections, attempts to give some such sense of authorization.[192]

Part VIII, "Other Main Features," which finally turns almost wholly to Columbus himself, opens with the chapter "The Shrine of the White City," which starts with: "The convent of La Rabida stands on a little promontory jutting into Lake Michigan, at the southern end of the Park. It is an exact reproduction of the monastry of that name, near Palos, Spain, where Columbus and his son Diego took refuge over four hundred years ago. As this building seemed to be more closely associated with the career of Columbus than any other known, the directors of the Exposition thought a fac-simile of that structure would be the most fitting shelter for all the relics of the great navigator that had been secured for exhibition at the Fair."[193] Columbus, too, like the cultures set out in the ethnology exhibits, was often displaced or recontextualized in the face of the utopian or future fiction of the vision of the White City. His place was, however, also honorific and an object of devotion and even religious observance: his relics were housed in a reproduction of a monastery. Industrial know-how had allowed this reproduction.

The official report is also suggestive in telling us about who helped to shape with care the representation of Columbus at the World's Fair. It indicates that "The inscriptions on the Columbus or Water Gate in the Peristyle were written by Charles William Eliot, LL.D., President of Harvard University."[194] Eliot's selection of inscriptions at the Water gate or Peristyle, "together with the names of the discoverers, Champlain, La Salle, Ponce de Leon, Cortez and Desoto, in the frieze," is about religious and civil liberty: here Columbus, in the context of the French and Spanish explorers who explored North America, becomes an agent of freedom.[195] On the panels over the four entrances to the Administration Building are four references to important parts of "the history of Columbus"—his birth in Genoa, his commission on April 30, 1492, his landfall in the western Atlantic (here the Bahamas) and his death in Valladolid.[196] It is perhaps best to end this discussion of the Columbus and the Columbian at the Chicago Expo of 1893 with a mention that at the base of St. Gaudens' statute of Columbus was a passage in the original Latin of Seneca's *Medea* (at 368), that mentioned Thule, which Columbus had gone beyond. Part of that beyond was the United States.[197]

VII

Social change over time had much to do with the different reception of Columbus. It is instructive to witness the ways that 1992 differed from 1892. As this is a vast topic in and of itself, I wish to call attention to a few examples of difference. For instance, as Robert Muccigrosso observes, "It seems ironic that the city of Chicago decided not to celebrate in 1992 the five hundredth anniversary of the voyage of Christopher Columbus to the New World."[198] This decision was not made in a vacuum. In 1990, the National Council of Churches in the United States recommended repentance to celebration for all the landfall led to—slavery, genocide and ecocide; different organizations representing Native Americans called 1992 the year devoted to indigenous people; in 1992, Berkeley, California changed Columbus Day to Indigenous Peoples Day, thereby shifting the focus.[199] The colonial, as we shall see particularly in chapter 7, is about the appropriation of land and culture and this has, in the figure of Columbus and of others from Europe, postcolonial implications.

In the 1980s and 1990s, there were still remnants of the homage paid to Columbus leading up to the Chicago Expo of 1893. Although culture in North America, and certainly in Canada, has in the past couple of decades tended to be more sensitive to the situation of Natives, there is still some division over the legacy of Columbus. At West Edmonton Mall, which long billed itself as the world's largest shopping mall, a model of Columbus' *Santa Maria* sits on an indoor lake or lagoon and has been rented for receptions. Its neighbors are dolphins and a group of submarines that, as Edmontonians like to say, is larger than that in the current Canadian navy, which, during World War II, was one of the largest in the world. This ship has a fascination for Canadians, as well as for tourists from the United States, Japan and elsewhere, while, for the Natives in Alberta and neighboring British Columbia and the territories, land claim settlements are being awaited or negotiated. Under the roof of this shopping pleasure dome—what would Marco Polo, Columbus and Kubla Khan have made of it?—Columbus is an attraction, as is an indoor skating rink, a water slide, and an amusement park. At the level of popular culture and "postmodern" consumption, the presence of one of Columbus' ships at this mall suggested that Canada, which, often considered itself an extension of western Europe because of its connections to Britain and its inheritance from France, could admit its Columbian, if not its British Columbian and American inheritance as the names on its earlier maps recognized. Owing probably to proximity in an age before air travel, Canadians had been the largest group of visiting dignitaries at the opening ceremonies of the Chicago Exposition in 1893 and they probably made up the largest group of foreign visitors to the Fair. Now, in a much smaller way, they and the tourists visiting West Edmonton Mall are consumed by Columbus. This time around, there are not the many scientific and educational exhibits, although there are a few such cases at the mall, but the ship is a display in an entertainment and shopping extravaganza, an indoor fantasy especially in the North American equivalent to Siberian cold in the dead of winter, a fantasy worth so much to Disney that it sued the owners of the mall for choosing "The Fantasyland Hotel" for a name.[200] Origins, possession and commerce have made it hard to remember the religious dimension, sometimes seeming so misguided half a millennium afterward. It is difficult to observe in the ether of the present our ideological blindspots and, hard as we try to see them and to identify them through the distance of critical thinking, the ones we identify are probably not as insidious as those to which we are blind. Each generation and century shifts in the wake of Columbus even if the world has shrunk with air travel and one reproduction of the ship sits on an indoor pond that does not make waves until people are asked for their opinion of it. There are, as we have seen, shifting contexts for Columbus, from his landfall forward.

The commemoration of 1992 is recent history, so I will not dwell on it too much. To focus my discussion, I will examine a few examples of materials available on the internet and I will also discuss film and television. Columbus has become technological. The article on Columbus in *Encyclopedia Britannica Online* makes an important point: "The period between the quatercentenary celebrations of Columbus' achievements in 1892–93 and the quincentenary ones of 1992 saw great advances in Columbus scholarship. A huge number of books about Columbus have appeared in the 1990s, and the insights of archeologists and anthropologists now complement those of sailors and historians. This effort has given rise, as might be expected, to considerable debate. The past few years have also seen a major shift in approach and interpretation; the older pro-

European and imperialist understanding has given way to one shaped from the perspective of the inhabitants of the *Americas* themselves."[201] This shift in scholarship cannot be denied, and such changes will probably continue over time as each generation and culture reassesses Columbus. Two films on Columbus were put together to represent Columbus in the early 1990s. In one, *Christopher Columbus—The Discovery* (1992), directed by John Glen, who had been the director on the James Bond movie *Octopussy,* Marlon Brando plays the inquisitor Tomas Torquemada, who questions an all too human but passionate Columbus (George Corraface) before he can receive the backing of Ferdinand (Tom Selleck) and Isabella (Rachel Ferdinand).[202] In the other, *1492,* Ridley Scot, who was the director of *Blade Runner,* produced an epic, and has Columbus (Gérard Depardieu) meet Antonio de Marchena (Fernando Rey) inside La Rábida— a far less sensational religious meeting than in the other film.[203] Apparently, Roselyne Bosch, a French journalist, had the idea for such a film in 1987 when she spoke with Tom Wolfe about *The Right Stuff* and astronauts. This was to show the fascination with Columbus as a complex figure rather than the earlier hero of *Christopher Columbus* (1949), starring Frederic March. The idea of adventure and discovery, despite the changing climate of opinion concerning Columbus, remained as key themes. Columbus Day, which in 1892 Benjamin Harrison called on the people of the United States to celebrate, has been celebrated annually since 1920 and was made a legal federal holiday there in 1971 only (the second Monday in October), so just as Columbus was being institutionalized nationally, he was also coming under greater pressure and being questioned as a symbol.[204] In Haiti and the Dominican Republic, despite a rejection of the term "discovery" and a preference for "commemoration," in 1992 there was a controversy over which part of Hispaniola Columbus landed on.[205] Another website is entitled, "1492–1992: Christopher Columbus slaver and thief."[206] With a wonderfully resonant title, which contains its own typology, John Curl's "Columbus in the Bay of Pigs" is a poem that proclaims in its opening lines that the Taíno language needs be heard and then proceeds to have passages in Spanish and English as well.[207] Native groups have continued their protest on the web, in the courts and elsewhere. For example, an essay from 1992, "500 YEARS OF INDIGENOUS RESISTANCE," whose author is not listed by name, is now on a website and asserts: "This article is intended as a basic history of the colonization of the Americas since 1492, and the Indigenous resistance to this colonization continuing into 1992. The author admits to not having a full understanding of the traditions of his own people, the Kwakiutl (Kwakwaka'wakw); as such the article lacks an analysis based in an authentic Indigenous philosophy and is instead more of a historical chronology."[208] Another article—by Russell Means and Glenn Morris—expresses regret that something better did not happen as a result of the encounter between Columbus and his hosts:

> When Taino Indians saved Christopher Columbus from certain death on the fateful morning of Oct. 12, 1492, a glorious opportunity presented itself. The cultures of Europe and the Americas could have merged and the beauty of both races could have flourished.
>
> Unfortunately, what occurred was neither beautiful nor heroic. Just as Columbus could not, and did not, "discover" a hemisphere that was already inhabited by nearly 100 million people, his arrival cannot, and will not, be recognized as a heroic and celebratory event by indigenous peoples.
>
> Unlike the Western tradition, which presumes some absolute concept of objective truth, and consequently, one "factual" depiction of history, the indigenous view recognizes

that there exist many truths in the world and many legitimate recollections of any given historical event, depending on one's perspective and experiences.

From an indigenous vantage point, Columbus' arrival was a disaster from the beginning. Although his own diaries indicated that he was greeted by the Taino Indians with the most generous hospitality he had ever known, he immediately began the enslavement and slaughter of the Indian peoples of the Caribbean islands. As the eminent Columbus biographer Samuel Eliot Morison admits in his book, Admiral of the Ocean Sea, Columbus was personally responsible for enslavement and murder of indigenous peoples. He was personally responsible for the design and operation of the encomienda system that tied Indians as slaves to the lands stolen from them by the European invaders.[209]

The death of indigenous peoples and the legacy of slavery became a focus of pain, regret and commemoration. There were a variety of polemical and carefully researched responses to the meaning and legacy of Columbus' landfall and the subsequent European expansion to the New World. *Time* produced a special issue on Columbus in late 1991 in conjunction with the "Seeds of Change" exhibit at the Smithsonian's Museum of Natural History in Washington, which provided historical background and analysis of Columbus and of the changes in diet, culture, flora and fauna thereafter.[210] I am partly backing up in time, from 1992, so it is fitting to call attention to two important documents, both produced by the settler culture of the United States, one by the church and one by the state.

The church document is devastating in its criticism of the legacy of Columbus. It is in the tradition of Antón Montesino, Las Casas, John Eliot and others who condemned the mistreatment of the Natives and it extends the critique further still. On May 17, 1990, the National Council of the Churches of Christ began its resolution:

> As U.S. Christians approach public observances marking the 500th anniversary of Christopher Columbus's first landing in the Western hemisphere, we are called to review our full history, reflect upon it, and act as people of faith mindful of the significance of 1492. The people in our churches and communities now look at the significance of the event in different ways. What represented newness of freedom, hope and opportunity for some was the occasion for oppression, degradation and genocide for others. For the Church this is not a time for celebration but a time for a committed plan of action insuring that this "kairos" moment in history not continue to cosmetically coat the painful aspects of the American history of racism.[211]

In May 1989 in Basel, the Final Document of the European Ecumenical Assembly, "Peace With Justice for the Whole Creation," recognized the detrimental effects on peoples and the environment of European expansion as a result of the voyages of 1492.[212] This is not the aspect of the church that Friar Vincent represented in the traveling trope or story of Atahualpa when he insisted the Native be killed for throwing down the Bible—Francisco López de Gómara narrated this conflict and Richard Hakluyt the Younger and the anonymous R. B. recounted this narrative in the sixteenth and seventeenth centuries, while Werner Hertzog took up a variant in *Aguirre, der Zorn Gottes* [*Aguirre Wrath of God*] (1972): in an interview, now part of the DVD, Herzog says (and I paraphrase here) that his character of the cleric, who equates the strong and the godly, is like the church's historic role in Latin America.[213] Controversy over Columbus and colonization made 1992 more volatile concerning the European legacy in the Americas than in 1892.

Chicago had hoped to host a new celebration of Columbus in 1992—Seville held an Expo in that year. In preparations for the 500th anniversary of Columbus' "discovery," a bill was passed in the U. S. Senate (67 in favor and 23 against) on February 1, 1984. It is instructive that the politicians did not necessarily see the protest coming, or at least the extent of it, because even those voting against the bill, objected for reasons other than of cultural sensitivity. The synopsis of the debate for those favoring the bill (H.R. 1492) stated:

> This legislation is designed to insure that the great event of 1492, which enlarged the globe as well as man's spirit, will be observed. In an appropriate and thoughtful way. Although the anniversary is still 8 years away, it is certainly not too soon to begin to plan for the observance of the 500th birthday of the New World. We should therefore support this bill. The total appropriation for the jubilee Commission is $2 million. The small expenditure that is involved year by year will be like bread cast upon the water: It will return to us manyfold in the number of visitors that will come to this country. Further, we will develop other important assets in the course of the commemoration. It is one of the ironies of history that Columbus' contemporaries never appreciated the enormous contribution Columbus made to the expansion of European civilization and, in fact, to the creation of a new civilization. We who are the ultimate beneficiaries of his vision, courage, and travail must see that his memory and achievement do not suffer the same fate in 1992 that occurred in his lifetime. Not only will this celebration stimulate us to reflect on the meaning of Columbus' discovery, but it will also give us the opportunity to strengthen ties with Spain, Italy, and the countries of the Western Hemisphere. Finally, it should be emphasized that the Commission will complement—and not compete with—the 1992 Chicago World's fair. In sum, passage of this bill and the establishment of the Jubilee Commission will help us properly observe Columbus' discovery, perhaps the greatest event in the history of the secular world.[214]

This synopsis shows the instability, or perhaps the stylistic elegant variation, of "commemoration" and then "celebration" (unless the second is displacing the first term rather than supplementing it). The desire of the Senate is to explore a "thoughtful and appropriate way" to mark this landmark of Columbus' landfall and outlines its financial benefits while being aware of "ironies of history." Columbus' "discovery," which led up to the United States, is seen as "perhaps" the culmination of secular history. This branch of government weighed historical meaning and fiduciary trust. Those who opposed the bill argued:

> The Senate should support the concept of celebrating the 500th anniversary of the wondrous discovery of America; but we should vote against the legislation. In view of the skyrocketing deficits and the mounting national debt, there is an urgent need to exercise spending restraint. Otherwise, we will drive up interest rates and exacerbate the problems arising from our overvalued dollar. To be sure, this $2 million allocation is a relatively small amount; but the point is that we must make a start, however feeble, on fiscal restraint. We can no longer afford to fund nonessential requests such as this one. From a fiscal standpoint, these are not normal times. If necessary, the Commission funding should come from private sources.[215]

The summary of the views of the opponents of the bill seems to use more laudatory, and less ambivalent, language concerning Columbus' landfall: there is no commemoration here for this "wondrous discovery of America." Fiscal prudence, rather than the awareness of cultural difference, seems to mark this opposition. Here was no equivalent to the largess leading up to the Chicago Exposition in 1893.

Instead, all that was left for Chicago were plans and artifacts from, and reissued stamps and records such as the websites on, the White City and the Chicago Expo of 1893. For instance, the United States Post Office issued a news release: "One of the most eagerly anticipated stamp issues in years will serve as the dramatic kickoff for 1992's premier U.S. philatelic event WORLD COLUMBIAN STAMP EXPO '92. On May 22, the U.S. Postal Service will reissue the entire Columbian Exposition series of 1893 as souvenir sheets. And for the first time ever, the United States will issue stamps jointly with three other countries: Italy, Portugal, and Spain."[216] This reproduction of a retrospective, along with websites looking back to the Chicago Fair in 1893, are the mark of a sea-change and the ruins of a hoped-for repetition. Columbus was in a new context. One of these websites, that of the Chicago Public Library, announces that in the six months the Fair was open, from May 1, 1893, it "attracted 27, 539, 000 visitors—almost half the total number of people then living in the United States."[217] This astonishing figure, while probably including many repeat visits from local people, indicted the level of interest in the 400th anniversary. The "Interactive Guide to the World's Columbian Exposition" is a site maintained by Bruce R. Schulman, which provides a wide variety of information, including law, about the exposition.[218] The Paul V. Galvin Library Digital History Collection at the Illinois Institute of Technology describes its aim: "The World's Columbian Exposition of 1893" website was created to provide world-wide access to thousands of illustrations and full-text images of the Chicago World's Fair of 1893 for purposes of teaching and research. The site highlights four works focusing on various aspects of the fair including two multi-volume sets."[219] American Studies at the University of Virginia gives access to a site, "The World's Columbian Exposition: Idea, Experience, Aftermath, " that proides its own representations in the form of a tour, reactions and legacy, while providing notes.[220] The White City—which burned and vanished and left a literal ruin, a legacy for debate and a virtual reality—was controversial and is still. The Columbian, like Columbus, is a matter of free speech and shifting signs, inviting reassessment in each generation and among different and even conflicting cultures, always under pressure. As in Shakespeare, in Columbus what was a minority position once can, all of a sudden, become a majority view—as in a change as unexpected as the tempest that shipwrecks the unsuspecting passengers long before Prospero drowns his book and even longer before he became part of a controversy over empire and colony.

VIII

Columbus was not the only figure in the ambivalent example Spain set for other would-be European colonizers of a seaborne empire: Philip II later joined the list of famous Spaniards, such as Hernán Cortés, Bartolomé de Las Casas, the Pizarros and others. About Richard Hakluyt the Younger's long unpublished state document, "A Discourse on Western Planting" (1584), I wish to mention one aspect among many but one that relates to the cover of this book, a portrait of Philip II of Spain.[221] Unlike Richard Eden, who hoped for some benefits from the marriage of Philip II and Mary of England, Hakluyt did not in "Discourse" display much trust in the king of Spain. In this text that king, the greatest threat to England, had to be faced with brave words.[222] Columbus was part of the representation of the ambivalent role of Spain in Europe and the New World.

The power of Spain and the homage to Spain, among mimetic themes, involved the legacy of Columbus, which could be seen in written and visual representations. Maps could also show the puissance of Spain, for instance the one apparently made for Mary Tudor that displayed the extent of the empire that her husband, Philip II, reigned over.[223] The Columbian contact became various signs of difference and change marked on the world before that moment. This encounter created new contexts in which to view events, images and texts, so that Columbus' texts helped to generate new conditions for their own reception and a work, like Shakespeare's *The Tempest,* while not ostensibly about the New World, could in time (after a long time) be viewed as being part of the production of colonialism and its production as well as a site of controversy between empire and colonies, tradition and postcolonialism. This is a point I will return to in the last part of this study. The aesthetic of empire and the empire of the aesthetic, especially in great works of art and literature, were not, and have not been, easy to distinguish. Columbus became a figure for imagination, and not just the history, of Europe, and his legacy was not always obvious and direct.

Coming after Columbus, and the Spain he represented, meant that, like it or not, the world had undergone a sea-change, something difficult to configure or represent, something passing strange but that could not be passed off. Columbus had been Janus-faced, representing himself to the Natives and to readers, clerics, courtiers and monarchs in Spain and Europe, so that he was between cultures. In what follows we will turn to the sexing of America, or the representation of gender and sexuality in the New World, and then to those, European or Native, who became go-betweens, translators and mediators, who were also met with ambivalence. The double signs doubled and it was difficult for those involved and for us now to understand what was going on. A refractoriness, not just concerning Columbus and Spain, but in their representation in the context of the New World and Europe, Natives and Europeans governed and governs the interpretation of interpreters. A strangeness can occur within a culture and not only between a familiar culture and another that is not. Being between cultures can be the distance between our cultural present and past as well as that between our culture and another. Before discussing Natives who were kidnapped, mediated, acted as interpreters and translators, those who went between their various cultures and those of different European groups, I now turn to another mediation between cultures—the rendering of America in sexual terms, something that begins with Columbus and takes many interpretive turns in subsequent texts and images. The tension that Shakespeare represents between Caliban and Miranda, which bears on Sycorax, Prospero and Ferdinand, is one manifestation of this sexual mimesis, even if Shakespeare's island is—through source, allusion and analogy—related to America in a typology of the Old World and the New World.

Chapter 4 ～

Sexing America

The "sexing" of America, that is the gendering of America in erotic terms, where the New World and its peoples are available for sexual pleasure and exploitation, whether homoerotic or not, by the Europeans is something I wish to explore using a comparative method. At first, when I began to consider this question, the surprise was to see it in so many instances of European textual and visual representations of the Americas and its peoples in erotic and sexual terms, but, later, it became important not to stress too much the concern with the sexual, yet to give it its due. This balance is always before us, but is particularly true of thematic history, criticism and theory. By placing this theme within the context of others throughout the book, it should find a balance, that it is significant but something among other important aspects of the European and Native encounter in the New World. Sex is one sign of speech in this cultural exchange and reading the sign is not always so easy. The rhetoric of seduction was not the only dimension of the representing of sex and gender in America. A complex of anxiety, voyeurism, attraction and repulsion entered into the texts and images of this early contact between European and Native. Although this kind of language helped to promote travel to readers as romance and ethnology, how much it was part of the promotion of empire is hard to say.

"Sex" is a word to be interpreted as well as a physical act, and even this bodily activity has psychological, imaginative, ideological, cultural and interpretative dimensions that occur simultaneously and involve conditioning and may change over time. Although making a distinction between "sexuality" and "sex" may be fruitful, I am not sure that this distinction holds, as suggestive as it might be.[1] "Sexing," too, is imperfect, but here it embraces the close relation between the physical and interpretative. The history of sexuality is about sex, which is mental, spiritual and physical in its scope, and history is both event and narrative. Although sex might exist without appropriation and cultural appropriation, it might be difficult to find it in such an ideal or prelapsarian state.[2] Appropriation, as we shall also see in chapter 7, is itself seductive and vexed: individuals and groups often desire to avoid, circumvent and escape its properties as property but have trouble doing so.

"Sexing America" is partly about the snares of desire and the representations of desire, which might wish a separation from desire but are implicated in it. There are troubling figures in such a landscape or other metaphors we might choose to talk about the subject at hand. The focus of what follows is about one kind of figure—Amazons, the women who would be men or would displace or devour men, but they appear beside cannibals, sodomites and other kinds of "aboriginal" women as these texts by European males suggest a mix of longings, hopes and fears. To discuss alone America as a woman, ready to be ploughed and cropped, to use a Shakespearean idiom, or to be raped, while these elements of the discourse were important, would be to tell part of the story. The debate over the nature of women, which included misogyny, began long before Columbus landed in America: Plutarch's *Mulierium virtutes* and Boccacio's *De mulieribus claris* (ca. 1380) set out worthy women.[3] While points of view are always partial, this perspective needed to be wider. I begin with Columbus and the Spanish and also talk about the French, discussing other instances of sex and gender than those that focus on the rape of virgin land or of Amazons, so the remarks so well known in English that Walter Ralegh made about Guiana as a woman ready to be taken by force can find a broader context. Such an intellectual milieu should provide another dimension to the complex relation between Ralegh and Elizabeth I both in his text and outside it.

Besides the pleasures of the flesh was the disgust over the eating of flesh, what Columbus described in his texts when he came back to cannibals over and over again. Jean de Léry set out a typological view of such flesh eating, on the one hand in the New World but, on the other, a worse case in the civil wars in France.[4] While a fear of sodomy occurs in a couple of the texts I discuss and while a lust for and fright of women happens in a number of the works, some instances suggest an alternative or opposition to such a view. Some of the responses to sex in these texts and images may be stock, but they often point to some social, physical or psychological aspect of those that generated the texts or reproduced the images and others who consumed them. I choose all these verbs knowingly and have considered this problem in connection to Shakespeare's poetry: how in an erotics in poetry, or in what I have called the rhetoric of seduction, does the reader, then and now, not become implicated in what is put on display.[5] The act of reading or viewing may become part of the act of seduction.

How much are we back with the romance writer to whom Marco Polo is said to have dictated his memoirs of his travels? The thin and jagged line between the exotic and the erotic, between the world and the imaginary is one that we will meet once more here. The fantastic calling up short the real may be a reason for the production and consumption of these images of sex in America. This sexing of America may be as much about domination as about dominion. Lures and excesses might call for expansion even as the mixing, reversal or overturning of sex roles show the very complexity of motives. The excesses might just be the wide gap between word and world in which dystopic and utopian projections and exaggerations return to the very actuality from which they seek to depart. Not, of course, that actuality is without fantasy. Amazons, cannibals and sodomites, to take three figures from this landscape, were images and "asserted realities" in the dreams and texts of breathing men in the first 100 years or so after Columbus' landfall. This figuration occurred before and beyond Columbus but took on a certain urgency and intensity after the shock of discovery.

I

There were, to be sure, figures of Amazons long before the birth of Columbus or his landfall in the Caribbean. The myth of the Amazons derives from classical antiquity. For instance, in Book 6 of the *Iliad*, Hercules and Bellerophon fought against them and Herodotus discussed them in Book 4 of the *Histories* and described how the Amazon mothers burned the right breast of their daughters with a copper device, a practice that helped their archery.[6] During the Middle Ages, the travel accounts of Marco Polo and John Mandeville, both of which are problematic regarding authorship and textual transmission, represent this theme of female warriors.[7] Columbus, who apparently read both these writers, made notes on Polo's work.[8] When reaching land in the western Atlantic, Columbus seems, as his *Journal* and *Letter* suggest, to have thought that he had come to the territory of the Grand Khan that Polo had described.[9] In fact, Polo's descriptions of the East—whether of the Great Khan's palace, Zipangu or commodities like spices and precious metals—affected accounts of scholars in the late Middle Ages, which, like Columbus' *Journal* and *Letter,* copied or translated them.[10] Polo's representation of two islands, Male and Female, seems to have influenced, or at least have been analogous to, Columbus' twin islands at the entrance to the Indies on the voyage from Europe, the one containing Cannibals and the other Amazons. Polo's islands, however, have Christian inhabitants but both are related to the fable of the Amazons.[11]

The land of the Amazons finds a place in the various texts—the Egerton, Paris and Bodleian texts, to name a few—of Mandeville's *Travels,* a text Columbus seems to have read. While source studies can be over-zealous in finding allusions, parallels and echoes in the shadows of the text, Columbus does describe subject matter that is similar to that which Mandeville represents. Textual instability occurs in Mandeville's work, as it does in the Columbus texts. Certainly, Columbus, as we saw in chapter 2, liked the word "marvellous" as well as marvels: a contemporary, Andrés Bernáldez, who claimed to have been close enough with Columbus in Spain to have been left certain of his papers, provided a context for Columbus' desire to see "the province and city of Catayo, which is under the dominion of the Grand Khan, saying that he could reach it by this route. Of it is read, as John Mandeville says and others who have seen it, that it is the richest province in the world and the most abounding in gold and silver, in all metals and silks."[12] Riches and marvels were on the minds of monarchs, sailors, merchants as well as romance and travel writers. Mandeville, whose identity has been contested, gives, near the beginning of his narrative, a list of places to which he traveled after 1332: one of these locations is Amazonia.[13] Later, Mandeville described its geographical situation: "Under Sythia, from the sea of Caspian unto the flood of Thanay is the land of Amazon, and that is the land of women, where women dwell by themself and no man among them."[14] This would be an expected location based on Herodotus' descriptions of the Sythians and Amazons. Like the Egerton text, the Paris text, which is very close to the English version, includes "Amazone" in the early list of Mandeville's destinations.[15] The Paris text also places Amazonia near to Sythia: "Et puis dessouz Sithie, de la mer Calpie iusques au flueue de Thanay, est Amozonne, cest la terre de Femenie, ou il na nuls hommes, fors femmes seulement."[16] This classical story had traveled, like a mobile trope, into Mandeville's discourse.

The description of the land of the Amazons occurs in all three major manuscripts. In the Egerton, Paris and Bodleian texts of Mandeville many of the elements adumbrate those that, as we shall soon notice, occur in Ralegh's description of Amazons. The Bodleian text will serve in giving us a sense of the ambivalent representation of Amazonia and its inhabitants: "Beside the rewme of Caldee is the rewme of Amazon, that we call Maidenlonde. And in that londe the women wil suffre no man to haue gouernaunce of that londe."[17] Besides the separation and the independence from men, these Amazons came to be warriors as a result of a war in which the king and his lords were all slain, so that in Mandeville, this story of Amazons is one of grief, survival and self-reliance—a result of trauma—and not a situation begotten of rebellion and repulsion. There is almost admiration or matter of fact reporting in Mandeville's account. One of the variants here is that Mandeville's Amazons have one breast removed according to class—"they cutte awaey the lift pappe of women of gret estate" to let then bear their shield better and remove the right breat of "comoun women" to help them to shoot their bows better.[18] The women seem to enyoy their separate existence, their "quene is chosen be eleccion as she that is doubtyest in armys" and, despite eschewing living daily with men, they satisfy their "lust" with them, although they keep male children until they can make sounds or speech, at which time they send them back to their fathers or slay them.[19]

Amazons and other amazing inhabitants, such as dragons, hydras and griffins in far-off lands, the lore of medieval legends, persisted in the mental landscapes of late-fifteenth-century Europe. To "discover" new lands at this time meant to possess new knowledge, seek out those who did not know Christ and to find treasure and commodities. In Spain of this time and beyond, chivalric romances played upon this theme in the representation of courageous and upright hidalgos in fabulous places, returning in glory and a fortune they once lost or had now gained.[20] "Conquest," or "*conquista*" was the establishing of lordship, or *señoría*, over the land and people by force, and this was done in the framework that the Reconquest and subjugation of the Canaries had provided. Extending Christendom and the dominions of Christian monarchs by defeating pagans and infidels and exacting tribute and booty from the conquered represented the aim of conquest. The Spanish did not use the term "conquest" in describing their dominion in Italy.[21] Medieval legends and chronicles filled the heads of Spanish discoverers with the search, in new lands, for Amazons, Gran Quivira, the Seven Cities of Cíbola and El Dorado. This was the mental world, or *mentalité,* in which Columbus found himself as he set sail for the western Atlantic and in which Cortés worked as he marched on Mexico. In December of 1541 Francisco de Orellana began his descent of the Amazon from its tributaries to its mouth, which he reached in August 1542: the river's name bears testimony to the power of the myth of the Amazons. On this journey, the Spanish reported to have seen Amazons on the banks of the river.[22] Walter Ralegh, a would-be English conqueror of parts of New Spain, would also inherit this legacy decades after these two formidable Spanish antecedents. "Discovery" and "conquest" were not then problematic terms as they are now. The sexual aspects of these endeavors constitute the central concern here.

Amazons and cannibals, threats to civility, hierarchy, order and peace, often inhabited the same European texts about the New World. On his first voyage, Columbus, as we observed in chapter 2, said that he heard reports that on the island of Quaris there are "a people who are regarded in all the islands as very fierce and who eat human flesh."[23] Although Columbus admits that he has not found "human monstrosities, as many expected," these harsh inhabitants "are no more malformed than the others, except that they have the custom of wearing their hair long like women."[24] This casual suggestion of effeminacy is complicated when Columbus, possibly taking up the lead from Herodotus' discussion of the sexual relations between the Sythians and the Amazons, created a reproductive union between these "cannibals" and these Amazons. These men "are those who have intercourse with the women of 'Matinio' . . . in which there is not a man. These women engage in no feminine occupation, but use bows and arrows of cane, . . . and they arm and protect themselves with plates of copper."[25] There is, at the first contacts between the Spanish and the Natives of the Caribbean, some anxiety in Columbus (with all the textual problems noted in chapter 2) about gender boundaries, strains that go back to Herodotus and beyond. Here are men who are effeminate

but eat other men and women who are manlike and who, in the neighboring first islands encountered by Columbus on his first voyage, produced offspring. These are the
enemies of Spain whose peoples and territories might provide opposition to Spanish dominion over the islands.

Nor did this Amazonian motif evaporate in the coming decades. Diego Velázquez instructed Hernán Cortés, as part of his mission, to search for Amazons.[26] In his fourth
letter to the king of Spain concerning his conquest of Mexico, Cortés reported a captain's account, based on the "word of the lords of the province of Ciguatán, who affirm
that there is an island inhabited only by women, without a single man, that at certain
times men go over from the mainland and have intercourse with them."[27] This report,
founded on a Spanish interpretation of the chiefs' oral accounts, also maintained that
the female children of such intercourse remained on the island and the male offspring
were sent away and that the island was full of gold and pearls. To conclude his own description of this Amazonian island, Cortés pledged to the monarch to learn the truth
about the island, and it is not certain whether the riches were of more interest to Cortés
than the "Amazons" were. Cortés, according to Anthony Pagden, probably learned
about the legend of the Amazons from *Deeds of Esplandían* [*Sergas de Esplandían*], a romance, a sequel to *Amadis of Gaul* that describes the Amazons, for the first time, explicitly in America.[28]

Like Columbus, Fray Gaspar de Carvajal connected indigenous resistance to the
Spaniards with the Amazons, those women who had dared to take the virility of war
upon them against the natural order. Carvajal described Indians that defended themselves against the Spanish because they were "subjects and tributaries of the Amazons"
and refused to combat because the Amazons, who "went into battle in advance of the
other Indians, like captains," would kill those who turned and fled "before our eyes."
This eyewitness report appears suspect because of the description: the Amazons—very
large, robust and white with very long and disorderly hair—"went totally naked, with
their shameful parts covered, holding a bow and arrows in their hands and fighting each
like ten Indians."[29] The mythical strength of these women invites admiration but also
subjugation, although, unlike the Sythians in Herodotus, the Spanish do not mate with
them and create a new people. A different return to natural order occurs in the face of
strangeness: the Spanish will need to rule the Natives to save them from this world of
reversals. The traveling trope of the Amazons suggests a mythological dimension to European ideology in coming to terms with the New World. The Spanish account here represents the mythical as witnessed experience and makes the outlandish an explanation
for the behavior of Indians that does not comply with the Spanish wish for lordship or
dominion over them.

As in many areas concerning the New World, the Portuguese and Spanish developed
their textual repertoire or archive before the French and English. In the English-speaking world Walter Ralegh's description in the 1590s of Amazons in Guiana is well known,
but earlier Iberian examples often are relatively neglected or left out of the discussion.
One such important instance is Antonio de Herrera's description.[30] His account of Francisco de Orellana's journey down the Amazon River provides an editorial filter. The description of this encounter with the Amazons contained a built-in gloss or commentary:

These women appeared to be very tall, robust and fair, with long hair twisted over their
heads, skins round their loins, and bows and arrows in their hands, with which they
killed seven or eight Spaniards. This account of the Amazons I repeat as I found it in

the memorials of the expedition, leaving the credibility of it to the judgement of others . . . some of the Spaniards were of the opinion that Captain Orellana should not have given the name of Amazons to these women who fought, because in the Indies it was no new thing for the women to fight, and to use bows and arrows; as has been seen on some islands of Barlovento, and at Carthagena, where they displayed as much courage as the men.[31]

The report contradicted Captain Orellana, who did not get to tell his story in the first-person, as Ralegh did, and did not really leave Orellana to tell his own story as found in the memorials. This is the kind of editorial impulse we observed in chapter 2 surrounding the Columbus texts. Herrera said that in the Province of St. John, Orellana "learned that the land was subject to women, who lived in the same way as Amazons, and were very rich, possessing much gold and silver. . . . The tales of Indians are always doubtful . . . but each reader may believe just as much as he likes."[32] This is ideological editing at its baldest even if Herrera apparently left the last judgment to the reader. The tales of the Natives may have been unreliable, if they were, as a protection against having gold at hand. If they could tell tales of fierce cannibals or Amazons and of gold far away, then they might watch the Spaniards move on and leave them in peace.

Another account of the Amazons occurred in Father Cristoval de Acuna's "A New Discovery of the Great River of the Amazons," which is quite different from Herrera's report of Orellana's journey. Of the Amazons themselves, Acuna wrote:

These manlike women have their abodes in great forests, and on lofty hills, amongst which, that which rises above the rest, and is therefore beaten by the winds for its pride, with most violence, so that it is bare and clear of vegetation, is called Yacamiaba. The Amazons are women of great valour, and they have always preserved themselves without the ordinary intercourse with men; and even when these, by agreement, come every year to their land, they receive them with arms in their hands, such as bows and arrows, which they brandish about for some time, until they are satisfied that the Indians come with peaceful intentions . . . they receive the Indians as guests for a few days. . . . The daughters who are born from this intercourse are preserved and brought up by the Amazons themselves, as they are destined to inherit their valour, and the customs of the nation, but it is not certain what they do with their sons.[33]

As in classical examples, this description of Amazons is not a one-dimensional instance of misogyny. The strength and independence of the Amazons here caused admiration and awe with some uncertainty and perhaps imputation or ill-ease over the fate of the sons of the Amazons. These women are valorous even if they need men for reproduction of their sex in order to ensure that Amazons have a future.

The real villains of the piece, for Acuna, are the Portuguese men, not the Amazons. The Black Legend of Portugal never caught on the way the Black Legend of Spain did, but Acuna tried even if he did not give the offenders the kind of space Las Casas did. Acuna told of Portuguese abuse of the "Indians": these fellow Iberians "cruelly abused the wives and daughters of the unfortunate captives, before their very eyes. . . ."[34] Acuna then referred to "the cruelty of the Portuguese" twice before moving into a direct address to "your Majesty," and the necessity for the Spanish king to restore peace to the land that was so troubled by the cruelty, and tyrannical rule, of the Portuguese.[35] This is a similar argument that Ralegh will use to move Elizabeth to action against the "cruel" Spaniards in Guiana.

God, gold, the land as woman and exploitation continue to be important themes in European writings about the New World more than 100 years after Columbus' landfall. Ralegh's *The Discouerie of the Large, Rich, and Bewtiful Empyre of Guiana* (1596), even as it tended toward the anti-Spanish and pro-Native position of the literature of the Black Legend, echoed the Spanish dreams of gold, God and a land to be exploited.[36] In the "Epistle Dedicatorie," Ralegh set for his goal, "*that mighty, rich, and beawtifull Empire of* Guiana, *and . . . that great and Golden City, which the Spanyards call* El Dorado, *and the naturalls* Manoa."[37] In the address "*To the Reader,*" Ralegh connects political expansion and breaking the hymen of a virgin. Charles V "has the Maydenhead of *Peru,* & the aboundant treasures of *Atabalipa*" and his successor has consequently held power over Europe: "It is his Indian Golde that indaungereth and disturbeth all the nations of Europe, it purchaseth intelligence, creepeth into Councels, and setteth bound loyalty at libertie, in the greatest Monarchies of Europe."[38] The Spanish rape of America makes all Europe quake. Ralegh also speaks about the minerals he saw in Guiana as "*El madre del oro* (as the Spanyards terme them) which is the mother of golde."[39] The body of Ralegh's *The Discoverie of Gviana* includes Ralegh's regret that he did not have the opportunity to go to the city of Manoa or to take other towns on the way. Anyone, like Ralegh, given such a chance, "he shall performe more then euer was done in *Mexico* by *Cortez,* or in *Peru* by *Pacaro.*"[40] Clearly, Spanish goals and influences affected English views of the New World even if Ralegh wanted to exceed Spain in the Americas. The Amazon River also reminds Ralegh of the women warriors that prompted the Spanish to give it a new name. He encapsulates the background and "history" of this mobile trope and myth: "The memories of the like women are very ancient as well in *Africa* as in *Asia:* In *Africa* those that had *Medusa* for *Queene:* others in *Scithia* neere the riuers of *Tanais* and *Thermadon:* we find also that *Lampedo* and *Marthesia* were *Queens* of the *Amazones:* in many histories they are verified to haue been, and in diuers ages and Provinces."[41] A transference of Amazons in a translation of empire marks Ralegh's typology. Like the lost tribes of Israel, the Amazons await the Europeans in the new lands. These female warriors also threaten the role of men in the raising of offspring and can also make them redundant on the battlefield. As Ralegh continues this passage, the story is familiar from antiquity through the Middle Ages to the Renaissance:

> But they which are not far from *Guiana* do accompanie with men but once in a yeere, and for the time of one moneth, which I gather by their relation to be in Aprill. At that time all the Kings of the borders assemble, and the Queens haue chosen, the rest cast lots for their *Valentines.* This one moneth, they feast, daunce, & drinke of their wines in abundance, & the Moone being downe, they all depart to their owne Prouinces. If they conceiue, and be deliuered of a sonne, they returne him to the father, if of a daughter they nourish it, and reteine it, and as many as haue daughters send vnto the begetters a Present, all being desirous to increase their owne sex and kinde, but that the cut of the right dug of the brest I do not finde to be true.[42]

The separation from, and expendability of, men is a recurring theme in descriptions of the way Amazons mate. Like Herodotus, Ralegh did try to make his ethnological work more believable by showing some skepticism in his oral sources or informants. Here, Ralegh questioned the usual detail that the Amazons cut off the right breast. Next, he did, however, side-by-side, report on the Amazons as a threat in war and a source of wealth:

It was farther told me, that if in the wars they tooke any prisoners that they vsed to accompany with those also at what time soeuer, but in the end for certaine they put them to death: for they are said to be very cruell and bloodthirsty, especially to such as offer to inuade their territories. These *Amazones* haue likewise great store of these plates of golde, which they recouer by exchange chiefly for a kinde of greene stones, which the Spaniards call *Piedras Hijadas.*[43]

The Amazons are cruel and hard to invade and are, therefore, Ralegh implied, unnatural: thus, they deserve the invasion. That intrusion is attractive, and perhaps necessary, because they have a dowry of gold. These women warriors can be taken when the English displace the Spanish, who trade with them.

In Ralegh's implied, and sometimes explicit, logic, the conquest of these women and the land as woman leads to gold, glory and pleasure. In addition to reading the Spanish, Ralegh also made use of French texts, like the work of Thevet: "And vpon the riuer of *Amazones Theuet* writeth that the people weare *Croissants* of gold."[44] "Those commanders and Chieftaines, that shoote at honour, and abundance, shal find there more eich and bewtifull cities, more temples adorned with golden Images, more sepulchers folled with treasure, then either *Cortez* found in *Mexico,* or *Pazzaro* in *Peru:* and the shining glorie of this conquest will eclipse all those so farre extended beames of the Spanish nation."[45] This model of conquest—of outconquesting Spain—has a sexual as well as military and economic dimension. The motif of finding more gold and glory than the Spaniards, a theme throughout this text, mixes with the image of rape and seduction of the land. As Ralegh builds toward his conclusion, he declares:

To conclude, *Guiana* is a Countrey that hath yet her Maydenhead, neuer sackt, turned, nor wrought, the face of the earth hath not beene torne, nor the vertue and salt of the soyle spent by manurance, the graues haue not beene opened for gold, the mines not broken with sledges, nor their Images puld down out of their temples. It hath neuer been entred by any armie of strength, and neuer conquered or possessed by any Christian Prince.[46]

Although Ralegh dedicated his work to his kinsman, Charles Howard, and to Robert Cecil, his text, like Hakluyt's "Discourse," was ultimately meant for the notice of the queen. The virgin queen is the Christian prince whom Ralegh wants to possess the maidenhead of Guiana. The queen is a woman and a prince, which Elizabeth herself made clear in her speech at Tilbury in anticipation of the Armada's attempted invasion of England.[47] In this passage in Ralegh's work the verbs "conquered" and "possessed" occur side-by-side. Like Shakespeare's typological or even stereoscopic image of the siege of the city and the siege of the women in *Henry V* a few years later, Harfleur and Katherine, Ralegh's description identified land and woman. The plunder is sexual and economic: both involve desecration and exploitation. A few sentences later, Ralegh spoke about "the conquest of *Guiana,*" so that this model from Spain persisted in Ralegh's thought.[48]

It is important to take these few and brief but significant sexual allusions and passages in context. They are part of a rhetoric of expansion, displacement and domination that is military, political and economic. The English, as I have mentioned in earlier chapters, regretted the Spanish lead in the exploration and colonization of the New World. Past regrets should lead to future benefits: the queen can rely on her servant, Ralegh, to help right wrongs, make profit and displace the Spanish, who got there first: "The west Indies were first offered her Maiesties Grandfather by *Columbus* a straunger, in whome there might be doubt of deceipt, and besides it was then thought incredible that there were such and so many lands & regions neuer written of before."[49] Xenophobia and ignorance are the defense that Ralegh offers in this missed opportunity with Columbus. This regret over Henry VII not having Columbus in his service is a much-rehearsed regret in the annals of the English colonization of America.[50] Next, Ralegh swore his allegiance and truthfulness: "This Empire is made knowen to her Maiesty by her own vassal, & by him that oweth to her more duty then an ordinary subiect, so that it shall ill sort with the many graces and benefites which I haue receaued to abuse her hignes, either with fables or imaginations."[51] The next step in this passage was to advocate a displacement of the Spanish with the help of a Native uprising: "The country is alreadie discouered, many nations won to her Maiesties loue & obedience, & those Spanyards which haue latest and longest labored about the conquest, beaten out, discouraged and disgraced, which amonge these nations were thought inuincible."[52] In Ralegh's rhetoric the rape of Guiana by Elizabeth and England now became a materalistic/paternalistic love. The Indians sought Elizabeth's protection from the Spanish.

Appealing to specifics in order to make the assault more credible, Ralegh then argued that Elizabeth use soldiers and gentlemen, such as the younger brothers. Ralegh held out a tangible and immediate goal: "after the first or second yere I doubt not but to see in London a contration house of more receipt for *Guiana,* then there is nowe in ciuil for the West indies."[53] London will displace Seville: the English will beat the Spanish at their own imperial game. The great Native leader could not be ignorant of the Spanish "cruelties to the borderers."[54] The Black Legend of Spain made its appearance in Ralegh as it had in Hakluyt's "Discourse." To this liberational narrative, Ralegh added the prophecy among the Incans that the Spaniard Berreo confessed to him and others: "from *Inglatierra* those *Ingas* shoulde be againe in time to come restored, and deliuered from the seruitude of the said Conquerors."[55] Concerning Guiana, Ralegh exhorts Elizabeth to "defende it, and hold it as tributary, or conquere and keepe it as Empresse of the same."[56] In Ralegh's view, if Elizabeth were to act and take Guiana and beyond, she would gain reputation and, as part of her secular cult of the Virgin Queen, she would be the virginal queen over the Amazons, who would help her to invade other empires. Here, the sexual roles were reversed. Ralegh had described Guiana as a land who still had her maidenhead and needed to be entered, but now the virgins were to invade other, presumably male-dominated, countries.[57] The English should drive out the Spanish and deliver the people from "the seruitude of the said Conquerors," so that the queen could be "Emperesse" of these lands: "For whatsoeuer Prince shall possesse it, shall bee greatest, and if the king of Spayne enioy it, he will become vnresistable."[58] Possession of the land and its goods leads to pleasure and power. Elizabeth's "great and princely actions" will "confirme and strengthen" the opinion in which other nations hold her.[59] There was a European as well as American dimension to this dominion.

Ralegh made explicit the connection between Elizabeth as Virgin Queen and the Amazons. The climax of the book approached in this stereoscopos: "And where the fourth border of *Guiana* reacheth to the Dominion and Empire of the *Amazones,* those women shall heereby heare the name of a virgin, which is not onely able to defend her owne territories and her neighbors, but also to inuade and conquere so great Empyres and so farre remoued."[60] As a great woman warrior, Elizabeth will be even more masculine than the Amazons and will be the ultimate conqueror. The implication is that she will conquer the *conquistadores,* themselves the inheritors of the great classical conquerors, like Alexander and the Roman emperors. By then appealing to God and Christ in royal imagery and implicitly conflating Elizabeth with the Virgin Mary as the "Lady of Ladies" and in the form of a prayer and confession, Ralegh ended this plea. All the men who would serve the queen in such an action would, with her grace and leave, be kings. Furthermore, all these military plans and invasions would be done in the name of the "king of al kings."[61] If Ralegh trusted in God, then the queen should trust Ralegh.

The sexualizing of Guiana has an intricate geometry. Ralegh attempted to seduce the queen as he proposed that she, through her male lieutenants, rape Guiana, which begged for her to help throw off the slavery the country suffered under the Spaniards while, as a courtier and a favorite who did not have as much favor as he once had, Ralegh courted the queen. The rhetorical cross-dressing and the textual equation of sexual and economic exploitation made sex a matter of force and politics, a thinly disguised rape in the name of God. Rape and gold hid behind, or served as adjuncts, to God.

While being part of ambivalent representations in texts by men in the Renaissance, the Amazons were often subject to praise in works in the formal controversy that defended, rather than attacked, women.[62] Ralegh's Amazons were positive allies to be suborned beneath the virginal brilliance of Elizabeth, whereas in *1* and *2 Iron Age* Thomas Heywood began with a positive view of the Amazons and then subordinated them to a man in the masculine world of war. In this drama, at the beginning of the first part, the Trojans welcomed the Amazon warriors but, in the second part, Pyrrhus, defeated them singlehandedly and beheaded their queen, Penthisilea.[63] It was perhaps easier to deal with the killing of warrior queens in England in 1632 than it was in 1596.

II

Not every early author writing about the New World had Amazons on his mind. Often the texts would shift their focus on questions of gender and sex and present a multiplicity of concerns. There are ethnographic and mythological dimensions that are sometimes difficult to separate. Here, I would like to concentrate on texts representing Spanish exploration and settlement of the New World that show this kind of shifting of multiple perspectives as they lead the way among the Europeans in talking about America. These texts about the Spanish were not always in Spanish or by Spaniards, but, despite the multilinguistic and multicultural enterprise of Spain's colonization of the New World, these actual and textual efforts came under the aegis of the Spanish crown. It was the authority, power and wealth of the Spanish monarch that invested the colonization with its ability to set trends and legal and political frameworks in the New World. These writings were, then, in the service of Spain.

In 1494–95, Micolaus Syllacius, while relating the second voyage of Columbus to the western Atlantic, first equated the Natives with those peoples in the Golden Age.[64] In describing the Caribs, he said that the women among enemies were used as concubines and the children borne by them were eaten.[65] There is, in this description, another aspect, that is the sexual attraction and flirting between Natives and Europeans. Not surprisingly, some texts by European males represented aboriginal women as wanton and seductive, as temptresses who would lead European men astray. According to Syllacius, Indian women "are somewhat lascivious in their demeanour and movements. They jest with our people and coquet with great freedom, provided that no improper subject is treated. . . ."[66] He proceeded to describe their dancing, which involves moving "in a gracefully voluptuous manner, through winding mazes [in] a languid dance in beautiful order with multiform involutions. . . ."[67] Here, there is an admiration for the geometry of voluptuousness, but still with a suggestion that there are rules in this dance and "encounter" with Europeans.

A few years later, describing his first voyage, Amerigo Vespucci portrayed the athleticism of the aboriginal women he encountered. While representing the Natives as generally fit, Vespucci maintained that the women ran as well as the men and even swam better than they did and that sometimes women used bows to hunt. These women were not a sex object for the men but a partner in war: "When they go to war they take the women with them; not because they fight, but because they carry the provisions in rear of the men. A woman carries a burden on her back, which a man would not carry, for thirty or forty leagues."[68] In Vespucci's description the physical strength of the Native women was equal to or greater than that of the men.

In relations between men and women there is equality and reciprocity: there is no marriage, and a man can repudiate a woman without shame and "in this matter the woman has the same liberty as the man."[69] Just when the reader might expect to stumble on a utopian society where sexual and social relations are equitable and well balanced, Vespucci criticizes the Natives: "They are . . . lascivious beyond measure, the women much more so than the men. I do not further refer to their contrivances for satisfying inordinate desires, so that I may not offend against modesty."[70] Like Syllacius, Vespucci blamed Native women most for their wantonness. Nevertheless, he did so in a context that described these women as hard-working in peace and war. While they were prolific in childbearing and pregnancy, this did not prevent them from work. In giving birth they did not feel pain: how Vespucci knew this he did not say. These women are made to seem tough: "If they are angry with their husbands they easily cause abortion."[71] Moreover, Vespucci seemed to display a prurient interest in the women's nakedness, what is shown and not shown of their bodies, something that becomes a stock response in some European reports of Native cultures. During the second voyage, Amerigo Vespucci developed this fascination in a new direction. When the Spaniards encountered some unusually tall women, "Our intention was to take the young girls by force, and to bring them to Castile as a wonderful thing."[72] However, many inordinately tall men arrived, so this kidnapping, a practice that Columbus brought with him to the New World, was foiled. During the third voyage, the Spaniards arrived at a shore where Native women spoke with them. When the Spaniards sent one young man over to the women "to reassure them," one woman clubbed him to the ground while other women helped drag him away from the beach and then "[tore] the Christian to pieces."[73]

In a letter on his third voyage to Lorenzo Pietro Francesco di Medici, Vespucci observes: "Their women, being very libidinous, make the penis of their husbands swell to such a size as to appear deformed . . . and by reason of this many lose their virile organ and remain eunuchs."[74] The women deform and castrate their husbands, so it is no wonder that some early modern scholars today enlist Freud, Lacan and other psychoanalytical theorists to try to explain the fear of castration and the fantasies of what, in another connection, Janet Adelman once called "suffocating mothers."[75] My tack here, however, will be to suggest the contradictory and multifold nature of the representations of the sexing of America, a kind of related friction, but to another end.

There is a strange physicality, perhaps even an ethnography of sex and seduction in Antonio Pigafetta's account of Magellan's circumnavigation of the world.[76] Pigafetta observed a scene of a female bird who lays her eggs on the back of a legless male who floats around hatching them for her, perhaps implying an allegory about role reversals among the Natives.[77] In this rather mythological work, Pigafetta sought out the origins of the cannibal in South America: cannibalism was started by an old woman who bit the men who had killed her sons; it was then that eating the flesh of one's enemy became a habit among tribes.[78] Pigafetta's ethnological impulse found further expression in his description of a scene of the baptizing of a Native queen.[79] He also told a story that the Native women decreed that their men should wear bolts through their penises. Otherwise the women would not have intercourse with them: "Those people make use of that device because they are of a weak nature."[80] This criticism led to the inevitable preference of the Native women for the Europeans: "The women loved us very much more than their own men. All of the women from the age of six years up have their vaginas gradually opened because of the men's penisses."[81] The fascination with the body of male and female Natives and how that relates to intercourse and relations with Europeans is almost on display, a strange mixture of ethnographical detail and boastful machissimo. How prurient the discussion of bolted penises and opened vaginas is depends in part on the elusive matter of tone. The question of child abuse, however the sexual involvement of children was viewed in Pigafetta's time, would occur to many readers of our period.[82] There is a certain divide and conquer here that would make the peaceful relations between European and Native difficult to establish.

A wider array of allusions to women occurred in Peter Martyr's work.[83] In the First Decade, Martyr represented the first encounter between the Spaniards and indigenous women. When the Spaniards reached the Antilles, they chased some fleeing Natives and captured a woman and took her back to their ships, "where fyllinge her with meat and wyne, and apparelynge her, they let her departe to her company."[84] Why they had to dress her is something that is not explained, which is not unusual in the early writings about the New World: they can be gnomic. Cannibals and Amazons also coexisted in Martyr's text. Of cannibals, he says: "yet do they abstain from the eatynge of women and count it vyle. Therefore, such women as they take they keep for increase as we do hens to lay eggs. The olde women they make theyre drudges."[85] It seems that the cannibals were squeamish about women and used them like hens for increase or to do work for them. The classical antecedents about cannibals and Amazons, which I discussed earlier, informed how Martyr constructed the relations between these two taboo groups. He described an island inhabited only by women,

> to whom the cannibals have access at certain times of the year, as in old times the Thracians had to the Amazons on the isle of Lesbos. The men children they send to their fathers. But the women children they keep to themselves. They have great and strong caves or dens in the ground, to the which they fly for safeguard if any men resort unto them at any other time than is appointed. And there defend themselves with the violence of bows and arrows against any who try to invade them.[86]

This is like a stock narrative, a traveling extended trope, that developed classical themes in coming to terms with the New World. The male children fared better in this version than in some accounts, but the mating between cannibals and Amazons was cast in a form consciously reminiscent of Herodotus. These exotic and erotic inhabitants, fierce in their independence, appeared both to threaten and liberate the "staid" European authors and readers of travel accounts. But even the writer claimed adventure and the status of a participant and an eyewitness. These women as well as cannibal men were, according to Martyr, very good at shooting, and he proceeded to tell the story of being attacked by a boat full of "cannibals." In the vessel there were as many women as men: they had at their head a queen. When the boat was overturned, the women swam as well as the men.[87] Martyr reinforced the sense of the strength and toughness of the Native women in telling a story of the escape of Native women captured by the Spaniards: one of them led the others to swim three miles to safety. In trying to make the New World familiar even in its most fantastic and unusual elements, Martyr compared the aboriginal woman to Cloelia of Rome. The former attempted a much more difficult and dangerous adventure than did Cloelia of Rome, "which being in hostage to the King Porcena deceaved her keepers and rode over the river Tiber with the other virgins which were pledges with her. For whereas they swam over the river on horseback. This Katharyne with seven other women trusting only to the strength of their armes swam above three long miles and also at a tyme that the sea was rough."[88]

This typology of Old World antiquity and New World novelty is both reassuring in its homologies and anxious in its desire to find them. Martyr continued in this vein when he described a scene in which they were approached by naked virgins whom Martyr compares to Dryads.[89] Classical and biblical allusions were ways Martyr and his contemporaries used to make sense of this world that was new to them.

Ralegh's Amazons in the New World, who came after Martyr's, were part of a larger context that is sometimes forgotten in the pursuit of the context of Elizabeth I as the virgin queen or in discussions of national literature or history. That is one reason a comparative method can be suggestive. Martyr was not without his strong women: Queen Anacaona, who bears "no less rule in the governance of her brother's kingdom than does he himself," possesses treasure, not gold or precious stones but "things to be used."[90] Riches were to be found among the Amazon before Ralegh set down similar ideas.

Martyr also represented more strange images of sexing America, sometimes keeping these exotic and bizarre myths in typology with classical mythology. For instance, he recounted a local myth about a group of men separated from their womenfolk, who see "a great multitude of beasts in shape somewhat like unto women" who, when the men "try to use them for women," turn out to lack "women's privities. Wherefore calling the belders ageyne to conseyle, to consult what were best to be done in this case, theyre advice was that the bird which we caule the Pye, shuld be admitted with his byll to open a place for that purpose whyle in the meane tyme these men called Caracaracoles, shulde hold fast the women's thighs abrode with theyr rowgh handes. Full wysely therefore was the pye put to this office, and opened the women's privities, and hereof the women of the Islande have theyre original and offspringe."[91]

Martyr compared this story with similar Greek fables, perhaps to put it in a familiar frame, but this kind of creation of sexual parts and therefore sex through force is a type of rape. Like the story of Leda and the swan, it allowed for taboo social acts to find a sublimation or secret desire in a body of texts that represented pagan religion or cathartic stories for the Christian imagination of the time. Martyr was describing desire without doing so apparently or formally within the purview of Christianity itself. But the theological disapproval was not far off, for Martyr soon spoke about graven images "lyke unto paynted devils," which are called Zemes, and told of a female Zemes of great magical powers.[92] She is "wayted on by two other lyke men. . . . One of these, executed the office of a mediatour to the other Zemes whych are under the power and commaundement of this woman, to rayse wyndes, cloudes and rayne."[93] This female is elemental and appears to be associated in Martyr's discourse with a kind of black magic, devil's art or witch's craft.

In the Third Decade, Martyr amplified this variety of female figures. He reiterated the motif of athleticism and equality in another description of cannibal and Caribbean women, who "can dyve and swymme" as well as men.[94] They broke the mould European society placed on its women, something apparently attractive (if although sometimes threatening) to male authors like Martyr in their writing. Women, and more specifically virgins, were tokens and gifts in an exchange between men. The inhabitants of Cariarai, for example, sent the Spaniards two virgins, "signifyinge unto them that they might take them away if they pleased."[95] This is like go-betweens and "mediators" between cultures that we will observe in the next chapter. Apparently, children, virgins and slaves were fine for surrender, or interested the Europeans most. The land also caught the eye of the Spaniards. Martyr represented the place that Columbus had described: The island of Hispaniola "hath a thousande and agayne a thousande fayre, fayre, pleasant, bewtifull, and riche Nereides whiche lye about it on every syde, adournynge this theyre ladye and moother, as it were an other Tethis the wyfe of Neptunus, envyronynge her aboute, and attendynge aboute her as theyre queen and patronesse."[96] The Nereids were islands, but they are described in terms of womanhood. This island is a queen with her waiting women or attendant maidens.

But the zones of women persisted as they did in the First Decade. Martyr observed once more in this Third Decade that South American women shoot as well as the men and that women defend their coasts against invasion when the men go hunting. He noted that this may be the origin of the all-woman island he mentioned in the First Decade.[97] In Martyr's New World there were many distinctions among women, and what might have appeared to be an Amazon at first glance was not necessarily. He speaks about islands inhabited only by women

after the manner of the Amazons. But they that ponder the matter more wisely, thinke them rather to be certeyne women whiche have vowed chastitie and professed a solitary life as the nuns do wyth us, or as the virgins called Vestales or Bonae Deae were accustomed to do under the gentiles in oulde tyme. At certeyne tymes of the yeare, men of the other islands resort to them. But not for the intent of generation, but moved wyth pitie to help them dresse theyre gardens and till theyre grounde. The reporte goeth likewise that there are islandes of corrupte women to whom men resorte for carnall copulation: And that they cut off one of the paps of theyre women children lest it should hinder shootyng. Also that they keep only the women children and send away the men children."[98]

Here is a distinction between women who might be mistaken for Amazons but who were like nuns and those who were like prostitutes but sounded a lot like Amazons. Apparently, as in epic and romance, it was hard to tell what kind of woman was before a man. In the next instance he mentioned a town where the women were wonderfully chaste.[99] There was an Old World grid into which these women of the New World fit. The anxiety over what became of male children resurfaced. These cares and tropes translate over time in new contexts but almost as if temporal changes never were.

Martyr's women of the New World were not alone as serving as images and projected fantasies that some of these European males had concerning women. In *Chronicles of Peru* Cieza De Leon provided an account that combined the domination and devouring of women by men. He spoke about an Indian tribe who "collected all the women they could from the land of their enemies, took them home, and used them as if they had been their own. . . . In this way they had women solely to bring forth children, which were afterwards to be eaten."[100] As if this production of children for food were not bad enough (it is worthy of Swift), Leon then related an account of a chief who used three women to sleep on: "two of them laid one on a mat and the other across it to serve as a pillow. The Indian then made his bed on the bodies of these women, and took another pretty woman by the hand."[101] Not only does Leon's Native literally abuse two women as mats but he also subjects them to being witness to his lying with a "pretty woman." To make the story even less attractive, the Indian then confesses that he plans to eat his wife and the child he has by her. The sexual impulse of the Native male, and perhaps by implication the voyeuristic or creative European male who reports this "event," literally devours itself.

A catalogue of strange practices of, or regarding, women are scattered throughout Leon's work. Virginity, a recurring motif in European accounts of encounters with indigenous peoples, meant something different to Natives: "they do not hold virginity to be a thing of any estimation. When they marry they use no kind of ceremony."[102] Live women became part of a dead man's entourage: "when the chiefs die their bodies are placed in large and deep tombs, accompanied by many live women."[103] Their valuables were also part of this tomb. Leon, who asserted that the women of the province of Quinbaya were amorous, once again described men who eat their wives and infants.[104] The strength of these women, as compared with European females, was also a recurrent theme: "fifty of these women suffer less pain in bringing forth than one of our nation."[105] In one scene Leon presented a victim of the cannibals: an attractive Indian girl gave herself up to her cannibalistic tribesmen rather than cross paths with the Spaniards and is duly killed and eaten—"they ate her heart and entrails raw"—after she had "knelt down and awaited her doom, which they gave her."[106] It is telling that Leon might be showing the violence of the cannibals but he raises the question, without stating it, of why the girl would chose them over the Spaniards she wanted to avoid. Native women given to "love" recurred: the women of Llacta-cunga "are very amorous and some of them are very beautiful" and those women of the Canaris are "very pretty, amorous and friendly to the Spaniards."[107] Leon, as we have seen, did not spare the Spaniards from criticism. He noted the Spaniards' "avarice and . . . desire for pretty women."[108] Throughout, Leon repeated references to the Native custom of burying wives alive, along with their dead husbands. The bravery of some indigenous women also recurred in Leon's narrative: he described "some women who were like valiant men. Taking up arms they subdued those who were in the district where they lived, and, almost like what is told of the Amazons, they made homes for themselves, without husbands."[109] The irrepressible Amazons were what might be called shadow-sisters to other Native women because they were often part of an implied or direct comparison in the early descriptions by European men. Leon then recounted how they built fortresses but eventually were conquered and died out. Some Natives seem to have told this story to the Spaniards, who were asking about the remains of the fortresses. One last example will suggest how Leon shifted his emphasis on various aspects of women. When discussing the Incas, he mentioned how their princes took their sisters as wives to ensure that any child born of the queen was the legitimate heir. But also, "none of these lords had less than 700 women for the service of their house and their pleasure."[110] This notion of amorousness and pleasure was a leitmotif amid discussions of sacrifice and cannibalism: the erotic nature of the Native woman was part of the exoticism that Leon and his fellow Spaniards and Europeans presented to the reader as an initiation into the "new" and distant America. Notions of the sacrifice of live wives to a dead

husband occurred elsewhere. For example, Pascal de Andagoya referred to this Native practice.[111] The strength and dominance of women also occurred in his text as, in Nicaragua,
for instance, "the husbands were so much under subjection that if they made their wives
angry they were turned out of doors and the wives even raised their hands against them. . . .
The wives made their husbands attend on them, and do everything like servant lads."[112]
This reversal is like *Twelfth Night*, where the Lord of Misrule upsets the social hierarchy:
here it is the gender order that was topsy-turvy. Sodomy, as we shall see, was another challenge to the old order that seemed both to fascinate and repel some of these early European
writers about the New World.

III

The French exploration and settlement of the New World in the sixteenth century also
described women in relation to the land. The two principal examples that should best
illustrate this description are Jacques Cartier's voyages to Canada in the 1530s and 1540s
and Jean de Léry's experience in Brazil in the 1550s. Both Cartier's account and the
Spanish narratives represented indigenous women as basic to the Europeans' economy
in the new land. Whereas the French wooed the women with gifts (and got some flattering responses for doing so), the Spanish seemed to want to take the women as gifts
in their own right. The differences among the Europeans or among the Natives is something that is easy to elide in comparative studies of the New World.

Cartier's accounts focused closely on the land and its animal and human inhabitants,
and women were an integral part of that environment. The northern climate of Canada
affected Cartier's descriptions. For instance, on the first voyage of 1534, in describing a
place he called Blanc Sablon, which he called "the land God gave to Cain," Cartier spoke
of the dress of the Natives: "They clothe themselves with the skin of animals, both men
as well as women; but the women are wrapped more closely and snuggly in their skins;
and have a belt at their waists."[113] European accounts of Native women are not necessarily sexual, something that can be forgotten in the current cultural climate, but is a
caveat I want to place at the center of my chapter on sexing America. Here, there is the
image of the exile in a strange and barren land, if Cartier's biblical attribution is to be
taken even metaphorically. Cain is about murder, not sex.

In another location, among another group of Natives, Cartier reported that 300 Native men, women and children came to see the French. Speaking about the women,
Cartier divided them into two groups:

> Some of their women, who did not come over, danced and sang, standing in the water up
> to their knees. The other women, who had come over to the side where we were, advanced
> freely towards us and rubbed our arms with their hands. Then they joined hands together
> and raised them to heaven, exhibiting many signs of joy. And so much at ease did they feel
> in our presence, that at length we bartered with them, hand to hand, for everything they
> possessed, so that nothing was left to them but their naked bodies, for they offered us
> everything they owned, which was, all told, of little value. We perceived that they are peo-
> ple who would be easy to convert, who go from place to place.[114]

The translation shifts the punctuation, so that it makes it even harder to distinguish between Native men and women in this scene with the French.[115] In the French there is a
semicolon after "joy," where Biggar, the English translator, begins a new sentence, so

that in the French it looks as though the French were playing a kind of strip-trade rather than strip-poker with the Native women, whereas in the English translation it is ambiguous whether the text is talking about Natives generally going away naked. Whatever the context, this nakedness is mild beside the Spanish remarks about female bodies and, sometimes, their own desire for sex with Native women. Cartier's text is quite sexless. The women may dance and sing and cook, but they are decidedly not Amazons or sex goddesses from a male fantasy. Cartier makes most people like animals and plants—a resource—or, if something more, a pawn to impress the king, François I, of the importance, riches or resources of this new land.

Cartier was a kidnapper as were Columbus, Cabot and others. On the first voyage, Cartier took back to France two captive Natives in what is today Gaspé Harbour: on the second voyage, he seized Donnacona, a chief, and some of his leading people, and removed them to France, where they all died except for one little girl, whom I will get to in a while.[116] Cartier could be a chief subject of my next chapter on mediation and kidnapping, but I leave that to a larger study.[117] He seemed more interested in possessing the land legally and symbolically with crosses than with taking possession of women. Cartier described political theater, trade, the beauty and the abundance of the land, his mastery over the Natives and their ready nature for conversion (tabula rasa) as means to promote his voyages and to convince the king of their benefits for France. What is striking, even though the text depends on certain tricks and lies to control the Natives, is the absence of "locker-room" chat or worse.

The women Cartier has just been describing were part of an Iroquoian group. Their men and women, according to him, "go quite naked, except for a small skin, with which they cover their privy parts, and for a few old skins which they throw over their shoulders."[118] Cartier then described their hair in detail, including a long tuft he likened to "a horse's tail."[119] Although the Natives were almost a part of the land like animals in this account, Cartier also thought of them in terms of conversion, so he recognized their humanity. His interest was ethnographical or proto-ethnographical: he did not use any disparaging analogies between these Natives and animals in any of his texts. Cartier appeared to see the Natives as natural, but treated them with the mixture of suspicion and hope he would other people. When the French went ashore, the Native men danced with joy but

> they had made all the young women retire into the woods, except two or three who remained, to whom we gave each a comb and a little tin bell, at which they showed great pleasure, thanking the captain by rubbing his arms and his breast with their hands. And the men, seeing we had given something to the women that had remained, made those come back who had fled to the woods, in order to receive the same as the others. These, who numbered some twenty, crowded about the captain and rubbed him with their hands, which is their way of showing welcome. He gave them each a little tin ring of small value; and at once they assembled together in a group to dance; and sang several songs. We saw a large quantity of mackerel which they had caught near the shore with the nets they use for fishing. . . . [120]

The original French, "qui est leur facon de faire chère," which the translator rendered as "which is their way of showing welcome," can also imply a way of giving cheer to or fêting someone. This interpretation, which cannot necessarily be suggested in a translation where the translator must chose one word, is borne out by a definition given in a dictionary of sixteenth-century French: "To give a good expression [look], good welcome, to show affection, to celebrate."[121] There is nothing explicitly sexual about this encounter, but "faire chère" did have some connotations that might have left this phrase more open: Ronsard, as the dictionary quotes him, wrote in his Sonnets: "I cannot love those to whom you show affection [vous faites chere] . . . /I curse their favours, I abhor their happiness."[122] Cartier saw it as a welcome and, in this context of gift-giving and expressions of joy, he felt quite comfortable eyeing the fish in their nets as proof for his French audience of the abundance and potential of this country. Outside of the kidnapping, which is something disturbing, there is in these texts no show of French force or proof that they wanted to dominate the men or the women they met along the way. They put up crosses to claim the land for the French king, but they did not go out of their way to provoke violence. That is not always the story told in the Spanish accounts.

IV

Visual representations of America as woman also complicate the "sexing" of this New World. A few instances will suggest the ways in which these images complemented and created another dimension to the verbal descriptions of the New World. Title pages and illustrations, often allegorical, attempted to appeal to the imaginations of European readers in their "encounter" with America. There is no one America, verbal or visual, so that if there were stereotypes of America as a woman, there was no single image above others that prevailed.

Study and collection connect our time with earlier fascinations with images of America. Libraries, museums and galleries, as recent controversies, such as the Elgin Marbles at the British Museum have shown, suggest that these institutions have imperial connections, that learning and collection may be a blur of causes and effects in the course of empire. Earlier scholars have collected or discussed some of these works from a vast array of images, for instance, Jan van der Street's "America";[123] Godfried Maes' "America, " a pen and ink wash;[124] and "Wild Naked People," a woodcut illustration to a German translation of Amerigo Vespucci's letters to Pier Soderini, published in Strassburg in 1509.[125] Museums and libraries have collected images of America. For example, "Vespucci Discovering America" by Jan van der Street, called Stradamus, in pen & ink, in 1589; a plaquette, "America," produced in Germany 1580–1590 in lead with gilt; "America," by Marcus Gheerarts, an engraving, about 1590–1600, and one of eleven etched playing cards representing parts of America by Stefano de Bella in 1644; "America, " by Nicolaes (or Claes) Berchem in black chalk and ink, which appeared in the period between 1640 and 1650; and many eighteenth-century representations of America as a woman can be found in the New York Metropolitain Museum of Art.[126] "America" in pen and ink by Maarten de Vos, about 1600, may be found in the collection of the University of Michigan Museum of Art in Ann Arbor.[127] The New York Historical Society's collection includes two important engravings, "America," Phillipe Galle, from about 1579–1600, and "America, " by Cornelius Visscher, from the period about 1650–60, which contains a poetic inscription.[128] The Galle engraving also includes an inscription describing America as a female glutton who devours men. In the late seventeenth century and early eighteenth century and beyond the fascination with images of America persisted in book illustrations, tapestries and paintings: significant instances are "America" (ca. 1700), a tapestry by Ludwig van Schoor, in the collection of the National Gallery of Art in Washington; "America" (ca. 1730–38), Francesco Solimena's painting—oil on canvas.[129]

Two further examples warrant particular attention. The first instance is the title page of Abraham Ortelius' *Theatrum Orbis Terrarum* (Antwerp 1570), which is the first known allegorical depiction of America. A naked woman in the foreground, America, looks both restful and vigilant. Holding an arrow in her hand, she is watching two parrots in the tree above. In the background, a few naked people appear to be talking and panning for gold. In this pastoral idyll the Natives look more European than in many other images. This is a world of civility apparently without strife. The second instance is two images by the Flemish artist, Philippe Galle. The first image is an American allegory from circa 1579–1600, and is of a naked and armed Amazon carrying the head of a man. An inscription portrays America, endowed with gold, as a gluttonous female who devours men. The second image, engraved about 1580, contains a woman with a club, who is situated at the center of a variety of other creatures, human and non-human, in the New World.[130]

America as a woman finds many representations in various media and forms in different situations. The first painting of America as woman occurred in 1574: it is in a fresco at the palace, built for Cardinal Alessandro Farnese, at Caprarola, near Rome. Jost Amman, a Swiss artist, produced four prints of the four continents as landscapes with figures (1577). Giovanni de' Vecchi represented the Western hemisphere of a world map with allegories of the continents (1574). Maarten de Vos' (1594) sketch was, according to Lynn Glaser, " . . . copied and recopied into the 18th century . . . the commonest allegorical depiction of America."[131] There is a panel that takes America as its subject in tapestries made after cartoons by Ludwig van Schoor, woven first at Brussels and then widely imitated elsewhere: between 1699 and 1709, fifty-eight were sold.[132] Lorenzo Vaccaro produced a sculpture in silver, "America" (1692), for the cathedral in Toledo; in 1694, Andrea Pozzo painted a fresco, "America," on the ceiling of Saint Ignazio, in Rome.[133] The representation of America as a woman extended to royal festivals and spectacles, and many of these images of the feminized New World had wide diffusion in books, or were transposed onto tiles or tankards. As Hugh Honour has noted, there are many representations of America as a woman in the eighteenth century.[134] The persistence of this image, even in the Enlightenment, suggests how deep this cultural grammar went.

The figure of the Amazon, as we observed earlier in the chapter, is another recurring motif in representations of America as a woman: this tendency is found in images as well as texts. Sometimes verbal and visual signs work together to emphasize doubly the Amazonian theme. "Cannibal America," in Ferdinando Gorges, *America Painted to the Life* (London 1659), contains an Amazonian figure. On the verso of this print, a poem suggests an identification of cannibalism with the Natives and the land.[135] The image of Columbus still haunts the encounter with America as a woman centuries after his first landfall. In Gottfried Bernhardt Goetz's "America" (Augsburg, ca. 1750), a woman on an alligator offers the plenty of the land to those arriving: the image portrays Columbus in the background. She, rather than the Europeans, is doing the seducing: like the New World, she appears to be, in Katy Emck's words, "a cornucopia of sensual promise."[136] In later images of America as a woman, she looks more European, less robust and more delicate. Many images that depict America in terms of fecundity and wealth, feminize the figure.

Maps also included America as a woman. A few examples will suggest that this practice occurred in various European countries over a long period. For instance, Diego Gutierrez's map of 1562, which is a decorative representation of the Spanish possessions in northern America, includes "Victoria," fierce, European-looking and with wings, who occupies much of the top left corner of this map, where she is embracing a coat of arms with a crown on it.[137] In these European maps sometimes the female figures are Amazonian, sometimes more indeterminate. Jacobus Meursius' map (1671–73; Amsterdam 1673), in the German edition of Montanus' "Die unbekante newe welt," focuses on a female figure seated on what at first appears to be a horn of plenty; Pieter Schenck's map of 1700 represents three figures apparently identified with harvest and war; in Pieter van der Aa's map (1706–1728) there is a picture of a half-naked, crowned, Amazonian woman to the bottom left, aiming her bow at the Americas.[138] Women, and Amazons in particular, could suggest a threat or even war, a kind of violence that opposes that which Ralegh represents in his narrative concerning Guiana. There are, as Gillian Hill has noted, a good number of maps portraying Europe as a woman as well.[139] The different continents also appeared as women in various images. It was not, then, simply a matter of colonization that determined this aspect of the representations of gender. Domination, degradation, allegorization and idealization took on many forms in a typology between Europe and her sisters. Europe often appeared as a dominating, but not necessarily domineering, woman over her sisters or fellow female continental icons. Europe could be domestic and delicate but strong, with or without the imperial dimension. As late as 1761, a map appeared that depicted the Spanish Empire as a queen.[140]

The iconography of empire was not simply one of males as conquerors. Men may have enlisted idealized images of women in empire, but powerful women, like the queens, Isabella of Spain and Elizabeth I of England, played a key role in the exploration, exploitation and colonization of America. Trompe d'œuil is something with an irony of its own, not just shifting perspective in images, but it might have fooled the eyes of the European beholders, at court and throughout the societies, as it fools us still, as a technique and a metaphor, about ways of seeing, just who is doing the looking and who and what really are being seen. In the sexing of America, nothing was necessarily simple or fair.

There is a kind of moment that often occurred among these multifold images of women in the New World that might have partly to do with the anxiety over absent presence of European women, or the desire to justify taking land or women from Native men, or the closeness of European men on these voyages: the homoerotic and even sodomite scenes. In The Third Decade, Peter Martyr, amid his many descriptions of Amazons, cannibals and women of many kinds, described the house of a king "infected with the most horrible and unnatural lechery. For he found the king's brother and many other younge men in women's apparell, smoth and effeminately decked, which by the report of such as dwelt about hym, he abused with preposterous Venus."[141] This gave Martyr a pretext to describe the ferocity and bestiality of the Natives, as if these attributed were connected to this "unnatural lechery."[142]

In *The General and Natural History of the Indies,* Gonzalo Fernández de Oviedo accused the Natives of the mainland of being "sodomites" and taking great "pride in this sin."[143] To prove this proud and perverse behavior, he pointed to physical proof: "just as other people are accustomed to wearing jewels or precious stones around their necks, in some parts of these Indies they wear a jewel made of gold, representing one man on top of another in that base and diabolical act of Sodom."[144] Moving from the general to the specific, Oviedo then claimed eyewitness status, maintaining in great detail his evidence: the port, the armada, the captain and the year (1514). So when he said that he had seen "one of these jewels of the devil," he expected to be believed.[145] One of these jewels

Oviedo saw "weighed twenty pesos of gold" and was "acquired" in a way that Oviedo neglected to specify.[146] Moral indignation also led to profit, a literal smashing and melting pot of Native culture. Of this sodomite gold ornament from Castilla del Oro, Oviedo said: "And since it was brought to the heap of gold that was taken there, and they subsequently brought it to be smelted before me as a royal official and overseer of gold smelting, I broke it with a hammer and pounded it up with my own hands on an anvil in the smelting house in the city of Darien."[147] This is a side of Darien whose Keats' "stout Cortez" missed and, as we shall see, was later challenged, as was much of Keats' geography in his poem. How much of this outrage, like that over Amazons and cannibals, became a rationalization for colonization and dominance?[148] While it might be stretching the argument, it is not hard to see why some might think that the Spanish invasion was, at least metaphorically and materially if not always sexually, a kind of (male) rape of the Indies and mainland America. In the God and gold complex I have discussed elsewhere, there is a seizure of gold in the name and glory of God, and, for all the talk of God and virgins, there is sometimes a taking of the Native women for the pleasure and excesses of the flesh so denounced in adjacent sentences of texts. The exchange of a woman from Native man to Spanish male, as Vespucci and others mention over and over, is, in Eve Sedgwick's terms, a kind of homoeroticism, something between men.[149] How much there was an exchange of boys or any homosexual practices that the Spaniards engaged in, if any, they did not say in these texts.

The existence of this gold ornament, for Oviedo, proved a longstanding and common practice among the Natives. As disgusted as he said he was by this sodomite practice, he did not spare any ethnographical or voyeuristic interest in it: "You should know that the man who consents and takes the burden of being the woman in that bestial and perverse act takes on the status (*oficio*) of a woman and wears *naguas*."[150] Oviedo then explained that naguas are pieces of cotton that Native women wear from their waist to halfway down the leg or, if they are important, to their ankle "in order to cover their shameful parts."[151] Oviedo's notion of shame amid the Natives seems to be contradictory. The Native women who are most significant cover up most, but "The girls who are virgins, as I said in another place, do not wear anything over their shameful parts, nor do the men, since not knowing what shame is, they do not employ any defense for it."[152] Do some of the Natives know shame and others not, or is shame in the eye of the beholder? Are heterosexual Native males shameful as well as their homosexual counterparts? They are, perhaps, like Adam and Eve before the Fall. Oviedo did return to the topic of sodomy, which he said "was commonly practiced among the Indians of this island, but it was hateful to the women, more out of their interest than for scruples of conscience."[153] Oviedo amplifed this critique of the women, who were apparently more interested in sexual desire than in moral scruples, but it may be that he was blind to the comparison between these indigenous women and the Spanish men whose desire for gold idols might be said to outweigh any moral indignation over homosexuality. Oviedo himself might have profited from breaking up such images or for asserting the existence of such gold figures, which Las Casas contexted. Oviedo's amplification was that although some of the Native women on the island behaved well, this place "had the most shameless and lustful women that have been seen in these Indies."[154] The lust of the Spaniards was not mentioned here. Michele de Cuneo described how he whipped a Carib woman that Columbus had given him during the second voyage, for she had resisted him mightily, and how he and she finally "came to an agreement" and she behaved as though she had "been brought up in a school of harlots."[155] Cuneo found a way to

convince himself that this rape was really something the woman had always been want-
ing and had been trained to accept as a pretext to her harlotry. This is not the Columbus enterprise of the Indies that was presented to the monarchs and the people of Spain
by his family and friends and editors, like Las Casas, for his time and for posterity, nor
the Columbian voice we encountered at the beginning of this book. Nor is this the
Oviedo, the naturalist and promoter of empire, but these are parts of the story. I began
the body of this book with Swift: it is for the cultural historian and literary critic to accept satire as a satire on himself or herself, so when I point out these possible interpretations, I do so from the logic and language of the texts and not from a sense that I, or
anyone else afterward, is not capable of bad faith, ill-gotten gains and poor behavior. No
one is, but for critical moments here and there, she or he is a katascopos or overviewer.
As I will suggest at the end of this study, we share some of the same frailties with the historical figures that inhabit this book. It is one thing to recognize frailty in all of us, but
it would be a "shame," to use Oviedo's phrase, to pass over bad or even criminal behavior. For Oviedo, that is the sodomite's: in our time and culture, it might be Cuneo's.

Las Casas, while asserting that the Natives were not cannibals, contradicted Oviedo
by saying that no one except him said that the people of Hispaniola, Cuba, Puerto Rico,
Jamaica and the Lucayos practiced sodomy: this Oviedo "pretended" to record the history of what he neither knew nor saw so that this accusation of sodomy was reckless because in Cuba Las Casas himself knew the people and the Spaniards, like his own father,
who had come with Columbus, who praised the indigenous peoples for their virtue and
kindness.[156] Like Oviedo, he appealed to his own status as an eyewitness and bolstered
his evidence with details of his inquiries with other people on the island about the possibility of sodomy in Cuba. To clinch his argument, Las Casas, who did not tell here of
his time as a landowner, set out an exchange he had with an old "Indian" woman of high
status who had been married to a Spaniard while he was taking her confession. Obviously the stakes were high in convincing the court and the elite in Spain of the virtue or
vice of "los Indios." Las Casas' debate with Sepúlveda in the early 1550s over the nature
of these "Indians"—were they natural slaves in Aristotle's terms or virtuous people waiting for the true light of the Scripture?—showed the importance of this debate. Las Casas
used all the rhetorical weight he could find to make his witness reliable: she was old,
high-born, married to a Spaniard so probably a friend, and at confession so she would
not lie. What Las Casas was doing using the confessional in this way is something to
wonder about. His question was also leading because he asked whether, before the
Spaniards had arrived, the Natives had practiced sodomy. It was as if Las Casas were implying that the Spaniards had introduced this "vice." Her answer, which I paraphrase, is
that sodomy had not existed among the Native men because if it had, the women would
have eaten them until they had died.[157]

Sodomy became a problem of representation, mediation and evidence, which recurs
in encounter literature, so that the image of the Native remains uncertain, stereotypical
or obscure. About fifty years after Cortés' conquest of New Spain, Bernal Díaz, who had
been with Francisco Hernandez, Juan de Grijalva and Hernan Cortés, resumed this story
of the conquest because he thought that Gómara and Gonzalo de Illescas had misrepresented it.[158] The Spaniards on Hernandez's expedition to Mexico were there because
they did not have a grant of Indians in Cuba. Indians were the means to wealth. About
their first contact with the Indians of Yucatan and Mexico, Díaz says that they thought
them more civilized than the Cuban Natives because they covered themselves with cotton clothing. The Indians seemed friendly to the Spaniards just before they ambushed

them and, after fierce fighting, retreated. The Spaniards then found gold, including idols, in the Indian prayer-houses. These houses "contained many idols of baked clay, some with demons' faces, some with women's, and others equally ugly which seemed to represent Indians committing sodomy with one another."[159] The treachery and cowardice of Indians, the danger of idols, the disturbance of gender boundaries were as much in Díaz as in Columbus. It is as if the Europeans had an image of the Natives that they expected the Natives to fulfill, so that they could justify taking their gold and riches and occupying their lands. The Spaniards, and later other European groups, clashed in their views of the Americas and that engendered some self-criticism and heavy polemics. This is another example of this phenomenon.

In writing about the French among the Tupinamba in Brazil in the 1550s, another religious, Jean de Léry, discussed sodomy in his chapter on marriage. In his account he tried to be balanced:

> I will add that, considering the hot region they inhabit, and in spite of what is said of Orientals, the marriageable young people of that land, boys as well as girls, are not so much given over to lust as one might think; and would to God it held more sway over here. Nevertheless sometimes when they are greatly vexed with each other they call each other *tyvire*, which is to say "bugger"; one can conjecture from this (for I affirm nothing) that this abominable sin is committed among them.[160]

Like Las Casas and Montaigne, he liked to turn the question around and see how the European mores came out in the examination of social and cultural practices. This double vision or typological method of comparison and implied similitude between the Old World and the New was a favorite technique. Oviedo, Las Casas, Díaz and Léry all abhorred sodomy, but they used it in different ways to position Natives and Europeans in a comparison or in the internal economy of a discourse about Europe itself. America was often a means of talking about Europe.[161]

The range of sexing America is wide, from the erotic and violent representations of Amazons and cannibals to images of America as a woman and to anxieties over sodomy. By making the enemy or the peoples whose lands the Europeans invaded into sodomites or effeminate figures in the landscape, some of the invaders could better justify conversion, war and economic exploitation. The Natives who helped the Spanish explorers could then be supplanted, exploited or blamed just as, on Shakespeare's island, Prospero came to blame Caliban, who once helped to show him the secrets of the isle. Miranda and Prospero accuse Caliban of sexual treachery and disloyalty before Prospero's authority, and Columbus himself came to see monsters, cannibals and Amazons in the paradise he proclaimed. The sexual anxiety and the proclamation of purity coexisted in Columbus' *Letter* and Shakespeare's *The Tempest,* two seminal but problematic texts that I am attempting to place in various contexts so these and other representations of the New World, the speech and signs and the heart of this study, might be seen anew. Before arriving at Shakespeare's island, it is important to set out a wider context for this representation of sexing, which is one significant part of a cultural exchange or mimesis only, a moving between cultures.

Chapter 5 ～

Between Cultures

The contact between Natives and Europeans in the New World after Columbus was not as one-sided as many might now think. The mixing of cultures or mediation through kidnapping, interpretation, translation, trade, sex and marriage constituted a complex and changing set of cultural practices. In the first years of contact, often Natives, who were sometimes exploited by the Europeans, gained an advantage from, and even the upper hand in, the exchange with the explorers and settlers France and England sent to the Americas. In James Axtell's words: "But the Indians, despite all odds, succeeded in seducing French and English colonists in numbers so alarming to European sensibilities that the natives were conceded to be, in effect, the best cultural missionaries and educators on the continent."[1] The existence of ambivalent and resistant voices in the documents surrounding the European arrival in the New World suggests that doubts and oppositions in the text involve all kinds of mediation. Images of the Native in European texts are translated, ventriloquized, refracted and occluded.

Kidnapping, mediation and *métissage* are important in the discussion of French and Native contacts in the first two centuries of French and Native relations in the New World. This chapter is a coming to terms with some important examples of hostages, go-betweens and the mixing of cultures. The title of the chapter hangs on "between," which is and is not neutral and ambivalent. Natives and Europeans, even if it is grammatically convenient to speak of the groups as two opposing and homogeneous cultures, were multifarious even if they shared, on each side, family resemblances or homologies. The "between" can also suggest a contest or conflict, but also a suspension in the relation of both groups. Several meetings between different European and Native groups over time tend to destabilize a firm sense of a unified cultural identity in such encounters. This examination begins with mediators, who are members of either European or Native cultures, because they seemed like examples of hope between the invaders and the indigenous cultures. These go-betweens served as translators, peace-makers, negotiators, roles that also could make them in both groups the target of suspicion and sources of anxiety and misunderstanding. As much as the mediators were figures of hope, they were also often victims of kidnapping and suggested that the anxiety of going between cultures was also one of the creation of new cultures through sex, the forming of mixed groups unmoored from traditional European and Native cultures, or *métissage*. This was another cause of anxiety. It is this disturbing of boundaries that is the fascination and raison d'être of this exploration of betweenness of cultures.

Once more theory and examples qualify each other. They mess each other up: and that is good. Theory without test cases floats without grounds, and examples without theory extend without shape and method. Where my use of these mutual supports converges is in example as *exemplum,* a model and illustrative story, and *théoria,* as something beheld or observed. There is then, in examples and the theory that shapes them or is derived from them (depending if the method is deductive or inductive), the common sense of sense, either from the picture or from the narrative.

Theory should not flatten out different groups into others. This chapter also attempts to understand the lost opportunity for cooperation and mediation between Natives and Europeans, something that Las Casas and Montaigne saw in the sixteenth century and that historians like Robert Royal, James Axtell and Wilcomb Washburn hope for today. Rather than simply use the theory of the Other, I am trying to develop a new framework.[2] In addition to my inductive method of trying to formulate a theory of mediation from Renaissance texts, I recognize the need to reach my audience by making use of the theoretical contexts of our time. In this chapter I attempt to complicate the awareness of the difference of the past while doing so in a language that is necessarily contemporary. On the other hand, an explication of rhetoric and textual strategies should allow for an understanding of the various possibilities open to speakers and writers in the past and present. Rhetoric is mediation and persuasion: it can communicate and overpower.[3] The literary theorist, anthropologist and the intellectual or cultural historian have to work with history, which means that they carry Aristotle in one hand and Brecht in the other.[4] This chapter offers a few concrete examples of mediators, which form the basis of inductive work toward a theoretical and practical mediation in order to provide a context for the manuscript work needed to introduce new Native and European perspectives to the topic of mediation in the encounter. There are apparent transhistorical similarities in historical change.[5]

Mediators or go-betweens are sometimes made into scapegoats and can become excluded in any cultural negotiation.[6] This one theoretical insight helps to characterize one of the difficulties some of the other mediators in early America find themselves in. The temptation is to scapegoat the mediator and to deny any possibility of coexisting with a different cultural group. The consequences of such polarization were and are disastrous. Here, I want to suggest four ways of talking about mediation, or going between cultures, both textually and historically and the relation of the mediated with *métissage,* the mixing or coexistence of two or more cultures within an individual or group: textual mediation, kidnapping Natives, mediators or go-betweens, White Indians and Métis. The Métis, who acted as go-betweens, sometimes became an excluded group in negotiations between European and Native.

Interpreters, that is Europeans, Natives or those of mixed backgrounds who interpreted signs and languages in negotiations and other cultural mediations, became important from Columbus onward.[7] In sixteenth-century writers we find suggestions on cultural practices that propose an alternative to stereotyping, so that the ideological othering of mediators is not inevitable. Communities found meaning in and resistance to negotiation. Mediators allow for a dialogue, a possible community, between two interlocutors from different cultures. The difference between scapegoater and scapegoated can be viewed in terms of mediation within a community: the scapegoat is a member of the scapegoating community, so that scapegoaters are potential members of a scapegoated community. Through a politics of invitation, the scapegoated group transvalues its difference from the scapegoating group into a new difference that forms the ground of a possible communitarian or cooperative dialogue.[8] Whether this desire in postmodern discourse theory to transform mediation into a politics of invitation and community works in an early modern setting and sufficiently takes into account the material dimension of the historical record is something worth examination. Before we can get to mediators or interpreters, it is important to see how mediated our texts in Spanish, French, English and other languages are in the representations of mediation: they contained interpretations before the interpreters.

I

Textual and cultural mediation play a key role in the speech and signs of the New World, but whereas elsewhere I have focused on Columbus to elaborate on this aspect of coming to terms with the Americas, here, I shall briefly recapitulate some elements of the problem only. Editors, collectors, printers and institutions all affected the interpretation of the contact between Europeans and Natives in the New World. The question of written and oral sources among indigenous groups is also vexing.

The case of Columbus, who is an originary figure in the European historiography of expansion, served as an illustration. Columbus' texts were highly mediated, so that his views of the Natives came to us through collective eyes. Those first meetings and conflicts between the Spaniards and the inhabitants of the Caribbean still arouse interest centuries later. A recognition of ambivalent and resistant voices in the documents surrounding Columbus' four voyages to America reminds us that these doubts and oppositions in the text involve all kinds of mediation. The image of the Native was translated, ventriloquized and involved a high degree of mediation and textual uncertainty, so that when we say that "Columbus" said this or that about the Natives, it should be stated with much care and skepticism and even more than usual with a suspicion of the "author" as an individual agent. The voices of Natives are reported in European texts, so that it is important to consider the problem of mediation in the writing and reading of the accounts of the contact between indigenous Americans and the European invaders.

The European representations of the Native also relate to the Native representations of the European arrival in, and colonization of, America. Unfortunately, even the most informative among pre-Conquest Native documents were mostly redone under Spanish influence during the 1540s and after.[9] Europeans and their American settlers often wrote about the Natives from the vantage of conquest and triumph.[10] The Europeans developed a myth that the Amerindians had no writing because these records threatened the Scripture and European authority and tradition.[11] From 1492 to 1519, there was no Amerindian chronicler of the exchange. It was Bartolomé de Las Casas who rose to write a defense of the Native population.[12] Against Juan Ginés de Sepúlveda, Las Casas also defended the Natives at Valladolid, where the debate centered on whether the Indians were human beings with culture or brutes, as Aristotle defined them, who could become servants to the civilized nations. Since 1492, the Europeans had viewed the Natives from a theological perspective in which they were identified with the lost peoples of the Old Testament or as brutes who originated in the "Americas."[13] Las Casas insisted on a place for the Amerindians as members of a human civil society.[14] The Spanish set the tone for debates among the French and English. The conflicted and contradictory voices of Columbus, Las Casas and Sepúlveda and Oviedo find their echoes in Cartier, Thevet, Montaigne, Ralegh, Hakluyt, Purchas and Shakespeare.

The represented also represented. Native images of the Europeans have not been widely disseminated, but they are coming to light more and more. For instance, as we saw in chapter 2, there are a number of important cases, such as the annals of the Valley of Mexico (1516–25), a Tupi taunt of French missionaries in Brazil (1612) and an Algonkin account of Europeans entering North America (seventeenth century): these instances represent but a small portion of the Native texts that describe the early contacts with the Europeans.[15] The written response to 1492 is much more varied and mixed than it was in 1792 and 1892. In a preface to a 1992 collection of Native responses to Columbus, Ray Gonzalez notes that official versions of the glory of Columbus' expedition have long been out of print and that the goal of the book is to promote understanding and reconciliation, in which Native history is heard as American history and not just as something that was in the path of Europeans: "Five hundred years have passed, and these writers know it. Five hundred years of native and foreign languages have already created voices of mixed cultures, the true sound of the Americas, as its artists and writers mark history with honest visions of what it means to be citizens of the Americas, not American citizens."[16] The view of mixed races and tongues leads Gonzalez to suggest mediation, a new understanding of the past in the Americas and the opportunities there, a practical utopianism, perhaps, rather than a continued rift of violence and misunderstanding.

It is an unpleasant turn, but hardly surprising, that Native written documents are also fraught with textual uncertainty and mediation. Like the texts of Columbus, the documents written in Nahuatl about the first exchanges with the Spanish and gathered together by Miguel Leon-Portilla as *Broken Spears* are problematic.[17] Thirty-five years ago, Leon-Portilla collected various of Angel Maria Garibay K.'s translations into Spanish of Nahuatl oral accounts of this conquest. Who is speaking and when?[18] From about 1524, the Franciscans trained some of the Nahua noblemen to read and write Nahuatl, presumably in a way that owed a debt to Latin and Spanish writing and grammar. Time mediates this cultural exchange, so that when speaking about mediation, it becomes difficult to know how much editing and changes in transmission have affected the earliest Spanish and Nahua accounts. For instance, the *Codex Ramirez* preserved a few Spanish fragments of an older indigenous text in Nahuatl about the Spanish March to Tezcoco, inluding Cortés' visit there.[19] The text was already hybrid and *métissé*. Early on, Europeans and Natives began to live among each other and sometimes literally abducted each other and kidnapped meaning.

The sources of Amerindian views of Europeans also depended on filters and editorial decisions made in the context of Europe and its colonies. Whether in a European language or in the making of a book in Native languages or in its translation into European tongues, the representation of the contact between the two groups was and is problematic. Peter Martyr reported the prophecy of people coming to do violence against them and to enslave them that the Taínos of Hispaniola ultimately interpreted as the arrival of the Spaniards, which Martyr notes laconically was not wrong.[20] In Mexico the Tarascan also had a prophecy of men, who, coming to earth, "will spare no end of the earth."[21] After contact, an Aztec account, as reported by Bernardino de Sahagún, focused on the physical features of the Spaniards, their steel armor, white faces, yellow hair and large dogs, but the report shifts to the Spaniard's revulsion at Moctezuma's [Montezuma's] offering of blood-soaked food to them as gods.[22] Two conflicting registers— Native and Spaniard—occur side by side in the text, but the European ascendancy is asserted in their revulsion and Moctezuma's treatment of them as divinities. The shift in narrative technique belies the overlay of European cultural and historical perspectives. The Natives would not have understood the revulsion of the Spaniards any more than the Spanish would have comprehended the meaning of the sacrifice. Both sides would have made the newcomers part of their mythological and ideological worlds, and this figurative kidnapping happened along with more literal hostage-taking.

II

Kidnapped Natives trouble the cultural boundaries of traditional cultures before the contact between Europeans and Natives in the Americas. This capturing and attempted use or assimilation of others from the other cultural group occurred for centuries in the New World. Whereas the Europeans began immediately to take back Natives as *exempla,* trophies, show-cases, translators, tokens and so on, they also grew suspicious of those, like Gonzalo Guerrero and Etienne Brulé, who went Native or "Indian." Natives and Europeans alike took hostages or prisoners, so that some of their captives were held against their will even if they became integrated or coexisted peaceably with their captors. This section examines the kidnapped while the next section concentrates on mediators (including White Indians).

In the *Letter* of Columbus there were contradictions. Later, Bernál Díaz spoke of Montezuma's divided mind, which became a trope in the Spanish view of the fall of the Mexican empire, but Columbus' letter suggested a division in his mind (or perhaps in the corporate Spanish editorial project on Columbus and the encounter). After saying how timid the Natives were, Columbus then admitted that he took some of them by force: "And as soon as I arrived in the Indies, in the first Island which I found, I took by force some of them, in order that they might learn and give me information of that which there is in those parts, and so it was that they soon understood us, and we them, either by speech or signs, and they have been very serviceable."[23] Columbus then reiterated that the Natives still treated him like a god and said that they inclined to Christianity, but what he did not emphasize was why he thought it necessary to use force to capture Indians as interpreters. Was it his ignorance of their timidity or was it a feeling that they were his property because they were, in his eyes at least, subjects and possessions of the crown? Columbus and the Spanish were not alone in this practice as John Cabot brought back captive Natives and the French used kidnapping as well in the New World.

The Spanish continued the practice of kidnapping. For instance, Oviedo reports an incident during Lucas Vásquez de Ayllón's last voyage when he tried to establish a colony north of 32 degrees (in the Carolinas). Even the name of the place seems to engender bitterness over the treachery of the Natives in Oviedo's interpretation: "That land which the licenciado Ayllón and his fleet went to look for is called in the treatise of the chronicler Peter Marytr *Chicora,* because the Indian, the false guide, that Ayllón took with him, and other interpreter-Indians from that area called it that."[24] The issues of abandonment and mistrust arise as Oviedo continues his excoriation of the Natives: "But the Indians fled inland after a few days, and left Ayllón and the others unsure whether to believe what they had said."[25] Ayllón expected the Natives to gain him advantage in his authority for his exploration and settlement, but Oviedo observed drily: "in the event this was the advantage that Ayllón got from the trust of the Indian Francisco de Chicora."[26] This yoking of the term "Indian" with the Spanish name of his baptism suggests an irony in the politics of naming. Ayllón and most of his men died in this attempt at colonization, so, Oviedo implied, such trust in Chicora and his fellow Natives was unfounded. The naming of places and peoples did not mean suasion or authority over them. Apparently, Chicora had been baptized in 1521 and lived for five years among his captors, finding favor at the Spanish court and with his master, Ayllón.[27]

This practice was well established. The Portuguese captured Natives, as a member of Gaspar Corte-Real's expedition, Alberto Cantino, reported to the duke of Ferrara: The explorers "forcibly kidnapped about fifty men and women of this country and have brought them to the king."[28] Another source, Pietro Pasqualigo, the Venetian ambassador to Lisbon, reported, in addition to the fifty that had not yet landed in Portugal, the explorers have "brought back here seven natives, men and women and children."[29] Pasqualigo also noted that the kidnapped Natives could be a boost to slavery in Portugal: "his Majesty here intends to draw great advantage from the said land, as well by the men, who will be excellent for labour and the best slaves that have hitherto been obtained."[30] In 1502 three Indians from Newfoundland were at the court of Henry VII of England, and, two years later, two were said to be "appaaylyd afftyr inglysh men in Westmynstyr paleys."[31] Other nations were quick to follow Columbus in the kidnapping of Natives, although taking captives and hostages was nothing new to European warfare. In this case the Europeans were not apparently at war, but although they denied their arrival in the Americas as being an invasion, some of their behavior was as much a part of the codes of war as the economic practices of slavery and serfdom.

Perhaps the most telling example of "kidnapping" is that performed by Binot Paulmier de Gonneville, a Norman who sailed to Brazil in 1504. He saw the bringing of Christianity to the Natives as the custom of all those who came to the Indies and said that the lord Arosca, a Native leader, wanted his son, Essomericq, to return to France to live in Christendom. This "kidnapping" was like Columbus'. The French promised the father and the son that Essomericq would be returned home after twenty moons at the latest. Arosca, according to Gonneville, was interested in the French tools and weapons, which to them were as gold, silver and gems to Christians. After Arosca had asked the captain to swear to return at the promised time and the ship was departing, "all the said people made a great cry, and gave their word that they would conserve well the cross; making this sign by crossing two fingers."[32] Like Columbus, Gonneville read the signs, but their meanings were not always as simple and clear as these European captains thought. After *l'Espoir* was shipwrecked, Essomericq settled in Honfleur and married one of the close relatives of Gonneville, his godfather, whose name and some of his goods he inherited. In 1658, Essomericq's descendants contested paying taxes because they were foreigners and because their ancestor had wanted to return home as Gonneville had promised him. They presented the journal for evidence.[33]

This kind of kidnapping persisted. In 1508 the *Pensée* sailed from Dieppe to Cape Bonavista: this ship, belonging to Jean Ango, later viscount of Dieppe, returned to France with seven Natives and their arms, canoes and belongings.[34] Jacques Cartier, who may have been to Brazil and Newfoundland before going to the mainland of Canada, kidnapped Taignoagny and Domagaya, sons of Donnacona, chief of the Stadacona, an Iroquian group—after the cementing of what the Iroquois would have thought to be an alliance with the French—and this would probably have appeared to the Stadaconans as treachery.[35] The brothers survived in France and returned to the St. Lawrence River valley, where they did not want to be with the French on their ships. This change caused some friction between the French and Stadaconans, who did not want Cartier to go to Hochelaga. In an effort to strengthen the alliance with the French and perhaps as a means of trying to dissuade them from going upriver, Donnacona offered the French the daughter of his sister and two boys, including a younger brother of the two sons who were taken back to France, a practice that Amerindians used to forge alliances. The chief then promised Taignoagny and Domagaya to guide Cartier to Hochelaga if the French left behind a hostage, which the French leader refused to do.[36] The Stadaconan tales of the kingdom of the Saguenay, with its gold and riches, may have made Cartier think that a colony was possible as a base for trade with the interior, where the kingdom was supposed to exist, and that Donnacona himself would be a great aid to establishing such a settlement. Perhaps dreams of emulating Cortés' conquest of Mexico influenced Cartier, who kidnapped Donaconna and his sons. Cartier returned to France in May of 1536 with ten Iroquois on board, and even though Donnacona's stories apparently influenced François Ier to seek to colonize North America and thereby challenge Spain, he would not let the chief and his sons return to their home.[37] These exchanges and cultural signs were so complicated and suggested the gaps between French and Iroquoian expectations and practices. In 1541, when Cartier set out with several hundred male and female colonists, he seemed to have learned something of the Iroquoian customs as he left two French boys at Hochelaga, probably to learn the culture and language to be go-betweens and interpreters but perhaps also as a sign of an alliance.[38] Violence was the ultimate outcome of this meeting of cultures, and the French, despite their reputation for cultural sensitivity with aboriginal peoples, did much to aggravate the situation. The Stadaconans told Spanish Basque fishermen, with whom they were trading, that thirty-five of Cartier's settlers had been killed.[39] By 1542 Cartier had given up and in the following year, after another attempt at colonization (without Cartier the French did not seem to know the Native cure for scurvy), Roberval also left New France. The Stadaconans appear to have found more compatible trading partners with the Basques, and even the Iroquois at Hochelaga had attacked the French, so that this pattern of trade and war complicates stereotypes of Europeans and Natives as two coherent and unified groups. Hostility and friendship were not constant and monolithic.

Later in the sixteenth century, the French and the English continued the practice of kidnapping. For instance, writing about the French experience in Brazil during the 1550s, Jean de Léry mentioned the French receiving Native slaves:

> I want not to omit the mention here of ten savage boys, nine to ten years of age and younger, who had been captured in war and sold as slaves to Villegagnon by savages who were friendly to the French. Minister Richier had placed his hands on them at the end of a sermon, and we had prayed God all together that He might do them the grace to be the first fruits of this poor people, and to be drawn to the knowledge of their salvation. They then embarked in the boats that left on the fourth of June to return to France, where upon their arrival they were presented to King Henry II, who was reigning then. The latter made a gift to them to several great lords; among others, he gave one of them to the late Monsieur de Passy, who had the boy baptized, and after my return I recognized him there.[40]

Léry's description shows the place of the French in the structure of warfare in Brazil as allies to the Tupinamba and foreshadows the way in which the Native allies of the French in North America used to send Pawnee slaves to New France or kidnap English colonists in exchange for something. This was a kind of slave trade that did not involve Africa at first. Léry made it sound as though the boys were redeemed so they could have redemption. The Native boys also became gifts of exchange between the Tupinamba and the French and within France itself, for the king gave them to several lords, and Léry himself recognized one of the boys, whom Monsieur de Passy had had baptized.

A couple of other examples will suggest that the taking of Native captives back to Europe was not unusual. Martin Frobisher's first expedition departed England on May 15, 1576, in search for the Northwest Passage, a goal that preoccupied the English, French, Spanish and Portuguese and was an aim of Giovanni Caboto's or John Cabot's voyage in 1497. Cabot himself had kidnapped Natives. In October 1576, Frobisher returned to England having thought that he had found the Northwest Passage, having brought with him an Inuit and having discovered what he thought was gold. Michel de Montaigne told of the three Natives who spoke with Charles IX in Rouen, but in recounting that event, Montaigne emphasized their ignorance of how knowledge of French corruption would cost them repose and happiness, of how the commerce would lead to their ruin, which Montaigne assumed was already advanced, and of their misery for having quit their mild air for that of France. These three wise men exposed the French by turning the ethnological glass back on itself. Montaigne said that he remembered two of their three comments. First, why would strong well-armed men obey a child rather than choosing one among them to assume power? Second, why do the hungry beggars outside the gates of the well-fed great not seize them by the throats or burn their houses down? The Native observations suggested French corruption even if that decay and barbarism might be applied to all of Europe. Montaigne ended "Des Cannibales" with the modest celebration of great warriors among the Natives and with their near nakedness.[41]

These kidnapped Natives from various nations became in the reports of different European cultures means of impressing the king with the necessity or success of colonization or as a kind of display of cultural difference, a theater of the New World, in the pageants of the courts. This drama of exoticism possessed many layers. It was as if the explorers had to have the Native there to prove the truthfulness of the captain's story as well as to furnish intelligence for further exploration. Paradoxically, as in the case of Donnacona's sons, the taller the tale, the more chance for further exploration and the way home. Taignoagny and Domagaya seem to have played on the French desire for riches. Another function of the representation of Amerindians in European texts, as in the case of Montaigne's portrayal, was a weapon in the arsenal of satire. This kidnapping could be, on an existential level, a form of betrayal and treachery: many of the Natives died of diseases or never saw their home again. Such a situation put at risk the very alliances the Natives had probably hoped to forge with "gifts" of their relations, adult and children. Some of these captives became mediators and interpreters, another predicament that could be ambivalent and contradictory.

III

When in 1899 Francis Parkman wrote that "Spanish civilization crushed the Indian; English civilization scorned and neglected him; French civilization embraced and cherished him," he was calling attention, inadvertently or not, to stereotypes in the relations between Natives and various European nations.[42] This statement challenges us to find the exceptions and the complex mediatory roles with various Amerindian nations.[43]

Some examples of mediators or go-betweens should, through induction, suggest ways in which mediation in the period was partly a matter of gender but also moved beyond it. La Malinche was a woman and a mediator. She helped translate and interpret Native culture while being Cortés' mistress and on his campaign to conquer the Aztec.[44] In the *Conquest of Mexico* Bernal Díaz suggested that she may not have been a Nathua or Aztec and may have been seeking revenge for their exploitation of her people. Thirty-five years ago, Miguel Leon-Portilla collected various of Angel Maria Garibay K.'s translations into Spanish of Nahuatl oral accounts of this conquest. *Broken Spears* gives the Aztec version of events, including a portrait of La Malinche from another point of view. Apparently, she was from the coast and spoke Nahuatl and Mayan. None the less, she translated from Nahuatl into Mayan, so that Jeronimo de Aguilar, a Spaniard who lived among the Mayas for eight years and one of the two captives Cortés had wanted to ransom, could translate the Mayan into Spanish for Cortés.[45] The European had crossed the boundary to Native culture and the Native to European culture. They now worked together. Nevertheless, tensions existed between European nations and between Native nations: both "sides" were also in conflict. Mediation often involves various interlocking stages. It is often precarious as it occupies a place between resistance and capitulation.

Cortés came upon two Spaniards, Jeronimo de Aguilar and Gonzalo Guerrero, who had been taken captive: one wanted to return into the Spanish fold and the other wished to remain in Native society. The Spanish and the Aztecs (Mexicas or Nahuas) were soon able to communicate. The Aztec messengers communicated with La Malinche and Aguilar as she spoke Mayan and Nahuatl and he had learned Mayan over the eight years since his shipwreck in Yucatan in 1511. After La Malinche translated the messengers' Nahuatl into Mayan for Aguilar, he translated it into Spanish for Cortés. Even during the siege of Tenochtitlan, where apparently hundreds of thousands perished, Cortés used La Malinche and Aguilar as interpreters.[46]

One interpreter leads to another. Once again, the reliability of an account of an exchange is open to question. Bernal Díaz's account, remembered years later as a clarification of earlier representations of the conquest of New Spain, gave the following view. Years earlier, the Spanish had captured a Native at Cape Catoche, now called Melchior, whom Cortés used to find out from the chiefs whether any Spaniards had survived from the expedition under Francisco Hernandez de Cordoba.[47] In fact, two Spaniards had become slaves under different *Caciques*. A *Cacique* advised Cortés to send a letter and ransom to their owners, so the two Spaniards might come. The letter had the desired effect on Aquilar but not on Guerrero, whom he sought out. This transformation from Spanish pauper to Indian prince suggests that dimensions of class also influence the crossing of boundaries and the roles of mediators.[48]

The story of Aguilar is also the tale of his shipwreck. The Natives were said to have sacrificed many of his companions to their idols. Other companions perished from disease; two women died of overwork; Aguilar escaped sacrifice and fled to a *Cacique*, who protected him as a slave. The only other survivor of the shipwreck was Gonzalo Guerrero. Aguilar and Guerrero become the good son and the bad son, Abel and Cain in the New World. Aguilar is thankful to be saved by the Spanish, Guerrero is not.[49] Cortés could never resist using his interpreters and mediators as scouts for his military campaign. The chiefs were pleased to discover that Aguilar could speak their language. He advised them to revere the image of the Virgin and advised them to ask Cortés for a letter of recommendation that would protect them from any Spanish mistreatment.[50] In this advice we can observe the ambivalence and double vision of a mediator: he speaks to them of Spanish religion and tries to seek protection for them from Spanish cruelty. He had worn a loincloth and kept his Bible in his cloak, at least according to Díaz.

Guerrero was much more successful in the Native world. That is probably one reason he did not want to leave it. He had risen in the world by "going Native." The question of class is also important to mediation. Cortés wants to find out from Aguilar more about Guerrero.[51] Guerrero comes to us through a triple filter—the narratives, descriptions and reactions of Díaz, Aguilar and Cortés. Cortés does not like Guerrero's kind of mediation, although he will take Native help against Native as often as he can find it. La Malinche and Melchior are examples of his Native mediators, both of whom Díaz described in considerable detail. Melchior prefigures Squanto's fate but only more tragically for him personally. Guerrero is a traitor, a dangerous precedent, especially for the soldiers of more humble origin. The New World might offer them freedom from the religious ideology and economic system they left in Spain. No more is heard of Guerrero in Díaz's narrative. The White Indian is a problem that haunts the Europeans from the beginning.

Mediation does not, then, rely completely on race or culture but also depends on class. In fact, the reluctant Spaniard has literally been treated as a prince owing, it seems, to the mediation of a Native woman, so that he has no desire to return to his far more humble place in Spanish society. This phenomenon of "going Native," or the "White Indian," was a concern that persisted into the eighteenth century and beyond amid the French and English administrators.[52] Tecuichpotzin or Isabel Moctezuma, daughter to Moctezuma II, had two Native and three Spanish husbands.[53] Her children crossed the bounds of race. Some of her descendants became titled in Spain. She was an Aztec princess. Her class allowed her to claim the lands Cortés had claimed on behalf of the Spanish crown. The Spaniards often wanted her to be a symbol of the assimilation of Aztec culture into the new Spanish Mexico, but it was not so simple. She was a Christian, but she also became involved in a long lawsuit with the Spanish crown over her land claims. Mediation does not preclude some resistance and assimilation. Sometimes, as we have observed, attempts to use abduction to find mediators and interpreters created terrible events with a baleful irony.

The Norman interpreters, or "trucements de Normandie," in sixteenth-century Brazil moved into the Tupinamba villages, learned their language, and lived with their women and had children with them.[54] In *History of a Voyage to the Land of Brazil* Jean de Léry reported on the mixing between the Normans and the Tupinamba in the mid-sixteenth century.[55] In the context of a discussion of the behavior of Villegagnon, the leader of the French expedition to Brazil of 1555, Léry described a scene between cultures: "Certain Normans, having escaped from a shipwreck long before his [Villegagnon's] arrival in that country, had remained among the savages, where, having no fear of God, they lived in wantonness with the women and girls (I have seen some who had children by them already four or five years old)."[56] Although Léry and his Calvinist brethren were generally disappointed with Villegagnon, they did not fail to see his strengths. Léry disapproved of this arrangement and praised Villegagnon's forbidding on the pain of death that a Christian man live with a Native woman unless she were baptized, in which case a marriage could then occur.[57] This conversion did not happen: "But in spite of the remonstrances that we have made several times to this barbarous people, there was not one of them who would leave her old skin and confess Jesus Christ as her savior; thus, in the whole time that I lived there, not a single Frenchman took one of them to wife."[58] The efficaciousness of this edict was something Léry extolled, but we do not hear of what happened to the Normans who already went Native. This anxiety of becoming like the aboriginals is a recurring theme of French narratives of the New

World. As if to defend Villegagnon against his critics in the rhetoric of religious strife between Protestants and Catholics that, along with actual violence, overtook France in the last half of the sixteenth century, Léry, having gone back to France, protected Villegagnon's honor in the face of rumor: "whatever I have heard said of him since my return—that when he was in America he defiled himself with savage women—I will bear this witness for him, that he was in no way suspected of it in our time."[59]

For Léry, Villegagnon was above the Norman interpreters and the Tupinamba women with whom they consorted. Even though, according to Léry, the so-called Americans "have no other law than that of nature," the husband, whose wife committed adultery, could kill her or repudiate her by sending her away in disgrace.[60] These women, however, had no such constraints before they were married, which prompted Léry to return to the relations between the Tupinamba and the Normans:

> It is true that before they marry off their daughters, the fathers and relatives have no great scruples about prostituting them to the first comer; as I have already mentioned elsewhere, although the Norman interpreters had already, before our arrival, taken advantage of them in several villages, nonetheless their reputations were not ruined. But, as I said, once they are married they take care not to stumble, under pain of being beaten to death or sent away in shame.[61]

While Léry was displeased with Villegagnon for abandoning the interests of the Calvinists in Brazil, he could see more positives in this contradictory leader, who both championed and undermined the Protestants, as compared with the Norman interpreters and the Native women with whom they lived. Going Native meant turning one's back on Christianity, of being converted away from the example of Christ rather than converting others to his way.

These Norman interpreters were, then, in Léry's view, worse than the wild Americans, or "savages" as the French called them. In the context of describing the cruelty of the Tupinamba to their enemies in war, Léry mentioned how he and his fellows had to refuse partaking in cannibalistic practices that were designed to exterminate their adversaries, the Margaia, and how this made them seem unloyal to the Tupinamba.[62] This show of principle was not, however, something the Normans cared to display:

> to my great regret I am compelled to recount here that some Norman interpreters, who had lived eight or nine years in that country, accommodating themselves to the natives and leading the lives of atheists, not only polluted themselves by all sorts of lewd and base behavior among the women and girls (by whom one of them had a boy about three years old when I was there), but some of them, surpassing the savages in inhumanity, even boasted in my hearing of having killed and eaten prisoners.[63]

These Norman go-betweens were even more inhumane than their hosts, and one had helped to bring a child into a world of cannibalism that was far from France. Léry himself was, however, ambivalent and full of contradictions. In just a few pages Léry mentioned cannibalism in France during the Wars of Religion and, in the editions after 1585, he added more cruelties in the Old World while, in the edition of 1611, Léry created a new chapter on the Spanish cruelties in the New World that Las Casas had described and that became part of the Black Legend of Spain.[64] Increasingly, as Léry's book changed, he created a great twist in his moral against the Tupinumba and certain Norman interpreters as cannibals. He asked, "what of France? (I am French, and it grieves me to say it)," and described in detail the St. Bartholomew's Massacre on August 24, 1572, and how, for instance, "the fat of human bodies (which in ways more barbarous than those of the savages, were butchered at Lyon after being pulled out of the Saône)—was it not publicly sold to the highest bidder?"[65] After the climax of atrocities, which followed on this one and which damned the French most, Léry pointed the moral:

> So let us henceforth no longer abhor so very greatly the cruelty of the anthropophagous—that is, man-eating—savages. For since there are some here in our midst even worse and more detestable than those who, as we have seen, attack only enemy nations, while the ones over here have plunged into the blood of their kinsmen, neighbors, and compatriots, one need not go beyond one's own country, not as far as America, to see such monstrous and prodigious things.[66]

Like Thomas More's satire on gold in *Utopia* and Montaigne's discussion of cannibalism, Léry's righteous indignation over cannibalism had a typological quality that was weighted even more against his compatriots. The diptych of the Old World and the New World involved a critique so savage of the French that any of the transgressions of Tupinamba and Norman interpreters, while to be lamented and denounced, grew pale by comparison. Léry's anxieties transformed with each edition and, in time, the barbarity of the civil war in France magnified in his mind and occupied a more central place in his rhetoric. In this context Léry's language became as extreme as that of Las Casas. It was almost too raw to be simply an imitation of Juvenalian satire.

The French also made use of interpreters as much as Léry criticized them. In describing the embarkation for Brazil, he noted that the approximately ninety people who were setting out "included ten young boys, whom we took along to learn the language of the savages."[67] Translation was already an important part of the relations between French and Tupinamba cultures. Léry also relied on interpreters to allow him a window to the world of the Natives and to help him to interpret their culture: "Now I had heard from the Norman interpreters who had lived a long time in that country that our Tupinamba held a solemn assembly every three or four years."[68] Along with Jacques Rousseau and an interpreter, Léry spent a night in a village where such an assembly was occurring. He commented on "certain false prophets that they call *caraïbes*," who were at this gathering, and likened them to "popish indulgence-bearers" who make the villagers believe that they can give them the power to communicate with sprits, vanquish enemies in warfare and grow large fruits and roots.[69] The *caraïbes* presided over a ritual in the assembly that separated the men, women and children in three separate houses, leaving Rousseau, the interpreter, and Léry in the house with the women, about two hundred of them. When the women replied to the cries of the men with identical sounds and then howled, shook and fainted, Léry concluded: "I can only believe that the devil entered their body and that they fell into a fit of madness."[70] This sense of possession that by implication requires an exorcism or something else just after Léry has claimed he will "show in the fourth place how, despite the utter darkness in which they are plunged, the seed of religion (if, after all, what they do deserves that name) germinates in them and cannot be extinguished."[71] Léry is caught in a bind because he would like to demonstrate that the Tupinamba have enough religion that they will make ready converts but cannot help wondering that if what they were displaying was really a kind of demonic observance that needs to be eradicated, punished or even eliminated through violence. Not that Léry recommended this directly but, as Janet Whatley has noted, from the edition of 1585 on, he commented thus on a witches' sabbath in Jean Bodin's *De la démonologie des sorciers* (1578): "I have concluded that they have the same master: that is, the Brazilian women and the witches over here were guided by the same spirit of Satan; neither the distance between the places nor the long passage over the sea keeps the father of lies from working both here and there on those who are handed over to him by the just judgment of God."[72] This is a typology of demons between the Old World and the New World. Léry had blamed Norman interpreters for their way of living and now he has needed one to take him to a village to make his own interpretation of a culture in which he has been for a very short time "more than a half a year" by his own admission.[73] Although between cultures, Léry did not always recognize the dangers of the leaps of his own mediation or interpretation. He often surprises the reader with twists of irony and introspection, and here he does not disappoint, for after having said that, hearing "these chaotic noises and howls," he had wished that he were back at the fort, he also marvels at the harmony of "the sweet and gracious sounds" to which the Tupinamba returned.[74]

But the twists are not over. Léry, drawn by such sweet sounds, attempted to go out of the women's house to see the men even though the women restrained him and the interpreter warned against it. It seems that Léry had such confidence that he had become wiser than the Tupinamba women and more daring than his own interpreter, who "said that in the six or seven years that he had been in that country, he had never dared be present among the savages at such a ceremony: so that, he added, if I went over there I would be behaving imprudently and exposing myself to danger."[75] Undecided for a while, Léry then decided that the interpreter had given him no good reason and that Léry himself could count on "certain kindly elders" whom he had visited four or five times in this village.[76] The interpreter, not to mention the Tupinamba women, were to be brushed aside. In fact, the other two Frenchmen were "emboldened" by Léry 's example.[77] The male Tupinamba did nothing and Léry and his compatriots were able to observe a long ceremony. Léry described how 500 or 600 Tupinamba men danced and sang with a harmonious melody even though they did not know music, but, despite this underestimation of the relation between theory and practice, Léry suggests once more how he can surprise as much as be surprised. Of the song he said: "When I remember it, my heart trembles, and it seems their voices are still in my ears."[78] Their music moved Léry, who admitted that he still needed his interpreter to explain "several things" in the Tupinamba language.[79] The songs included religious context that appeared promising to Léry and his Calvinist view. He tried to undermine the *maracas* or idols of the *caraïbes*, whom he persisted in calling false prophets as opposed by implication to himself, "the true servant of God," by eating their offerings and showing how they could not affect the French or do all that the sorcerers had claimed to the Tupinamba.[80] Animosity between the *caraïbes* and the French had thus arisen at Léry 's bidding and he took their food left for the idols and complained that the sorcerers fed "gluttonously and idly with their whores and bastards."[81]

Léry recalled his first visit to Tupinamba villages, to which another unnamed interpreter took him, three weeks after Léry had arrived at Villegagnon's settlement.[82] He spoke about one village that the French named "Gosset" after an interpreter who had stayed there.[83] While Léry showed great admiration for the Tupinamba and described them vividly, he described the cannibalistic rituals they performed on the body of an enemy prisoner killed six hours before.[84] On this trip, Léry's interpreter, "who was not new to the customs of the savages, and who, moreover, liked to drink and *caouiner* as much as they did," left his compatriot without saying a word.[85] *Caouiner* is to drink *caouin,* which much earlier in the narrative Léry had explained was a strong red or white drink made of roots and millet that the Tupinamba drank to such excess that it would put any of the most avid European carousers to shame and that was sometimes consumed as they devoured a prisoner of war in ceremonies.[86] This *cacouinage* led Léry to tell a number of humorous anecdotes about drunkenness and to compare the making of wine and *caouin* in ways that are balanced toward and praising of the Tupinamba.[87] Returning to Léry's later description of caouiner, we find that a Tupinamba has offered him a "victim's foot in hand, cooked and *boucané,* asking me (as I learned later, for I didn't understand at the time) if I wanted to eat some of it."[88] In setting out this description of horror and disgust, Léry said that he did not comprehend the situation and that this Tupinamba "wanted to make me understand that I was about to be similarly dealt with."[89] And what happens in the next sentence in Léry's narrative becomes a commonplace in writing about the New World—an expression of suspicion against the interpreter that the writer/speaker has had to rely on: "As one doubt begets another, I suspected straight away that the interpreter, deliberately betraying me, had abandoned me and delivered me into the hands of these barbarians."[90] Although Léry realized that he had read the situation wrongly, he was not afraid to show his fear and error in interpretation.

This errancy and ambivalence continued to inform his view of his interpreter and his hosts. Léry set a scene in which, while he was calling on "God in my heart" for fear of being a victim of cannibalism, his interpreter was out enjoying the company of the Tupinamba:

> At daybreak my interpreter (who had been off carousing with those rascals of savages all night long in other village houses) came to find me. Seeing me, as he said, not only ashen-faced and haggard but also feverish, he asked me whether I was sick, or if I hadn't rested well. Distraught, I answered wrathfully that they had well and truly kept me from sleeping, and that he couldn't understand at all; still as anxious as ever, I urged that we get ourselves out of there with all possible speed. Thereupon he told me that I should have no fear, and it wasn't us they were after.[91]

Léry showed his anger to his interpreter and the Tupinamba, the one for going off to carouse and leaving him and the others for being "rascals" and scaring him with their celebration. While criticizing his compatriot for the abandonment and for not being able to understand Léry himself and his Native hosts for making him sleepless and anxious and while displaying his own fallibility and testiness, Léry did represent the calmness and compassion of the interpreter, who reassured him. Even more, Léry was able to suggest a bond between the Tupinamba and the interpreter, who told them what Léry had thought and said: "When he recounted the whole business to the savages—who rejoicing at my coming, and thinking to show me affection, had not budged from my side all night—they said that they had sensed that I had been somewhat frightened of them, for they were very sorry. My one consolation was the hoot of laughter they sent up—for they are great jokers—at having (without meaning to) given me such a scare."[92] Léry was capable of seeing the joke on himself and did not allow himself to become too self-righteous. Even in a passage where he criticizes the Tupinamba, he is able to show their generosity of spirit.

Although Léry said that the interpreter and he went to other villages, he set this story out as a "sample" and went on "to generalities."[93] In fact, Léry praised the steadfast friendship the Tupinamba showed toward the French, even if mutual benefit in trade and safety might have partly underlain it for both sides. The relations between the two groups were, however, intricate and sometimes full of twists, turns and misunderstandings. In one village Léry "came across one of those little French boys whom we had brought along in the ship Rosée to learn the language of the country and who was now living in this village."[94] On the boy's advice, Léry took and killed one of the ducks from the village in the expectation that he would have to pay some knives for it. As it turned out, when Léry joined the *cacouiner,* he found that the owner of the duck made life difficult for Léry and even the interpreter and the boy could not help: Léry deemed the interpreter "mistaken."[95] The Tupinamba who owned the duck changed his mind, asking for one knife then another and then a pruning hook and then threatened Léry's life with "a wooden club five or six feet long."[96] This confrontation was, as Léry had noted, "the greatest danger I ever found myself in among them."[97] At the peak of this action, Léry said he knew he could not show fear, but it seems that his interpreter was instrumental in teaching him this point:

> Thereupon the interpreter, seated in a cotton bed suspended between the quareller and me, and warning me about what I didn't understand, said to me: "Hold your sword in your fist, and show him your bow and arrows, and let him know just who he is dealing with; as for you, you are strong and valiant, and will not let yourself be killed as easily as he thinks." So I bluffed my way through, and after a few more exchanges between this savage and me (without any attempt from the others to reconcile us), he left to sleep off the *caouin* that he had been drinking all day. The interpreter and I went off to dine on the duck with our companions, who were waiting for us in the village and knew nothing of our quarrel.[98]

The interpreter is literally caught between his countryman, Léry and the Tupinamba, whom Léry has deprived of his duck. While the interpreter could not put a stop to the tension, he could help Léry bluff his way through and could share the meal of duck with him. Whereas the other Tupinamba would do nothing to stop the quarrel, the rest of the French knew nothing about it. Immediately after describing this confrontation, Léry explained how the Tupinamba knew that if they killed one of the French, their supply of goods, like axes, knives and pruning hooks, would dry up as the Portuguese were their enemies, "so everything my man had done was in jest."[99] Apparently, when the owner of the duck "woke up about three hours later, he sent a message to me saying that I was his son, and that what he had done to me was only to test me, and to see by my countenance whether I would be valiant in war against the Portuguese and the Margaia, our common enemies."[100] Léry did not want this kind of thing to happen with this man "— for such jokes are not very pleasant—" so he told him would have nothing to do with him and the next day "gave little knives and fishhooks to the others right in front of him, who got nothing."[101] This is not a great sign of Léry's generosity and shows a certain toughness and penchant for judging. Still, he once more reiterates the loyalty of the Tupinamba but does so in the context of his own lack of knowledge—"out of ignorance of the standing that our nation had among them, I thought I was in danger"—and the reliance the Natives have for French tools they lacked beforehand.[102] As much as Léry enjoyed displaying his own limited understanding of his situation among the Tupinamba, especially in the first part of his sojourn, he distinguished between good jokes and bad jokes in a way that probably differed from the manner in which his hosts would see them. Differences in understanding and interpretation could cause divisions within the French and Native cultures as well as between them even as they relied on each other.

This situation also held true in the next century. The mysterious fate of Etienne Brulé among the Hurons in the first part of the seventeenth century in New France demonstrates in the various "explanations" the breach of mediation. He was a prime example in New France or Canada of someone who lived with the Natives. Samuel de Champlain says that in about 1610 Brulé was sent among the Huron in exchange for a young Huron. Brulé left no accounts of his career, so that all we have are missionary reports. Their dislike for his Native way of life, as the model for the *coureur de bois,* affects the rhetoric and content of their representations of Brulé. In one traditional version he is reputed to have been eaten (cannibalism) for mistreating the chief's daughter (the mixing of sex and politics).[103] Brulé may have disappeared because the Hurons did not like his political connections with the Iroquois. The representation of the relation between Native and European priests, writers and historians is another form of mediation.

A source for the representation of Brulé that I want to examine here is the works of Samuel de Champlain, a French explorer who traveled in the Americas in the late sixteenth and early seventeenth century and whose crowning achievement was the founding of Quebec in 1608. One of the first possible references to Brulé occurs when Champlain wrote about his third voyage in 1611, where he spoke about the Natives returning his youth or boy. Whether this person was Brulé or not, the account provided an image of the mixing of cultures, of the White Indian: "I also saw my French boy who came dressed like an Indian. He was well pleased with the treatment received from the Indians, according to the customs of their country, and explained to me all that he had seen during the winter, and what he had learned from the Indians."[104] Champlain showed less anxiety over this Native dress than Cortés did, but he, too, wanted intelligence of the country and its inhabitants. Brulé might also be the youth Champlain sent, not against his will, to live among the Algonquin in order to learn their language and customs.[105] He may also have been the interpreter who begged Champlain to allow him to go among the Natives.[106]

In recounting the events of 1618, Champlain portrayed Brulé as a heroic explorer and interpreter who was doing Champlain's work in the wilderness. He explained that Brûlé had spent eight years among the Natives "both as a pastime and to see the country and learn their language and mode of life."[107] Brulé's heroism in surviving two attacks by enemy Indians, the second for being suspected of being French, is something Champlain celebrates at length. Here, Brulé was an explorer and a man who suffered torture, only to be delivered by a storm sent by God. The storm so distracted the Natives that they relented, and Brulé became friends with them and a man who promised to make peace with the French who had been making war on them.[108] Champlain's narrative of Brulé is of a French patriot saved by God in the face of death, but that story was soon to change. Even in this narrative Brulé, knowing that these Natives were enemies of the French, is flexible about his identity in order to survive. According to Champlain, the Natives asked Brulé "whether he were not one of the French nation which was making war on them? Thereupon he made reply that he belonged to another better nation that was desirous only of their acquaintance and friendship, which they refused to believe, and rushed upon him, and tore out his nails with their teeth, burned him with red-hot firebrands, plucked out his beard hair by hair, contrary nevertheless to the wish of their chief."[109] The other neglected mediator in this story is the chief who prefers talk to torture. But one of Brulé's attributes, flexibility to survive, may have led to lies, and came to trouble Champlain.

In 1623 Champlain once again named Brulé explicitly and called him an inter-preter.[110] He now described Brulé, who had been among the Hurons or Ouendat, in un-flattering terms:

> amongst others the interpreter Brûlé, who was receiving a hundred pistoles a year to incite the savages to come down and trade. And the influence of example was very bad in send-ing out such evil-livers, who ought instead to have been severely chastised; for this man was recognized as being very vicious in character, and much addicted to women. But what will not the expectation of gain make men do, a passion which tramples under foot all other considerations?[111]

Champlain's representation of Brulé's role as interpreter shows a conflict that Las Casas outlines in relation to the early Spanish colonization, between religion and commerce, between different ethical codes. Like Guerrero, Brulé is depicted as a traitor, somebody who can give the enemy information, in this case the English in 1629, when Kirke takes Quebec. Champlain reviled his former protégé: "Here I saw Etienne Brûlé, the inter-preter to the Hurons, who had placed himself at the service of the English, as had also Marsolet, with both of whom I remonstrated on their faithlessness to the King and to their country. They replied that they had been taken by force, which is incredible; for any one who takes a man by force and puts him in a position of trust may rather expect some ill turn than fidelity."[112] Champlain reported his remonstrance in which he told these two, as any relative would, that they are without religion and have indulged in de-bauchery and libertinism, so that God will punish them: "And then, besides, to think of you, brought up from early boyhood in these parts, turning round now and selling those who put bread into your mouths!"[113]

He also warned them that the English would use them for their knowledge of the country and then drive them away. Brulé is like a Native whose knowledge the English and French are fighting over. It is possible that he identifies more with the Hurons than he does with the French or English. In the New World his knowledge of Native ways and lands is what makes him valuable, not his French heritage. For Champlain, he is nothing but a turncoat who has betrayed him. Champlain also mentioned Louis, the Native the Jesuits had instructed, how he was living in the free fashion of the English ("se licentier en la vie des Anglois"), how he promised to prove his commitment to Catholicism if the French ever returned to Quebec.[114] The English were sending Louis back to his people: his father had come to see him, and rejoiced to see him. Louis told his people great sto-ries about what he had seen in France and England ["il fit de grands discours de ce qu'il auoit veu tant en France qu'en Angleterre"].[115] Champlain's last sentence about Brulé is that he went back with Louis to the Hurons. If the English were so interested in these two men who had turned their backs on the French, then why did they not keep them in Quebec? Both knew the French and English and both went back to Huronia or Ouen-dake. In Champlain's narrative, the rest is silence for Brulé. The boy he taught to be a me-diator has, in his view, become a traitor. In war especially, the middle space between opponents is hard to find. What is Native about Brulé and Louis is forgotten in the ri-valry between European powers. This forgetfulness is, perhaps, a parody of mediation, a kind of excluded third who is blamed for the conflict, the very friction of European op-position. The colonial governors can construe the White Indian as a traitor.

Despite having himself suffered badly at the hands of the English and having wit-nessed the decimation of his nation through pestilence, Squanto, unlike Don Luis de

Velasco, a Native kidnapped by the Spanish, chose mediation over revenge. A male Patuxent Indian, Squanto acted as a mediator—a translator and interpreter—for the Pilgrims at Plymouth. Champlain would have visited the lands of Squanto's nation in 1605 and 1606, while John Smith, a former leader of Virginia, was there in 1614. French and English both had interests in the area. Smith left Thomas Hunt in charge of the fisheries in 1614, and, acting against his superiors' wishes, he captured Squanto and about twenty other Natives. He took them to Malaga in Spain to sell them into slavery, but most were saved by friars. In 1617, Squanto was in London. He then traveled to Newfoundland. By 1619 he is back home, having convinced his English hosts of his value as a go-between. He found his people gone, victims of disease. He was taken captive several times by different anti-English Native nations. Eventually, as his position as a mediator weakened, Squanto made trouble to ensure the necessity of his mediation.[116] The fragility and vulnerability of the part the mediator played and his relation to the various Native and European cultures with which he came into contact suggest one reason why European settlers and Native leaders were tempted to attack moderation and mediation. The role of mediator depends as much on language and culture as on gender.

In *Of Plymouth Plantation : 1620–1647* (pub. 1847) William Bradford represented the ambivalent situation in which Squanto found himself. Unfortunately, Bradford's papers were not published for more than another 200 years, so that their portrayals of the relations between Native and European could not affect his immediate successors and their children. Bradford viewed this mediator as a divine gift to the Pilgrims: "Squanto continued with them and was their interpreter and was a special instrument sent of God for their good beyond their expectation."[117] The next sentence provides a juxtaposition not unlike the relation between gold and God in Columbus, that is a transition between the spiritual and the material, and leads into a description of Squanto's past, before Samoset, the Algonkin sagamore of Pemaquid Point who had learned English from fishermen, introduced him to Bradford at Plymouth.[118] Of Squanto, Bradford said:

> He directed them how to set their corn, where to take fish, and to procure other commodities, and was also their pilot to bring them to unknown places for their profit, and never left them till he died. He was a native of this place, and scarce any left alive besides himself. He was carried away with divers others by one Hunt, a master of a ship, who thought to sell them for slaves in Spain. But he got away for England and was entertained by a merchant in London, and employed to Newfoundland and other parts, and lastly brought hither into these parts by one Mr. Dermer, a gentleman employed by Sir Ferdinando Gorges and others for discovery and other designs in these parts.[119]

Despite this kidnapping, a practice enacted and recorded by Columbus, Cartier, Frobisher and others, Squanto survived to help keep the peace between the English and the various Native nations. Squanto's life was as hard as the much-buffeted hero of a romance. He was caught between the two groups: to different groups of Natives and English, he was a go-between or a turncoat.

Bradford quoted Dermer at length about Squanto, failing to mention that this mediator had jumped Dermer's ship in 1618 and had then made his way to Plymouth, where he found his Patuxet nation to have been wiped out by pestilence (this happened the previous year):[120]

I will first begin (saith he) with that place from whence Squanto or Tisquantum, was taken away; which Captain Smith's map is called Plymouth; . . . The Pocanockets, which live to the west of Plymouth, bear an inveterate malice to the English, and are of more strength than all the savages from thence to Penobscot. Their desire for revenge was occasioned by an Englishman, who having many of them on board, made a greater slaughter with their murderers and small shot when as (they say) they offered no injury on their parts. Whether they were English or no it may be doubted; yet they believe they were, for the French have so possessed them. For which cause Squanto cannot deny but they would have killed me when I was at Namasket, had he not entreated hard for me.[121]

Although the tensions between Natives and Europeans is rectangular, between four nations with all their rivalries, even in Dermer's denial of English culpability and his blaming of the French (something akin to the technique used to build up the Black Legend of Spain), he admitted the opposition of the Pocanockets and the charges they had laid against the English. He also portrayed Squanto as someone with two names (probably neither he would recognize in his own language) and someone who was so modest or careful that he would not admit strife between the Pockanockets and the English or his mediatory role in keeping the peace between them. Dermer credited Squanto with saving his life. Despite having himself suffered badly at the hands of the English and having witnessed the decimation of his nation through pestilence, Squanto chose mediation over revenge. For some reason, mediation is more difficult and controversial than the lightning strike of revenge, although there is always a tension between the two means of settling a wrong or dispute. In *A Briefe Relation of the Discovery and Plantation of New England* (1622), Dermer also related more about how he was nearly killed when the Nausets took him prisoner and how, in 1619, he seized some of them in order to escape, which shows how tense the region was at the time Squanto was acting as a mediator.[122] In fact, Bradford reported that while Dermer was going ashore to trade in what is now called Martha's Vineyard, with Squanto at his side, "he was betrayed and assaulted" by the Natives, his usual trading partners, so that all but Squanto, a boatman and Dermer were killed.[123] But Bradford does not say who betrayed Dermer, but the Natives are blamed. No censure is attached to Squanto. Later, having arrived in Virginia, Dermers died from wounds or disease. Bradford drew this providential moral: "By all of which it may appear how far these people were from peace, and what danger this plantation was begun, save as the powerful hand of the Lord did protect them."[124]

The relations among the Natives and Europeans were strained. Bradford reported that the Natives kept aloof from the English because they had killed French castaways on Cape Cod and enslaved the three or four survivors, of whom Dermer redeemed two. The Natives, according to Bradford, confessed all this and that they thought that the Mayflower was coming to revenge their act against the French. He also said that the Natives later let it be known that "before they came to the English to make friendship, they got all the Powachs [Powows or medicine men] of the country, for three days together in a horrid and devilish manner, to curse and execrate them with their conjurations, which assembly and service they held in a dark and dismal swamp."[125] Witches and sorcery do not seem too far from Bradford's mind. None the less, if Bradford is right about their treatment of the French, the Natives were not entirely in training for a role in Rousseau *avant la lettre*.

Squanto's help was indispensable. His mediation was material. In 1621, after the Mayflower departed, many of the Pilgrims

> began to plant their corn, in which service Squanto stood them in great stead, showing them both the manner how to set it, and after how to dress and tend it. Also he told them, except they got fish and set with it in these old grounds it would come to nothing. And he showed them that in the middle of April they should have store enough come up the brook by which they began to build, and taught them how to take it, and where to get other provisions necessary for them. All which they found true by trial and experience. Some English seed they sowed, as wheat and pease, but it came not to good, either by badness of the seed or lateness of the season or both, or some other defect.[126]

Squanto became necessary for the very survival of the English. They could not transplant their ways and needed a mediator.[127] The peace was established. We never hear the mediators' side of the story.

Captain Miles Standish continued to use Squanto as a guide and interpreter. On one expedition, Standish became ill and Bradford had to take over, but neither he nor Squanto could find his way about the shoals of Cape Cod. As a result, they put into Manamoyick Bay: "In this place Squanto fell sick of an Indian fever, bleeding much at the nose (which the Indians take for a symptom of death) and within a few days died there; desiring the Governor to pray for him that he might go to the Englishman's God in Heaven; and bequeathed sundry of his things to sundry of his English friends as remembrances of his love; of whom they had a great loss."[128] Even in death Squanto is represented as being between Native and English: his sickness is Indian and the heaven he hopes for, English. He was lost in another mission of mediation. Bradford told his story, and, not surprisingly, it is one of reconciliation, friendship, love and redemption. We hear of Squanto's mediation through Bradford's mediation, his acculturation through the Governor's culture. But in this account, there are glimpses of the struggle and the predicament in which Squanto found himself. Although the ultimate hero of Bradford's story is Plymouth Plantation, he showed that its founding was difficult. He displayed affection for Squanto and represented the troubles, oppositions and mediations along the way, even if his explanations might differ from those some might choose today.

Through a few examples of mediators, especially of Aguilar, Guerrero, Brulé and Squanto, we can observe the refractory and multiple nature of mediation in the Spanish, French and English contact with various groups of American Natives in the early modern period in terms of the contexts of other Europeans. In this chapter, I have presented shards of representations of the lives of these mediators, which are mediated in someone else's story. Mediators find room to maneuvre as go-betweens, interpreters and peace-makers, but they are often subject to scrutiny, control or condemnation by those who command power, the chiefs and governors in the exchange. They are of the system and against it. By finding alternatives, sometimes the middle way, they work against the extremes that the logic of stereotypes, conflict and war work toward. In Cortés' view, Aguilar was good to return to the fold and Guerrero was a turncoat for not doing so. Champlain praised Brulé as a great patriot saved by God in the cause of France and, later, reviled him for being a Godless turncoat. Squanto saved the Pilgrims and alienated certain Natives. Later, Bradford and Standish were split on whether he could be trusted, as he may have been playing the two ends against the middle. The mediator is subject to the distrust of both sides, the two poles between which he attempts to mediate.

IV

Are the mediators discussed here related to those writers and historical figures like Garciolaso, part Spaniard and part Incan, in the sixteenth century and Louis Riel, part Cree and part French, in the nineteenth? Some of the mediators performed intellectual work and some, like the French traders of the seventeenth century, took on the Native life and were entwined in their families and commercial life. They helped create, at least technically speaking, a Métis community. For instance, from the 1620s through to 1650, when the Iroquois decimated the Hurons or Ouendat in war, the French traders married into Huron households according to Native law, and these sexual alliances created a social and economic network and led to better understanding between the French and Huron involved.[129]

In examining the relations between cultures in the New World, whether of kidnapping or mediation, the problems of identity, crossing cultures, ambivalence and contradiction are themselves full of enigmas and paradoxes. While I have held up mediation as a utopian hope of cooperation between cultures and against notions of purity and of insider and outsider, it would be naive to see the various European and Native cultures as breaking down into two oppositional cultures. There is some truth to this enmity or division along European and American lines, but figures on both sides complicate these distinctions. Guerrero is a striking case. He fought a war against his former compatriots, the Spanish, with great persistence and resolve. Bernal Díaz has another captive, Aguilar, reporting that Guerrero had prompted the attack on Cordoba at Cape Catoche.[130] Another Native, Melchior, whom the Spanish had brought from that same place, fled Cortés' expedition to the Indians, "advised them that if they attacked us by day and night we should be beaten, for we were few in number. So it turned out that we had brought an enemy with us instead of a friend."[131] Uprooted, Melchior had nowhere to run: he could not find peace with the Spaniards or with the Natives. Díaz reported Melchior's fate: "Cortes ordered them [the Natives] to bring this man before him without fail. But they answered that when they saw the battle going against them he had run away. Search had been made for him, but they did not know where he was. We discovered, however, that they had offered him as a sacrifice because his advice had cost them dear."[132] Aguilar, who was said to have been so happy to regain the Spanish fold after being enslaved by the Indians, acted as interpreter on this campaign. As for Guerrero, he remained an elusive enemy for a long time. In about 1534 or 1535, after a battle south of Yucatan, the Spanish surveyed the Indian dead and found among them a tatooed white man: Guerrero. According to Inga Clendinnen, "His hatred of his countrymen had been so compelling that he had led a canoe-borne attack far beyond his own territory, and had died for it."[133] Clearly, this White Indian was unruly and hostile to his European culture.

The relations among various European and Native groups were at least triangular and this multiplicity persisted for centuries. In describing King William's War (1690–97), Francis Parkman noted the role of the French in the relations between the English and Indians:

Early in the war, the French in Canada began the merciful practice of buying English prisoners, and especially children, from their Indian allies. After the first fury of attack, many lives were spared for the sake of this ransom. Sometimes, but not always, the redeemed captives were made to work for their benefactors. They were uniformly treated well, and often with such kindness that they would not be exchanged, and became Canadians by adoption.[134]

The rivalry between the French and English also included ambiguity and porous boundaries of identity. In Parkman's narrative the French rescue the English from Native savagery, but there are other accounts that make the Indians seem like such wonderful hosts and such effective cultural assimilators that Europeans generally refused to return willingly to their own after captivity among the Natives. For example, Pierre de Charlevoix, a French Jesuit, noted the onesidedness in the conversion of Europeans to the Native way of life and Hector de Crèvecoeur observed that while thousands of Europeans had become Indians, "we have no examples of even one of those Aborigines having from choice become Europeans!"[135] According to Benjamin Franklin, "When an Indian Child has been brought up among us, taught our language and habituated to our Customs, yet if he goes to see his relations and make one Indian Ramble with them, there is no perswading him ever to return," whereas the English of both sexes, even though ransomed by friends, would rather be among the Indians and take the first opportunity to escape.[136] Going between cultures, in light of these views, or a mediation between two sides, while a useful description of the practical effects of kidnapping and the use of interpreters, does not seem to have been a choice that went two ways between Europeans and Natives. While Europeans appear to have chosen to become acculturated to Native customs and communities, the opposite does not appear to have been true. The Native fleeing European captivity is a figure encountered in Díaz in the sixteenth century as much as it is in Franklin in the eighteenth. That context has implications for Native-settler relations to this day.

This figure of the person between cultures is still with us. As a gesture toward chapter 7, which will discuss *métissage* at greater length, I will mention an important figure in North American history—Louis Riel—who was mediator, renegade, resistor—Métis. Part Cree, part French, Riel lived when Canada was emerging from its colonial period. People now are supposed to inhabit a postmodern and postcolonial world and are encouraged to think about these relations and see beyond them as oppositions. The crossing of boundaries and the flexibility of mediation can suggest one way to live in the world and to respond to movements and mixing of culture in the global village. Louis Riel, who is a mythical and controversial figure in Canadian culture, led the Northwest rebellions in 1869–70 and 1885. The very ambivalence of Riel made and makes him problematic. He combined progressive aspects such as a politics of liberation and nostalgic and conservative religious elements. The images of Catholicism and France coexisted with his declaration of rights and his vision of independence for the Métis and the Northwest. He was rebel and mystic, prophet of a new age and a throwback to a religious past, French and Amerindian.[137]

The eruption of the early modern and of modernity in the postmodern is an important historical element that is too often neglected. If history is really available to us in a postmodern age, then it should not be used ornamentally or citationally if it is to be an effective aspect of our analysis. Mediation is something that relies on textual transmission and reception and depends on the difficulty of translation, so that mediators, who cross boundaries or are cultural Métis, find resistance in themselves and in their societies. The dream of purity persists, and the kidnapping of language is no easier and ultimately no more successful than the European kidnapping of Natives from Columbus onward. It may be, then, that earlier forms of mediation and métissage can be suggestive for a world that lives with terms such as multinational and multicultural, postcolonial and neo-colonial.

Fictional "indigenes" like Shakespeare's Caliban, who are taught a new language and who are under the influence of another culture, had actual predecessors. Caught between Europe and Africa, the Old World and the New, Caliban has been the center of a debate on the legacy of colonialism and has been given a role in postcolonial cultural studies. Chapter 6 will discuss Caliban in the aesthetic and political contexts of Shakespeare's *The Tempest,* but will suggest, as this chapter has, that the geometry of culture is not simply bi-polar, so that the relation between Caliban and Prospero will be refracted in the context of many other connections. The actual figures of mediation in this chapter, from La Malinche to Brulé and beyond, should provide a larger milieu for Ariel, Caliban, Miranda, Prospero and others who find themselves in situations that are no longer the cultural contexts they knew before their contact with the other culture. Shakespeare's fiction should read Columbus' truth as much as Columbus' truth reads Shakespeare's fiction. If, to use Natalie Zemon Davis' phrase, there is fiction in the archives, there are also archives in fiction.[138] The past erupts in the present enacted in the repeated enactments of Columbus, Shakespeare and others in each generation. The issue of interpretation continues to be reconfigured in new aesthetic and political frameworks: the very tension between poetics and ideology are still being played out. From sexual representations in and of the New World, which I have called the sexing of America, a moving sign and target, and the overlapping, entwined and liminal spaces between cultures, we now move on to the relations among Caliban, Miranda, Prospero, Ariel and others, another kind of complex mediation and interpretative betweenness that deserves notice.

Chapter 6 ～

Shakespeare's Island

As Jamestown was hanging on precariously as an English settlement on the Atlantic seaboard of North America, being part of the plan of the "American party" at the English court, which, over the years, included Humphrey Gilbert, Walter Ralegh, Richard Hakluyt, Francis Walsingham and others, Shakespeare wrote a play, perched precariously between a Virgilian nostalgia and a contemporary anxiety over the shipwreck on Bermuda: *The Tempest*. This play, set in the Mediterranean and torn between Italy and Tunisia in a storm, also has, through echoes of William Strachey and scarce allusions to the New World, American dimensions. Regardless of the empirical evidence, this play has become as much a controversy in colonialism and postcolonialism as it had been an aesthetic icon in the revolutionary age of the Romantics. Shakespeare, unlike Columbus, seems never to have gone to the New World or to have written more than a few allusory words about it or, at best, a play that has in recent times been interpreted as an allegory about the European "discovery" of the New World. Shakespeare does not really say much of anything about Columbus, but he is now almost as much a part of the debate over colonization of the New World as Columbus is and perhaps more so in Africa. This situation would probably have surprised Shakespeare. Whatever the reckoning says literally, *The Tempest* is a play about the meeting, if not the clash, of cultures. The go-betweens here are principally Ariel and Caliban. Various groups have claimed the play and playwright, or some of his characters, as their own in a cultural struggle over who can say and interpret what. The question of between or among cultures persists.

Given to interiority in an age of political turmoil, many Romantics regarded Shakespeare's play, which is perched between empire and creation, in artistic terms. Shelley did not write a treatise on the revolutionary mode of this drama in the spirit of his sonnet satirizing the political corruption of England. Instead, the Romantics forged a criticism of Shakespeare's *The Tempest* that was allegorical, a type that subsequently dominated views of the play. Perhaps taking their cue from Coleridge, who said that the appeal of the play was to the imagination, subsequent critics appealed to fantastic and the aesthetic allegories. Schlegel identified Ariel with air and Caliban with earth; Campbell saw *The Tempest* as Shakespeare's farewell to his art; Lowell equated Caliban with brute understanding, Ariel with fancy and Prospero with imagination. When I was an undergraduate the Romantic reading of this play as the playwright's farewell to his art was still going strong. But for some time another kind of allegory was going on, that is the political allegory. Once a minority position, the political allegory has, in the last decade or so, overtaken the aesthetic allegory. My task is to find a version of *The Tempest* that acknowledges the political and aesthetic dimensions of the play but that discovers a middle ground between them. Although allegorical interpretation may be unavoidable in regard to *The Tempest*, I want to minimize it, as others have mined this vein, and to try to point up its stresses and intricacies as a means of moving along to a different type of critique. This attempt, then, is to redeem *The Tempest* from too much redemption.[1]

As the traditional aesthetic allegory of this play has been synthesized into the history of Shakespearean criticism, I wish briefly to outline the shift to political allegory, particularly in light of postcolonialism, before proceeding to my own analysis. Between about ninety and a hundred and twenty years ago, a shift seems to have happened in interpretations of *The Tempest*. Whereas in 1873 Daniel Wilson thought that *The Tempest* was a social Darwinist work, in 1904 W. T. Stead objected to the imperialism and sided with indigenous cultures. In the twentieth century a central debate over the use of canons as a means of promoting tradition and empire has occurred in English-speaking countries. Shakespeare has been at the heart of that debate as in those countries he occupies the center of literature and education in the humanities. In traditional criticism, Prospero's art and power were sometimes identified with Shakespeare's and Europe's while Caliban was sometimes associated with the physical, moral and political dependency of non-European peoples. As an understandable reaction to this European position, some writers in Africa and the Caribbean set out to use *The Tempest* for their own literary and political purposes. Between 1957 and 1973, most African and large Caribbean colonies won their independence. Dissenting intellectuals and writers from these regions decided to appropriate *The Tempest* as a means of supporting decolonization and creating an alternative literary tradition.[2] In *The Tempest* African and Caribbean writers saw hints of pre-European traditions and European colonization. These "proleptic" signs suggested raw material for retrieving repressed traditions and inventing new ones. In Europe itself, as I have suggested, there was already opposition to the imperial view, so that, as usual, there were not two monolithic sides to this debate, Europe on the one hand and Africa and the Caribbean on the other. For forty years or more—in Spanish, French and English—African and Caribbean writers and critics have, directly and indirectly, appropriated or discussed the appropriation of Shakespeare's play. For instance, in 1961 Aimé Césaire's *Une Tempête: D'après "la Tempête" de Shakespeare—Adaption pour un théâtre nègre* was published in Paris.[3] During the 1970s, *The Tempest* was not used as much as a tool of opposition in decolonizing cultures. Nonetheless, such work persists and the mark or trace of Shakespeare's play is still with us: in "Calypso for Caliban," which is in *Highlife for Caliban*, Lemuel Johnson shows what Caliban has done with Prospero's language, life and history: "papa prospero/jig me mama."[4] From the mid-1970s, the interest in colonization in the Renaissance, and in *The Tempest*, begins among scholars, later known as new historicists. This tradition of dissent from within continues among scholars of European descent and seems to have culminated with the five-hundredth anniversary of Columbus' arrival in America. In this most recent manifestation White North American scholars, like the White American-born élite of the Spanish colonies or *criollos* of the late eighteenth century, find themselves in the position of identifying with Amerindians as a means of vindicating the wrongs done to, and prejudices against, those peoples in the past and as a declaration of independence from their own European past.[5] While this position is understandable and even laudable, it is difficult to avoid contradiction and to erase the European contact with the first Americans so readily and with an exercise of conscience.

My aim in this chapter is to do something much more modest. The aesthetic and political allegorists have created a vast body of secondary literature: in this brief space, I
wish to set out the intricate problems of interpretation in the play. This argument is cautionary, as much to me as to any other critic. The recognition here sought is not a new
world of religious, aesthetic or political redemption from the sins of our parents but
more a chronicle of the difficulties and contradictions in interpreting what appears on
the surface to be a well-wrought and self-contained comedy or romance.

The aesthetic has historical contexts, some of which I have explored in my other
work on Shakespeare and on the New World. The colonial in the postcolonial is something I have advocated: this is a historical context for later breaks from empire and considerations of whether the postcolonial is neocolonial.[6] For the purposes of this essay,
which concentrates more on aesthetics and politics as opposed to history, I wish to call
attention to a few brief contexts of Shakespeare's *The Tempest* before proceeding to the
question of the aesthetic. The promotion of English colonization in Virginia had literary associations. Thomas Campion addressed an epigram to Strachey, who had literary
aspirations, having composed a sonnet in commendation of Ben Jonson's *Sejanus*. Campion was also connected to the theater in London, for he was a shareholder in the acting company, the Children of the Queen's Revels, which, in 1606, had taken over the
Blackfriar's Theatre from Shakespeare's associate, Richard Burbage. John Marston was
also a shareholder and Ben Jonson wrote for this company.[7] In a deposition Strachey testified that he usually attended Blackfriars, "sometymes once, twyce, and thrice in a
weeke," which suggests that he knew the theater company, including Shakespeare, who
later used William Strachey as a source for *The Tempest*.[8] Samuel Purchas, who continued Hakluyt's work on collections of travels and navigations, published the Strachey letter to a certain "noble lady" that Shakespeare is thought to have used as a source for *The
Tempest*.[9] It is to Shakespeare's play that I now wish to turn.

The ethical and aesthetic dimensions of *The Tempest* have been and will be part of
the reception of the play, but it is the interplay of the two that demonstrates how intricate the task at hand is. Rather than side with Prospero or Caliban, who both feel
wronged, the one that he has lost Milan and the other that he has lost his island, I will
examine them both, as well as Ariel, who is a frustrated figure caught between rebellion
and obedience, and other characters. *The Tempest* is of the historical moment and is a
putative space away from the cares of Milan and Europe. Moreover, the island is a place
that lives in the sources of the European past in double exposure with the New World.
The play contains much narrative, so that story as meditation, report and description
stands in for many actions. The Shakespearean play that represents the so-called classical unities most looks forward to a new world.

Perhaps the nub of the problem of interpretation of *The Tempest* derives from the
stresses between the rules of genre and the historical changes that have transformed the
audience for the play. Frank Kermode notes this stress: "In romance there survives that
system of ideal correspondences and magic patterns which in actuality could not survive
the scrutiny of an informed and modern eye."[10] For contemporary critics, it has become
increasingly difficult in the face of political and ideological issues arising from *The Tempest* to concentrate on the genre of the play, which some have called a comedy, others a
tragicomedy and still others a romance. Although the generic or aesthetic dimension
seems to be obscured at the moment, it would be surprising if it disappeared entirely.
Rather, like the neglect of the political and historical aspects, the generic question will
endure dismissal and oversight.

If *The Tempest* is considered to be a romance, it does not fit entirely Northrop Frye's characterization of the genre even if he thought that it was a romance. Romance, according to Frye, dominates the Elizabethan and Jacobean periods of English literature, for instance by taking over Sidney's *Arcadia,* Spenser's *The Faerie Queene* and the plays of Shakespeare's last phase. This genre was successful even though it was scorned for its extravagance, neglect of the unities, incredible actions and characters and attention to "nature."[11] Unlike *The Winter's Tale, The Tempest* more or less obeys the classical unities, but, as Frye implies, it is extravagant, represents unbelievable characters and actions and focuses a great deal on nature. To nature it adds the nurture of art. Romance, in its narrative and dramatic forms, suggests the intricate relation between, and refraction of, classicism and popular culture. Like *Cymbeline, The Tempest* hints at *translatio imperii,* taking up the westering journey and the movement of empire found in Virgil's *Aeneid.*[12] Romance and the imperial theme, as Wilson Knight argued, do meet.

The temptation in contemporary criticism of *The Tempest* is to seek out Caliban as a hero and to see in Prospero the idealization of Europe at the brink of empire.[13] My view is that the stress between the ideals and wish-fulfillment of romance on the one hand and the political objections of modernity and postmodernity on the other suggests additional productive ways to view this play. What my reading attempts is an interpretation that takes into account the aesthetic question of genre and the political question of authority and rebellion but through the literary and dramatic text of *The Tempest* itself and not through external sources. When discussing historical analogues and contexts, the chapter will do so from and through Shakespeare's play and not the other way around.

II

My method is to discuss the problems as they arise from act to act in order to show how bound up the aesthetic or generic dimension is with the political or historical one. The details of the *seriatim* of language are as important to consider as the structural movement of comedy and the ideas of politics, colonialism and postcolonialism. The very inconvenience of language, structure and content for one another suggests a productive and dramatic friction that I hope to raise through this mode of interpretation. It is the very contradiction and ambivalence, and not a one-eyed ideological or structural reading, that I hope emerges. Although I bring in contextual material and indeed the rest of the book provides a context for this chapter as it should cast some light on the volume as a whole, I am affirming the importance of close attention to the text. It is as inconvenient for me as for anyone else but it provides evidence that asks me to be honest and, I hope, keeps me so.

The play opens with the Ship-master and the Boatswain trying to save the ship from the storm. In the first line the Master asks the Boatswain to speak to the mariners briskly or the ship will run aground. After the Master exits and the Mariners enter at line 4, the Boatswain, who has not replied to the Master, follows the order by giving the appropriate instructions to the mariners. At line 9, Alonso, Sebastian, Antonio, Ferdinand, Gonzalo and others enter: here begins the disobedience after only a few lines in which the chain of command seems to have been working. As far as the Boatswain is concerned Alonzo, the King of Naples, is in the way in the fight for survival: "Hence! what cares these roarers for the name of King? To cabin: silence! trouble us not" (I.i.16–18). When Gonzalo, the old counsellor, reminds the Boatswain that he has the king aboard, the Boatswain, with some sarcasm and under pressure to work while the storm is raging, says he loves no one more than himself and reminds Gonzalo of his apparent impotence:

> You are a counsellor; if you can command these elements to silence, and work the peace of the presence, we will not hand a rope more; use your authority if you cannot, give thanks you have lived so long, and make yourself ready in your cabin for the mischance of the hour, if it so hap. Cheerly, good hearts! Out of our way, I say. (I.i.20–27)

Authority is a matter of context, convention and use. The king and his counselor have no authority in the storm because they hinder, rather than help, the survival of the crew. Gonzalo may pun on the gallows the Boatswain will face, but the nobles are almost comic in the way they presume to assert authority where they have it in name only. By insisting on authority, Gonzalo is showing up its fissures. Fate may, as Gonzalo wishes, save them and hang the Boatswain. The Boatswain's authority in seamanship is not respected. He has four lines of peace before Sebastian, Antonio and Gonzalo re-emerge in another comic brawl with him. He meets them with more sarcasm and they counter with condescending insults. Antonio concludes that "We are less afraid to be drowned than thou art" (I.i.44–45) and adds later that "We are merely cheated of our lives by drunkards" (55). Gonzalo and the others show their nobility by joining the king and the prince in their prayers. Even though the nobles seem to have asserted their honor and courage, Gonzalo ends the opening scene with the contradictory: "The wills above be done! but I would fain die a dry death" (I.i.65–66).

The audience is reminded of motifs of romance in the opening words of Act One, scene two, which Miranda speaks to Prospero: "If by your Art, dearest father, you have/ Put the wild waters in this roar, allay them" (I.ii.1–2). The child orders the father, even if it is after a conditional clause. The motifs of magic, suffering and survival, regeneration and wish-fulfillment occur in Prospero's magical storm and Miranda's desire that it cease (see I.ii.3–20). Part of the genre of romance (which is closely related to epic and comedy) is the quest for identity. In this play, Prospero and Miranda have been shipwrecked and both have had new identities thrust upon them, he knowingly and she not. So Prospero has promised to tell about Miranda's past. She reminds him that "You have often/ Begun to tell me what I am, but stopp'd" (33–34). He now tells her the story of her early life in a dialogue where he leads her to see "the dark backward abysm of time" (50). Prospero chronicles his brother Antonio's perfidious usurpation of Prospero's dukedom (66–139). His "library/ Was dukedom large enough," so that Prospero neglected his kingdom until his brother, with the help of the King of Naples, took Milan by expelling Prospero and Miranda (109–10). The personification of the winds that Prospero creates is supposed to move Miranda and the audience in the theater to lamentation and indignation over the wrong (149–51). So too is the appeal to Miranda as a cherubim and to Divine Providence as the reason for their survival (152–59). Prospero tells her how Gonzalo helped save them by sneaking them food and books, which allowed Prospero to study on the island (160–74). Miranda wants to know the reason for Prospero's storm, and he thanks Fortune for bringing his enemies to him, and then casts his daughter into a sleep (175–86).

The first appearance of Ariel is one of obedience. He carries out Prospero's art. When Prospero asks Ariel to come, the spirit replies: "All hail, great master! grave sir, hail! I

come/ To answer thy best pleasure" (189–90). When Prospero inquires whether he has performed the tempest as he was bade, he enumerates, amid his master's exclamations of joy, its execution, so that the audience is also well informed. Like Prospero's narrative, Ariel's is a device to compress the action of the play, to let the classical unities obtain in a way that Shakespeare had not done since *The Comedy of Errors.*[14] In fact, in keeping with romance, Ariel assures Prospero that his actions were regenerative, as those tossed in the water now have fresher garments than before (218–19). In this account, Ariel makes the only allusion to the Bermoothes or Bermuda. In a nook, where Prospero once summoned him "at midnight to fetch dew/ From the still-vexed Bermoothes," Ariel has hidden the ship, while he has put all the other ships on the Mediterranean "Bound sadly home for Naples" (228–29, 235). Bermuda is an allusion in a subordinate clause, a kind of association with storms in a story-fragment, and with no grid of where the island is located. Here is the only direct and obvious evidence of the New World in the play and it is passing, and perhaps not far for a spirit who can go from here to there, from Mediterranean to Bermuda, in a glance.[15] Even Ariel is rebellious, as he reminds Prospero of his promise to grant him liberty (242–50). Prospero reacts to what he views as ingratitude by reminding Ariel of the torments that Sycorax had devised for him and of the way Prospero rescued him. The phrase, "Thou liest, malignant thing," illustrates the vehemence that Prospero shows to Ariel and the quickness with which his mood can swing (257). According to Prospero's account, he found a tyranny on the island. For a crime, Sycorax was banished from Algiers and, pregnant, was brought to the island, where Ariel was her servant. As Ariel would not enact her terrible commands, she imprisoned him in pain in a cloven pine for a dozen years, during which time she died. Only Caliban had a "human shape" on the island when Prospero found it, and only Prospero's "Art" could free Ariel from his howling captivity (284, 291, see 256–93). Even after Ariel responds, "I thank thee, master," Prospero threatens to do unto him what Sycorax had. After Ariel swears his obedience, Prospero gives up the threats and promises to free Ariel in two days. He also commands Ariel to make himself invisible in his next enactment of Prospero's magic. Prospero claims the barely inhabited island from the bestial yet human Caliban as if it were *terra nullius* or, in John Winthrop's words, *vacuum domicilium.* Just as the Portuguese had claimed "discovery" of populated areas of the African coast in the fifteenth century, so too had the Spanish, English and French used the legal fiction of *terra nullius,* that nomadic Amerindians ranged but did not inhabit the land as Europeans did, so that their land could be possessed.[16] If we are sympathetic to Prospero, we can say that he usurped the remnants of a penal colony, founded as the result of some unnamed crime, and became the de facto ruler through justice. On the other hand, his magic is a deterrent and becomes the force of law, especially in relation to Caliban, the son of the tyrannous Sycorax of Prospero's official version, but also to Ariel.

Prospero wakes Miranda after Ariel leaves and in order to find Caliban, whom Prospero calls "slave" to his face five times in this scene (310, 315, 321, 346, 376). As in the opening scene, a conflict between classes occurs here, but in its most unsavory manifestation (at least for a modern audience), that is in the relation between master and slave. Prospero understands Caliban's indispensability, whereas Miranda feels repugnance.[17] Ariel makes a brief entrance as a water nymph, as if to provide a contrast with Caliban (318–20). According to Prospero, Caliban is the offspring of a witch and an incubus, a fiend whose mother is in many ways a witch from the classics.[18] Prospero and Caliban curse each other (323–32). Caliban claims the island was his: he was a king who has now become Prospero's only subject. He curses Prospero, whom he once loved and showed the fruits of the island, for detaining him in a rock. For Prospero, this state arose because Caliban attempted to rape Miranda, an attempt that Caliban wishes Prospero had not thwarted. This rape is a reversal of the sexual violence Cuneo showed the Carib woman on Columbus' second voyage. Sexual violence was one of the frictions between Natives and invaders (or newcomers). Here, however, the rape is attempted but not executed, as in Cuneo's case, and the Carib woman did not seem to have a Prospero or Ferdinand there whose authority and power could protect and right her situation. Miranda (some editors make it Prospero) curses Caliban as "Abhorred slave" and upbraids him for his betrayal of trust (353–64). Here, then, is an irreconcilable dispute over the history of the island, a meeting of two sides who are incommensurate, whether this irreconcilable difference possesses any dimension of an allegory of the New World. Caliban makes his position clear: "You taught me language; and my profit on't/ Is, I know how to curse" (365–66). He then proceeds to do just that chiasmically, for he curses Prospero (and Miranda) for teaching him their language. But even then Shakespeare weighs the debate rhetorically in Prospero's favor, making Caliban almost too much of a tabula rasa. As in the case of Ariel, Prospero threatens Caliban with physical pain if he does not obey him. Even if there is no direct evidence that this Old World island is also of the New World, it seems that the berry drink Caliban remembers as a gift of Prospero is like the one the Bermuda castaways drank in Sylvester Jourdain's *A Discovery of the Bermudas* (1610) and that Caliban must obey Prospero, who could control Sycorax's god, Sestebos, whom, as Richard Eden mentions in *History of Travaile* (1577), in his description of Magellan's voyage, the Patagonians summoned for help.[19] But, like Ariel's stopover in Bermuda, Caliban's allusion, which is more unconscious, is part of a diffuse context of Shakespeare's reading rather than a distinct fictional world based in the New World.

The next segment of the scene involves Ariel leading Ferdinand to Prospero and Miranda (377–504). His songs of wild waves and drowning remind Ferdinand of his father, who was apparently lost in the storm (377–411). Miranda thinks that Ferdinand is a spirit, and, as Prospero has planned it, she considers the young man "A thing divine" (420). For Ferdinand, Miranda is a wonder, and more wonderful still for speaking his language (429–33). His wish fulfillment is that of the traveler who hopes to find a paradise that speaks his language and bears his names. The Europeans began to rename the New World, but Ferdinand does not need to in this scene that Prospero has made for him. Prospero is so pleased that in asides he promises to set Ariel free for his good work: he also calls Ferdinand a spy who wants to usurp his island and tests him in case he takes Miranda too lightly for having wooed her so easily (422–69). Nor does Prospero fail to test Miranda as he says that she has seen two men, Ferdinand and Caliban, and this young man needs to be obedient (469–501). The scene closes with Prospero promising freedom to Ariel if he does exactly "All points of my command," which Ariel promises "To th' syllable" (503). Prospero controls the freedom of all the other characters in the play.

That Prospero has almost the power of a god or a playwright using dramatic irony is something that critics have noticed for over 200 years. In this he is like Henry V and Duke Vincentio of *Measure for Measure*. The dramatic power and almost providential control that these characters possess allows them to exercise authority over those who question their right to rule and decide the fates of other people, Bates and Williams in IV.i. of *Henry V*, Lucio in III.ii of *Measure*, and Caliban through much of *The Tempest*. Although I do not wish to get ahead of the end of *The Tempest*, each of these rulers attempts to have others acknowledge his power to rule. The notion of authority depends on the relation between playwright and audience, something we shall return to in discussing the end of this play. How much did Shakespeare's audience rebel against authority, or was that something firmly to avoid, even through catharsis, as the strict censorship of Elizabethan and Jacobean theater would suggest?

III

The political themes of authority and rebellion or freedom and slavery continue to interact with the romance themes of survival, regeneration and wonder. This very interaction enriches the drama of the language and of the play as a whole. Another thing to remember about politics in *The Tempest* is that they take place in a comedy or romance that is not shy about expressing its ideas about love, marvel and authority through humor. Whereas it is one-sided to treat the play in terms of dramatic structure, it is equally partial to examine the ideas of characters as if they were persons speaking in a debate or as though the ideas occurred in pamphlets. There is a fictional side to a play, so it is a different kind of text from a non-fictional document no matter how much fiction is in the archives. Prospero will outlive us all but he never breathed. The actor embodies and enlivens him, and the character is not just a string of discourse rules with a name tacked on to make him interesting, as fascinating as his language games might be, but he and his fellow characters in *The Tempest* live in the living relation between actors and audience. Laughter and wit are as much a part of comedy as is structure. There is a dramatic and dialogic livingness that defies the reduction of rivals to representatives of static and impersonal ideas.

In Act Two, scene one, Gonzalo tries to cheer Alonzo with thoughts on the miracle of their preservation, while the king will not be so easily humored. Sebastian and Antonio make fun of Gonzalo's efforts and wit in a satirical running commentary made in asides, until they make fun of the old counselor directly as Hamlet does with Polonius. Gonzalo notes the freshness of the garments as Ariel had (II.i.1–68). The first 185 lines of this scene involve a diversion in which Antonio and Sebastian send up Gonzalo, thereby showing their youthful impatience with him, indirectly their opposition to Alonzo, whom Gonzalo serves, and their impatient and sharp characters as opposed to Gonzalo's well-meaning but official character. The marriage between Claribel and the King of Tunis, to which Gonzalo alludes, is the pretext for the journey in which Prospero has trapped them by means of the storm. Gonzalo's comparison of the couple to "widow Dido" and Aeneas causes Antonio, Sebastian and Adrian much merriment. They were not married but were lovers—and Aeneas abandoned Dido to found Rome and to become part of the translation of empire. As Adrian points out, Gonzalo confuses Carthage with Tunis. In Antonio's and Sebastian's response the subsequent allusion to the miraculous harp of Amphion, which raised the walls of Thebes, reveals that Gonzalo's gaffe has made a new city. Antonio and Sebastian also make fun of his wondrous geography, suggesting his magical mistakes (66–97). Just as Gertrude grows impatient with Polonius' logorrheia, so too does Alonzo tire of the surfeit of words. He is lost in his grief and he will not abide Gonzalo's verbal insistence (102–09). Not even Francisco's hopeful description of Ferdinand's possible escape from the storm will placate the doleful Alonzo. It is his distraction that has allowed Gonzalo to be the butt of the jokes for so long in this scene as the men wile away the time until the king's grief abates. Alonzo's brother, Sebastian, blames the king for marrying his daughter to an African, for not listening to all of them who argued against the marriage and for not heeding his daughter, who "Weigh'd between loathness and obedience" (126). Besides this aspect of obedience, the theme of widows recurs, as Sebastian reminds him of the men lost at sea, but his bluntness earns him Gonzalo's gentle rebuke—to think of the king's feelings (118–36).

When Gonzalo speaks of his ideal commonwealth, he draws on Montaigne's *Des Cannibales,* which John Florio published in translation in 1603 (143ff).[20] Montaigne, and therefore Gonzalo, draws on reports of cannibals in the New World. Those critics who emphasize the New World in *The Tempest* have seized on something important in the play. The notion of Europe's connection with Africa and America occurs in passing and in brief allusions and sources. It is a significant subtext that Shakespeare uses but does not stress explicitly. For ethical and political reasons, critics have increasingly felt the need to focus on the theme of colonizer and colonized. The ideal commonwealth, which Gonzalo borrows from Montaigne, is something Antonio and Sebastian scorn in their continued mockery of the old man. Whether Shakespeare is satirizing Montaigne's natural commonwealth is unclear. Nature is abundant and sufficient to ensure human happiness. Is Gonzalo a good man who is wrong about the ideal state or are Antonio and Sebastian as errant in their mockery as they are in their plot against Alonzo? It is true that Gonzalo would need the authority not to admit sovereignty, which would be a trick of government this world has not yet seen. Sebastian and Gonzalo treat Gonzalo as an upstart king of his dreams, and tell him they laugh at him (139–79). They willingly literalize Gonzalo's words, beginning in his first words about the commonwealth with their equation of "plantation" with planting and forgetting its equivalence with colonization, so to ridicule his ideas. But Gonzalo is good-natured as he asks his two mockers to laugh him to sleep (180–85). It is, however, Ariel who lulls Gonzalo and then Alonzo to sleep with solemn music (179–93).

It does not take Antonio long to tempt Sebastian with Alonzo's crown (193–203). Sebastian thinks that Antonio is speaking a language of sleep in this torpid place. Antonio says that Ferdinand is dead and that Claribel is in Tunis and therefore out of the way from Naples, so that Sebastian could be king; he also replies to Sebastian's remark that Antonio supplanted Prospero and his question about conscience by representing himself as happy and without regret (204–275). The audience experiences dramatic irony as it knows that Ferdinand is alive and that Prospero has orchestrated the storm to trap Antonio and to redeem his lost kingdom. Whereas Antonio is hyperbolic, Sebastian is not. He would kill Alonzo while Sebastian killed Gonzalo. But, as Ariel says, Prospero has foreseen this rebellion, so that Sebastian's agreement will get him nowhere. Ariel wakes Gonzalo with song, and the two guards, who had promised Alonzo his safety, have to lie about drawing the swords against bulls or lions (276–320). The scene ends with Ariel promising to report his work to Prospero, and his wish: "So, King, go safely on to seek thy son" (322).

Ariel may be obedient, but Caliban, like Sebastian, is not and is open to suggestion. Yet another rebellion is simmering. Caliban opens Act Two, scene two with a curse on Prospero (II.ii.1–4). Caliban mistakes Trinculo for one of Prospero's spirits, and Trinculo does not know whether Caliban is a man or a fish. In England, Trinculo says, a monster makes a man rich: there, when people "will not give a doit to relieve a lame beggar, they will lay out ten to see a dead Indian" (32–34). John Cabot kidnapped Natives, and from Frobisher onward (1576), the English brought many Indians home and exhibited them as long as they lived, which was not always very long. Montaigne spoke with some Amerindians who visited France. As Indians became more familiar, they replaced the wild man in masques and pageants.[21] This comic incident of the fishiness of Caliban demonstrates that, through allusion, he was at least in part associated with the Amerindian in Shakespeare's mind. When Stephano enters with his bawdy sailor's song, Caliban mistakes him as well for one of Prospero's tormenting spirits. Stephano misapprehends the four-legged beast under the gabardine, that is Trinculo and Caliban: "Have we devils here? Do you put tricks upon's with salvages and men of Ind, ha?" (58–59). Stephano wonders how the "monster of the isle" learned "our language," an astonishment not unlike Ferdinand's when he hears Miranda speak (66–68). Like Trinculo, Stephano is thinking of how a show of this "monster" will make him rich at home (69–80). On stage the humor is more apparent as the monster that Stephano is talking about is Trinculo and Caliban under cover, and Stephano thinks it the devil when it calls him by name (99–100). In an aside, Caliban considers Stephano a god who "bears celestial liquor" (118). Stephano admits that he escaped the storm on a butt of sack, a comic gesture for a drunkard but also a detail from the Bermuda narratives.[22] Rather than swear on the Bible, Caliban declares uninvited: "I'll swear, upon that bottle, to be thy true subject; for the liquor is not earthly" (126–27). Here is a parodic oath of allegiance, a kind of comic inversion of the obedience Caliban once gave to Prospero. Shakespeare represents a kind of parodic first encounter between Amerindian and European:

> Caliban   Hast thou not dropp'd from heaven?
> Stephano   Out o' the moon, I do assure thee: I was the man
>   i'th'moon when time was.
> Caliban   I have seen thee in her, and I do adore thee.
>
>   (137–40)

Other Europeans had thought that they had beguiled the Natives so, but that might have been hubris on their part.[23] The famous *Letter* of Columbus concerning the first voyage represents the first contact with the Amerindians in similar fashion: "And they do not know any creed and are not idolaters; only they all believe that power and good are in the heavens, and they are very firmly convinced that I, with these ships and men, came from heaven."[24] It is questionable whether the Natives thought of the Europeans in the grandiose ways that the Europeans represent for themselves.

Trinculo insults Caliban as "A most poor credulous monster!" while Caliban asks Stephano to "be my god" and swears to be his subject (146, see 142–59). Thus Caliban promises to serve Stephano as he had served Prospero by exploiting the island's resources for him. Amid these promises and his curse of Prospero, whom he calls a tyrant, Trinculo comments: "A most ridiculous monster, to make a wonder of a poor drunkard!" (165–66). Once again, dramatic irony limits the usurpation of new authority. The audience knows that the king and company live even as Stephano tells Trinculo the contrary and that "we will inherit here" (175). Trinculo thinks that Caliban is drunk (179). Although Caliban sings that he will make no more dams for fish, he has promised to fish for Stephano (161, 180). In this drunken scene of mistaken identity, there is comedy from the ironic blindness with which Caliban and Stephano end it:

> Caliban   *'Ban, 'Ban, Cacaliban*
>   *Has a new master:—get a new man.*
>   Freedom, high-day! high-day, freedom! freedom,
>   high-day, freedom!
> Stephano   O brave monster! lead the way. (183–88)

Here the class delusions of Stephano are as great as the illusions of Caliban. The divisions between Native and European have already become more complex, even if they are a laughing matter, because a connection develops among Stephano, Trinculo and Caliban. They are rebels against Prospero's authority, which has much to do with his education and social status. A tension between Shakespeare's England and Western democracies today is that the position of monarchy and aristocracy has changed and diminished into constitutional or social prestige and ceremony from great political and social power. This may explain another link among Caliban, Trinculo and Stephano: the post–Second World War audience for literature and theater, having descended more from classes and backgrounds more analogous to these three than to Prospero, tends to have shown more empathy for them than for the duke. Dramatic irony leads the audience into laughter at the ironic inferiority of the three rebels to Prospero, but social and political change have made the reception, at least among many of the critics from the 1960s and beyond, more aware of his control in terms of class and colonization. The rebels revel and are drunk with freedom, but the comic bluster has also led to a political discourse among more and more critics.

III

The innocent love of comedy and romance, which the relation between Miranda and Ferdinand represents, has also come up against political criticism that reflects and refracts social changes. After the woman's movement of more than a century, it is hard to receive without qualification Prospero's narrative and actual control over his daughter and the magically arranged marriage that he has over the couple. Once again, a friction occurs between content and form in *The Tempest.* Prospero's magic is closely connected with that most powerful of theatrical tools—dramatic irony, which creates a bond between the playwright and the audience, a connection that calls for superior knowledge of the characters. One variant of dramatic irony is when the dramatist and the audience share superior knowledge with one or more characters and together they are aware of the ignorance of other characters. Moreover, the audience experiences Prospero's magic and wisdom, and to a lesser extent Ariel's, a key to understanding the predicaments of other characters, Stephano, Caliban and Trinculo in the last scene we examined and Ferdinand and Miranda in the one we are about to discuss. The structure of romantic comedy and romance is such that the young couple usually overcomes the parental blocks to their marriage. *The Tempest* is a little different from that, as there are no conventional blocks as is the case in *A Midsummer Night's Dream,* but is more like the way the shipwrecks of *Twelfth Night* and *A Winter's Tale* affect the union of lovers. The movement toward marriage is so strong in Shakespeare's romantic comedy and in his romances, which the First Folio did not recognize as a genre but classified plays like *The Tempest* as comedies, that some of the marriages, like that between Touchstone and Audrey in *As You Like It,* are eccentric, or, like those between Viola and Duke Orsino and Olivia and Sebastian, are good-natured but arbitrary. The structural imperative of comic endings from New Comedy onward, with the conventions of shipwrecks, twins, magic and other miraculous devices, devours solemn content and matter. The seriousness occurs paradoxically through laughter.

Here is a context for the aesthetic and generic concerns of comedy and romance that qualify the solemnity and denunciatory aspects of colonial and postcolonial critique. It is one thing to be wary of structures of authority but in a comedy or romance it is ill advised to ignore the dramatic structure and the strong imperatives of comic conventions. Courtship and marriage are central to comedy and romance (tragicomedy), the genres by which critics almost always classify *The Tempest*. Such courtships, as a prelude of or prelude to marriage, occupy the center of this play. Act Three, scene one represents Ferdinand as he performs his labors cheerfully for Miranda, though he is not without criticism for Prospero (1–14). She bids Ferdinand rest and circumvent her father's orders because Prospero is studying but he is actually observing them at a distance unseen. She tells Ferdinand her name against her father's wishes. They swear their love and Prospero asks heaven to shower its grace on this pair. Prospero is less happy with their promise to marry than they are (15–96). Like Caliban and Stephano, the lovers are full of wonder, but their oaths will see them farther than the two rebels because in the context of romance, they are the young who will regenerate the world through marriage. Their obedience in comedy would not be so necessary as they could circumvent the *senex,* but here in romance, the magus helps their love with his spell, which also heals the impotent king.[25]

This courtship is not to occur in solemn isolation. Shakespeare represents misrule, exuberance, and irreverence here as much as he does in the tavern scenes of *1* and *2 Henry IV.* This comic misrule becomes part of the aesthetic and politics of the island in *The Tempest* as it did in the England of those history plays. Shakespeare surrounds the love scene in the middle of the play with the antics of Stephano and Caliban and the satirical comments of Trinculo. Folly continues to be Trinculo's theme: "They say there's but five upon this isle: we are three of them; if th'other two be brain'd like us, the state totters" (III.ii.6). Both Caliban and Stephano are reeling with drink. Of Trinculo, Caliban says, "I'll not serve him, he is not valiant" (22–23). He appeals to Stephano when Trinculo abuses him, and Stephano warns the offender: "if you prove a mutineer,—the next tree!" (33–34). Ariel plays tricks on the three so that when he says "Thou liest" to Caliban's lament, that Prospero is a tyrant who cheated him of the island, Ariel is mistaken for Trinculo and this brings about new threats from Stephano (40f). By repeating this phrase at key times, Ariel disrupts Caliban's plot to deliver Prospero to Stephano and raises the new master's ire against Trinculo. Caliban wants Stephano to possess and burn Prospero's books, "for without them/ He's but a sot, as I am" and promises that Stephano will have Miranda in bed and produce "brave brood" (90–103). Stephano declares that Miranda will be his queen after he kills Prospero and that Caliban and Trinculo will be viceroys. This is the kind of advancement that expansion by war, usurpation or colonization might have enabled. Ariel's invisible presence makes this all unlikely and increases the dramatic irony. Thoughts of Prospero's death by violence makes Caliban "full of pleasure," and Stephano cannot remember the song Caliban wants but comes up with a nonsensical catch that ends "*Thought is free*" (114, 120). Stephano and Trinculo are afraid of Ariel's music, so that Caliban must tell them not to be afraid of this island so "full of noises" (131–32). As in the scene before the pledges of Ferdinand and Miranda, Caliban leads Stephano, to make the inversion complete.

Not surprisingly, the next scene represents more rebellious thoughts. Gonzalo is tired and Alonzo out of hope: Antonio and Sebastian plot to kill them. Now Prospero and Ariel put on a banquet for them and play more tricks. This time Prospero's asides point out the evil in Alonzo's party. He leaves the banquet behind, but Alonzo does not want to touch it. Gonzalo, however, tries to reassure him that this feast is not more strange than "men/ Whose heads stood in their breasts" (III.iii.47). This Mandevillian motif also occurs in Walter Ralegh's *The Discovery of Guiana* (1596) and in Othello's Anthropophagi, so that it combines Old World fiction with New World rumor (I.iii.144–45).[26] When Alonzo decides to eat, Ariel, as a Harpy, makes the banquet vanish. Ariel appeals to himself as an agent of Destiny and Fate. He reminds the three that they "From Milan did supplant good Prospero" and tells Alonzo that for such actions the ministers have taken away his son and leave the father to perdition (70). Ariel vanishes; the spirits reappear and carry out the table; Prospero praises Ariel's role as harpy and speaks of his control over his enemies and his impending visit to Ferdinand, whom they suppose drowned. Another case of dramatic irony shows the limitations of those who oppose Prospero: the conventions of romance check political rebellion. Alonzo thinks the events "monstrous," that the wind seemed to call out the name of Prospero and make him so aware of his guilt that he will seek his son in the deep. Sebastian and Antonio think that they are fighting fiends. Realizing that Alonzo, Antonio and Sebastian are desperate and that "their great guilt,/ Like poison given to work a great time after,/ Now 'gins to bite their spirits," Gonzalo sends Adrian to restrain the three (104–06).

There are three "revolts" in the play: the usurpation of Prospero's dukedom before the action began that occurs in Prospero's version of events and in allusions in the play; the plot of Antonio and Sebastian; and the attempted rebellion of Stephano, Caliban and Trinculo. Each has an aesthetic as well as a political dimension. The wound of the usurpation stays with Prospero and occupies his art, his narrative in an Osiris effect, and these bits of story are also connected to Miranda's memory as a child of almost three years old of the women who tended her before the political exile she and her father suffered (I.ii). This is a political wound that Prospero will use his magic to heal. The second revolt occurs when Ariels' music puts everyone but Sebastian and Antonio to sleep, so Prospero's brother, Antonio, can urge and aid Sebastian to usurp the realm of Alonso just as Antonio had taken Prospero's dukedom. With a song, Ariel awakens Gonzalo, who saves Alonso from his fate and causes Sebastian to say he heard the sounds of bulls or lions and for Antonio to claim he heard a monster (II.i). Ariel has been able to save Alonso so he can see his son, Ferdinand, which will help make possible the marriage with Miranda, which has dynastic as well as romantic dimensions. The third revolt has a comic aesthetic, not in the structural sense like a marriage to lend harmony to the end of comedy, but in the drunk Stephano's misconstrual of the form of Trinculo taking cover from the storm under Caliban's gaberdine as a four-leged monster (II.ii). This inauspicious beginning to yet another monstrous form of rebellion has an ending that is no better for the rebels as, through Ariel, Prospero stings and drives these three before him. Trinculo and Stephano are exposed in the fine clothing they have stolen from Prospero and that is as close to his authority as they get.

This political containment of monstrosity, in the play's terms at least, occurs through aesthetic and meta-aesthetic means, that is, through Shakespeare's use of magic and music within the larger aesthetics of the play as a way of limiting usurpation and restoring Prospero to his dukedom while creating a dynastic alliance between Milan and Naples through the marriage of Ferdinand and Miranda. Both fathers, curiously without the mothers of their children to lend their authority, can bless the marriage that will take place on the return to Italy. There is an element of history play to this comic marriage. But Caliban, like Falstaff, Jacques and Malvolio, is a comic scapegoat and makes the ending less single, and to some, less satisfying. Like those other characters, Caliban has learned to curse and has a great personality in his language. Shakespeare's very brilliance in creating language and character complicates the division or friction between structure and content that I have discussed.

Comedy (romance) possesses a strong structural imperative, but the power of language, even within the convention of a comic scapegoat, that Shakespeare brings to this and other plays creates another level of sympathy. The great debate over the rejection of Falstaff that went on so many years in Shakespearean criticism has all but faded away about the time that the subjugation of Caliban has arisen. Both debates have different content—the defense of an old fat knight and a lord of misrule being a call for carnival and riot, whereas the case for Caliban is the abuse of a Native who has been called a monster and subjugated. Both rebellious figures, Falstaff and Caliban, are sexually unruly and have a gift for invective, insult and catalogues of wrongs. They both challenge the order of the government that rules them. They are subversive. Each evokes in the audience a kind of empathy at different times in the reception of Shakespeare's work. During the American Revolution, Maurice Morgann, who served in that war, defended Falstsaff and argued he was not a coward, and so began a long series of defenses of the fat knight that have, for now, been somewhat stemmed.[27] While popular in Shakespeare's time and soon after, if title pages and the promise of Falstaff in another play made in the Epilogue to *2 Henry IV* are a proper gauge, Falstaff took a long time to defend. Caliban took even longer to develop a band of defenders. His empathy has grown in the independence movements in the Caribbean and Africa from the 1950s and in the movement, in English studies, from Commonwealth literature to postcolonialism. Caliban throws off the colonizer even if in the play he does not quite. As with Falstaff, the character, owing to shifts in the sensibilities and political circumstances of the audience as well as to the power of his language and personality, engenders a following well beyond what his author might have imagined or intended.

IV

Falstaff and Caliban question the dominant notions of honor in the world they inhabit. While they are powerful characters that have, at different times in the reception of their respective dramas, almost hijacked the plays in which they appear, their views of honor are not the only ones the audience has to consider. This is also true of loyalty. Whereas Falstaff is loyal to Prince Hal only to be rejected by him, he enacts his own rejection of Peto, Bardolph and Poins toward the end of the great tavern scene of *I Henry IV* (II.iv). He is loyal to Hal but not necessarily to his other friends. Hal, of course, says that he does and will banish Falstaff but is interrupted by the knocking when the "sheriff, with a monstrous watch," to quote Bardolph, comes to the door. Prince Hal's loyalty to Falstaff is not enduring: he chooses to be loyal to his father and his state. Prospero uses Caliban as Hal, Falstaff: the scapegoat teaches the master about a certain world he could not know otherwise. Both Caliban and Falstaff feel unjustly used and spit out. Caliban as the exploited Native is an aspect of the character that Shakespeare might have considered: while he may not have known Bartolomé de Las Casas' defense of the "Indians" or Jean de Léry's complex observations that refused to make the indigenous peoples of Brazil simply into devils, heathens, pagans or caricatures, Shakespeare was apparently familiar with Montaigne's satiric technique of showing up the barbarity of Europeans. Shakespeare seems to echo Montaigne concerning the ideal commonwealth in one part of the play, so he might not have been surprised if another aspect of that writer, the Natives as satirical chastisement of European folly and corruption, could be used. This aspect of Caliban has been taken up both by writers whose people were throwing off European colonial regimes and by "European" and settler critics in various parts of the world.

The texts in their specifics do not always make it so easy for Falstaff or Caliban. The audience can have empathy for them but sometimes do so against the grain of the text or at least in a modfied context. In other words, Shakespeare structures his texts to contain Falstaff and Caliban. Both are scapegoated and are not part of the new order that comedy makes from the old order. They are the chaos that order must pass through. They may linger and question the very order of the texts themselves, just as William Blake claimed in his marginalia that in *Paradise Lost* Milton was of the devil's party without knowing it presumably because of the subversive power of his Satan, that great rhetorician of seduction. Nonetheless, the details of Shakespeare's text, as contrary as they might be to the revolutionary, radical and subversive cause, need to be considered. This is like the great debate in the theory of irony in the late eighteenth century and early nineteenth century about whether irony was in the speaker or the audience, in the words or their interpretation. My position here, as good and as difficult as this question is, constitutes a rhetorical view that the relation between speaker and audience, text and interpreter is key. As so much interesting work has been written in recent years on Caliban as the hero of Shakespeare's paradise lost, I would like to set out a reminder of some of the details in the text, especially, in the immediate context, concerning expressions of what is loyal and honorable as I discuss the last two acts of *The Tempest*.

Shakespeare has been contrasting the loyalty and honor of Ferdinand with the treachery of Caliban, Sebastian and Antonio. In Act Four, scene one, he intensifies this comparison. Prospero tells Ferdinand that he has passed his tests and now has won Miranda's hand, a daughter who "will outstrip all praise" (IV.i.10). Still, Prospero threatens Ferdinand not to break Miranda's virginity before the marriage ceremony, and Ferdinand swears by his honor that he will not (13–32). Prospero, the trickster, still needs Ariel to perform tricks, so that he can regain Milan and ensure the dynastic marriage for his daughter. After checking the young couple's resolve, Prospero arranges for the masque. It is stylized, its verse in rhymed couplets. Iris, Juno's messenger, speaks of Ceres, the goddess of the harvest, in appropriately pastoral imagery. Juno descends. Ceres asks Iris why Juno has summoned her, and Iris replies that "*A contract of true love to celebrate;/ And some donation freely to estate/ On the blest lovers*" (83–5). Ceres wonders whether Venus or Cupid now attends Juno as they plotted to allow Dis or Pluto, the ruler of the underworld, to carry off Ceres' daughter Proserpine to be his queen. Thus, Ceres has foresworn their company, and Iris assures her that Venus and Cupid will not carry out their vows to put a "*wanton charm*" on the young couple, for they are defeated (95). Juno asks Ceres to go with her to bless the couple's marriage, and they do with images of increase and agricultural bounty. Ferdinand praises this "most majestic vision" and asks Prospero whether these are spirits, which the magician says he has summoned. The audience response or interruption, so common in Shakespearean plays-within-plays, ends with Ferdinand's praise of Prospero's ability to make this place "Paradise," and Prospero's call for silence for fear that the spell will be broken (118–27). On behalf of Juno, Iris calls forth the Naiads, or chaste nymphs, to "*celebrate/ A contract of true love*" (132–33). This emphasis on chastity amplifies Prospero's lesson to Ferdinand and Miranda. The reapers join the nymphs in a dance, but at the height of harmony, which would usually end a comedy, Prospero starts and ends the vision because of his memory of Caliban's conspiracy (139–44). The political theme will not let the romance theme alone.

Miranda tells Ferdinand that she has never seen Prospero so distempered, and to cheer up his newfound future son-in-law, Prospero comments with his famous speech, beginning "Our revels now are ended" (148f). The spirits dissolve just as the masque did, but from that Prospero makes his well-known generalization about human life, "We are such stuff/ As dreams are made on; and our little life/ Is rounded with a sleep" (156–58). This metatheatrical moment calls attention to the metaphysics and aesthetic experience of drama. The politics of ingratitude, which Caliban and Antonio represent for Prospero, break in on the theatrical illusion but do so in the self-conscious space of the theater.

After Miranda and Ferdinand have gone, Ariel enters and says that he did not want to anger Prospero by mentioning Caliban. Ariel left Caliban and his cohorts up to their chins in a foul lake and in their conspiracy. Prospero dismisses the idea of Caliban as "A devil, a born devil, on whose nature/ Nurture can never stick" (188–89). He thinks that the outward decline of his body reflects the inward decline of his mind. There is now great dissension among the three conspirators, and even Stephano has begun to threaten Caliban. Caliban wants Stephano to kill Prospero, but his would-be king is drawn to what his monster knows to be a trashy wardrobe. It is as if Stephano and Trinculo cannot measure up to Caliban. Prospero and Ariel drive the three conspirators out. Prospero wants them to feel pain, and he reminds Ariel one more time that he will soon be free (264–65).

The pain and endurance, not to mention the loyalty of Ariel, can be forgotten, especially if the play is made into a strictly postcolonial allegory, for he becomes a *vendu,* a member of a colonial class that sold his independence for comfort. But to feel empathy for Caliban, Trinculo and Stephano, even as the play is ridiculing them on the surface and structurally, does not mean that a multiple and ambivalent reading of Ariel cannot also occur. The friction of the imperatives of the genre of comedy/romance, which move toward rewarding Ariel and punishing Caliban, against the political content engenders a more intricate view of the play. Further, within the politics, there is the authority of Prospero that the play is establishing with the colonial critique that Montaigne and others make and that is taken up in a later context and a different shape by postcolonial theory. It is easy to allegorize out of existence the close examples I am presenting here. One of the reasons I have incorporated *explication de texte* into my reading is to show the ambivalence, contradiction and messiness of *The Tempest* in the context of other works. In western culture Columbus and Shakespeare read each other even if neither men could read each other. They are great figures in the landscape and that is why so much is at stake. It is, however, always best to seek out as much evidence as possible, even when it embarrasses each of our own arguments. Contradiction is dramatic; so is ambivalence, which is very close to dramatic irony. Messiness may be another critical metaphor but I am using it because of the rage for order in comedy and in allegory. One of the things I am saying is that sometimes there is unresolved friction and that something does not quite fit in an interpretation, including in my own reading. This unfit or unfitted reading allows some room to breathe.

V

Prospero's control and the order of the play or of comedy/romance more generally is something that can be called into question. Critics of Shakespeare, beginning with Boas in the 1890s and developing with W. W. Lawrence in the 1930s, found some of Shakespeare's comic dramas to be problem comedies or problem plays, perhaps taking the term from some of Bernard Shaw's social plays. After Romanticism and the French and American Revolutions, and to some extent even after the Reformation, the established order was thrown into doubt. Order itself, from the point of view of content and politics, especially in the 1960s, was a value to be challenged. The structure of comedy moves from an old order through chaos or a challenge to that order to a new order that incorporates some of the elements of that challenge. Unless an interpretation of a comedy is anti-comic, order cannot be thrown out entirely. In this discussion of the end of *The Tempest* I would like to follow the logic of the order Shakespeare gives to his romance through Prospero.

The fifth and final act shows Prospero in control as he had planned. Ariel tells him about Alonso and his other prisoners and says that Gonzalo's tears have moved him and should therefore move Prospero, who is human. The magician orders his spirit to release his prisoners from the spell. Alone, Prospero chronicles his power as a magician and concludes: "But this rough magic/ I here abjure;" he says he will break his staff and drown his book (V.i.50–57). Ariel brings Alonso and the others to Prospero, and he notes how the charm dissolves. The nub of Prospero's meditation is the loyalty of Gonzalo and the unnaturalness of his own brother Antonio, who resembles Caliban in this: "I do forgive thee,/ Unnatural though thou art" (78–79). This act of forgiveness is spoken for the benefit of Prospero and the audience because Antonio is still spell-bound. Prospero will dress as he did as Duke of Milan (86). Politics lie behind his art of magic.

Ariel sings while attiring him in ducal dress. Prospero says he will miss Ariel and promises him freedom once more. The last bit of magical business that Prospero wants Ariel to perform is to awaken the crew and bring them to him. Gonzalo and Alonso wake to Prospero, dressed as the Duke of Milan. Understandably, Alonso is confused whether Prospero is an apparition or the person himself, but he gives up Milan's tribute. Here is the ultimate recognition scene, in which Alonso asks pardon for his wrongs (112–19). Prospero's generous welcome yields to his reproach for his brother, Antonio, who is blind to recognition of his faults and does not answer or make amends (129–34). But Alonso deflects the confrontation by asking Prospero to tell his story (134). The greatest moment of dramatic irony occurs in this scene. Alonso has lost his son, and Prospero says he has lost his daughter. The audience knows his double meaning: Alonso does not. He wishes that they were both alive to be King and Queen of Naples. Prospero will not tell his story in full "For 'tis a chronicle of day by day,/ Not a relation for a breakfast, nor/ Befitting this first meeting" (163–65). When speaking about the recovery of his dukedom, Prospero uncovers the final piece in the comic *cogito*, or discovery. As the stage direction indicates, "he *discovers* FERDINAND *and* MIRANDA *playing at chess*" (171). This game of chess as moment of recognition is wonderful theater and is also a romance motif. Like the resurrection of Hermione in *The Winter's Tale*, this scene is, as Sebastian says, "A most high miracle!" (176). More than the similar scene in *The Winter's Tale*, this scene involves two-way recognition. Alonso learns that Ferdinand is alive, but the son also sees that the father still lives. And Miranda discovers her "brave new world," even if it is new to her and not to Prospero (183–84). Ferdinand and Gonzalo, who says he is speechless with inward weeping, claim that it is Providence that has brought Miranda and Ferdinand together.

Gonzalo summarizes the comic triumph of this romance. Through this good counsellor, Shakespeare represents, for the characters if not for the audience, the comic catastrophe, how events driving toward tragedy reverse themselves to a happy ending:

> Was Milan thrust from Milan, that his issue
> Should become King of Naples? O, rejoice
> Beyond a common joy! and set it down
> With gold on lasting pillars: in one voyage
> Did Claribel her husband find at Tunis,
> And Ferdinand, her brother, found a wife
> Where he himself was lost, Prospero his dukedom
> In a poor isle, and all of us ourselves
> When no man was his own.

(205–13)

Alonso and Gonzalo bless the much-blessed couple as if to amplify the blessings of Prospero and Juno and Ceres in the masque. But Shakespeare keeps his lightness of touch by having Gonzalo confront the foul-mouthed Boatswain, who arrives after an absence since the first scene of the play. The Boatswain ignores the confrontation and is glad to see his king safe. The chaos, which began with the storm that made him question the use of his ruler and the counsellor on deck, is over. In asides that punctuate this part of the scene, Prospero praises Ariel's work. In response to the Boatswain's wondrous tale about what happened to the crew in the storm, Alonso gives another perspective on events: "This is as strange a maze as e'er men trod;/ And there is in the business more than nature/ Was ever conduct of" (242–44). He asks for an oracle to make all clear, and Prospero says he will later give every detail of events.

The final loose end is the three rebels, Caliban, Stephano and Trinculo. Ariel drives these drunkards on stage. After Sebastian and Antonio return to their sardonic repartee (this time on these three) as if nothing happened, Prospero tells of Caliban's origins and how he plotted to take Prospero's life (263–74). This parodic Saturnalia must have an end. In a kind of comic accommodation, but with some political tensions in our day, Prospero says of the three drunken plotters: "Two of these fellows you/ Must know and own; this thing of darkness I/ Acknowledge mine" (274–76). Prospero is probably referring to darkness as evil because he has called him "this demi-devil " (V.i.272), but some critics, like E. K. Chambers, have thought that Prospero is referring to Caliban's skin.[28] Despite Prospero's assertion that Caliban's ill shape reflects his ill manners, he sees that Caliban looks "To have my pardon" (293). Perhaps as part of the logic of the comic ending of romance, which may be generally seen as part of general comedy, Caliban asks forgiveness and seems to be assimilated into the comic triumph. He will obey Prospero and go promptly to his cell: "and I'll be wise hereafter,/ And seek for grace. What a thrice-double ass/ Was I, to take this drunkard for a god,/ And worship this dull fool!" (294–97). The comic imperative can also allow Sebastian, who was part of Antonio's plot to kill Alonso and Gonzalo, to correct Alonso, who asks the three drunkards to take their luggage, saying that they stole it. Prospero invites everyone to his cell to rest for a night and to hear the story of his life. Unlike the end of *Cymbeline,* where Shakespeare represents a long narrative to enlighten the characters about events the audience already knows, here the narrative is but a promise for the future. In the morning Prospero hopes to go to Naples, to see the nuptial solemnized and give every third thought to his grave. Alonso continues to do what he has done in this scene: he speaks of the strangeness of the events, a reminiscent theme of the endings of Shakespearean comedy and romance, something, for instance, much evident in *A Midsummer Night's Dream* : "I long/ To hear the story of your life, which must/ Take the ear strangely"

(311–13). Once again, Prospero promises to "deliver all" and he hopes for good winds. His last act is to set Ariel free (313–18).

But of course that is how the body of the play ends. The Epilogue, which Prospero speaks, is famous for his request that the audience set him free from the island through its applause. The breath of the audience in his extended metaphor will blow his ship and make his project succeed, because his magic has left him. Prospero is out of character and out of magic. He needs the audience's mercy and prayer to be free him from his faults. His last two lines are *"As you from crimes would pardon'd be/, Let your indulgence set me free"* (19–20). This is metatheatrical pleading along the lines of Rosalind's Epilogue at the end of *As You Like It.*

Here is the imperfect perfection beyond the bounds of the body of the play: the audience rounds off the illusion of drama with a mediation back into the world. I have tried to take the middle way and look at the intertwined themes of romance and politics, the two allegories of Shakespeare's art and taking leave and of the politics of colonizer and colonized. These two allegories, especially Shakespeare's return to Stratford, are understandable ways of reading the need for pardon in the play and in the Epilogue. But as an audience, we have to remember that we too have faults, aesthetic and political, for which we need pardon and understanding.

VI

Here, I wish to return to the comparison of the three rulers, Henry V, Duke Vincentio and Prospero, who served as examples of characters who exerted the control of Providence or dramatic irony in the plays. Each of these plays enacts a kind of control of subversion or critical questioning of the authority of the ruler. When Henry catches Williams through disguise and dramatic irony, the soldier proclaims in IV.viii: "Your majesty came not as yourself." Although Vincentio says he forgives Lucio's slanders, he finds a punishment for them in the last speech of *Measure for Measure,* because "Slandering a prince deserves it." After Prospero pardons Caliban in the last scene of the play, Caliban says, "he will seek for grace" and reproaches himself for being "a thrice-double ass . . . to take this drunkard for a god/ And worship this dull fool!" Even though Caliban admits Prospero's authority, he satirizes his own mistakes for taking these lesser Europeans for gods, a motif, without this realization and irony, that Columbus, Jacques Cartier and others repeat. Each of these plays has a movement toward triumph and order, like comedy itself, but this structural imperative, complicated by epilogues in *Henry V* and *The Tempest,* coexists with an order that is also rhetorical. By this I mean the relation between writer and audience through the expression of the characters. How much Shakespeare's audience accepted the authority of these player kings and differentiated them from actual monarchs is difficult to say, but those who receive the play do not end with the playwright's contemporaries. The ruler like Prospero who reasserted his order might believe in the roles they played, as the speaker in Sonnet 55 noted, that "your praise shall still find room/ Even in the eyes of all posterity/ That wear this world out to the ending doom." The audience might insist on its judgment until the Last Judgment, but that is a projection that could not predict the shifts and revolution of the times.

For over 100 years, some critics have questioned the comic imperative of the ending of *Measure* partly because they see an abuse in Vincentio's power; after World War One some critics began to read *Henry V* as ironic and the eponymous king's authority as questionable—even if Olivier's great film did play the king as a hero from E. M. W. Tillyard's hero of epic English history before the onslaught of Hitler's forces—and this critical view gained ground in and from the 1950s; and from that period, Caliban became the focus of liberational and anti-colonial readings of *The Tempest*. The "eyes of posterity," then, constitutes one of the reasons for interpretative friction between aesthetics and political allegory, between the imperial theme and the opposition to empire. In this intricate space between then and now, aesthetics and politics, Shakespeare, unable to know the future except as a projection or shade of the past, inserts a couplet that catches us as an audience of his time and other times, like ours: "As you from crimes would pardon'd be,/ Let your indulgence set me free." This is a historical sense: the present knows that the past is different and can and cannot judge it the same way. We the audience are judged as we judge Prospero. Even with a pardon it is a long way from crimes to freedom, and the more the audience feels in the metatheatrical estrangement of the Epilogue superior to Prospero, or Caliban for that matter, as its members return to the world, the more it deludes itself and blinds itself from the errors of its own aesthetics and politics.

It is possible that in regarding this play of cultural appropriation and colonialism, the postmodern and postcolonial sensibilities that imbue the turn from the twentieth century appropriate and colonize in some ways that we are, by definition, blind to, so that the cultures of past and present are in an inbetween state of flux. Some of the ironies that define interpretation are historical. In the thematics of the present, the father-daughter relation between Prospero and Miranda, the class divisions between the sailors and their governors and between Stephano and Trinculo and their masters, the family strife between Prospero and his brother all qualify the master-slave dialectic—to return to the nineteenth-century with Hegel, between Prospero and his servants, Ariel and Caliban. Language, which has poetic and ideological power, and Shakespeare's language, which concentrates and intensifies this power, both in expression and reception, haunt the speech and signs of imperial expansion and cultural conflict. Beauty and force, in the hope of grace and in the service of profit, dwell in tension, perhaps never quite reaching synthesis except in a dialectical dream. Romance is a familiar form in travel literature, in epics like Homer's *Odyssey* and in accounts that claim historical truth, like those by Marco Polo and John de Mandeville, so that *The Tempest* is in good company in the shadowlands between fiction and truth, the story in history. This is a play that does not claim to be about Bermuda but is often taken to be in a typological reversal between the Old World and New World. If Jean de Léry, Montaigne and the translators of Las Casas could have what happened in the Americas also "be" in Europe, either potentially or actually through typological analogy or imagination, then why not Shakespeare in this play? *The Tempest* is temporarily colonial or imperial even if it is actually in the Mediterranean, and the contemporary shipwreck in Bermuda (and the slight allusion to that island) gives the play an American dimension that it inscribes and effaces. Granting that, it is a highly aesthetic work of an apparent simplicity wrought from the most intricate materials. The enactment and reenactment of Shakespeare's drama restages the tension between the seduction of aesthetics and the drive of politics in changing contexts. Shakespeare's island, like Bermuda, has been revisited and resettled since the first shipwrecked figures left its shores, people and characters left to the script in fiction and archives, being what they are in words but also subject to the shifting winds of interpretation. No one and no words really possess the island or the wake even as they represent them. A little like Columbus' Hispaniola.

Chapter 7 〜

Cultural Appropriation:
Colonialism and Postcolonialism

Changes in historical circumstance, for instance the growth of English then British then American economic, political and linguistic power affected the translation of Shakespeare's imperial theme and has become another "chapter" in the translation of empire. Like Columbus, Shakespeare has been and is appropriated by those who would explore, affirm and resist empire. Sometimes 1492 and 1611, or any significant dates in the early modern expansion of Europe, seem remote. The various celebrations and, later, commemorations of the anniversary of Columbus' landfall—the last great burst being in 1992—provide a reminder that the present is always past and that the postcolonial contains the colonial in many senses. The postcolonial here will be something opened up and not something discussed mainly in and of itself. Perhaps, as Terry Eagleton recently suggested, "It is remarkable how hard it is to find an unabashed enthusiast for the concept among those who promote it."[1] Colonialism involved self-critique and contradiction so that a study that comes after colonialism in both senses might well be expected to exhibit some of the same tendencies. Interpretation of Shakespeare's *The Tempest,* as we observed in the last chapter, had become in recent decades as much a part of a movement from colonialism to postcolonialism as a Romantic aspect of Shakespeare's farewell to his art that many previous generations had garnered from the play. The questions of cultural and intellectual property make this imperial past more immediate. Who speaks for whom? and Who tends to or owns what? are questions that still reverberate. This chapter will help to draw this study, which has ranged from Columbus through Shakespeare and beyond, to a close and will, I hope, suggest that types and shadows have and have not their endings. While focusing here on appropriation, I will suggest that context prevents closure and that this sense of an ending, to borrow Frank Kermode's phrase, will be open.[2]

The focus of this chapter will be on setting out what cultural appropriation is and its role in imperialism, colonialism and postcolonialism. As this topic is vast, perhaps the most effective strategy is to provide one possible map of this role or relation.[3] One of my primary concerns here will be the colonial in the postcolonial and the story in history, exploring the fictions and properties where culture and law meet. Cultures cross and get cross or crossed over in contact, exchange, encounter and invasion. Being self-possessed and being possessed, as person and nation, and the properties of culture, land, body and thought, is not a seamless continuum over time or in various places.

Sometimes, as we saw in chapter 5, people and peoples are caught between cultures: this betweenness can lead to new potential or scapegoating, or both. Hybridity, *métissage* and creolization might be cause for utopian hope but also for a concern over contradiction: there is a narrow, shifting and invisible line between ambuiguity and ambivalence. Sometimes in periods of stress or crisis the two-way or multivalent become one-way and the rules set into conformity. The question of survival can close the very openness that made certain cultures so vital. What about our cultures in Europe, North America and elsewhere and what of the former colonies of European empires and adjacent countries affected by the most recent, but not the only forms, of imperialism? Cultural appropriation becomes something lived with and to live with as well as something studied and to study.

A residual function of what follows will be to suggest ways in which the history of colonialism also bears significantly on making a property of someone else's culture in a world that calls itself postcolonial, and the resistance to that practice. To separate postcolonialism from its context would be to leave out part of the story. Imperialism is about the expansion of political property through the acquisition of colonies. That colonization involves setting up the cultural example of the imperial center while that center also appropriates aspects of the colonized cultures officially and unofficially. In the wake of empire and in the migration of peoples that has happened, especially in the twentieth century in the "postcolonial" period, the debate on what constitutes cultural appropriation by the dominant culture has become an important concern in multicultural societies. These societies in the West are most often the imperial centers, their colonies in the Americas and Australia, New Zealand and South Africa.

Cultural appropriation becomes a question of cultural rights and difference and enriches or makes problematic, depending on the view, the possibility of community. Can all the claims of different cultures find expression in a community or nation? Perhaps the postmodern and postcolonial nation finds its greatest hope in such expression. None the less, some views show anxieties that the controversy over cultural appropriation reflects fault lines in contemporary multicultural societies that will lead to ethnic conflicts like those in the former Soviet Union and Yugoslavia. In keeping with the framework of the study as a whole, this chapter will set out some of the ambivalences, contradictions, conflicts and contours of the topic in its historical and cultural contexts and will continue to imply that all of us, then and now, are implicated in these dilemmas and paradoxes that have material as well as textual implications.

I

Some general remarks about cultural appropriation should help to set out the shape of the debate. Before proceeding, let me give working definitions of key terms that this chapter will use, to come to terms with the speech and signs of colonialism and postcolonialism. "Cultural appropriation" is a debate over whether speaking for others or representing them in fictional as well as legal, social, artistic and political work is appropriate or proper, especially when individuals or groups with more social, economic and political power perform this role for others without invitation.[4] Appropriating culture probably occurred before human records but has also been a function of "tribal," national and imperial expansion.

Something about cultural appropriation raises anxiety. The upset can take the form of worry over cultural negotiations, wanted and unwanted, over general issues of race and gender or specific examples like arts funding and music. "Between cultures" is not simply about Native and European groups coming to terms with each other in the wake of Columbus, but is something that occurs even still. The controversy over rap music in the United States, where the record companies, the artists and the groups calling for censorship have collided. Should White American record executives profit from a music that exploits tensions and violence in the Black community, or are Black artists using these outlets as vehicles for wealth and free expression? The anxiety in debates over culture and who owns it, who gets to speak and who gets to listen, is frequently political in nature: the people involved in the debate often take the matter personally.

"Culture" and "appropriation" are notoriously complex terms. This chapter is no place to rehearse this intricate history, so, instead, it offers working definitions. Culture is the material, spiritual and artistic expression of a group, which defines itself or which others define as a culture, both in its daily lived experience and in a longer historical view, that is according to practice and theory. Culture is and is not self-conscious: some group must identify it. Appropriation is making what belongs to another or a different group into the property of another individual or group. It is making something else proper to oneself. That something can be tangible or intangible property. The appropriating can be achieved through ventriloquy, translation or the dispossession of lands and other property.[5] It can be figurative or literal. Cultural appropriation occurs when a member of one culture takes as his or her property a cultural practice or theory of a member of another culture as if it were his or her own or as if the right of possession should not be questioned or contested. This same appropriation can happen between groups as groups. The debate over cultural appropriation is a matter of whether the term describes anything that exists, or, if it does exist, is it harmful?

Two opposing views should help to focus the debate: a dominant cultural view that all cultures should be available to us and a marginal view that minorities should speak for themselves because the "majority" has misrepresented them. At the heart of the discussion is artistic and intellectual freedom in relation to cultural integrity and who obtains what funding or other resources in the production of art, thought and culture. The "dominant" position is an aesthetic and political argument, claiming that those who proclaim cultural appropriation as an ill to guard against would limit artistic freedom.[6] Moral grounds take precedence over aesthetic grounds in the "marginal" counterscheme. This view is that more minority voices are needed in the debate on cultural appropriation. These positions can potentially share some middle ground in their differences: the need to understand and consider carefully minority cultures. This conclusion, which comes from members of the dominant cultural group, is designed to be sensitive to different cultures in a multicultural and postcolonial society. Often this debate occurs about minorities without minority participation and can itself be a form of ventriloquy and cultural appropriation. In other words, the debate embodies itself. Whether it is possible to prevent one culture from assimilating ideas and culture from its own interpretations of another culture, rather than from representations of minority cultures by members of those cultures, is an open question. Who can represent whom is an intricate epistemological and ontological problem. In part, it hinges on experience.

In keeping with the last chapter, which centered on *The Tempest,* it might be suggestive to focus for a moment on this mutuality, and mutual, suspicion of cultural exchange, in terms of appropriation in and of Shakespeare, a forbear of my own cultural "group." Could William Shakespeare alone represent himself? What would that do to the Shakespeare industry around the world in various cultures and languages? Should other cultures be allowed to represent him? Certainly, in the early phases of postcolonial writing and critique people of many linguistic, racial and ethnic groups adapted Shakespeare to write back against the European empires that had, until so recently, governed them. The Japanese built a reproduction of Shakespeare's Globe Theatre before the "English" did. Can the English today, who are culturally different from their ancestors, bridge the difference of time and interpret Shakespeare? What is the difference between the interpretation that goes into writing, reading and critique? Should Shakespeare have tried to represent ancient Greeks, Egyptians and Romans or, in later history, the French, Italians, British, Moors and others, or should he have limited himself to stories about his boyhood in Stratford? Perhaps Shakespeare's era bounds his potential cultural appropriations: he did live at a time before theories of historical difference had taken hold or when copyright law prevailed. Through historical imagination, it is possible to see that the postmodern period will possess certain concerns over the debate on representation (or *mimesis*) and that subsequent ages will take different views of the question.

The debate on cultural appropriation needs to be encouraged as a sign of freedom rather than a screaming across the abyss. It would be hypocritical of the dominant culture to assert totalitarianism while shutting down debate over the issue. In the debate over the appropriation of the "Other," even the putatively transverbal world of music is now debated.[7] This political debate over appropriation tries to implicate even the putatively apolitical spheres of instrumental music and lyric poetry. The drama of Shakespeare, the symphonic music of Beethoven and the lyric-driven rhythms of rap all turn into points of friction in multicultural societies. If an Asian American is a great pianist, does she avoid Beethoven because of his European origins and because she does not want to appropriate European culture, or, for historical and political reasons, is it necessary to redress the inequities of cultural exchange in the past? It is patronizing not to consider how other cultures used and use "Western" cultures. It's only the arrogance and insecurity of "Western" countries that have led to the stating of the obvious: Chinese and European cultures, both ancient and rich, meet in the Americas partly through this musician. Chinese and European cultures have also developed important technological breakthroughs, but technology is one aspect of culture even if it has driven dominance and empire. Technical development might be inversely proportionate to cultural development. Some of the most complex cultures have only recently begun industrial and technological development. In speaking of cultural appropriation, it is necessary to complicate the debate with specific examples and with history and then to proceed with some caution. This is a world where each country contains uneven "development," so to talk about "post" this and that is only one part of the story.

II

Postmodernism is not the first instance of a period and method that made connections between law and the commodification of culture. Long before colonies and modernism, culture was a commodity. The pots and knifes of everyday culture, however much their decoration and ornament appeal to us now as art, were useful in daily work and as objects of trade. Perhaps only the split between high art and craft, which is comparatively recent in Western culture, created this notion of the commodification of art. Nineteenth-century theories of alienation from labor, such as Marx's, might have romanticized farm labor and some pastoral era before industrialization. As horrific as the industrial revolution was—the working and living conditions in Salford, Manchester and elsewhere, the use of child labor and the mortality rates attest to this horror—to think that the serf, peasant and tenant farmers in England and Continental Europe felt fulfillment in, and control over, their labor, is a kind of pastoralism. This fall and return to Eden—even in its secular forms—has biblical and theological antecedents, such as Saint Augustine. There was a gap between the desire for wholeness and the hard particulars of existence long before Marx, capitalism and the industrial revolution. It is also the case, however, that colonialism and postcolonialism present particular instances of alienation and commodification.

The politics of postmodernism and postcolonialism have uncertain and multiple valences. Similar techniques and forms in theory and practice can be used for opposite political ends. "Postmodernism" assumes the recycling of writing and history, "postcolonialism" a movement, at least politically, beyond the colony as the empire's property. If utopian vision beyond the old properties of politics and history resides in these two "post" terms, a presumption and triumphalism, which characterized imperial narratives and themes, might also threaten to make problematic these after-discourses. Before suggesting that the ancient question of property underwrites the rhetoric of cultural appropriation, I want to use cross-cultural terms and images to unsettle the relation between colonizer and colonized that is often represented in colonial and postcolonial studies.

In a time when the prefix "post" is everywhere, as if our period were epochal or apocalyptic, it is important in the arts, humanities and social sciences to examine self-consciously this urge to be beyond or after in technique or time and to analyze and complicate the intellectual property of terms like postcolonialism. There are days when I think that postmodernism is not just another aftermath and that postcolonialism is as intricate as quipu. In speaking about cultural appropriation I use "aftermath" and "quipu" as a means of showing the stress between the nostalgic essentialism of identity politics and the displaced hybridity, if not hybrid displacement, of words and art. "Aftermath" is literally grass growing after the harvest, and I use this agrarian image in counterpoint, to emphasize the urbanity of this age after the modern. Quipu (ke-poo), which is an image from the ancient history of the "New World" and involves a metonymy for writing, should represent something from the past that complicates the already complex world of postcolonial studies. The ancient Peruvians used quipu as a substitute for writing/recording by variously knotting threads of various colors.[8] As etymology shows, English is a language that is built on cultural appropriation. To use this language, like so many others, especially in this age of rapid travel and information exchange, is to bear witness, consciously or not, to culture as a commodity to be traded, fairly and freely or not. Words and names become a form of displacement. Place-names are especially revealing in this regard. In this so-called New World or the Americas, it is often a practice for the descendants of Europeans to use aboriginal names like Mexico and Canada for the places they live in while obliterating others. It is difficult to know whether such investment and divestment of indigenous names is systematic or situational. It is possible that the theft or borrowing returns as a reminder of what has been stolen from the other culture. There is a history that returns with lands, names, images and ideas. The quipu can and cannot be appropriated in the alphabetic world of English.

The borrowings, lendings and enforcement of property may be an idea that owes too much to the development of Western law, whether through the biblical tradition of the Jews or the laws of Greek and Roman law-givers like Solon and Justinian, or more vernacular and national versions that King John or Napoleon may have devised. Thou shalt not steal. Let the peers decide. Guilty before proven innocent. From physical property the idea of cultural property develops, although the distinction was never so clear. In English-speaking countries the copyright law of 1709 leaves its traces in squabbles over photocopying and the protection of individual, if not group, intellectual property.[9]

Cultural appropriation has complex legal dimensions. Property can be intellectual, cultural and physical ("tangible"). The debate over voice or cultural appropriation, in which James Young and John Rowell participated, has implications for other related controversies. For obvious reasons, in a situation where intellectual property has become associated with cultural appropriation, legal judgements, scholarship and theory have made and will make contributions to what we can say about, and do with, culture. Rosemary J. Coombe argues that the models of authorship that dominate Anglo-American laws of copyright are those that incorporate possessive individualism, which is recognized in 1814 under the influence of Romanticism—authors can find plots, characters and themes from others as long as they do not copy another's expression.[10] For Coombe, the cultural essentialism and possessive individualism (the latter being a central concern for C. B. Macpherson) of this tradition, which define legal categories of property, do not account for the forms the Natives in Canada employ to seek recognition.[11] Western histories of colonialism and imperialism do not consider Native ideas of identity, authenticity and culture, and in this view societies, like Canada, need new conceptual and legal tools to accommodate the needs of Natives in a postcolonial and postmodern world.[12] Cultural borrowing, then, needs to be understood in its historical context. For Natives, ecology, spirit and territory are part of the culture in cultural appropriation.[13] Aboriginal title, as Loretta Todd contends, represents "the term under which we negotiate with the colonizers . . . which asserts a reality that existed before Native peoples were positioned as Other."[14] In response to Todd, Coombe says that non-Natives should comprehend the contingency and historical specificity of their laws, especially their implication in colonialism and imperialism. Essentialism and individualism are not the only properties of culture, so Aboriginal title presents a new possibility.[15] The structure of the law precludes recognizing claims based in culture, as Amanda Pask argues—the law must not continue to wish for the disappearance of cultural difference but should respond to those, like the Natives, who are culturally different,[16] so that the ultimate problem of cultural appropriation arises from a failure to acknowledge other ways of doing things.[17] The law is another systematic textual, epistemological, conceptual and material means of perpetuating stereotypes and of continuing to colonize those who would refuse colonization. A postcolonial law would attempt to find other ways and incorporate alternate cultural traditions.

In my view, there might also be an excavation of legal history to understand the religious and secular reasons given to the settlement of the New World. The papal bulls and the treaties between the Portuguese and the Spanish dividing up the colonial world in the fifteenth and sixteenth centuries and the subsequent French, English and Dutch challenges to them, especially the notion of *terra nullius* or "unoccupied" lands, might provide ways in which to include alternative laws from other traditions. The specific historical intentions of the European popes, monarchs, advisors and colonizers will show dissention from within nations, and rivalries between them.[18] As we observed earlier in the book, the famous debate between Brother Bartolomé de Las Casas and Juan Ginés de Sepúlveda for the benefit of the Spanish king over Aristotle's concept of natural slavery and whether it applied to the aboriginal inhabitants of the New World demonstrates the dissention from within. The creation of the Black Legend, which the French, English and Dutch based in large part on Las Casas' denunciation of Spanish treatment of the Natives after Columbus, illustrates the rivalry between European nations and still has resonances in our culture through Montaigne, Rousseau and others. Later treaties and laws in Spanish, Portuguese, British and French America, especially in the new nations in the Western hemisphere from the late eighteenth century onward, will probably receive increasing legal scrutiny. In Canada, like Australia, this reassessment has taken and will take the form of land claims.[19]

In Australia the High Court judgments of the Mabo case, published in June 1992, involved Eddie Mabo's complaint that the state of Queensland's annexation of the Torres Strait in 1879 had not legally extinguished his customary ownership of a part of Murray Island that his family passed on to him. The nature of Native title in Australian law and the judgement in favor of Mabo have brought about a reinterpretation of sovereignty and common law. In the Coe case of 1979 the High Court had interpreted sovereignty in terms of international law and had therefore ruled Coe's challenge to the sovereignty of the Australian state over the continent to be outside its jursidiction. In the Mabo case the judges found the common law to be within their jurisdiction. Concerning the Mabo case, two judges of the High Court of Australia, Justice Sir William Deane and Justice Mary Gaudron, do not, according to Tim Rowse, "dispute the historical persistence of a doctrine of *terra nullius* in our judicial culture; rather, they question the quality of legal reasoning which has allowed it to become doctrine."[20] The High Court was split over a nation based on legal tradition and one based on an imagined moral community. In the Australian legal system the doctrine of *terra nullius* was confirmed in 1979 and rejected in 1992.[21] As I have argued, the colonial persisted in the postcolonial: perhaps the postcolonial reinterpreted the colonial. In Australia, as in the Americas, the legacy of Portuguese and Spanish expansion, which was also to be found in the empires like those of Britain, France and the Netherlands, was being reinterpreted in the years leading up to the five-hundredth anniversary of Columbus' landfall. The relation between settler and aboriginal cultures was being redefined in the courts. What is property and what is appropriation have become central questions in history, literary theory, ethnology and other disciplines beyond the law.

Some of the questions that arose in this phase of a debate that we have seen occurred on a philosophical, theological and legal level in the first six decades of the Spanish empire in the Americas persist today. These problems apply to the clashes of cultures beyond the experience of European expansion. A culture has to have a home and some resources and property to protect itself. The reparations of war and invasion have occurred in international law, but where does one stop going back in history? In terms of cultural appropriation, can we connect the Norman invasion, the spread of Islam into Northern Africa and southern Europe, the European invasion of the New World and the Chinese invasion of Tibet? What time limitations and doctrine of reparations and natural justice could the law develop in these clash of cultures? The law bears some relation to the society it represents, so how can we expect an international law that takes into account all these cultures? The notion of what is legal and what is just is something discussed in Western philosophy since Plato, but these ideas change over time. Aristotle's idea of natural slavery is a kind of natural justice that no one in Western culture, let alone other cultures, would endorse in the early twenty-first century. In the multicultural nation new systems of law might supplement the dominant legal system, but not without difficulty. Given the stakes, however, such an attempt is worthwhile.

Cultural appropriation through law is only one aspect of culture as property. Culture has long become a commodity. Traditionally, cultural exchange has followed trade routes. But the weight of culture is more than simply the balance or imbalance of trade. In practical arts, like pottery, where yesterday's urn is today's art, this commodification has long been the case, but in more abstract matters of the mind or spirit, the division between use and ornament is less clear. Techniques and ideas have crossed borders and followed trade routes for thousands of years. When anyone confronts European colonizers with the metaphor or political argument of cultural appropriation, is he or she using European concepts to criticize European colonial practices, or have Europeans obscured various traditions of intellectual or cultural property or of property law? Is it possible that the colonized are appropriating European culture to criticize it? Perhaps European intellectuals are taking up alternative or oppositional techniques from within their tradition to oppose European or Western imperialism past and present. Quite possibly, they are also ventriloquizing indigenous peoples and other colonized peoples as a means of activating change now.

It would be misguided to think that any useful answer to these questions can be simple or extreme. The mixing of cultures has always brought about such forms of resistance and ventriloquy, but whether cultural appropriation might also enact mediation and understanding is a problem worth considering in the context of postcolonialism and postmodernism. Even that objective is probably too large. It is more likely that I can set out a typology of cultural appropriation in that context that might be suggestive of the possibility of dialogue and mediation between various groups. While saying that, I am not denying resistance and repression. On the whole, however, I will focus on a typology of appropriation and not on the ethical wish of its utopian form. Whereas elsewhere I have discussed postcolonialism and postmodernism more generally, the rest of this chapter will discuss these matters strictly in relation to appropriation.

The body of this book began with Columbus: from his initial projections on the indigenous peoples he encountered at the first landfall, something that would have been difficult for any of us to avoid, the Americas have been a place where Europeans have read their signs on the Natives, displaced them and celebrated and mourned that displacement. The aboriginal peoples have long spoken up against being signs in that interpretation and their voices seem to be heard increasingly. Appropriation has been going on since the first meetings of cultures in war and peace, somewhere beyond the reach of the archive in the realms of pre-history, paleontology and anthropology. The search for origins can create myths and nostalgia among researchers.

In exploring cultural appropriation it is easy to devise a nostalgia or be sublimated in a utopia, forgetting in an imagined past and future what's difficult here and now. Who gets to say who owns what and for how long is a sobering question beside the human yearnings for the golden age and the promised land, the union of individual and community, unity without uniformity. For whatever reason, the mirages vanish and others take their place. Somehow the teleological urgings of Christianity and Marxism sometimes become circular, the future becomes the past and the past the future in a present that is never quite present. Dramatizations and self-dramatizations, explorations of individual and cultural identity recur in essays on postcolonialism and on cultural appropriation. Self-conscious examination and problematization are two strategies in facing these terms and the debates they represent.[22]

Perhaps it is difficult for writers on this topic to avoid being part of a Criollo effect, that is resembling the Spanish-American elite who identified with the Indians they had

displaced as a means of differentiating themselves from Spain and Europe and of de-
claring their cultural independence.[23] These problems can be dilemmas that are not, by
definition, easily solved. The problems I am about to examine arise in postcolonial studies in two contexts, first, in the colonial and postcolonial and, second, in European history and its representations of the translation of empire. Here, I would like to make
some more basic comments that might help in thinking about cultural appropriation
and the relation between colonialism and postcolonialism. Issues of cultural appropriation in a postcolonial world, as my study as a whole would suggest, benefit from an
awareness of elements in the classical cultural background of *translatio imperii,* or the
translation of empire, and the development of European colonies in the "New World"
during the early modern period. One area of this debate is Europeans and their descendants in their former colonies speaking for non-Europeans.

<h1 style="text-align:center">III</h1>

Cultural appropriation is a central facet of colonialism. In discussing the background to
the appropriation of culture and to colonization, one aspect is particularly important:
translatio imperii, or the translation of empire. This classical myth of the western movement of empire from Greece involves later European appropriations of the myth of empire and the "civilization" of the barbarian. As I think that colonialism has to be
understood before postcolonialism can be more fully understood—one of the main
premises of this book—I would like to turn to a few classical, medieval and early modern instances of the trope of *translatio imperii* or the translation of empire. Perhaps even
this brief sketch will testify that if by moving back to Conrad's representations of empire in *Heart of Darkness* and *Nostromo,* we can, as Edward Said suggests, see our own
relations to present imperialism and the persistence of empire, then by moving forward
from the Greeks we can further that understanding. In *Orientalism* Said himself looked
at the Greek understanding of barbarians, as Anthony Pagden also did in *The Fall of
Natural Man,* as a means of explaining the European views of another culture.[24] The
translation of empire begins for the West in the earliest times and continues today, and
finds critics of empire like Said.

   Increasingly, the opposition from within or alternative critique has developed more
along the lines of what I might call the Essomericq principle.[25] Essomericq was the
Native Paulmier de Gonneville brought back from Brazil in 1504 and whose family,
in 1658, contested paying taxes in France because they were foreigners and their ancestor had wanted to go back to Brazil as Gonneville had promised.[26] It is not as
though the "advance guard" of the imperial centers still kidnap and bring back people from their former colonies or their economic dependencies, but the movements of
people, especially since the Second World War, from colonies and former colonies or
from former colony to former colony (something often overlooked), have created
writers of double and multiple perspectives who are American, Canadian, Australian
or European and something else. They are bilingual or multilingual and are of two or
more cultures. Like Essomericq and his descendents, they are at home and displaced.
Derrida, Said, Spivak, Bhabha and others write an alternative critique that crosses
boundaries and is at home with exile or is exiled at home, perhaps philosophically,
culturally and existentially. Such may be the postmodern and postcolonial condition
for the interpreters of culture, although probably not for most of the people, especially
those living in the former colonies of the European empires. Consciously or not, those

who press for economic expansion, or have a nostalgia for empire or are trying to rewrite the history of European expansion, can reinscribe that history and help to re-produce the future of stereotypes and uneven relations between people and among peoples.

One of the main recurrent imperial themes is the ways in which colonizers, whether they have been the colonized, identify with earlier empires and create a myth of conti-nuity. The colonized justify their transformation into colonizers by appropriating the political and military culture of earlier regimes. This is a vast area that stretches back to the earliest history of the Middle East and Europe and may also apply to other cultures. By appealing to European history, I am focusing on European colonialism, one of the underpinnings of postcolonialism. The connection between postcolonialism and colo-nial expansion from classical to modern periods is often neglected. In such a brief space, all I can do is sketch the Western tradition or trope of *translatio imperii*. This is not something I have seen done anywhere in postcolonial studies. I wish to appeal to the an-cient and early modern as a means of seeing where the rupture might happen in the colonial moment that allows ways of thinking toward a postcolonial state even in the midst of empire and therefore representing a prolepsis to postcolonialism. This reaching back may help to ground the postcolonial and make the postcolonial problematic a lit-tle clearer.

The Athenians were not interested in empire in the sense that Alexander the Great was and that the Romans later were. Greece was a loosely related group of city-states and the Greek world was in many ways a commercial "empire." Anthony Pagden's discussion of barbarism is instructive here. Aristotle discussed the term "barbarian," as did Aquinas and the neo-Aristotelian commentators. The word is, as Pagden notes, unstable as it was applied over time to the Berbers, the Turks, the Sythians, Ethiopians, Irish and Nor-mans, but these uses had one thing in common—"implication of inferiority."[27] The word "barbarian," which was coined in the seventh and sixth centuries B.C., meant for-eigner, including the Egyptians, whom the Greeks respected. By the fourth century B.C., however, it had come to mean, and still means, someone of cultural and mental inferiority. The *barbaros,* for the hellenistic Greeks, meant a babbler who could not speak Greek, someone devoid of the *logos,* of speech and reason. Barbarians lacked *civis* and *polis,* the civil society of the Greek family of humankind, the *oikumene.* The Greeks' failure to admit the *barbaroi* or barbarians into the Hellenistic community was "a denial of their humanity."[28] Aristotle thought that the birds watching over the temple at Di-media were able to differentiate between the Greeks and barbaroi because while the one group had access to the mysteries through the *logos,* the other did not.[29] Although Aris-totle considered the barbarians to be human, he thought that they behaved like beasts, so that the Achaeans and the Heniochi, tribes of the Black Sea, had gone savage and en-joyed human flesh.[30] Cruelty and ferocity, as Pagden says, are the marks of barbarism, and behavior is the key difference between the civilized and the barbarous. The word "civilized" should also provide a clue to the importance of civic and civil life of the city or *polis* to the Greeks who dwelt there first and to the shaping of the views of those peo-ple who lived beyond them. When the barbarians lived in cities, they did so under tyran-nous conditions and devoid of freedom. The idea of the barbarian, as Said and Pagden recognize, is crucial for an understanding of xenophobia, of projections on to others and of imperialism. It is also important for my problematic of translation. Pagden is explicit about this link: "The definition of the word 'barbarian' in terms that were primarily cul-tural rather than racial made its translation to the largely non-Greek speaking Christian world a relatively easy business."[31] Here, the narrative of conversion or of spreading Christian civilization began. In order to pursue translation of empire, there had to be a sense of the civilized world and those barbarians beyond it. Before taking up the Christian notion of a chosen people of the *logos* (appropriated from the Jews), it is also necessary to acknowledge the move from Athens to Rome of the imperial theme.

Although each subsequent empire expressed some anxiety over the influence of the earlier empire, the Romans borrowed from the Greeks and emergent "empires," and European and American nations from medieval and Renaissance onward have incorporated this myth of the translation of empire. Humanism and classicism are partly built on that foundation. Literally, the architecture of the Capitol building in Washington expresses that imperial genealogy. The are hundreds of individual examples of rulers in the West picking up on this trope of the translation of empire.[32] As an illustration, I will continue with the strand of European contact with the Americas.

My contention is that the European contact with America soon revealed that this translation of empire and this assimilation of new peoples into a successor to the Greek and Roman empires would be a difficult if not new balancing act. The Amerindians represented new peoples whom the Europeans knew nothing about. Even though the American experience was novel, many of the Europeans tried, for obvious reasons, to fit the Amerindians and their lands into the framework of European experience. Having discussed Columbus at some length earlier in this study, I shall move on to other figures.

In 1519 Charles of Spain became Emperor Charles the Fifth of the Holy Roman Empire. In 1521 Magellan's voyage around the globe uncovered a world of diverse peoples that the classical chronicler, Eusebius (ca. 263–339), and his successors did not know. Still the idea of a universal Spanish monarchy persisted into the 1700s, a rule in which universal meant European. The universality of the past was not the same as the universality of the future, and this was a problem that the Spanish and Europeans generally had a hard time facing. Peter Martyr (ca. 1455–1526), an Italian humanist, wondered whether the Amerindians were inhabitants of the Golden Age who had escaped corruption as their land had long ago been severed from Europe. Gonzalo Fernández de Oviedo, a leading figure in the promotion of empire, wrote his universal history with an understanding of "empire" in its traditional Mediterranean and Western European meaning and spoke of Charles as being part of a direct line of emperors from Caesar. But Oviedo and colonial administrators and missionaries came to see that the Amerindians had their own traditions. The debate between Las Casas and Sepúlveda over the treatment of the Amerindians represented two ways at incorporating America into European history. Las Casas saw the contact as fulfilling Christian universal history in the conversion of the Indians, who were human and had souls to be saved. Sepúlveda argued for the growth of the Spanish monarchy and empire and did not consider important the conversion of the Indians, whom he thought were not completely human.[33]

Here began European migration on a scale not yet seen. What is remarkable is that the Europeans could not shake the incommensurability of their representations of the "New World" with what they experienced. Although experience and observation modified the image of the Indians of America as being in a state of nature as opposed to civilization, it was hard to give up old ways entirely. There might be understanding and misunderstanding now, but incomprehension persisted in new forms. The Europeans experienced what Pagden has called the problem of recognition.[34] Europeans of each age brought with them a set of expectations. Many of the fantastic natural phenomena, like fauna and satyrs, pygmies, cannibals and Amazons, that the Europeans expected to see in America during the late fifteenth and early sixteenth century came from popular oral tradition via travel writers and scientists from Pliny to John de Mandeville. The specter of a new barbarian raised itself repeatedly in the colonial world.

It is the image of the barbarian projected and the empire translated that postcolonial theorists see in the world then and now. I could go on with hundreds if not thousands of examples, but only a few will make my point. These notions met with resistance within European culture from the earliest times, as we have seen, and continued to be resisted into the present. Vico's cycles moved toward a new barbarism in a *corso* that would be followed a few hundred years later by a *ricorso,* but he thought certain cultures escaped this cycle by experiencing a stop in its development, like the Carthaginians, whom the Romans destroyed, and the American Indians with the coming of the Europeans. Turgot, the *philosophe,* did not care about the coming and going of empires because that pattern did not alter the progress of reason and knowledge.

A large number of examples of myths of imperial translation occur after the Enlightenment as European imperialism expanded at an unprecedented rate. The growth of Russian, German and American power also complicated this expansion of empire. What we have with cultural appropriation is a discussion that arises mainly from the wake of these European empires. As cultural appropriation is tied to empire, are discussions of it as vulnerable as those about empire? In *History of England from the Accession of James II* (1849–61), Thomas Macaulay said something that is a warning to all who write about empire, that those who neglect the art of narration should remember "that histories of great empires, written by men of great ability, lie unread on the shelves of ostentatious libraries."[35] If discourse might have once been underestimated in a Western philosophy dominated by notions of *mimesis* and *reality,* as Derrida, Foucault and other poststructuralist theorists assert, it is possible that it is now over-estimated as a force in the world. This observation applies to what might become an increasing gap between the theory and practice of cultural appropriation. To be moral critics, like Chomsky and Said, is an important but difficult task. The problem for all of us writing on cultural appropriation, colonization, postcolonialism and imperialism is, How does one advocate historical change that recognizes the difference between then and now, the very historicity of experience, and maintain a moral view that has a transhistorical standard that allows such ethical judgement? If we allow for moral progress in history, will our blindnesses not seem foolish to those who come after?[36]

In this debate on cultural appropriation and colonialism, the very nature of syntax, grammar and rhetoric is called into question. Are Portuguese, Spanish, French and English by their very nature agents of appropriation because they are languages of empire (often cannibalizing Latin and Greek as well as, for English, early Germanic) and have absorbed words from other cultures they have conquered? English is an amalgam of the languages of Roman, Germanic and Norman conquerors but also an absorption of the languages of the peoples of the British empire. The cultural property of English involves traces of the colonizer and colonized. From the beginning cultural appropriation seems to be a matter of ambivalence and instability. Language is at the heart of cultural appropriation. Who is speaking and from where? Trinh T. Minh-ha criticizes anthropology as a conversation about us—White men—and them—speechless subjects the "us" group invites to speak about their context.[37] This concern seems legitimate, especially politically, because the imbalance of power between the colonized and colonizer, particularly when they are from very different cultures and have disparate technologies, has been pronounced since the industrial and technical revolutions. Cultural mixing and the sphere of go-betweens, in evidence for centuries and millennia, have complicated this division, so that the we/they split is not as apparent as first appears.

Although my focus in this chapter is not on the relations between Native Americans and Europeans, I use this relation as a background to what is often seen more conventionally as postcolonialism, that is the aftermath of the French and British empires. My rationale is that both empires owed debts to those of Portugal and Spain (not to mention the classical antecedents of Greece and Rome), and that these precedents helped to build much of the imperial strategy in their early relations with the Natives. All the countries of the Americas have a postcolonial dimension that is often denied, particularly in the United States. It is difficult to read about the massacre of the American Indians in the early modern period without a sense of horror. Although more and more indigenous sources are coming to light, the Native side of the story has largely been silent or left to European representations. It is important to shed light on the Native part of the archive to achieve a greater understanding of the history of the European contact and settlement of the Americas.

There will be certain problems. First, the texts often derive from Native texts worked out in a Europeanized grammar of the original language, and Europeans will discuss them in European languages. Many Native groups have lost their languages and use English, French, Spanish and Portuguese or new dialects, which mix European and indigenous languages. Europeans transported African slaves to the New World, and they took the place of American Indians as a source of wealth through enforced labor. American history, which involves Native decimation by European disease and cruelty, affects the language of the Americas. So language fails us: the American Indian nations did not think of their lands as new; nor did they decide to name them after Vespucci. But while granting this political wisdom of not speaking for others from less dominant groups, the desire for responsible political action is also with "us" (I have used "us" and "them" consciously to demonstrate the point that language fails us and them). If the rich leave the poor to speak for themselves, will anyone hear them? Or will the affluent only represent the impoverished in their own language? There is in European thought a radical and liberal tradition that has argued for the abolition of slavery, for the rights of women and for the end of empire. Perhaps the political, economic and social structures demanded the change, and words were rationalizations of those forces or were irrelevant wishes. But perhaps they had some effect.

In the history of Spanish colonization, Sepúlveda and Oviedo argued against the humanity of the American Indian, whereas Las Casas defended them. The Synopsis of *A Short Account of the Destruction of the Indies* (1542, pub. 1552) says Las Casas spoke for Natives thus:

Everything that has happened since the marvellous discovery of the Americas—from the short-lived initial attempts of the Spanish to settle there, right down to the present day—has been so extraordinary that the whole story remains quite incredible to anyone who has not experienced it at first hand. It seems, indeed, to overshadow all the deeds of famous men of the past, no matter how heroic, and to silence talk of other wonders of the world. Prominent amid the aspects of this story which have caught the imagination are the massacres of innocent peoples, the atrocities committed against them and, among other horrific excesses, the ways in which towns, provinces, and the whole kingdoms have been entirely cleared of their native inhabitants. Brother Bartolomé de Las Casas, or Casuas, came to the Spanish court after he entered the Order, to give our Lord, the Emperor, an eye-witness account of these enormities, not a whisper of which had at that time reached the ears of people here. He also related these same events to several people he met during his visit and they were deeply shocked by what he had to say and listened open-mouthed to his every word; they later begged him and pressed him to set down in writing a short account of some of them, and this he did.[38]

Here, once again, is the contradictory voice of cultural appropriation. The Americas are a marvelous discovery, which is quite different from any Native perspective. This "discovery" of otherness is a matter of heroism and wonder, which evokes the traditions of natural history (Pliny), history (Herodotus), epic (Homer, Virgil) and travel literature (Marco Polo). But beside this is Las Casas' outrage at genocide and his defense of the humanity of the Natives, which defies Sepúlveda's application of Aristotle's theory of natural slavery and which draws on a radical New Testament distrust of class and race that institutional Christianity sometimes perverted. Here is opposition from within the "us" to stand up for "them." Las Casas did not have enough of an effect on Spanish policy to save the Indians. The mediation between "us" and "them" is also a possibility; for some a crossing of cultures is a sell-out, while for others it is the only hope any of us has.[39] Here is the tradition of the other from within.

Montaigne, a skeptic of imperial hubris, also opposed European abuses against the peoples they were subjecting. On his first voyage Columbus had divided the Natives into good and bad, depending on how pliable they seemed and how pro-Spanish they were. He sub-divided the bad Natives into Amazons and cannibals.[40] Montaigne's *On Cannibals* (1580) describes when Montaigne asked the Natives, who were in Rouen when Charles the Ninth was visiting there, what they found most remarkable:

> They mentioned three things, of which I am sorry to say I have forgotten the third. But I still remember the other two. They said that in the first place they found it very strange that so many tall, bearded men, all strong and well armed, who were around the King— they probably meant the Swiss of his guard—should be willing to obey a child, rather than choose one of their own number to command them. Secondly—they have a way in their language of speaking of men as halves of one another—that they had noticed among us some men gorged to the full with things of every sort while their other halves were beggars at their doors, emaciated with hunger and poverty. They found it strange that these poverty-stricken halves should suffer such injustice, and that they did not take the others by the throat or set fire to their houses.[41]

The other becomes a way of criticizing the injustice in European politics and economics. The colonized becomes, as Minh-ha and Said suggest, a medium for a discussion between Europeans, but, unlike later anthropologists, who are said to have valued scientific objectivity, Montaigne shows up his own awareness of the subjectivity and imperfection of his knowledge and his situation.[42] He admits to forgetting the third remarkable thing the Natives observed in Europe and later complains about how bad his interpreter was. His ethnographical turn, which came to be an aspect of anthropology as it developed as a discipline in the late nineteenth and early twentieth centuries, turns back the lens on Europe, but does he do so through cultural appropriation or does he avoid ventriloquy to counterbalance European prejudice? Some of the debate on cultural appropriation arises from this critical, alternative or oppositional tradition within European and Western culture, but in postcolonial, multicultural societies a new questioning of that tradition has recently occurred.[43]

Perhaps Montaigne foreshadowed the new movement in anthropology to use its own methods to look at European culture as an Other. As we saw in the first chapter on Columbus, Swift had the King of Brobdingnag complain about European ethnocentricism, which is something that Las Casas and Montaigne also criticized even though they were, by definition, very European in their cultural training.[44] Earlier in his essay on cannibals, Montaigne alludes to the old debate on barbarism and speaks about a new spirit that might escape ethnocentrism, perhaps the ideal of a scientific anthropology even if the practice must fall short: "I do not believe, from what I have been told of this people, that there is anything barbarous or savage about them, except that we all call barbarous anything that is contrary to our own habits. Indeed we seem to have no other criterion of truth and reason than the type and kind of opinions and customs current in the land where we live."[45] Is this cultural appropriation or the distance of criticism saying that we cannot get outside our cultures and times in matters as important as truth and reason?

The other group that shakes up the "us" and "them" are the mediators or go-betweens.[46] As we observed in the chapter "Between Cultures," mediation between European and Native in this early colonial period, which involved intermarriage, translation, interpretation and diplomacy, has left traces today. Mediators cross cultures in different ways and they confuse the "us/them" split of colonizer and colonized that lies at the heart of empire and has sometimes had too tight a grip on postcolonial studies. It is worth revisiting in a new context some of the mediators or go-betweens discussed a couple of chapters ago. La Malinche was Cortés' mistress during his campaign to conquer the Nahua or Aztec.[47] *Broken Spears,* which is a collection of Angel Maria Garibay K's translations into Spanish of Nahuatl oral accounts of this conquest, says La Malinche translated from Nahuatl into Mayan. Then Jeronimo de Aguilar, a Spaniard who lived among the Mayas for eight years and one of the two captives Cortés had wanted to ransom, translated the Mayan into Spanish for Cortés.[48] Native and European cross each other's cultural boundaries even if precariously and not without controversy. Aguilar gladly came back to Spanish culture when Cortés ransomed him, whereas Gonzalo Guerrero wanted to remain a *Cacique* with fine children than return to a life as a solitary Spanish pauper. In Champlain's narrative about New France, Etienne Brulé is either a French hero or a traitor. At the end of this account, the boy whom Champlain had taught to be a mediator has betrayed him. In *Of Plymouth Plantation: 1620–1647* (pub. 1847) William Bradford tells the story of another mediator—Squanto. In Bradford's narrative that tale is one of reconciliation, friendship, love and redemption. Through Bradford's mediation, we hear of Squanto's mediation: through the governor's culture, we witness Squanto's acculturation. Whether Squanto is a hero or a turncoat depends on which Native or English view the reader chooses to accept. Mediators are controversial.[49]

Mediation, which may allow for hope and possibility in colonization and its wake, also encounters problems of textual provenance, transmission and reception. This problematic is where the body of this book began. Cultural mediation and interpretation surround the text from the beginning. While this situation is true of texts generally, in texts that involve the crossing of cultures and cultural appropriation the problem becomes even more acute. The European representation of the Native (or any Other) also relates to the Native account of the European. Even the most informative among pre-Conquest

Native documents were mostly redone under Spanish influence during the 1540s: the Europeans developed a myth that the American Indians had no writing because these records threatened the Scriptures and European authority and tradition. From 1492 to 1519, there was no Native chronicler of the exchange—Las Casas was the principal defender of Native rights.[50]

The focus on the European use of language and symbolic systems in the exchange with American Indians and other indigenous peoples, while important, is only part of the story of appropriation and adaptation.[51] Increasingly, collections of Native representations of the contact or exchange with Europeans, like *Broken Spears,* and scholarly studies are beginning to provide a balance in the debate. Two examples of this movement to analyze the roles of colonial discourse as a means of resisting the European colonization of local populations or of adaptation through their own ideas to shifting cultural, social, political and economic conditions are Vincente L. Raphael's study of Tagalog society under early Spanish rule and Jorge Klor de Alva's essay on Nahua colonial discourse. Klor de Alva's work, which I will concentrate on here, emphasizes the Nahua appropriation of the European Other and of the Other's voices by way of the adaptation of the alphabet to Nahuatl as tactics to accommodate themselves to Spanish initiatives and to their own visions of truth and reality.[52] The European first encounter narratives, according to Klor de Alva, involved discontinuities because they moved from the unexpected through novelty, then discovery to justification of the imposition of modes of behaviors on the Other. These discontinuities were "cracks between an 'us' and a 'them' that needed to be filled with the mortar of Christian faith and set in the mould of the Spanish polity."[53] De Alva concludes that the Nahuas represented themselves as the only ones who could know what Natives said, so they could control Spanish translation of their intentions, language and customs, and that if disease had not struck, they might have survived into the twentieth century as a dominant bicultural and bilingual community. Instead, incorporation yielded to exclusion, and the Nahua were decimated.[54]

The relation between appropriation and mediation applies as much to people in a postcolonial world as it does to those in a colonial period. Mediation becomes as ambivalent for postcolonial subjects as between European and Native in the early modern period. This ambivalence has helped to lead me to emphasize the connection of the colonial and postcolonial in terms of mediation. Ross Chambers, a theorist of mediation, builds his theory on Nerval and other nineteenth-century writers but applies his model to modernist and postmodernist texts from Australia, Quebec, Argentina and elsewhere. Between seduction and irony he sees a mediation, and mediation in reading creates a conversion of a subject (a shifting), a room to maneuvre between desire and power, a crossing over between them.[55] Like Chambers, I see a connection between textual or semiotic appropriation and political appropriation. Columbus' diaries and Las Casas' editing of that text are just as indicative of cultural appropriation as the postmodern texts Chambers discusses.[56] The point cannot, however, be made enough about the link between semiotic (textual and visual signs) and political appropriation. Chambers sees the intricacy of the relation:

> But mediation is the necessary precondition and ally of appropriative practices. Unmediated discourse, if such a thing could exist, would be perfectly literal and so absolutely dictatorial; it is the fact of mediation that introduces into any discursive situation the element of distance and otherness that splits what is said into "what is said' and "what is under-

stood," and it is this possibility of understanding *otherwise* that makes appropriative (re-) interpretations possible.[57]

The connection between speaker or writer and audience is never literal and unmediated culturally. The discourse has a cultural context in which it is framed and received. Interpretation, which occupies the heart of the human sciences, is a form of mediation. The oppositional, alternative or critical tradition I have been outlining briefly in European culture is predicated on this otherness from within, what Chambers calls "understanding *otherwise*." Appropriation is available to all people and groups on the political spectrum. Chambers sees openness, provisionality and instability of outcome in appropriation and reappropriation. He cites this example: the civil rights movement appropriated TV, and the anti-abortionists have reappropriated these tactics, the going limp and being dragged off to police vans before the cameras, and who knows who will make it their property next? Thus, appropriation threatens those who seek stable and definitive meanings.[58]

For some, however, resistance and counter-hegemonic theory and practice are alternatives. This objective is to restore the colonized as subject rather than deconstruct the opposition of colonizer and colonized as a means of avoiding a simple inversion or reversal of this imperial cultural trap. The argument is, then, that the postcolonial critique that refuses and displaces European claims to constructing the colonized can deprive those who were colonized of their identities as autonomous individuals who have agency. Benita Parry looks at Frantz Fanon, who lived through the decolonization after the Second World War, and sees within his work a tension between Nativism and incipient postcolonial turning away from Europe as a source of ideas and models. For Fanon, Europe had not produced the whole person, who across the world had experienced an oppositional and emancipated humanism. Parry asks a question that resonates in our age, which is still caught between colonialism and postcolonialism: "What is less certain is whether the time for transnational politics had come when Fanon was writing, whether it has now, and whether the prospect of his post-nativist 'whole man' is one that wholly delights."[59]

The establishment of, and resistance to, empire expresses a movement of appropriation and reappropriation. Forms may remain the same but content can be opposite. The desire for mediation in postcolonial studies may also be implicated in appropriation but it, too, represents a hope that in the wake of empire people do not get caught up in the fight of oppositions. Whether this hope is pious or the basis for practical action is for each reader to decide. The next section will outline some of the problems of appropriation in relation to postcolonialism. In progressing from colonialism to postcolonialism and to the hybrid state, like the exhibition Anne McClintock describes, I am conscious of the tenuousness of the term "postcolonial" and how complex history is in its appropriations and reappropriations.[60]

IV

The relation between appropriation and postcolonialism is, then, fraught with difficulty. The debate over the crisis of representation involves a doubt over whether it is legitimate or just to describe or speak for others. But representation has always been in crisis. The Platonic Socrates, himself in the liminal region between fiction and dialectic called the "dialogue," thinks that representation that sings the literal praises of the state is good, while fictional representation is bad because it creates shadows, a copy of a copy of a copy and thereby deflects people away from the good and just. Aristotle opposed his teacher by making *mimesis,* or the representation of reality, the foundation of poetry, so that poets described the real. Both Plato and Aristotle thought philosophy to be greatest, the one because it guaranteed an understanding of essential ideas and the other because it expressed universals in human experience. Whereas Aristotle emphasizes detachment and catharsis, Longinus stresses identification and ectasis: the reader and audience have different options in these different interpretative modes in Western culture, an ideology of the aesthetic, to use Terry Eagleton's term, or a mythology of the creative.[61] "Representation" has always been contested, so that its instability in our time should come as no surprise. To use the term as a monolith—a temptation in some poststructuralist, postmodern and postcolonial discourse—is ill-advised, for it represents misrepresentation. Representation and its theory of itself have been, therefore, unstable long before late-twentieth-century theorists had called attention to its instability. In recent decades the reminder of the contradictions and fragility has been suggestive.

Great metanarratives and systems, essential truths and universals are all under attack in our postmodern age. While the "postmodern" and the "postcolonial" are difficult terms in and of themselves and are not synonymous, they do share some attributes. There is a new crisis in representation: unstable meanings are part of a postmodernist and poststructural perspective. Owing to the mediated nature of representation, some critics have suggested on political and epistemological grounds that mimesis is a dangerous or bad thing: by extension representative government is equally offensive.[62] Gayatri Chakravorty Spivak's exploration of whether the subaltern can speak mediates between the retreat of the intellectual from speaking for others and those who are dangerous and careless in speaking for others. Spivak prefers speaking *to* others where intellectuals neither deny speaking nor assert authenticity of the oppressed but are open to a new "countersentence" or history the oppressed can produce and to which the intellectuals should listen.[63] This dialogue allows for the possibility of alternative critique. Linda Alcoff attempts to extend Spivak's analysis by saying that people must be more aware of the dangers of speaking for others in the following four ways: the impetus or motive for speaking; the bearing of our location and context on what we are saying; accountability and responsibility for speaking: and the effects of the words in discursive and material contexts.[64]

Location is a central idea in a post-war world in which there has been a great movement of peoples. The language of exile and the shifting nature of place characterize the postcolonial world. Location ranges from the institutional to the geopolitical. Homi K. Bhabha argues for innovative theory and a crucial politics in thinking beyond narratives of initial or originary subjectivities by focusing on processes or moments produced while articulating cultural differences: he explores these spaces in between, especially those who live on the boundaries, and hopes for a radical revision of the idea of the human community.[65] Salman Rushdie speaks of "hybridity, impurity, intermingling, the transformation that comes of new and unexpected combinations of human beings, cultures, ideas, politics, movies, songs."[66]

Cultural hybridity and mediation, which involve an in-between identity (not an essential one), oppose an essential view of cultures that are situated in old oppositions and that appropriate and are appropriated. Annie E. Coombes examines hybridity in regard to the difficulties arising from the curatorial strategy of presenting exhibitions that produce an exchange of cultures by claiming to disrupt radically the boundaries of the West and Other. In this analysis she assumes that the recognition of hybridity is a significant cultural strategy for the politics of decolonization. Coombes advocates, as Benita Parry and Stuart Hall have, strategic essentialism.[67] Power and transgression lie at the heart of this question. For Coombes, one of the troubles with appropriating "hybridity" as a sign of postcolonial self-determination is that it is a term from art history and anthropology to describe a cultural concept and the cultural object. Museums of fine art and ethnographic museums, both implicated in capitalism and colonialism, are homes to exhibitions. To relocate with success the cultural sign of cultural assimilation, appropriation and transformation demands a self-consciousness in which cultural objects assigned to the Other are, at any particular moment, already circumvented.[68] Coombes thinks that an exploration of the hybridity of all cultures should allow for an examination of its specific conditions and not as a monolithic repetition of hybridity as an encounter between the West and the Other.[69]

V

Appropriation has an intricate relation to colonialism and postcolonialism. One view of the shift from colonialism to postcolonialism is that the first group of writers imitate texts from the imperial center, the second group abrogates them and the third appropriates them. By discussing nineteenth-century "postcolonial" writers, Gareth Griffiths uses this successive model to show how for postcolonial authors, at least in the present sense, to go beyond abrogation, they must appropriate imperial texts for their own uses.[70] Another kind of appropriation is, as we have seen in the last chapter, Shakespeare's *The Tempest*, which used as sources a pamphlet on Bermuda and Montaigne's "On Cannibals." In turn, Shakespeare's play became a trumpet for empire and the White man's burden and then was adapted by postcolonial writers in several languages to write back against the empire. Caliban was appropriated as a tragic hero of the triumph of European colonialism.[71]

In the French-speaking world, postcolonialism has not caught on as a term, but interesting new work on hybridity in culture, such as studies of Creole, is being done.[72] Françoise Lionnet calls attention to the work of writers in Francophone countries who have represented displacement, exile and intercultural exchanges, and, observes, more generally: "The global mongrelization or *métissage* of cultural forms creates hybrid identities, and interrelated, if not overlapping, spaces."[73] Lionnet draws on examples from contemporary postcolonial Francophone women who have different perspectives on multiculturalism from those in the United States. Cultural appropriation in the Francophone world is not simply one of assimilation of the Francophone to France. It is no longer a matter, as in the colonial context, of mimicking or imitating the colonizer.[74] The local and the global are interrelated and the old opposition of center and margin is no longer tenable.[75]

One of the difficulties is that with colonization both Europe and the cultures it came into contact with changed. Indigenous traditions need to be acknowledged and understood, so that postcolonialism does not become a property, a kind of front, for neo-colonialism. But these traditions have also changed over time, before and after contact with the Europeans. To talk of an essential tradition, then, is problematic. Change has also occurred in European culture, which is also not an essence. There are also differences between Europeans and indigenous cultures, which are sometimes erased more for ideological than for historical reasons. On both sides the notions of culture and property have altered, so that cultural appropriation has changed in history.[76] The present can also appropriate the past. The best way to look at cultural appropriation is as an interaction between changing cultures over time and not simply as a static transaction between two sides.

VI

Terms and movements coexist while also appropriating each other. In this age of "post" everything, in which there is the proclamation of being after the modern, after structure, after empire, perhaps after all, it is seductive to think that everything is present and that, in the empire of technology, if not, in Roland Barthes' phrase, the empire of signs, people have moved beyond history as they had conceived it before. This appropriation of progress without progress (because in postmodernism liberal or Whig progress is to be moved beyond) finds itself in a kind of satiric position—a movement without movement. The dilemmas abound, and theorists and historians find themselves in appropriating or inappropriate positions.

In a world given to capital the commodity world of postmodernism might suggest that there is an ever-changing world of empire where property and appropriation prevail over other political and economic forms. It is, then, difficult to address postcolonialism without saying a few words, no matter how inadequate, about postmodernism. Both terms are slippery and do not define adequately what they stand for. In my view, postmodernism involves two things, first, a coming after and, second, a recycling of techniques. The coming after is a subsequence to all periods but bears a more direct relation to modernism, which, as an avant-garde, postmodernism must criticize. The recycling is usually of techniques that are pre-modern, and more often than not, early modern. Sometimes even the Enlightenment is recycled against the heirs to the Enlightenment. Sterne is refitted to trim Joyce's sails just as Cervantes is recalled to show that the Victorian novel was not the culmination of the tradition of the novel. Postmodernism is heir to modern technological developments, so that it revolves around instant communication, which differentiates us from previous ages, though again not entirely from our Victorian and modernist parents and grandparents, who gave us the telegraph and telephone. But this is a world of uneven developments, even within countries, so that to speak of one unified postmodern world would be misleading. Instead, we need to recognize what I have elsewhere called "our living archaeology" and what I might call here our simultaneous worlds. So many of us and our societies are primitive, modern and postmodern at once.[77] It is also true that in repressing modernism, postmodernism has gone too far in equating modernization with modernism, in stressing the nationalist, organicist or fascist aspects of modernism and not its experimental, fragmentary and alienated elements.

It is a current interest to relate postmodernism to postcolonialism. A commonplace too often forgotten is that the beginnings of the term "postmodernism" are in architecture, that is the critique of high modernism as a celebration of advanced technology and the affluence of capitalism.[78] Postmodernism, in which Habermas' pursuit of truth and Lyotard's questioning of the grand narratives contend, has affinities with postcolonialism.[79] Postmodernism can be appropriated to be used against new radical movements, just as postcolonialism is in danger of being packed in the belly of the Trojan horse of neo-colonialism. Some voices oppose relating the postcolonial to postmodernism. Arun P. Mukherjee argues against grouping postcolonial texts under "postmodernism" because of this last term's genesis from White European males and thinks that this classification will not do for the non-White writing.[80]

Postcolonialism can be ironic and may not use postmodern deconstruction to go beyond existing orthodoxies into areas of social and political action. One danger is that postcolonialism can be appropriated, consciously or not, by those of us who write about it in the institution as part of a paradigm shift that becomes domesticated among granting agencies, institutes, publishers, journals, museums, galleries and universities. Voice appropriation becomes a question of mobile maneuvres as institutional identities threaten to ossify anti-essentialist or strategic essentialist tactics of postmodern postcolonialism. Irony and ambivalence, whether adopted from Friedrich Schlegel, Walter Benjamin or William Empson, is a Socratic or German Romantic tool negotiated through modernism and displaced into the repertoire of postcolonialism and postmodernism. The rhetoric of temporality occupies postcolonialism as much as it does history and the philosophy of history. If Lyotard questions the grand narratives of the European Enlightenment, Edward Said looks at how postcolonial strategies question the nature of representation, cultural property and property itself, while Spivak and Bhabha discuss agency and the interruption of the narration and reading of nation and empire. Whereas Robert Young considers postcolonialism's critique of European historiography and of otherness to be subsumed under postmodernism, as in Bhabha's work, Henry Louis Gates thinks that Western academic interest in making colonialism a field of all writing may yet be another project of European universalism. Literary criticism and theory have appropriated the form and content of rhetoric, philosophy, history and literature itself. Postcolonialism, which is a kind of cultural critique or cultural studies, is cross-disciplinary theory and practical criticism. It appropriates from these traditional sources.

A key question is whether postcolonial theory, which is centered in the Western university, has not appropriated postcolonial fiction. Is this another case of the critic feeding off the artist? Or do we need cultural mediators to create an audience or to go between writers/artists and readers/viewers? Spivak has wrestled with this difficult question with sensitivity. None the less, it is hard to know whether any form of irony or ambivalence is subversive or evasive or both. Do postcolonial critics provide models in countries subject to economic colonialism or is their discourse an institutional and professional discourse of privileged Western universities? As I have argued, from the first contacts between Europeans and Native Americans, to use just one example of "first encounters," the role of mediators is important but precarious. By attempting to unmask, contain and circumvent ethnic and racial suspicion and hatred, the postcolonial theorists are attempting something significant and problematic. Crossing boundaries and understanding those translations are the tasks of postcolonialism. In postcolonial studies, theorists use subaltern voices, European high theory, the fiction of the former colonies and European fiction, so that cultural appropriation is fine if it criticizes empire and essentialism in race, nation, religion.

No one has done more to establish postcolonial studies than Edward Said, a mediator who has crossed many boundaries.[81] To understand the foundation others have built on his work (I could use the metaphor of appropriation here), I want to comment briefly on his importance to the field, especially as it relates to hybridity and property. What distinguishes postcolonialism most is its focus on empire and its attempt to see beyond empire or read the wake of empire even while new forms of empire may be in the making. Edward Said's landmark works, *Orientalism* (1978) and *Culture and Imperialism* (1993), mark the take-off and the power and velocity of postcolonialism. Much has been said about *Orientalism,* and others, including Said, have revisited and supplemented it.[82] It wasn't as if the discussion of British and French imperialism was new with Said. And he never said it was. Said himself returns to the narratorial voice in Conrad's *Heart of Darkness,* where, for instance, the idea of empire lies as a religion to bow down to, and offer sacrifices to, in the "conquest of the earth."[83] Although imperialism has, thanks largely to Said, recently become a central concern of literary studies, he reminds us of the early critical work by historians and others in the field, such as J. A Hobson's *Imperialism: A Study* (1902). He also departs from Raymond Schwab's *La Renaissance Orientale* (1950). Nor does Said think that empires began with the British and French, but he is particularly interested in those as imperial kinds whose vastness and whose dominion over so many different peoples had never occurred in the world.[84] But it is Said's work that has helped to inspire a generation of English-speaking students to look into imperialism in literary texts. He has brought Conrad, Aimé Césaire and Frantz Fanon into classroom and critical discourse in North America and beyond.

Said makes some important points in his Introduction to *Culture and Imperialism.* For instance, he wants to emphasize the resistance to empire that he did not address in *Orientalism,* the mutual relation and response to imperialism of the heirs to colonizer and colonized, and the new ways of seeing texts like Dicken's *Great Expectations* (1861) and Conrad's *Nostromo* (1904) (the former as a tale of banishment, alienation and living through empire and the latter as a critique and celebration of empire). Said is interested in moral criticism.[85] Here is such a moment in Said's Introduction: "To the extent that we see Conrad both criticizing and reproducing the imperial ideology of his time, to that extent we can characterize our own present attitudes: the projection, or the refusal, of the wish to dominate, the capacity to damn, or the energy to comprehend and engage with other societies, traditions, histories."[86] Here is a call for an understanding of historical difference between Conrad and us in conjunction with an assumption that history translates, that a kind of transhistorical ethic can be taken in this comparison of then and now. Imperialism mutates but remains the same. But Said is too subtle to make such a bald statement. The world has changed, he says, because for some time globalization has brought non-White immigrants into the heart of the metropolitan centers of Europe and the United States. Therefore, Said asserts, "For the first time, the history of imperialism and its culture can now be studied as neither monolithic nor reductively compartmentalized, separate, distinct."[87] The implied question becomes, Whose place is this anyway? The division of territory and culture as the property of the colonizer in opposition to the colonized is no longer the case. Said's quest is to map the relation between narrative and empire, especially as they appear in his life, that is the British, French and American imperiums. He focuses on their shared idea of overseas rule.

More than in previous work, Said looks at American imperialism. He also celebrates the new work in Middle East and Indian studies by women and makes the apt point that narratives of emancipation have been about excluded groups fighting for integration. With a humanistic view of the university as a utopian space in which to explore possibilities, which is not too different from Northrop Frye's, Said also alludes to New York, the city of his exile, as a state for his meditation that he offers to the reader as a possible "salutary alternative to the normal sense of belonging to only one culture and feeling a sense of loyalty to only one nation."[88] Said writes from the utopian space of the university that is and is not of the world and in the putative dimension between his "Oriental" and "Western" selves and experiences. Connected hybridity and hybrid connection is Said's ideal as a means of facing the new reality that faces us in the global village. It is, as he notes, empire that has brought us together to study about empire.[89]

Ambivalence and contradiction, as I have argued in this study and elsewhere, characterize imperial expansion.[90] The imperial theme makes us uncomfortable, but the consequences of empire have been part of the economic and political systems that have created the very institutions, such as universities in the Americas, Australia, South Africa and elsewhere, that foster research that enables military, technological and scientific foundations for the state and for global companies and that criticizes these very organizations. These bring us back to the Aristotelian distance and the Longinian engagement that representation and writing embody. Perhaps interpreters of colonialism and postcolonialism are caught between identity and estrangement. Empire might have a fascination amid the revulsion over its excesses and abuses. It is important to guard against a colonial pastoral while realizing that empires, even if they constitute a typology, differ one from the other and can also bring benefits. This last point, especially in light of the horrors of slavery and the destruction of peoples, is the hardest to admit, but if empires were uniform and entirely negative, they would not be so elusive and would not have attracted so much mixed commentary over the ages.

VII

This intractability and ambivalence also relates specifically to postcolonial irresolution, indigenous identity and the hybrid. It may be possible to see more clearly several key relations in the connection between cultural appropriation and postcolonialism: the colonial and postcolonial; Native rights and the postcolonial; identity and hybridity; mediation and resistance, to name a few. Rather than wind these relations into a tight dialectic, I have tried to weave them. To conclude, I will leave off with an important figure in North American history—Louis Riel—mediator/renegade/resistor/Métis. By looking at this figure, part Native, part European, as Canada is emerging from its colonial period, the reader, who is supposed to inhabit a postmodern and postcolonial world, can think about these relations and see beyond them as oppositions.

Has the postcolonial escaped the dilemmas of the colonial? Simon During sees the emptiness of postcolonial culture and the tendency of postcolonial identity toward irresolution and paradox: as Northrop Frye asked of Canadian culture so many years ago—is there any here here?[91] Post-structuralist and postmodernist notions of self or subject reveal a discomfort with Renaissance or modern claims for identity and individualism. But this is a European view that is not accepted by all, let alone all Europeans, not even by those who work in the rarefied world of critical theory. There are levels of qualification in views of the person and the state. For instance, Tom King is an aboriginal novelist who has moved between the United States and Canada, whose borders for Natives are more porous and imaginary than for settlers. He does not like the term "postcolonial" because it assumes that in relation to Native culture the time to begin is with the arrival of Europeans in North America. Nor does King approve of the term "postcolonial" because he argues that it implies that Natives now forget their own traditions and write entirely about their struggle as "wards" with their "guardians." Thus postcolonialism neglects Native traditions, which have survived colonization. For King, Native writing is an alternative and not a construct of oppression, so that it should not be held hostage to the nationalism that postcolonialism suggests for it. King sees Native writing as a counter-narrative or as a counter-classification. Riel may be a narrative and counter-narrative.

Perhaps, then, it is not necessary to have an either/or between traditional nationalism, in which people die in the streets because they are supposed to have a certain identity, and postmodern/postcolonial self-invention and hybridity. But I think the crossing of boundaries and the flexibility of mediation can suggest one way to live in the world and to respond to movements and mixing of culture in the global village. This is where I wish to turn to Louis Riel, who is a mythical figure in Canadian culture. He led the Northwest rebellions in 1869–70 and 1885.[92] Having lived in British North America, the United States and Canada, Riel remains a controversial figure in Canada and a key representative of aboriginal and Métis history and culture.

The very ambivalence of Riel makes him problematic. He combines progressive aspects such as a politics of liberation, and nostalgic and conservative religious elements. The images of Catholicism and France coexist with his declaration of rights and his vision of independence for the Métis and the Northwest. He is rebel and mystic, prophet of a new age and a throwback to a religious past, French and Amerindian. As Thomas Flanagan says, Riel listened to his mother's stories about his descent from the French nobility, but in his "later life, compassion for the Irish as fellow unfortunates alongside the French Canadians within the British empire was to be a hallmark of his thinking."[93] He was hanged as a rogue in the view of Orangemen from Ontario and died as a martyr for the Catholics of Quebec. For many of the Métis, he was the last chance at the dream of being heard as the European settlers moved West.

Riel is a figure who disturbs the opposition of colonizer and colonized, the simple division between European and Indian that could be an excuse for conscious or unconscious racism, exploitation and even genocide, because he was a Métis, part French and part Indian in a country that was supposed to have two founding nations and languages and to be making treaties with the Indians, nation to nation. Here was a man who was and was not European, was and was not an Indian. He was part of a group that confounded the oppositions that built Canada and put its indigenous peoples on reserves. In the history of colonization there are many figures like Riel. He questions the category of race, the destiny of Europe and the "purity" of culture. The figure of Riel unsettles the demands of imperialists and nationalists, of too many traditional cultures, European and other, to set up a situation of either/or and we/they, to build an ideological wall around a nation, cast out those who have not been allowed into the definition, and pretend, sometimes in a ghastly fantasy with the grossest consequences, that culture is not oblique, complex and ambivalent.

Riel, then, becomes like the figure of the hybrid. Hybrid languages break down the opposition between a European and an indigenous language.[94] The potential of hybrid or Métis discourse is to mix European and other cultures; the difficulty, as in Riel's case, is that the European cultural element is given too great a sway. But as times have changed since Riel, it is possible to look to analogous figures and writers today at a time when there can be more exchange between the cultures because the British and American empires are traces. Only the influence of American political power, something Riel does not seem to have concentrated on as Britain was the world power then, affects the Creole and Métis. The danger and liberation may now lie in American popular culture, which has made such inroads into Native households as everywhere else. In Riel there was a narrative of liberation but also the eruption of the colonial and the feudal. This figure that disrupted colonialism at the height of the British empire is, like Columbus and Shakespeare, even if he is less well known, appropriated by nationalists and post-colonialists. Riel is disturbing to all sides and as ambivalent as empire itself. He appealed to authority while calling and acting for liberation. Some of his yearning was for the past life of the Plains Indians that was being destroyed and for the lost grandeur of the French empire in America—both sides of his family—while his American republicanism and his identification with subjected peoples constituted part of a utopian yearning for a better future. Like Riel, many of us are caught between cultures and find it difficult to resolve our own contradictions and those of the cultures and nations in which we live. Perhaps the irresolutions and dilemmas can suggest better ways to become and coexist and need not end tragically.

There have been narratives of resistance to empire and narratives of imperial celebration for three thousand years or more in Western culture. To come after empire and to get beyond it may be far more difficult than we recognize. In the meantime, even while the term "postcolonial" seems inadequate because the colonial has not entirely left us, neo-colonialism may still be with us and strange manifestations of pre-modern and modern identities may remain with us like an archaeology. The translation of empire and the resistance to it should be studied, even if that study is marked with a disjunction between ethics and history, because no matter how short we fall of the mark, it is too important an area to let alone. Cultural appropriation is at the heart of debates on postcolonialism and neo-colonialism: Who speaks for whom? Can we get past old ways of exchanging culture? Our futures depend on this debate, but they have to come to terms with our pasts. The postcolonial should see through itself in the colonial. Quite possibly, the appropriation of the past is at the center of human cultures as they meet.

Afterword

A s this book was in its final preparations, New York and Washington were attacked and, after some time, Afghanistan was subject to bombing. It is not for this book to interpret this suffering.

Others, none the less, have interpreted these events. One result of this situation is some articles in newspapers and magazines questioning hybrid and multicultural societies, one of the legacies of Columbus' landfall in the western Atlantic. In times of crisis, cultures are put under immense pressure. After 1492, European, African and Native Americans lived through vast and painful changes in the New World. Native and African workers and slaves suffered most. At the heart of this book is a strand about mediators and go-betweens, which I hope to amplify in one of my subsequent studies of the New World. These figures, with such potential to bring disparate cultures together, were often held in suspicion or actively opposed. They presented, and present, an alternative to division. These people of *métissage* or hybridity and cultural interaction may well come under pressure again and again.

Whereas there is a wide gap between past and present, there are some filiations or traces between them. Although the past in its strangeness reads the present by its very difference, it is also the object of present attention. Few ready morals can be pointed in the messiness of history and the texts and documents we have as representations of that past. Columbus, Shakespeare and others left complex texts and images of the New World and suggested a typology with Europe and other places. Fictions, pictures and descriptions yielded traces of fractures and imagined cultures. The utopian impulse as well as the inconvenient artifacts of history are especially under strain in times of crisis. Myth, the story in history, slips back into the rhetorical relation we have in oral, visual and written culture.

It may be hubris to think that any of us are post anything. The globe, which Columbus and subsequent explorers, writers and scientists have helped to shrink, is also distracted. Globalization, and this has been obvious for some time, is not simply about utopian unity. Various cultures and the differences between the hungry and the fed face each other, and representations on television and in newspapers are almost instantaneous. The eruption of the pre-modern as well as earlier phases of the modern in each of those cultures makes the interpretation of culture something vexed. If Columbus had trouble interpreting speech and signs, often without knowing it, so do any of us. As with any shattering events there will be much in the hearts and minds of those who witnessed them. While texts and images represent the world, they are not synonymous, and to think that they are the world is something that such events throw into stark relief. They may be part of and impart the world but are not the world whole. It is, however, a time for remembrance and reflection. Perhaps there is still some room for the in-between, a mediation between one human and another, no matter how disparate.

Notes

Chapter 1

1. See Anthony Pagden, *The Fall of Natural Man: The American Indian and the Origins of Comparative Ethnography* (Cambridge: Cambridge University Press, 1982, rev. ed. 1986), 10, where he speaks about the problem of recognition for the Europeans.
2. See Jonathan Hart, *Representing the New World: The English and French Uses of the Example of Spain* (New York and London: Palgrave, 2001).
3. See, for instance, Keith Thomas, "Anthropology and History," *Past and Present* 24 (1963): 3–24 ; Natalie Zemon Davis, *Society and Culture in Early Modern France* (Stanford: Stanford University Press, 1975); Robert Darnton, *The Great Cat Massacre and Other Episodes in French Cultural History* (1984. New York: Vintage, 1985), esp. 4; Pagden, *The Fall of Natural Man,* esp. 14–26; Carlo Ginzburg, *Clues, Myths, and the Historical Method,* trans. John and Anne Tedeschi (Baltimore: Johns Hopkins University Press, 1989, rpt. 1992), esp. 186.
4. In this study I may take advantage of irony, satire and skepticism to be aware of my own cultural and personal blind-spots, but, despite whatever effort to achieve understanding and communicate that "recognition" to others over time, these attempts may fall short, partly because of the apparent limitations and changeability of time itself. But I began with assumptions and how they were somewhere to begin, implying that they should beget a heuristic approach and not already be a conclusion if that is possible. This is not a treatise about being or becoming in time, but I wanted to mention, however briefly, some of the snares that await those who write about the past.
5. Bernal Díaz del Castillo, *The Discovery and Conquest of Mexico,* trans. A. P. Maudslay (New York: Farrar, Strauss and Cudahy, 1956) or Maudslay's translation in 5 volumes, *The True Story of the Conquest of New Spain* (London: The Hakluyt Society, 1908); another clear and readable translation is J. M. Cohen's in Penguin. Tzvetan Todorov, *The Conquest of America,* trans. Richard Howard (1984; New York: Harper & Row, 1992).
6. I have chosen *The Broken Spears* here partly because it is accessible to readers and has been used over the years on courses throughout North America. See *The Broken Spears: The Aztec Account of the Conquest of Mexico,* ed. Miguel Leon-Portilla, expanded and updated edition (1962; Boston: Beacon Press, 1992).
7. *Ibid.,* 64. Throughout my study, I have chosen to use different variants of Montezuma's name to show the instability of representations of him and to abide by the various choices of those writing about him. This choice could also be made for Columbus (Colón, Colombo) and Shakespeare, but I have done so with Motecuhzuma because, even if in a Romanized alphabet, there are Nahua (Native) as opposed to European ways to represent his name.
8. Miguel Leon-Portilla, "Introduction," *The Broken Spears,* xxxiii.
9. Here I am borrowing Anthony Pagden's apt phrase.

10. See Lysander Kemp, "Translator's Note," ix; J. Jorge Klor de Alva, "Foreword," xi-xxiv, esp. xiii, xvi.
11. Miguel Leon-Portilla, "Introduction," *The Broken Spears,* xlvi-xlvii.
12. *Ibid.,* xlv.
13. See Davis, *Society and Culture* and Darnton, *The Great Cat Massacre.*
14. For a useful discussion of the role of rhetoric among classical historians like Thucydides, Cicero, Sallust, Livy and Tacitus, see A. J. Woodman, *Rhetoric in Classical Historiography* (London: Croom Helm, 1988).
15. See Jonathan Hart (with Terry Goldie)"'Postcolonial Theory," *Encyclopedia of Contemporary Literary Theory* (Toronto: University of Toronto Press, 1993), 155–8.
16. British Library, MS Yelverton No 131 Add Ms. 48116 [554 c], 34 recto. Philip II is a controversial figure. There have been positive portraits and assessments in English then and now: Richard Eden hoped to flatter him; see his *The Decades of the newe worlde of west India,* . . . London, 1555; "The Lion's Cub," an episode of *Elizabeth R,* a popular television series written by John Hale, makes Philip the champion of Elizabeth. While interested in her as a woman in this representation, Philip wants to protect Elizabeth against her fanatical sister, Mary, who is extreme in her Catholic faith, partly because he fears the deleterious effects such mistreatment of Elizabeth, a Protestant, might have on Catholicism in England (London: British Broadcasting Corporation, 1971).
17. Richard Eden, *The Decades* (1555); Richard Hakluyt, *The Principall Navigations Voiages and Discoveries of the English Nation* . . . (London, 1589 [Princeton copy]); Samuel Purchas, *Purchas His Pilgrimes. In Five Bookes* . . . (London, 1625 [Princeton copy]); Melchisédech Thévenot, *Relation de divers voyages cvrievx, qvi n'ont point esté pvbliees; qui ont esté tradvites d'Haclvyt; de Purchas, & d'autres voyageurs Anglois, Hollandois, Portugais, Allemands, Espagnols; et qvelqves Persans, Arabes, et avtres avteurs Orientaux* . . . (Paris, 1663).
18. The article by Adam Hopkins is a full page and is on page 1. For more on Philip II and Spain see the other books in my series, *Representing the New World* (2001) and *Comparing Empires* (forthcoming)—both with Palgrave.
19. *Ibid.*
20. J. H. Elliott, *Europe Divided: 1559–1598* (Glasgow: Fontana/Collins, 1968, rpt. 1974), 265–76. For a general view of the economics in the Spanish empire, see John R. Fisher, *The Economic Aspects of Spanish Imperialism in America, 1492–1810* (Liverpool: Liverpool University Press, 1997).
21. A. J. R. Russell-Wood, *The Portuguese Empire, 1415–1808: A World on the Move* (1992; Baltimore: Johns Hopkins University Press, 1998), 6.
22. Jeremy Belknap, *A Discourse, Intended to Commemorate the Discovery of America by Christopher Columbus; Delivered at the Request of the Historical Society in Massachusetts, on the 23rd Day of October 1792, Being the Completion of the Third Century Since that Memorable Event* (Boston: Belknap and Hall, 1792), 10–11. I originally consulted the copy in Houghton Library Harvard in 1992 and checked it against the copy in Special Collections in Princeton in 2001. Another interesting work at about this time, which received notice in the new American republic, was Thomas Morton's play; see Thomas Morton, *Columbus: Or the Discovery of America: An Historical Play, as Performed at the Theatre-Royal, Covent-Garden, London* (Boston: William Spotswood; Philadelphia: H. & P. Rice, 1794). The original London edition was printed for W. Miller in 1792, was reprinted in Dublin for P. Wogan in 1793 and for J. Barker in London in 1799.
23. The making of modernity on both sides of the Atlantic and the opposition to "divine-right monarchy" have philosophical origins as well, as Jonathan Israel suggests in *Radical Enlightenment: Philosophy and the Making of Modernity 1650–1750* (Oxford: Oxford University Press, 2001), esp. 72–73. The moment of modernity or even the sea-change of modernity over a period of generations or a century can be a vanishing horizon. The importance of the Enlightenment, which Israel argues for and with which I concur, can sometimes be obscured in a reaction to it or even in a useful critique of Enlightenment

ideals and accomplishments. For an economic analysis of transitions to "modernity," see Robert S. Duplessis, *Transitions to Capitalism in Early Modern Europe* (Cambridge: Cambridge University Press, 1997). The period of the late fourteenth century is a good time to see breaks with traditional ideas and systems, but Columbus and his time are not the only possibilities in the debate on the modern. Modernity has an uneven development and has, I would argue, not fully arrived even in an age that is, perhaps, passing beyond the "postmodern." There are eruptions of tribalism and the pre-scientific or intense global interaction (great trade networks existed long before Columbus or multinationals with name brands and the fate of international trade was subject to vicissitudes).

24. Quoted in A. J. R. Russell-Wood, 5.
25. *A Short Relation made by the Lord De-La-Warre, to the Lords and others of the Counsell of Virginea, touching his vnexpected returne home, and afterwards deliuered to the generall Assembly of the said Company, at a Court holden the twenty fiue of Iune, 1611.* Published by authority of the said Counsell, C verso-C2 recto; see *The Relation of the Right Honourable the Lord De-La-Warre, Lord Gouernour and Captaine Generall of the Colonie, planted in* VIRGINIEA (London: William Hall for William Welbie, 1611) [Princeton copy].
26. *Ibid.*, B3 verso-B4 recto.
27. The British Library has a copy of the Florence edition.
28. For a brief but helpful discussion of the woodcuts, which includes reproductions of these two images, see Ron Tyler, *Visions of America: Pioneer Artists in a New Land* (London: Thames and Hudson, 1983), 10–11. Tyler reiterates the point about stereotypical use of woodcuts and thinks that the figures in the Florence woodcut are giants. It is also possible that they are roughly represented and that proportion is not precise here.

Chapter 2

1. Jonathan Swift, *Gulliver's Travels,* Philip Pinkus, ed. (Toronto: Macmillan, 1968), 141–42.
2. *Ibid.*, 7–8.
3. *Ibid.*, 7.
4. *Ibid.*, 126.
5. Bartolomé de Las Casas, *Historia de las Indias,* Gonzalo de Reparaz, ed. (Madrid, 1927), 3 vols., vol. 3, ch. 29; see Kirkpatrick Sale, *The Conquest of Paradise: Christopher Columbus and the Columbian Legacy* (New York: Random House, 1990), 157; Tzvetan Todorov, *The Conquest of America: The Question of the Other,* Richard Howard, trans. (1984, rpt. 1992), 141; for the original see *La Conquête de l"Amérique* (Paris: Seuil, 1982).
6. James Lockhart, *The Nahuas After the Conquest: A Social and Cultural History of the Indians of Central Mexico, Sixteenth Through Eighteenth Centuries* (Stanford: Stanford University Press, 1992), 330.
7. Vine Deloria, Jr., "Afterword," *America in 1492: The World of the Indian Peoples Before the Arrival of Columbus,* ed. Alvin M. Josephy, Jr. (1991. New York: Random House, 1993), 429–30.
8. Gordon Brotherston, *Image of the New World: The American Continent Portrayed in Native Texts* (London: Thames and Hudson, 1979), 15.
9. *Ibid.*, 21; see Carl Ortwin Sauer, *Sixteenth Century North America: The Land and the People as Seen by Europeans* (Berkeley: University of California Press, 1971).
10. Deloria, 432–35.
11. Anthony Pagden, *The Fall of Natural Man: The American Indian and the Origins of Comparative Ethnology* (Cambridge: Cambridge University Press, 1982), 119.
12. Brotherston 28–32, 48–53.
13. Three recent works on Columbus include important discussions of Columbus' texts; see Cummins, Zamora, and Fernández-Armesto (listed below). Their views are quite different from Henige's: see David Henige, *In Search of Columbus: The Sources for the*

First Voyage (Tucson: University of Arizona Press, 1991). Cummins has tried to reconstruct as closely as possible Columbus' *Journal* from the evidence available, mainly in Las Casas and Ferdinand Columbus: "My version, therefore, is not Columbus's original, but then neither is Fernando's, nor the Las Casas manuscript, nor any of the myriad translations which have slavishly followed the slapdash Las Casas text. What follows is, I hope, a version corresponding as closely in content to the original as it is possible to produce while that original remains lost." (John Cummins, "Introduction," *The Voyage of Christopher Columbus: Columbus' Own Journal of Discovery Newly Restored and Translated* [London: Weidenfeld and Nicolson, 1992], 76). Unlike Jane and Henige, Cummins believes in an original text by Columbus. Zamora sees two editorial camps that have not reached a consensus: "the Columbian texts have been deemed both very reliable and largely untrustworthy testimonies on the Discovery" (Margarita Zamora, *Reading Columbus* [Berkeley: University of California Press, 1993], 3). Zamora gives a clear account of the status of the text of the "Letter to Luis de Santángel" (February 15, 1493)—the main text in my essay—and the "Letter to the Sovereigns" (March 4, 1493) (5–6). The "Letter to Santángel" was in Spanish and was translated into Italian prose and verse and Latin prose very soon after its appearance. Zamora argues that this letter was probably based on the one addressed to the crown the following month and that someone other than Columbus substantially revised, if not composed, it. The February letter, which we have in Santángel's hand, was lost or suppressed and stood in for the letter to the crown for 500 years (Zamora 5–6). Rather than undermine my argument, Zamora's attribution of the "Letter to Santángel" to someone other than Columbus makes the importance of Columbus as an author function and a collective cultural production even more important. We do not know whether Columbus wrote this or other texts. Even the textual status of the "Letter to the Sovereigns" is uncertain and may be questioned. Zamora admits as much (Zamora 9–20, 211). One of the provocative points Zamora raises in her comparison of the letter to Santángel with that to the Sovereigns is that the latter emphasizes more the connection between the discovery of the New World and the reconquest of Jerusalem (19–20).

Felipe Fernández-Armesto tries as much as possible to present Columbus in his own words, that is to pare him down to those passages that seem to be in keeping with Columbus' style (Felipe Fernández-Armesto, *Columbus on Himself* [London: Folio, 1992], 9–16). He warns of three major scruples that have made historians suspicious about the status of this document: it was datelined near the Canaries when Columbus was off the Azores; the postscript is dated March 14 and claims that Columbus had just reached Lisbon when he had been there for ten days; no copy in Columbus' hand has endured. None the less, although one should read the document with these problems in mind, "There is no reason . . . to see it as other than wholly or substantially Columbus's work" (Fernández-Armesto 101–03).

These textual differences over the Columbian canon do not prevent new characterizations of Columbus the man or his writings. For Djelal Kadir, Columbus is the first in a line of "American" prophets come to the New World who plead in "a rhetoric of prophetic injunction" (Djelal Kadir, *Columbus and the Ends of the Earth: Europe's Prophetic Rhetoric as Conquering Ideology.* [Berkeley: University of California Press, 1992], 64). I use the different variants of the name of Columbus' son Ferdinand, Fernando and Hernando as other critics and historians have done.

14. Cecil Jane, "Introduction," *The Four Voyages of Columbus,* Cecil Jane, ed. (1929 and 1932; New York: Dover, 1988), vol. 1, xiii-cxxii, esp. xcvii-xcviii.

15. There are, as John Fleming has noted, many Columbuses: "Like Julius Caesar, Shakespeare, Napoleon, and others whose lives and works have throughout history intrigued small armies of admirers and detractors, Columbus has been remade in the image of every

age and every group of his investigators"; see John Fleming, "Christopher Columbus: The Man and the Myth," *1492: An Ongoing Voyage,* ed. John R. Hébert (Washington: Library of Congress, 1992), 94–109. I wish to thank John Fleming for sharing his exemplary knowledge and for our conversation about Columbus at Princeton.

16. *Ibid.*, 95; see 98.

17. In keeping with my decision to refer, whenever possible, to images that are accessible to most readers, I have referred to these portraits that face the first page of John Fleming's fine essay; see *ibid.*, 64. See also Everette E. Larson's helpful note, "Six Images of Columbus," as part of that essay—*ibid.*, 95–96. The books on Columbus keep coming: here are a few studies since I first wrote on the topic: David M. Traboulay, *Columbus and Las Casas: The Conquest and Christianization of America, 1492–1566* (Lanham, MD: University Press of America, 1994); Ignacio Solares, *Columbus* (México: Alfaguara, 1996); Miles H. Davidson, *Columbus Then and Now: A Life Reexamined* (Norman: University of Oklahoma Press, 1997).

18. Luis Marden, "Foreword," *The Log of Christopher Columbus,* trans. Robert H. Fuson (Camden, ME: International Marine, 1992), xv; see Robert H. Fuson, "The *Diario de Colón:* A Legacy of Poor Transcription, Translation, and Interpretation," *In the Wake of Columbus: Islands and Controversy,* Louis De Vorsey, Jr. and John Parker, eds. (Detroit: Wayne State University Press, 1985), 51–75 and Fuson, "The Log," *The Log of Christopher Columbus,* 8–11.

19. Peter Hulme, *Colonial Encounters: Europe and the Native Caribbean 1492–1797* (London: Routledge, 1986, rpt. 1992), 17; see also Fuson, "Log" 5–11.

20. Henige x. I wish to thank Daniela Boccassini and her co-organizers of the Pacific Northwest Renaissance Conference (PNRC) for inviting me to present a briefer version of this chapter. I thank Ian MacLaren, who afterwards made me aware of a similar view to my own on the difficulties the text of Columbus' writing presents to us: see Henige. My thanks to the editors and anonymous readers at *Ariel* who in a related and earlier version allowed me to take Henige's and other work into consideration. More generally, though less perceptibly here, I benefited from conversations with the President and Fellows of Clare Hall and with members of the Faculty of History at the University of Cambridge, most notably with Peter Burke and Mark Kaplanoff. My thanks also to Marjorie Chibnall, who invited me to a session on discovery at the British Academy, and who, in response to my reading in medieval voyages from Europe, alerted me to a good summary: see Seymour Phillips, "European Expansion Before Columbus: Causes and Consequences." *The Haskins Society Journal* 5 (1993): 45–59. I want especially to thank Anthony Pagden for directing my attention beyond Columbus, Cabot, Cartier and other explorers to the intellectual assimilation of America in Europe during the sixteenth century. Those audiences in England, France and Australia who heard me give various papers in the field know how much humanists, collectors and administrators have entered my study.

21. Columbus, Jane ed., 2. The original reads:

SEÑOR, porque sé que avréis plazer de la gran vitoria que Nuestro Señor me ha dado en mi viaje, vos escrivo esta, por la qual sabréys como en.xxxiii. díaz pasé de las islas de Canaria á las Indias con la armada que los ilustrísimos rey é reyna nuestros señores me dieron, donde yo fallé muy muchas islas pobladas con gente sin número; y d'ellas todas he tomado posesión por Sus Altezas con pregón y vandera real estendida, y no me fué contradicho. á la primera que yo fallé puse nombre 'San Salvador', á comemoración de Su Alta Magestad, el qual maravillosamente todo esto ha dado; los Indios la llaman 'Guanahani'. (Jane ed. 3)

22. Columbus 4. The original reads:

de adonde enbié dos hombres por la tierra, para saber si havía rey ó grandes ciudades. andovieron tres jornadas, y hallaron infinitas poblaciones pequeñas y gente sin número, mas no cosa de regimiento; por lo qual se bolvieron. Yo entendía harto de ostros Indios, que ya tenía tomados, como continuamente esta tierra era isla. (5)

23. Columbus 6, 8. The original reads:

La gente d'esta ysla y de todos las otras que he fallado y he avido noticia, andan todos desnudos, hombres y mugeres, así como sus madres los paren, aunque algunas mugeres se cobijan un solo lugar con una foja de yerva ó una cofia de algodón que para ellos fazen. ellos no tienen fierro, ni azero, ni armas, ni so(n par)a ello, no porque no sea gente bien dispuesta y de fermosa estatura, salvo las armas de las cañas, quando est(án) con la simiente, á (la) qual ponen al cabo un palillo agudo; é no osan usar de aquellas. (7, 9)

24. Columbus 8. The original reads: "y allende d'esto se fazan cristianos, y se inclinen al amor é servicio de Sus Altezas y de toda la nación castellana, é procuren de ayuntar é nos dar de las cosas que tienen en abundancia, que nos son necessarias" [9, 11]).

25. Stephen Greenblatt has directed our attention once again to the European desire to possess these marvels; see Stephen Greenblatt, *Marvelous Possessions: The Wonder of the New World* (Chicago: University of Chicago Press, 1991). The legal nature of the encounter cannot be underestimated. At the PNRC, William M. Hamlin gave an interesting paper on the marvelous and Renaissance romance, especially in Spenser's *The Faerie Queene:* see "Making Religion of Wonder: Reading, Writing, and the Divine Attribution in Renaissance Ethnography and Romance." I also want to thank him for exchanging comments on each other's papers.

26. Columbus 10. The original reads: "Y luego que legué á las Indias, en la primera isla que hallé tomé por fuerça algunos d'ellos, para que deprendiesen y me diesen noticia de lo que avía en aquellas partes, é así fué que luego entendieron, y nos á ellos, quando por lengua ó señas; y estos han aprovechado mucho" (11).

27. Columbus, Jane ed. 12.

28. Columbus, Jane ed. 14. The original reads: "é, aunque le mudase la volundad á ofender esta gente, él ni los suyos no saben qué sean armas, y andan desnudos, como ya he dicho, é son los más temerosos que ay en el mundo; así que solamente la gente que allá queda es para destroir toda aquella tierra; y es ysla sin peligros de sus personas, sabiéndose regir" (15).

29. Columbus, Jane ed. 14. The original reads: "he hallado hombres mostrudos, como muchos pensavan" [15]; see Columbus' annotations of *Imago Mundi* (Jane 14).

30. Columbus, Jane ed., 16. The original reads:

ási que mostruos no he hallado, ni noticia, salvo de una ysla 'Quaris', la segunda á la entrada de las Yndias, que es poblada de una gente que tienen en todas las yslas por muy ferozes, los quales comen carne humana. estos tienen muchas canoas, con las quales corren todas las yslas de India, y roban y toman quanto pueden; ellos no son más disformes que los otros, salvo que tienen costumbre de traer los cabellos largos como mugeres, y usan arcos y flechas de las mismas armas de cañas, con un palillo al cabo, por defecto de fierro que no tienen. son ferozes entre estos ostros pueblos que son en demasiado grado covardes, mas yo no los tengo en nada más que á los otros. estos son aquellos que tratan con las mugeres de 'Matinino', que es la primera ysla, partiendo de España para las Indias, que se falla, en la qual no ay hombre ninguno. ellas no usan exercicio femenil, salvo arcos y flechas, como los sobredichios, de cañas, y se arman y cobigan con launas de arambre, de que tienen mucho. (17)

31. Jacques Le Goff includes a miniature (Plate 11, between 172–73) that illustrates the medieval revival or translation of classical anxiety over monsters; see Jacques Le Goff, *Medieval Civilization: 400–1500,* trans. Julia Barrow (Oxford: Blackwell, 1988), and, for the original, see *La Civilisation de L'Occident médiéval* (Paris: B. Arthaud, 1964). The image is of human monsters from the ends of the earth. These surreal images, according to Le Goff, reflect "a subject conjured up by the inferior Roman vulgarizer Solinus in the third century and taken up again by Honorius Augustodunensis in the twelfth century." For the relation of patriarchal territories to images of the female in the Renaissance, see Peter Stallybrass, "Patriarchal Territories: The Body Enclosed," *Rewriting the Renaissance: The Discourses of Sexual Difference in Early Modern Europe,* Margaret Ferguson et al. ed. (Chicago: University of Chicago Press, 1986), 123–42; for other views of sexual difference in the period, see Ferguson et al. Annette Kolodny looks at the relation between the land of the New World and the woman's body and Patricia Parker examines the connection between women and the monstrous in male discourse; see Annette Kolodny, *The Lay of the Land* (Chapel Hill: University of North Carolina Press, 1975) and Patricia Parker, *Literary Fat Ladies: Rhetoric, Gender, Property* (New York: Methuen, 1987).

32. Ocular proof, as Othello came to recognize so tragically, depends on whether one is being framed and on the framework of the evidence. He says to Iago, when the two are alone at the end of Actus Tertia, Scæna Tertia (III.iii), "Villaine, be sure thou proue my Loue a Whore;/Be sure of it: Giue me the Occular proofe." William Shakespeare, *Mr. William Shakespeares comedies, histories, & tragedies. Published according to the True Originall Copies* (London: Isaac Iaggard, and Ed. Blount, 1623), 325 [t t 5 recto; there are, however, two pages that are marked t t 3 – on 319 and 321]. The title shows that Shakespeare's editors, Iohn Heminge and Henrie Condell, or perhaps Iaggard and Blount, the printers, want the readers to know that this edition was from Shakespeare's papers and has a certain authority. In "*To the great Variety of Readers,*" Heminge and Condell sought to praise Shakespeare's genius while attesting to the good order of his papers: "His mind and hand went together: And what he thought, he vttered with that easinesse, that wee haue scarce receiued from him a blot in his papers" (A 3 recto). I consulted the Princeton copy. The First Folio was published seven years after the death of Shakespeare, so that he could not, as Ben Jonson might have done with his own collected plays, overseen the editing and printing. Before 1623, about half Shakespeare's plays had not appeared in print, and the state of some of the quartos, which were apparently the property of the acting company (first the Lord Chamberlain's Men and then the King's Men), may explain why Heminge and Condell sought out to print this clean version as a memorial to their great friend and colleague (he had left them mourning rings), or may suggest that they inherited a much messier and more complex textual situation than they would say when entering into the public domain in print. The scholarship on Shakespeare's First Folio and texts more generally is vast and deep. For instance, see Chalton J. K. Hinman, "The Prentice Hand in the Tragedies of the Shakespeare First Folio: Compositor E," *Studies in Bibliography* 9 (1957), 3–20 and his *Printing and Proof-reading of the First Folio of Shakespeare* (Oxford: Clarendon, 1963); T. H. Howard-Hill, *Shakespeare Bibliography and Textual Criticism: A Bibliography* (Oxford: Clarendon Press, 1971); Peter W. M. Blayney, *The Texts of King Lear and their Origins* (Cambridge: Cambridge University Press, 1982). My thanks to Stephen Ferguson for his discussions of Shakespearean bibliography and textual criticism this year and last and to G. Blakemore Evans for sharing his expertise in these fields with me over the past seventeen years.

Chapter 3

1. There is a vast literature on textual studies in Shakespeare and fine editions, such as the Arden, Cambridge, Norton, Oxford and Riverside. Peter Alexander's edition has also been influential, particularly in Britain. These editions, as well as Shakespeare bibliographies, will give an idea of the scope of this scholarship. The editorial and textual work of Stanley Wells, John Jowett and Gary Taylor has caused debated over the past couple of decades. G. Blakemore Evans continues to contribute to his long and distinguished record of editing and research in the area. Rather than try to list all the important contributions to textual studies and bibliography generally and editing Shakespeare specifically, I will mention a few recent works that I did not note in the last chapter: see Randall McLeod, "UnEditing Shak-speare," *Sub-stance* 33/34 (1982): 26–55; Margreta de Grazia and Peter Stallybrass, "The Materiality of the Shakespearean Text," *Shakespeare Quarterly* 44 (1993): 255–283; Leah S. Marcus, *Unediting the Renaissance: Marlowe, Shakespeare, Milton* (London: Routledge, 1996). There are anniversaries for Shakespeare as there are for Columbus. For instance, on April 23, 1923, the three hundredth anniversary of the death of Shakespeare, Alfred W. Pollard delivered the annual Shakespeare lecture to the British Academy, and entitled it "The Foundations of Shakespeare's Text." In this address, he focused on what he considered the textual "Foundations of Shakespeare's Text": "We are left then with the Folio of 1623, and the forty-four editions of sixteen different single plays issued before it appeared. From the *Titus Andronicus* of 1594 to the *Othello* of 1622" (*Proceedings of the British Academy,* 2–3). The capitalization of the phrase "Foundations of Shakespeare's Text" is not simply a fetishization or aggrandizement of Shakespeare's work, because two sentences later Pollard reiterates it in lower case. For a recent interesting and suggestive interpretation, see Patricia Parker, *Shakespeare from the Margins* (Chicago: University of Chicago Press, 1997). A fine modern biography of Shakespeare is that by Samuel Schoenbaum, which includes the reproduction of documents pertaining to Shakespeare.

2. Michele de Cuneo, "Letter on the Second Voyage, 28 October 1495," in *Journals and Other Documents in the Life and Voyages of Christopher Columbus,* trans. and ed. S. E. Morison (New York: The Heritage Press, 1963), 212. For a pioneering work on gender and the land in America, see Annette Kolodny, *The Lay of the Land: Metaphor as Experience and History in American Life and Letters* (Chapel Hill : University of North Carolina Press, 1975).

3. V. E. Fuchs, Introduction to Felipe Fernández-Armesto, *Columbus and the Conquest of the Impossible* (London: Weidenfeld and Nicolson, 1974), 6.

4. Fernández-Armesto, *Columbus and the Conquest of the Impossible,* 215.

5. *Ibid.,* 205, 210–11, 214–15.

6. Hugh Honour, *The European Vision of America* (Cleveland: The Cleveland Museum of Art, 1975), 305n3.

7. This image is well known and is on the cover of my last book on America, *Representing the New World* (New York and London: Palgrave, 2001), but can also be found in a number of publications, such as Dennis Channing Landis, *The Literature of the Encounter: A Selection of Books from* European Americana (Providence: John Carter Brown Library, 1991), 22 and Susan Danforth, with an introductory essay by William H. McNeill, *Encountering The New World 1493–1800* (Providence: The John Carter Brown Library, 1991), 3. Other images I discuss can also be found in these collections.

8. For an instance of this "departure scene," from Part IV, Historia Sive of Girolamo Benzoni, *America* . . . , in case the original is out-of-reach, see Louis de Vorsey, Jr., *Keys to the Encounter: A Library of Congress Resource Guide for the Study of the Age of Discovery* (Washington: Library of Congress, 1992), 63.

9. See Honour, *European,* 155–56, 303–05; I am indebted to Honour's discussion; see Leicester Bradner, "Columbus in Sixteenth-century Poetry," *Essays Honoring Lawrence C. Wroth* (Portland, ME, 1951), 15–30.

10. See Honour, *European,* 306–07.

11. *Ibid.,* 313.

12. *Ibid.,* 312.

13. *Ibid.,* 314.

14. Everette E. Larson, "Six Images of Columbus," in John Fleming, "Christopher Columbus: The Man and the Myth," *1492: An Ongoing Voyage,* ed. John R. Hébert (Washington: Library of Congress, 1992), 95–96. For a text about the 1892 events, see Herbert B. Adams and Henry Wood, *Columbus and His Discovery of America* (Baltimore: Johns Hopkins University Press, [1892]). This book shows the scholarship of the time; see, for instance, the oration of Herbert B. Adams [7–39], that by Henry Wood [40–44]; M. Kayserling's "The First Jew in America," [45–50]; Vyrus Adler's "Columbus in Oriental Literature," [51–54]; as well, in an Appendix, work on bibliographies of the discovery of America and on Columbus public memorials by a then graduate student, Charles Bump, at this recent and first graduate school in the United States—Johns Hopkins. Here, then, is an important point in Columbus scholarship in the United States. I have consulted the copy at Princeton. A single-authored volume of the following year, with an appropriate title for work in this field, is also informative; see Richard H. Clarke, *Old and New Lights on Columbus. With Observations on Controverted Points and Criticisms* (New York: Richard H. Clarke, 1893). Columbus was controversial from the beginning, as I have argued in this study, and he continued to be: it was not in 1992 that the controversy started. The nature of the controversies changes over time.

15. I viewed this painting three times, in August and December 2000, and in December 2001 in order to see how it might relate to earlier works.

16. I discuss in more detail this larger context for coming after Spain in a chapter of the next book in my series on the New World, *Comparing Empires.*

17. See Bartolomé de Las Casas, *Narratio Regionem Indicarum per Hispanos quosdam devastatarum verissima* (Oppenheim: J. T. de Bry, 1614), 26.

18. Honour, *European,* 94–95.

19. Hugh Honour, *The New Golden Land: European Images of America from the Discoveries to the Present Time* (1975; London: Allen Lane, 1976), 22–24; see Honour, *European,* 30–32. For an extended discussion, see James Snyder, "Jan Mostaert's West Indies Landscape," *First Images of America: The Impact of the New World on the Old,* ed. Fredi Chiapelli, Michael J. B. Allen and Robert L. Benson (Berkeley: University of California Press, 1976), vol. 1, 495–502. Snyder favors Coronado's expedition of 1540 as the subject of Mostaert's painting. For this theme in literature, see Arthur Lovejoy and George Boas, *Primitivism and Related Ideas in Antiquity* (Baltimore: Johns Hopkins University Press, 1935) and Harry Levin, *The Myth of the Golden Age* in the Renaissance (Bloomington: University of Indiana Press, 1969).

20. Here I refer to William Shakespeare, *The Tempest,* ed. Stephen Orgel (Oxford: Oxford University Press, 1987, rpt. 1998).

21. Honour, *European,* 52–53. This map is in the collection of the British Library, Department of Manuscripts.

22. For an accessible image and description, see McNeill, *Encountering,* 18.

23. John Parker, *Books to Build an Empire: A Bibliographical History of English Overseas Interests to 1620* (Amsterdam 1965), 21–3. For *Of the new landes . . . ,* see Edward Arber, ed., *The first Three English books on America [?1511]–1555 A.D. . . .* (Westminster, 1895), xxiii-xxxvi.

24. *Ibid.,* c,i, recto.

25. On Belleforest and Thevet, see Olive P. Dickason, "Thevet and Belleforest: Two Sixteenth-Century Frenchmen and New World Colonialism," *Proceedings of the Annual Meeting of the French Colonial Society* 16 (1992): 1–11.

26. Thevet uses the phrase "cruels jusques au bout"; André Thevet, *La Cosmographie Vniverselle D'André Thevet Cosmographe dv Roy . . . Tome Second* (Paris, 1575), in *Les Français en Amérique pendant la deuxième moitié du XVIe Siècle: Le Brésil et les Brésiliens*, ed. Charles-André Julien, and notes by Suzanne Lussagnet (2 vols., Paris, 1953), II, 29.

27. The Natives were "thieves, robbers, and without faith, or loyalty, that their God was imaginary"; *ibid.*, 29. The Spanish names in South America marked their presence during the French expedition there; see *ibid.*, 218.

28. Francisco López de Gómara, *Histoire Generalle des Indes Occidentales et Terres Nevves, qui iusques à present ont estre descouuertes. Traduite en françois par M. Fumee Sieur de Marly le Chatel.* (Paris, 1578), āiv verso; my translation.

29. Urbain Chauveton, "Sommaire," *Histoire Novvelle dv Novveav Monde, Contenant en somme ce que les Hespagnols ont fait iusqu'à present aux Indes Occidentales, & le rude traitement qu'ils ont fait à ces poures peuples-la* (Geneva 1579), no pagination [1st page recto]. *Brief Discours* and *Requeste au roy* are numbered together and continuously after Benzoni's work, which was first published in Italian in 1565. For a discussion of Chauveton, see Benjamin Keen, "The Vision of America in the Writings of Urbain Chauveton" in *First Images of America: The Impact of the New World on the Old*, ed Fredi Chiapelli *et al.* (2 vols., Berkeley, 1976), I, 107–20.

30. Chauveton, 'Sommaire', no pagination [1st page verso]. My translation of Chauveton here and below.

31. Richard Hakluyt, *The Principall Navigations . . .* (London: George Bishop, 1589), no pagination; the actual Latin inscription is "AMERICA SIVE IN DIA NOVA Ao 1492 a Christophoro Colombo nomine regis Castelle primum detecta." "Noua Francia" appears to the east.

32. John Smith, *New Englands Trials . . .* , second edition (London 1622) in *Tracts,* ed. Force, II, 23.

33. Sagard, "Av Lecteur," 12. All translations of Sagard in the notes are mine. See also Sagard, 627.

34. *Ibid.*, II: 809.

35. *Ibid.*, II: 810, 815–16.

36. Walter Ralegh, *The Discoverie of the Large, Rich, and Bevvtifvl Empyre of Gviana, with a Relation of the Great and Golden Citie of Manoa (which the Spanyards call El Dorado . . .* (London: Robert Robinson, 1596), 99 [Princeton copy].

37. "Memorandum de Francois [T]ourillon of Marseille who made several voyages in Spanish Mexico, with the Spanish and in their service, having lived there several years both in the islands and on the main land [terre ferme] always in the company of the Spanish," November 2, 1669, [5]; no pagination; the document is seven pages, so I will create my own numbers in square brackets. Archive d'Outre Mer.

38. *Ibid.*

39. R. B. [pseudonym Richard Burton for Nathaniel Crouch], *The English Empire in America: Or a prospect of his Majesties Dominions in the West-Indies* (London: the Bell, 1685). I have consulted the first edition in the British Library, whose copy had been misplaced but is now back in circulation.

40. *Ibid.*, 42.

41. Anon., *The British Sailor's Discovery: or the Spaniards Pretensions Confuted* (London, 1739), 2–3.

42. *Ibid.*

43. David Ramsey, *The History of the American Revolution,* 2 vols. (Philadelphia, 1789).

44. Jeremy Belknap, *A Discourse, Intended to Commemorate the Discovery of America by Christopher Columbus; Delivered at the Request of the Historical Society in Massachusetts, on the 23rd Day of October 1792, Being the Completion of the Third Century Since that Memorable Event* (Boston: Belknap and Hall, 1792), 19.

45. *Ibid.*, 28.

46. *Ibid.*, 36–37.

47. *Ibid.*, 41.

48. *Ibid.*

49. *Ibid.*, 46–47. The "Ode" in Belknap occurs on pages 56–58. Stanzas VI-VIII, which I quote, are on p. 57.

50. See Anthony Pagden, *The Fall of Natural Man: The American Indian and the Origins of Comparative Ethnography* (Cambridge, 1982, rev. ed. 1986) and his "*Ius et Factum:* Text and Experience in the Writings of Bartolomé de Las Casas" in *New World Encounters,* ed. Stephen Greenblatt (Berkeley, CA: University of California Press, 1993), 87–100. Las Casas did change his mind about African slaves; see Wright.

51. I have discussed this aspect of the teleology of prophecy when the events are past in *Theater and World: The Problematics of Shakespeare's History* (Boston: Northeastern University Press, 1992).

52. Stanza 32, fifteenth booke, Torquato Tasso, Godfrey of Bulloigne, or The Recouerie of Ierusalem. Done into English Heroicall verse, by Edward Fairefax Gent. (London: Ar. Hatfield, for I. Iaggard and M. Lownes, 1600), 273. Canto XV is not found in the 1594 translation, which is a bilingual edition of the first five cantos; see *Godfrey of Bvlloigne, Or The Recouerie of Hiervsalem. An Heroicall poeme written in Italian by Seig. Torquato Tasso, and translated into English by R. C. Esquire: And now the first part containing fiue Cantos, Imprinted in both Languages* (London: Iohn Windet for Christopher Hunt of Exceter, 1594). Fairfax's translation, which is well exemplified in this canto, is literary and sometimes strays from Tasso's original syntax and diction.

53. Joel Barlow, *The Columbiad. A Poem with The Last Corrections of the Author* (Paris: F. Schoell, 1813), vi.

54. *Ibid.*, v.

55. *Ibid.*, x.

56. *Ibid.*, xii.

57. *Ibid.*, xix.

58. *Ibid.*, xxi.

59. *Ibid.*, xxxii.

60. *Ibid.*, xxxix.

61. *Ibid.*, xxxix.

62. *Ibid.*, xl.

63. *Ibid.*, xlii [unnumbered].

64. *Ibid.*, 1–2.

65. *Ibid.*, 362 (X:638).

66. Richard Snowden, *The Columbiad; Or A Poem On The American War, in Thirteen Cantoes* (Baltimore: W. Pechin, [n.d.]), 3.

67. For more on the history of Columbia University, see the *Encyclopedia Britannica.*

68. Harriet Munroe, *Columbian Ode* (Chicago: W. Irving Way & Co., 1893), 5 [unnumbered]. I have consulted the "Souvenir Edition"—which was produced on fine durable paper with uneven treated edges that give it an antique feel—in Rare Books at Princeton.

69. *Ibid.*

70. *Ibid.*, 7.

71. *Ibid.*, 8.

72. *Ibid.*, 9, see 8.

73. Ralegh, *Discoverie*, 101.

74. Munroe, 9.

75. *Ibid.*, 23.

76. Louisa Susannah Wells Aikman, *The Journal of a Voyage from Charleston, S.C. to London: Undertaken During the American Revolution* (New York: New York Historical Society, 1906), 11–12. I would like to acknowledge the work of the North American Women's Letters and Diaries and other resources that have made research so much easier in this area (*www.lib.uchicago.eduletts/asp/NAWLO/* or *www.alexanderstreet2.com/NWLOlive/*). I have not referred to references in databases but have provided the references to books under the assumption that not everyone has access to, or expertise on, the internet but readers will have libraries and interlibrary loan available to them.

77. Harriet Low Hillard, *My Mother's Journal: A Young Lady's Diary of Five Years Spent in Manila, Macao and the Cape of Good Hope from 1829–1834,* ed. Katherine Hillard (Boston: George H. Ellis, 1900), 190.

78. Frances Anne Kemble, Diary, September 2, 1832, *Journal of Frances Anne Butler* (Philadelphia: Carey, Lea & Blanchard, 1835), I: 43.

79. *Memoir of Anne Gorham Everett, with Extracts from Her Correspondence and Journal,* ed. Philippa C. Bush (Boston: privately printed, 1857), 125, see 124.

80. Relations between settlers and Natives in early New England were ambivalent, as I argue in the discussion of William Bradford in the chapter "Between Cultures."

81. *Memoir,* ed. P. Bush, 177.

82. Mother Theodore Guerin, "Letter from Mother Theodore Guerin to Louis Veuillot and Leon Aubineau, May 28, 1844," *Journals and Letter of Mother Theodore Guerin, Foundress of the Sisters of Providence of Saint Mary-of-the Woods, Indiana,* ed. Sister Mary Theodosia Mug (Saint Mary-of-the-Woods, IN: Providence Press, 1937), 157.

83. *Ibid.*

84. *Ibid.*, 157–58.

85. *Ibid.*, 158.

86. *Ibid.*

87. *Ibid.*, 159.

88. *Ibid.*

89. Mary Davis Cook Wallis, Entry of April 1, 1846, "Diary of Mary Davis Wallis, April, 1846," *Life in Feejee, or Five Years Among the Cannibals* (Boston; W. Heath, 1851), 194.

90. Catherine Elizabeth Havens, entry for August 15, 1849, *Diary of a Little Girl in Old New York* (New York: Henry Collins Brown, 1919), 26.

91. Susan Augusta Fenimore Cooper, entry for September 20[?], 1849[?], *Journal of a Naturalist in the United States* (London: R. Bentley & Son, 1855), 2:30.

92. Harriet Preble, Letter [undated], *Memoir of the Life of Harriet Preble: Containing Portions of Her Correspondence, Journal and Other Writings, Literary and Religious,* ed. R. H. Lee (New York: G. P. Putnam's Sons, 1856), 231.

93. *Ibid.*, 232; see July 4 [?].

94. Ellen Douglas Birdseye Wheaton, *The Diary of Ellen Birdseye Wheaton,* ed. Donald Gordon (Boston: privately printed, 1923), 359–60.

95. *Ibid.*, 360–61.

96. Catherine Ann Devereux Edmonston, Letter, March 20, 1864, *Journal of a Secesh: The Diary of Catherine Ann Devereux Edmonston 1860–1866,* ed. Beth G. Crabtree and James W. Patton (Raleigh, NC: North Carolina Division of Archives and History, 1979), 540.

97. Annie Adams Fields, *Memories of a Hostess: A Chronicle of Eminent Friendships,* ed. Mark A. de Wolfe Howe (Boston: Atlantic Monthly Press, 1922), 91.

98. Edmundo O'Gorman, *The Invention of America: An Inquiry into the Historical Nature of the New World and the Meaning of Its History* (Bloomington: Indiana University Press,

1961). He declares "the object of our inquiry is to test the scientific validity of the idea that what Columbus really did was to 'discover' America" (10).

99. Letter, January 3, 1873, *The Letters of Ellen Tucker Emerson,* ed. Edith E. W. Gregg (Kent, OH: Kent State University Press, 1982), 2: 37. For example, see her letter to her father on January 28, 1857, from Concord, Massachusetts, *ibid.,* I: 128.

100. *Ibid.,* 2:105.

101. Emily McCorkle FitzGerald, Letter, May 24, 1874, *An Army Doctor's Wife on the Frontier: Letters from Alaska and the Far West, 1874–1878,* ed. Abe Laufe and Russell J. Ferguson (Pittsburgh, PA: University of Pittsburgh Press, 1962), 6.

102. Helen Adams Keller, Letter, January 8, 1890, *The Story of My Life: With Her Letters (1887–1901) and a Supplementary Account of Her Education, Including Passages from the Reports and Letters of Her Teacher, Anne Mansfield Sullivan* (New York: Doubleday, Page & Co., 1903), 181.

103. Letter, December 28, 1893; *ibid.,* 223.

104. Fannie de C. Miller, entry for September 11, 1891, *Snap Notes of an Eastern Trip: From the Diary of Fannie de C. Miller,* (San Francisco: S. Carson Co., 1892), 99, see 100.

105. Florence Trail, diary entry for Tuesday, September 22, 1891, *Foreign Family Life in France in 1891* (Boston: B. Humphries, 1944), 22–23.

106. *Ibid.,* 23.

107. *Ibid.,* 24.

108. Ellen Tucker Emerson, *The Letters,* 652.

109. *Ibid.,* 652.

110. *Ibid.*

111. *Ibid.*

112. *Ibid.*

113. *Ibid.,* 652–53.

114. Susan Hale, Letter, February 4, 1893, *Letters of Susan Hale,* ed. Caroline Atkinson (Boston: Marshall Jones Co., 1919), 277.

115. Mary Perkins Quincy, Letter, May 23, 1893, *Pages in Azure and Gold: The Letters of Miss Gardiner and Miss Quincy* (privately printed), 26.

116. *Ibid.,* 28.

117. *Ibid.*

118. *Ibid.,* 29.

119. *Ibid.,* 30–31.

120. *Ibid.,* 30, see 31.

121. *Ibid.,* 70.

122. *Ibid.,* 73, see 72.

123. *Ibid.,* 74–75.

124. Laurette Taylor, diary entry for May 29, 1918, *The Greatest of These*—(New York: George H. Doran Company, [1918]), 50; see entries for May 13 and 14, 1918, 17–19.

125. Clare Consuela Frewen Sheridan, diary entry of February 22, 1921, *My American Diary* (New York: Boni and Liveright, 1922), 51.

126. Entry for June 23, 1921, *ibid.,* 141–42; see the entry for June 2, 1921, 133.

127. Rosalie Caden Evans, Letter, June 8, 1923, *The Rosalie Evans Letters from Mexico,* ed. Daisy Caden Pettus (Indianapolis IN: Bobbs-Merrill, 1926), 220.

128. Sheridan, diary entry for June 2, 1921, 133.

129. Mary Matthews Bray, diary entry for January 18 [?], *A Sea Trip in Clipper Ship Days* (Boston: R. G. Badger, 1920), 146.

130. *Ibid.,* 147.

131. Monica Storrs, entry beginning Sunday, September 29 [including events from other days], *God's Galloping Girl: The Peace River Diaries of Monica Storrs, 1929–1931,* ed. W. L. Morton (Vancouver: University of British Columbia, 1979), 2–3.

132. *Ibid.*, 3.

133. *Ibid.*, 68–69.

134. For instance, Storrs thinks that if Mrs. Millar's husband is a changed man—he now does the wash, because she ran away and came back, she asks :"Why don't we all run away more often?" See *ibid.*, 68.

135. Betty May Hale, diary entry of June 29, 1937, *My Trip to Europe, 1937* (San Francisco: W. Kibbee & Son, 1938), 228.

136. See information on the "Discovery of the Site," L'Anse aux Meadows National Historic Site of Canada: "It was nearly nine centuries later, in 1960, that a Norwegian explorer and writer, Helge Ingstad, came upon the site at L'Anse aux Meadows. He was making an intensive search for Norse landing places along the coast from New England northward. At L'Anse aux Meadows, a local inhabitant, George Decker, led him to a group of overgrown bumps and ridges which looked as if they might be building remains. They later proved to be all that was left of that old colony. For the next eight years, Helge and his wife, archaeologist Anne Stine Ingstad, led an international team of archaeologists from Norway, Iceland, Sweden, and the United States in the excavation of the site." See http://parkscanada.pch.gc.ca/parks/newfoundland/anse_meadows/english/discover_e.html.

137. Viola Chittenden White, diary entry August 12 [?], *Not Faster than a Walk: A Vermont Notebook* (Middlebury: Middlebury College Press, 1939), 126. The Thoreau comes from *Journals* (Boston: Houghton, 1906). The diary entry was probably written between 1906 and 1939, which does not narrow matters down much.

138. Robert Muccigrosso, *Celebrating the New World: Chicago's Columbian Exposition of 1893*, ix-x; see Claudia L. Bushman, *America Discovers Columbus: How an Italian Explorer Became an American Hero* (Hanover, NH: University Press of New England, 1992).

139. Norman Bolotin and Christine Laing, *The World's Columbian Exposition* (Washington, DC: The Preservation Press, 1992), 104–06.

140. *Ibid.*, 111.

141. *Memorial Volume. Dedicatory And Opening Ceremonies Of The World's Columbian Exposition. Historical And Descriptive. As Authorized By Board of Control: Edited Under The Direction Of The Joint Committee on Ceremonies Of The World's Columbian Commission And The World's Columbian Exposition. With Illustrations* (Chicago: Stone, Kastler & Painter, 1893), 8.

142. *Ibid.*, 53. I discuss this more in *Comparing Empires*.

143. A consideration of Columbus in preparation for the Columbian Exposition in Chicago in 1493 was not always direct or in evidence. Sometimes such an event was a pretext for a celebration of some other cultural landmark. For instance, one typescript in manuscripts at Princeton involved a marking of the achievement of women writers in New York. See Edward Hale Bierstadt (for and under the direction of Miriam Y. Holden), "A List of the Books Contained in The Library collected by the Board of Women Managers of New York for the World's Columbian Exposition of 1893, and afterwards given to the Library of the University of the State of New York." The title page states that "(The 'Women's Library' was subsequently destroyed in the Capitol fire of 1911)." It also notes that Bierstadt compiled this list from the *State Library Bulletin*, September 1894, which says "that these books were 'preserved as a permanent memorial of the literary work of New York women and contributions are asked from all authors and others interested to make the collection as complete as possible.'" Miriam Y. Holden Collection (C0071), IV. Papers of Others Persons. C. Miscellaneous, Box 64, Folder 1A, manuscript, n.d. Thank you to Stephen Ferguson and Meg Sherry Rich for their advice concerning archival material and rare books at Princeton about the Columbian Exposition.

144. For an interesting study of this contribution, see John E. Findling, *Chicago's Great World Fairs* (Manchester: Manchester University Press, 1994), especially chapters 2 and 4. For instance, Findling mentions that the Japanese replica of an eleventh-century temple at Expo 1893 kindled Frank Lloyd Wright's interest in Japanese design.

145. William Boldenweck and Maier Weinchenk, *"An Address to His Excellency, Grover Cleveland, President of the United States in Presenting the Historical World's Fair Medal in Gold at the Dedication of the World's Columbian Exposition at Chicago, on May 1st. 1893. By William Boldenweck and Maier Weinchenk,"* 2–3. This is the copy that Grover Cleveland presented to the Princeton Library. He retired to Princeton after his presidency.

146. *Ibid.*, 4.

147. *Ibid.*, 4–5.

148. *Ibid.*, 5–6.

149. *Ibid.*, 6–8.

150. *Ibid.*, 8–9.

151. *Ibid.*, 10–11.

152. *Rand, McNally & Co.'s A Week at the Fair Illustrating the Exhibits and Wonders of the World's Columbian Exposition with Special Descriptive Articles . . . Also Maps, Plans, and Illustrations* (Chicago: Rand, McNally & Company Publishers, 1893), 78. This article seems to have been written by Van Brunt & Howe, Kansas City, MO.

153. Wim de Wit, "Building an Illusion: The Design of the World's Columbian Exposition," in Neil Harris, Wim de Wit, James Gilbert, and Robert W. Rydell, *Grand Illusions: Chicago's World's Fair of 1893* (Chicago: Chicago Historical Society, 1993), 85. As part of a centennial assessment of Expo 1893, Wim de Wit says that besides the Statue of the Republic, a personification of national unity, and the Columbian Fountain, a representation of the ambitions of the United States, "Columbus, the historical figure who initiated the country's progress, was also present in the Court of Honor. His statue stood atop the central portion of the Peristyle, which, since it was shaped as a triumphal arch, elevated both the act of entering the fair and the voyage of Columbus to the status of triumphal processions. Accordingly, the sculpture of Columbus showed the navigator standing triumphantly in a chariot pulled by four horses. Texts inscribed in the walls of the arch clarified the importance of explorers such as Columbus"; *ibid.*, see *ibid.*, 87. Image and text were part of this carefully conceived typology of Columbus and the Columbian, of Spanish discovery and U. S. progress: "Names of explorers inscribed in the frieze over the arch were accompanied by odes that on the lake side (facing east, the direction from which the Europeans had come) were devoted to the explorers and settlers who had made America's development possible and on the court side to the 'Pioneers of Civil and Religious Liberty,' who had made America great"; *ibid.* For more on the MacMonnies or Columbian Fountain, see Bolotin and Laing, 61.

154. *Rand, McNally & Co.'s A Week at the Fair,* 111.

155. *Ibid.*, 113.

156. *Ibid.*

157. *Ibid.* A brief discussion of the Columbus Quadriga on the Peristyle occurs at *ibid.*, 129.

158. Littleton, N. H.: B. W. Kilburn, 1893), 8.7 X 17.8 cm. Collection: Photographs of American Indians (WC 064), Folder WA 1998: 156. Princeton University

159. James Gilbert, "Fixing the Image: Photography at the World's Columbian Exposition," *Grand Illusions,* 133. See Robert Rydell, *All the World's a Fair: Visions of Empire at American International Expositions, 1876–1916* (Chicago: University of Chicago Press, 1984).

160. John Eaton, *Education at the Columbian Exposition* (Washington: Government Printing Office, 1896), 1079. I am grateful to Stephen Ferguson, curator of Rare Books at Princeton, for sharing with me his knowledge and his file on the Chicago Expo of 1893. His characteristic generosity has helped to expand this section and has been a great help on other projects as well.

161. *Ibid.*, 1081; see 1079–80. See also "Princeton at the World's Fair," *Princeton College Bulletin* (January 1894), 1–37. I have viewed the Peale portrait on many occasions between 2000–2002 in the Princeton Art Museum.

162. "At Old Nassau, Princeton Gets Four World's Fair Awards for Her Exhibit . . . ," Dec. 11, 1893. See the Curtis scrapbooks—William Eleroy Curtis Papers—at the Seeley G. Mudd Manuscript Library, Princeton.

163. Quoted in Muccigrosso, *Celebrating,* 134, see 131–41. See Jeanne Marie Weimann, *The Fair Women* (Chicago, 1981). An interesting book of the time is Kate Brannon Knight's *History of the Work of Connecticut Women at the World's Columbian Exposition Chicago,* 1893 (Hartford, CT: The Hartford Press, 1898); Knight explains that states had to give their histories because of a decision by Congress to postpone the official reports and that the literature of the world's fair must "consist of impressions. Indeed, no other word so fitly describes this greatest of illusions" (1, 5). It is important to emphasize that people writing then were sophisticated and self-conscious about this Exposition. What is most difficult for any of us in any age is to see the illusions we have not already identified as such.

164. Quoted in Muccigrosso, *Celebrating,* 77, see 76.

165. Muccigrosso, 151, see 147–53.

166. Quoted in Bolotin and Laing, 147. Rydell notes that Native Americans from the Pacific Northwest were put on display: "Groups of people from cultures considered 'exotic' and 'savage' were displayed on the Midway as curiosities"; see Robert W. Rydell, "A Cultural Frankenstein? The Chicago World's Columbian Exposition of 1893, " in *Grand Illusion,* 142–43. He also states: "Despite the heat of a Chicago summer, members of the Innuit tribe, referred to at the fair as Esquimaux, were expected to perform with their huskies while dressed in the fur garments of their native land. When the concessionaires threatened to withhold food, some of the Innuits sued them and were released from their contract"; see *ibid.,* 158–60.

167. "To the Commissioners of the Columbian Exposition," [1891?], Frederic Ward Putnam Papers, Box 34, Harvard University Archives, quoted in *ibid.* While at Harvard in the 1980s and 1990s, I consulted archival material on Natives at Harvard and Native American discontent. There was also an exhibit at Harvard on the topic that I saw. Owing to limits of space, I leave some of this material to my next books.

168. *Ibid.*

169. *Ibid.*

170. See Wells and Douglass, "The Reason Why the Colored American is Not in the World's Columbian Exposition," cited in Findling, 28; see 27. For the original, see Frederic Douglass, Ida Wells, and Ferdinand Barnett, "The Reason Why The Colored American Is Not in the World's Columbian Exhibition" (no imprint, 1893). On Native and African-Americans in this period or at the fair, see Philip Weeks, *Farewell, My Nation: The American Indian and the United States 1820–1890* (Arlington Heights, IL, 1990); Elliot M. Rudwick and August Meier, "Black Man in the 'White City': Negroes and the Columbian Exposition, 1893," *Phylon* 26 (1965): 354–61; see also Rydell, *All the World's a Fair,* esp. 52–53 and Donald L. Miller, "The White City," *American Heritage* 44 (July-August 1993), esp. 85, see 71–87. See also R. Reed Badger, *The Great American Fair: The World's Columbian Exposition and American Culture* (Chicago: Nelson-Hall, 1979) and Weimann, *The Fair Women.*

171. Julian Street. Scrapbook, 1892–94. [Cover title: "Notes on Niagara"], Rare Books: Manuscripts Collection, Princeton University.

172. Bolotin and Laing, 96.

173. William Eleroy Curtis Papers, one of the four World's Fair Volumes, vol. 104 of the scrapbooks, Seeley G. Mudd Manuscript Library [n.d., n.p.].

174. *Ibid.*

175. *Ibid.*

176. *Ibid.*

177. *Ibid.*

178. *Ibid.*

179. *Ibid.*

180. *Ibid.*

181. *Ibid.;* see [Kate Field's Washington (in hand in ink)], "Relics of the Great Discoverer. Mr Curtis Collecting Columbiana for the World's fair. By Grapevine Telephone"; "Columbus Portraits. W.E. Curtis' Search for An Authentic One. Walter Wellman Here Presents Ten Examples of the Different Conceptions of America's Discoverer, Together with the Facts Regarding Them," [(in ink) Times. Sioux City, IA 7–31–91]. I discuss these in *Comparing Empires.* A replica of La Rábida, the Spanish monastery where Columbus visited, housed the Columbian relics, whereas Native artifacts were housed principally in the Anthropology Building.

182. Washington, October 24th [Anglo-American Hanover 11–8–91 (in pen)], Curtis, Scrapbook 1891 (as above), vol. 104.

183. [Union Springfield Mass Aug 28/91 (in pen)], Curtis, World's Fair Scrapbook, vol. 105. Actually this scrapbook contains material from 1890 into 1892. I also discussed the question of origins and these papal bulls in *Representing the New World.*

184. Curtis, World Fair Scrapbook, vol. 105.

185. Curtis, vol. 107.

186. *Ibid.*

187. *Ibid.,* 165.

188. *Ibid.,* 242.

189. *Ibid.,* 255.

190. *Ibid.*

191. *Ibid.,* 256.

192. See *A Week at the Fair,* 105.

193. Truman, 409.

194. Daniel H. Burnham, *The Final Official Report of the Director of Works of the World's Columbian Exposition in Two Parts* (New York: Garland, 1989), I:56.

195. *Ibid.,* IV: 76. I discuss this and other inscriptions more in *Comparing Empires.*

196. *Ibid.,* IV: 72.

197. *Ibid.,* IV: 77.

198. Daniel H. Burnham, *The Final Official Report of the Director of Works of the World's Columbian Exposition in Two Parts* (New York: Garland, 1989), I:56. See Muccigrosso, *Celebrating,* ix.

199. *Ibid.,* x–xi; see, for instance, Kirkpatrick Sale, *Conquest of Paradise: Christopher Columbus and the Columbian Legacy* (New York, 1990) and John Noble Wilford, "Discovering Columbus," *New York Times Magazine* (August 11, 1991), 24f.

200. See Walt Disney Productions v. Fantasyland Hotel Inc (1993), 141 A.R. 291.

201. At www.eb.com.

202. See www.rottentomatoes.

203. See Paul Chutkow, "Discovering Columbus: Ridley Scot, Cohiba in Hand, Directs Gérard Depardieu in 1492," at *www.cigaraficionado.com.* My discussion is indebted to this article here and below.

204. See www-unix.oit.umass.edu/~rtww/columbus.

205. See www.etext.org/Politics/NativeNet/1492/Misc/haiti-tourism.

206. Htpp://flab.blackened.net/revolt/ws92/columbus35.html.

207. See www.red-coral.net/Columb.html.

208. See page 1 of http://www.dickshovel.com/500.html; reprinted from *Oh-Toh-Kin,* vol. 1 No. 1 (Winter/Spring 1992).

209. Glenn Morris and Russell Means, "Why Autonomous AIM Opposes Columbus Day and Columbus Day Parades," website of the American Indian Movement at www.dickshovel.com/colum.html; at the end of the article, the following statement appears: "Russell Means and Glenn Morris wrote this position statement in 1991 on behalf of the American Indian Movement of Colorado, 1574 South Pennsylvania St., Denver, CO."

210. Robert Royal, "Consequences of Columbus," *First Things* 20 (February 1992): 9–11.

211. "A Faithful Response to the 500th Anniversary of the Arrival of Christopher Columbus As adopted by the Governing Board, May 17, 1990, A Resolution of the National Council of the Churches of Christ in the USA," opening paragraph; at http://www.indians.org/welker/faithful.html.

212. One website on the environment quotes the following excerpt from this document: "Let us nail the lie that we have unlimited freedom to exploit the natural world as we will. To deal with nature in the way of peace requires us to reject economic and social structures which are a threat to life. It has been borne in on us again in recent days that the present profligate waste of resources and energy must be drastically reduced. Of all of us is required a radically different and simpler life-style." See the website of the "european christian environment network" at http://www.ecen.org/ecenmain.html.

213. *Aguirre, Wrath of God* (1972); *Aguirre, der Zorn Gottes;* Director: Werner Herzog; Starring: Klaus Kinski, Cecilia Rivera, Ruy Guerra, Helena Rojo, Del Negro; Language: German; Germany, 95m, color. On this narrative in Gómara and others, see my *Representing the New World,* esp. 143–44, 269.

214. See www.senate.gov./~rpc.rva/982/9824.html.

215. *Ibid.*

216. "COLUMBUS SETS SAIL AGAIN: CLASSIC STAMPS REISSUED IN LIMITED QUANTITIES, FOR LIMITED TIME," Stamp news—1992, News Release, United States Postal Service, Washington, DC 20260–3122, Philatelic Release 92–033.

217. See www.chipublib.org/004chicago/timeline/columbianx.hmtl.

218. See http://users.vnet.net/schulman/Columbian/columbian.html.

219. See http://columbus.gl.iit.edu/about.html.

220. See http://xroads.virginia.edu/~MA96/WCE/title.html.

221. See my *Representing the New World,* chapter 4.

222. Richard Hakluyt, *Discourse of Western Planting,* ed. David B. Quinn and Alison M. Quinn (London, 1993), 36.

223. Honour, *European,* 52–53. This map is in the collection of the British Library, Department of Manuscripts.

Chapter 4

1. For this distinction between "sex" and "sexuality," see Gayle Rubin, "The Traffic in Women: Notes on the 'Political Economy' of Sex," *Toward an Anthropology of Women,* ed. Rayna Reiter (New York: Monthly Review Press, 1975), 157–210; Louis Adrian Montrose, "'Shaping Fantasies': Figurations of Gender and Power in Elizabethan Culture," *Representations* 2 (1983): 62; David M. Halperin, "Is There a History of Sexuality?" *History and Theory* 28 (1989): 257–59. See also Lynn Margulis and Doran Sagan, *The Origins of Sex* (New Haven: Yale University Press, 1985) and Merry E. Weisner, *Woman and Gender in Early Modern Europe* (Cambridge: Cambridge University Press, 1993, rpt. 1999), esp. 9–38, 239–55. Michael Foucault's *History of Sexuality* has also been suggestive and provocative in the field.

2. Halperin speaks of sexuality as "the *appropriation* of the human body and of its physiological capacities by an ideological discourse"; see Halperin 257. For other important discussions of sexuality, see Ian Maclean's *Woman Triumphant: Feminism in French Literature, 1610–1652* (Oxford: Clarendon Press, 1977) and *The Renaissance Notion of Woman: A*

Study in the Fortunes of Scholasticism and Medical Science in European Intellectual Life (Cambridge: Cambridge University Press, 1980); Alan Bray's *Homosexuality in Renaissance England* (1982; New York: Columbia University Press, 1995); Eve Kosofsky Sedgwick's *Between Men: English Literature and Male Homosocial Desire* (New York: Columbia University Press, 1985) and *Epistemology of the Closet* (Berkeley: University of California Press, 1990).

3. Weisner, 15. Juan Luis Vives', Erasmus' and Thomas Elyot's ideas of gender, which were sympathetic to women, provided a context for this Columbian moment: Christine de Pisan's *City of Ladies* (1405), which defends women, was not published in France in the early modern period but appeared in English in 1521. See Weisner, 16. Amazons and monstrosity do not really figure in Weisner's history of gender.

4. For a further discussion of this point, see the next book in my series on the New World— *Comparing Empires.*

5. See Jonathan Hart, *Shakespeare: Poetry and the Poet* (in manuscript). For interesting groundbreaking work in the field of gender and poetics, see Annette Kolodny, *The Lay of the Land* (Chapel Hill: University of North Carolina Press, 1975); Nancy Vickers, "Diana Described: Scattered Woman and Scattered Rhyme," *Critical Inquiry* 8 (1981): 265–79; Patricia Parker, *Literary Fat Ladies: Rhetoric, Gender, Property* (London: Methuen, 1987).

6. See Jean-Paul Duviols, *L'Amérique espagnole vue et rêvée. Les livres de voyages de Christophe Colomb à Bougainville* ([Paris], 1985), 43–4. He mentions a few classical examples.

7. In chapter 2, I have discussed textual transmission at some length. The textual messiness of Columbus' *Journal* is something that continues to receive more attention. John Cummins, for instance, does not think that Las Casas was summarizing Columbus as much as previously thought in the extant manuscript in which Las Casas changed, with lapses, Columbus' first-person to a third-person narrative. Cummins compares Bartolomé de Las Casas' changes to quotations from the original journal in Ferdinand [Hernando; I use these forms alternately] Columbus' biography in Italian of his father. His reconstruction of the *Journal* involves a translation of all first-person parts in Las Casas; changing back to first-person passages in which Las Casas changed wholly or partially to third-person; translation of Ferdinand's first person Italian version of parts of the *Journal* and their substitution for passages that appear in the third person in Las Casas; translation and insertion of material from Las Casas' *Historia* or from Ferdinand's biography that, in Cummins' view, were obviously from the original journal; deletion with a note that Cummins considers obvious comments by Las Casas; see John Cummins, "Restoring and Translating the Journal," *The Voyage of Christopher Columbus: Columbus' Own Journal of Discovery Newly Restored and Translated,* ed. John Cummins (London: Weidenfeld and Nicholson, 1992), 75–76. On the role of the *Historié* attributed to Fernando, see Ilaria Luzzana Caraci, *Colombo vero e falso: La costruzione delle Historie fernandine* (Genova: Sagep Editrice, 1989), esp. 15–27. Although Columbus' ship journal has long since disappeared, Las Casas' copy from the early sixteenth century has survived; see Biblioteca Nacional, Madrid, MS Sig Vitrina 6, n 7, which was published in facsimile—Carlo Sanz, *Diario de Colón* (Madrid 1962). About the time I was concentrating on this problem, Dunn and Kelley published a paleographic transcription of this source with a facing English translation; see Oliver Dunn and James E. Kelley, Jr., *The 'Diario' of Christopher Columbus's First Voyage to America, 1492–1493* (Norman, OK: University of Oklahoma Press, 1989). The editorial controversy and work continues. See also note 9 in this chapter.

8. *Raccolta di documenti e studi pubblicati dalla Regia Commissione Colombiana pel quarto centenario della scoperta dell' America* (Rome 1892–94), I.ii.446f. For an edition of his comments, see also *El Libro de Marco Polo anotado por Cristóbal Colón. Versión de Rodrigo de Santaella* (Madrid 1987).

9. See Cecil Jane, "Introduction," *The Four Voyages of Columbus,* trans. and ed. Cecil Jane (1930 and 1933; New York: Dover, 1988), 2 volumes bound as one, I:xcii–xciii. Jane proceeds with

his argument that disintegrates Columbus' text into the work of his editors, Ferdinand, his son, and Las Casas. Whatever the final determination of authorship, the textual Columbus or figure of the Columbian enterprise, speaks of Amazons, the Grand Khan and other themes from Mandeville and Polo.

10. For a similar view, see John Cummins, "The Orient and the Ocean Sea," *The Voyage of Christopher Columbus,* 9.

11. Marco Polo, *The Travels of Marco Polo: The Complete Yule-Cordier Edition* (1903 and 1920; New York 1992), 2 vols, vol. 2, bk. 3, ch. 31, 404–06 and 405–6n1.

12. Jane, "Introduction," *Four Voyages,* I: cxlix. Bernáldez's original reads: "la provincia y ciudad del Catayo, diciendo que la podría allar por allí, que es en el señorío del gran can, la cual se lee, según dice Juan de Mandavilla y ostros que la bieron, que es la más rica provincia del mundo, é la más abundosa de oro é plata, é de todos metales é sedas" (*Historia de los Reyes Católicos, Don Fernando y Doña Isabel, Capítulos* 123–31, in Jane, ed., *Four Voyages,* 117; see 114–6 for translation).

13. John Mandeville, *Mandeville's Travels: Texts and Translations,* 2 vols, ed. Malcolm Letts (London: Oxford University Press, 1953), 1:3 (Egerton Text or ET); for a discussion of Mandeville and the question of authorship, see Lett's Introduction, 1: xvii-xxvii.

14. Mandeville 1:102.

15. *Ibid.,* 2:231.

16. *Ibid.,* 2:310.

17. *Ibid.,* 2:457.

18. *Ibid.,* 2:458.

19. *Ibid.,* see 2: 457.

20. Lyle N. McAlister, *Spain and Portugal in the New World 1492–1700* (Minneapolis: University of Minnesota Press, 1984), 89. See also *Books of the Brave: Being an Account of Books and Men in the Spanish Conquest and Settlement of the Sixteenth-Century New World* (Cambridge, MA: Harvard University Press, 1949) and Wilcomb E. Washburn, "The Meaning of 'Discovery' in the Fifteenth and Sixteenth Centuries," *AHA* 68 (1962): 1–21.

21. McAlister, 89–90 and Manuel Fernández Alvarez, *Charles V: Elected Emperor and Hereditary Ruler* (London: Thames and Hudson, 1975), 188–90.

22. Jean-Paul Duviols, *L'Amérique espagnole,* 43. For a discussion of the etymology of the word "Amazon," a brief discussion of classical antecedents and of the Pizarros, Francisco de Orellana and Walter Ralegh in the context of Amazons and El Dorado, see Bardo de Santa-Anna Nery, *The Land of the Amazons,* ed. George Humphrey (London: Sands & Co., 1901), 3–7. It is important to remember, as Nery does, that Ralegh set out for El Dorado in 1617 as well as in the 1590s, but that this time, the negotiations for the marriage of the Infanta of Spain with Charles, the Prince of Wales, meant that when Ralegh was involved in friction with the Spaniards in America, it had much more dire consequences than his first expedition—his death. On Peru, gold and riches, see also Levini Apollonii, *De Periviæ, regionis inter Novi Orbis provincias celeberemæ, inventione et rebus in eadem gestis* (Antverpiæ: J. Bellerus, 1567), libri v.

23. Columbus, 14–15.

24. Columbus, 14–17.

25. Columbus, 16–17.

26. Hernán Cortés, *Letters from Mexico,* ed. Anthony Pagden with an Introduction by John Elliott (1971; New Haven: Yale University Press, 1986), 502n.21. Cortés also records how the council in Veracruz complained to Charles V that the Natives were sodomites as well as sacrificing men, women and children (see the letter of July 10). Richard Trexler also cites this instance in *Sex and Conquest: Gendered Violence, Political Order, and the European Conquest of the Americas* (Cambridge: Polity Press, 1995), 3. See also Irving A. Leonard, "Conquerors and Amazons in Mexico," *Hispanic American Historical Review* 24

(1944): 561–79 and *Books of the Brave;* G. C. Rothery, *The Amazons in Antiquity and Modern Times* (London, 1910).

27. Cortés, *Letters,* 298–300.

28. *Ibid.,* 502n.21.

29. Fray Gaspar de Carvajal, *Relación del nuevo descubrimiento del famosos río Grande de las Amazonas* (México: Fondo de Cultura Económica, 1955), 97. In his important study, Duviols, who discusses the Amazons at some length, makes Carvajal the implantation of the Amazonian myth in the New World, but the seeds occur in Columbus. See Duviols, 43–53.

30. Antonio de Herrera, "The Voyage of Francisco de Orellana down the River of the Amazons" (From the Sixth Decade of his "General History of the West Indies," Book IX) in *Expeditions into the Valley of the Amazons,* trans. and ed. Clements R. Markham (London: Hakluyt Society).

31. *Ibid.,* 36.

32. *Ibid.*

33. *Ibid.,* 122.

34. *Ibid.,* 126.

35. *Ibid.* This collection also contains an extract from Garcilasso Inca de la Vega's Royal Commentaries (the second part), but it has no references to women and Amazons.

36. Walter Ralegh, *The Discouerie of the Large, Rich, and Bewtiful Empyre of Guiana, with a Relation of the Great and Golden Citie of Manoa (which the Spanyards call El Dorado . . .* (London, 1596), L 2 verso—L 4 recto.

37. *Ibid.,* A 3 verso.

38. *Ibid.,* q 3 verso.

39. *Ibid.,* q 2 recto. Ralegh testified to all those in London who made many trials of the gold ore and found it to be of high quality and once more refuted the unnamed alderman who had tried to make a scandal. *Ibid.,* q 2 verso.

40. *Ibid.,* C recto.

41. *Ibid.,* D 4 recto.

42. *Ibid.,* D 4 recto-verso.

43. *Ibid.,* D 4 recto-verso.

44. *Ibid.,* D 4 verso.

45. *Ibid.,* N 3 verso.

46. *Ibid.,* N 4 verso.

47. Elizabeth's Tilbury speech is a good example. See Louis Adrian Montrose, "The Work of Gender in the Discourse of Discovery," *Representations* 33 (1991): 1–41.

48. *Ibid.,* 0 recto.

49. *Ibid.,* 0 2 recto.

50. See Hart, *Representing the New World.*

51. Ralegh, *Discoverie,* O 2 recto.

52. *Ibid.*

53. *Ibid.*

54. *Ibid.,* O 2 verso.

55. *Ibid.*

56. *Ibid.*

57. *Ibid.,* 0 2 recto, see O 3 recto.

58. *Ibid.,* O 2 verso-O 3 recto.

59. *Ibid.,* O 3 recto

60. *Ibid.*

61. *Ibid.*

62. See Linda Woodbridge, *Women and the English Renaissance: Literature and the Nature of Womankind, 1540–1620* (Urbana: University of Illinois Press, 1984), 15. On this controversy over the nature of women, see also Ruth Kelso, *Doctrine for the Lady of the*

Renaissance (1956; Urbana: University of Illinois Press, 1978); Ian Maclean, *The Renaissance Notion of Woman: A Study in the Fortunes of Scholasticism and Medical Science in European Intellectual Life* (Cambridge: Cambridge University Press, 1980).

63. See Thomas Heywood, *The Dramatic Works of Thomas Heywood.*, ed. R. H. Shepherd (London 1874), vol. 2, and Woodbridge 164–65.

64. Micolaus Syllacius, *De Insulis Meridiani atque Indici Maris Nuper Inventis,* with trans. by John Mulligan (New York, 1859).

65. *Ibid.*, 39.

66. *Ibid.*, 87.

67. *Ibid.*

68. Amerigo Vespucci, *The Letters of Amerigo Vespucci,* ed. Clements Markham (London: Hakluyt Society, 1944), 6–7.

69. *Ibid.*, 8.

70. *Ibid.*

71. *Ibid.*, 9.

72. *Ibid.*, 27.

73. *Ibid.*, 37.

74. *Ibid.*, 46.

75. Janet Adelman, *Suffocating Mothers: Fantasies of Maternal Origin in Shakespeare's Plays,* Hamlet *to* The Tempest (New York: Routledge, 1992).

76. Antonio Pigafetta, *Magellan's Voyage around the World,* trans. James A. Robertson (Cleveland: Arthur H. Clark, 1906), vol. 1. *First Voyage around the World. South America.*

77. *Ibid.*, 36–37.

78. *Ibid.*, 39.

79. *Ibid.*, 155–56.

80. *Ibid.*, 167–68.

81. *Ibid.*, 169.

82. Although not discussing sexual abuse directly, perhaps owing to different notions of what constituted a child and what was thought to be maturity over time, Colin Heywood has some interesting things to say about the kinds of sexuality allowed or disallowed to the young and about childhood more generally. See Colin Heywood, *A History of Childhood: Children and Childhood from Medieval to Modern Times* (Cambridge: Polity, 2001), 37–38. See also Jean-Louis Flandrin, "Mariage tardif et vie sexuelle: discussions et hypothèses de recherche," *Annales ESC* 27 (1972): 1351–78.

83. Peter Martyr (Anglerius), "The Decades of the Newe Worlde or West India," ed. Edward Arber, *The First Three English Books on America* (Birmingham 1885). I am using the Richard Eden translation of 1555, which Arber included. It is a filter of an earlier translation with Renaissance standards that are different than those today, but the Eden translation is really the beginning of a period in which the texts of Spanish colonization of the Americas began to take off. Spain's textual influence in England became more palpable in the last half of the sixteenth century.

84. *Ibid.*, 66.

85. *Ibid.*, 67.

86. *Ibid.*, 69.

87. *Ibid.*, 70.

88. *Ibid.*, 77.

89. *Ibid.*, 83.

90. *Ibid.*, 85.

91. *Ibid.*, 100.

92. *Ibid.*, 99.

93. *Ibid.*, 102.

94. *Ibid.*, 149.

95. *Ibid.*, 151.
96. *Ibid.*, 165.
97. *Ibid.*, 177.
98. *Ibid.*, 189.
99. *Ibid.*, 190.
100. Cieza De Leon, *Chronicles of Peru* vol 1, ed. and trans. Clements R. Markham (London: Hakluyt Society, 1933), 50–51. In contrast, in Pedro de Cieza De Leon, *The War of Quito*, ed. Clements Markham (London: Hakluyt Society, 1913), there is no mention of Native women.
101. *Ibid.*
102. *Ibid.*, 64.
103. *Ibid.*, 81.
104. *Ibid.*, 73, 86.
105. *Ibid.*, 74.
106. *Ibid.*, 79.
107. *Ibid.*, 152, 167.
108. *Ibid.*, 202.
109. *Ibid.*, II: 3.
110. *Ibid.*, II: 26.
111. Pascal de Andagoya, *Narrative of the Proceedings of Pedrarias Davila in the Provinces of Tierra Firme . . . the South Sea . . . the Coasts of Peru and Nicaragua*, trans and ed. Clements R. Markham (London: Hakluyt Society, 1865), 15.
112. *Ibid.*, 33. A footnote on this page notes: "Herrera also says that the men swept their houses and performed other menial services, and that in some places they even spun, having their arms naked and painted."
113. Jacques Cartier, *The Voyages of Jacques Cartier* (Toronto: University of Toronto Press, 1993, rpt. 1995), 10. This is a reprint and moderate revision of H. P. Biggar's translation in 1924 and 1930, which focuses on a few key words and which Ramsey Cook explains in his Preface, vii-viii. Having used an earlier text, I decided to switch to this one. Although I have consulted the originals, a practice that can be seen by my companion volume, *Representing the New World*, I have in this book, as part of my wish to reach a wider audience, used the most available sound translations possible. Only when my argument hinged on close interpretation of the original language or when a good literal translation was not available did I resort to an edition that was in, or included, the original language. For a good recent edition in French, see Jacques Cartier, *Voyages en Nouvelle-France*, ed. Robert Lahaise et Marie Couturier (Québec: Cahiers de Québec, 1977). For some striking descriptions of women in that edition, see 56, 58, 90, 102–03, 109. The third voyage of Cartier's accounts survives only in an English translation of the Renaissance and was translated into French after World War II. See Richard Hakluyt, *The Third and Las Volume of the Voyages, Navigations, Traffiques and Discoueries of the English Nation . . .* (London 1600), 232–37. As we saw with Columbus, the textual histories of some of the works in this study are complex and refractory.
114. Cartier, *The Voyages*, 22.
115. See Cartier (1977), 56. The Native women who "vinrent franchement à nous, et nous frottaient les bras avec leurs mains, et puis levaient les mains jointes au ciel, en faisant plusieurs signes de joie; et se fièrent tellement à nous, qu'à la fin nous marchandames, main à main, avec eux, tous ceux qu'ils avaient, de sorte qu'il ne leur restaient que leurs corps nus, parce qu'ils nous donnaient tout ce qu'ils avaient, qui est chose de peu de valeur. Nous reconnumes que ce sont des gens qui seraient faciles à convertir, qui vont d'un lieu à l'autre."
116. Cartier, *The Voyages*, 47, 80–87, 96–98.
117. This book on mediation and kidnapping is called *Between Cultures*.

118. Cartier, *The Voyages,* 24.

119. *Ibid.*

120. *Ibid.*, 25. Here is part of this passage in the original French (Cartier 1977, 58): To some Native women, "nous donnames à chacune un peigne, et une petite clochette d'étain, dont elles furent fort heureuses, remerciant le capitaine en lui frottant les bras et la poitrine avec leurs mains. Et eux, voyant ce qu'on abait donné à celles qui étaient demeurées, firent venir celles qui s'étaient enfuies dans le bois, pour en avoir autant que les autres, qui étaient au moins une vingtaine, qui se rassemblèrent autour dudit capitaine en le frottant avec leurs dit mains, qui est leur facon de faire chère. Et leur donna à chacune une petite bague d'étain de peu de valeur; et incontinent, se mirent à danser et à dire plusieurs chansons."

121. The dictionary actually defines "Faire chere" as "Faire bonne mine, bon acceuil, montrer de l'affection, faire fête." The example from Ronsard it gives leaves some room for ambiguity how warm this welcome might be as it makes the poet dejected. The meaning can become quite complex as "mine" can suggest an expression, look, demeanour, or appearance, and "faire fête" can mean to hold a high holiday or keep a holiday, whereas "faire la fête" means to have a fling or carouse, while "faire fête à quelqu'un" means to receive someone with open arms. See Edmond Huguet, *Dictionaire de la Language Françsaise du Seizième Siècle, Tome Deuxième* (Paris: Honoré Champion, 1932), 244. I have consulted various dictionaries by Robert, Larousse, and Harrap's to go further into these possible meanings.

122. Pierre Ronsard, Pièces retranchées, *Sonnets* (VI, 45) in Huguet, 244. My translation. The original is as follows: "Je ne puis aimer ceux à qui vous faites chere . . . Je maudis leurs faveurs, j'abhorre leur bon-heur." What Huguet leaves out is the line between these two verses—"Fussent ils mes cousins, mes oncles et mon frere": the sonnet is about jealousy, a kind of cold anger that overcomes the poet, when anyone is near his beloved, whether her family or his, and, as his perhaps anti-Petrarchan stance suggests satirically, he is even jealous of his own shadow, eyes and mouth. Even though the context could make the meaning of "vous faites chere" equivocal, its primary meaning, given the satire, is that of a warm and affectionate welcome. See Pierre Ronsard, *Oeuvres Complètes,* ed. Gustave Cohen (Paris: Éditions Gallimard, 1950), II:878.

123. In this section I have kept my general principle in this book that I want the sources to be available to students and readers. Most of the images I am describing have been reproduced in books that are readily accessible, so that the reader can confer there and see more examples than I have space to discuss here. Whereas it would be more convenient to reproduce the images here, I have taken the approach I have to combine accessibility with affordability. To reproduce the drawings here would have put the price of the book up considerably. See Claire le Corbeiller, "Miss America and her sisters: Personifications of the Four Parts of the World," *Metropolitan Museum of Art Bulletin* ser. 2, vol. 19 (1961): 209–223. Hugh Honour's important work and collecting of these images have been a great help.

124. Joshua C. Taylor, *America as Art* (New York: Harper and Row, 1976), 5.

125. "Further Representations of America as Woman" in Hugh Honour, *The European Vision of America* [all illus. in book] no. 3. "Wild Naked People." Illustration to a German translation of Amerigo Vespucci's letters to Pier Soderini. Strasburg 1509. Woodcut. British Library. See page 15 for more on this.

126. No 86—"Vespucci Discovering America." Jan van der Street, called Stradamus. Pen & ink, 1589. NY Metropolitan Museum of Art. Other less highly finished drawings in the Biblioteca Laurenziana, Florence (cod. pal. 75).—no.87. a plaquette: "America." Germany 1580–1590. Lead with gilt. NY Metropolitan Museum of Art.;—no. 92. "America." Marcus Gheerarts. Engraving ca. 1590–1600, NY Metropolitan Museum of Art—no. 93. One of eleven playing cards representing parts of America. Stefano de Bella. Etchings,

1644. NY Metropolitan Museum of Art.; NY Metropolitan Museum of Art.—95. "America." Nicolaes (or Claes) Berchem. Black chalk and ink, 1640–50. NY Metropolitan Museum of Art. This book has many eighteenth-century representations of America as a woman.

127. No. 89. "America" Maarten de Vos. Pen & ink, ca. 1600. Ann Arbor, University of Michigan Museum of Art.

128. "America," Philip Galle. Engraving ca. 1579–1600. New York Historical Society. 93A. "America." Cornelius Visscher. Engraving ca. 1650–60. With poetic inscription. New York Historical Society.

129. "America," frontispiece to Arnoldus Montanus, *De Nieuwe en Onbekende Weereld,* Amsterdam 1671. Engraving. Jacob van Meurs. Washington DC, Library of Congress. 128. "America." Ludwig van Schoor, ca. 1700. Tapestry. Washington DC, National Gallery of Art. 128. "America," Francesco Solimena. Oil on canvas, ca. 1730–38. London, private collection.

130. Title page of Abraham Ortelius' *Theatrum Orbis Terrarum* (Antwerp 1570). Bibliothèque Nationale. The first painting of America as woman is in a fresco at the palace at Caprarola, near Rome, built for Cardinal Alessandro Farnese (1574). Engraving by Etienne Delaune, of the Fontainebleu School (1575). Bibliothèque Nationale. Illus. in Honour, no. 76. Jost Amman (Swiss). Prints of the 4 continents as landscapes with figures (1577). Bibliothèque Nationale. Philippe Galle (Flemish); a print (1581). Bibliothèque Nationale. Illus. in Honour, no. 77. Works by Philippe Galle also in Lynn Glaser, *America on Paper,* Philadelphia: Associated Antiquaries, 1989, pp. 136 and 165. The first is an American allegory from ca. 1579–1600, and is of a naked and armed Amazon carrying the head of a man. Glaser writes, "An inscription describes America as a female glutton who devours men, is rich in gold and mighty with the bow. She rears parrots and wears garlands of feathers." The second was engraved around 1580 and, with a woman with a club at the center of many other New World creatures, human and non-human, it "is an early recognition of New World variety with his Indians ranging from Eskimos to Brazilians." Jan Sadeler (Flemish); engraved a drawing by Dirk Barendsz. Rijksmuseum, Amsterdam. Illus in Honour, no. 78. Giovanni de' Vecchi; Western hemisphere of a world map with allegories of the continents (1574). Illus. in Honour. Crispijn de Passe; early 17th century print. Rijksmuseum, Amsterdam. Illus. in Honour, no. 80. Theodor Galle; print after Stradamus (Jan van der Street); "Vespucci Discovering America." British Museum. Illus. in Honour, no. 81. Maarten de Vos (1594); sketch. Prentencabinet, Antwerp. Illus. in Honour, no. 82. [Also in Lynn Glaser, *America on paper* (Philadelphia: Associated Antiquaries, 1989), Contents page. Glaser writes that this image was " . . . copied and recopied into the 18th century . . . the commonest allegorical depiction of America"]. Stafano della Bella (1644). Metropolitan Museum, New York. Illus. in Honour, no. 83. Cesare Ripa; fig. of America accompanied by alligator, in his *Iconologia* of 1604 (a handbook for Baroque artists). Bibliotheque Nationale. Francois van den Hoeye, early 17th C. "Allegory of America." Illus. in Honour, no. 84. After Giulio Parigi, 1608. "The Ship of Amerigo Vespucci." Bibliothèque Nationale. Illus. in Honour, no. 85. Frans Francken II, "Allegory on the Abdication of the Emperor Charles V at Brussells." (c. 1636). Rijksmuseum, Amsterdam. Illus. in Honour, no. 88. Tapestries after cartoons by Ludwig van Schoor, woven first at Brussels & widely imitated elsewhere—58 sold between 1699 and 1709. cf. panel devoted to America. Jan van Kessel, "America" (painting; 1664–66). Alte Pinakothek, Munich. Illus. in Honour, xvii. Andrea Pozzo; fresco on ceiling of S. Ignazio, Rome. "America." (1694). Illus. in Honour, xviii. Lorenzo Vaccaro, "America" (1692). Sculpture in silver, Toledo Cathedral. Hazlett, Germany. Illus. in Honour, no. 100. Jean Dumont (1742), "America." Israel Museum, Jerusalem. Illus. in Honour. See also illustrations to Vespucci's letter to Soderini, Strassburg 1509, pp.10–11. Works by Philippe Galle also in Lynn Glaser, *America on Paper,* pp. 136 and 165.

131. Title page of Abraham Ortelius' *Theatrum Orbis Terrarum* (Antwerp 1570). Bibliothèque Nationale. Honour gives information on the representation of America as a woman in royal festivals and spectacles. He expands on the fact that many of these images had wide diffusion in books, or transposed onto tiles or tankards. And he cites many eighteenth-century representations of America as a woman.

132. Tapestries after cartoons by Ludwig van Schoor, woven first at Brussels & widely imitated elsewhere—58 sold between 1699 and 1709; cf. panel devoted to America. . . . Honour also notes the wealth of information about tapestries of the four continents in the Marillier tapestry archive, Victoria and Albert Museum, London.

133. Lorenzo Vaccaro, "America" (1692). Sculpture in silver, Toledo Cathedral. Hazlett, Germany. Illus. in Honour, no. 100;—Andrea Pozzo; fresco on ceiling of S. Ignazio, Rome. "America." (1694). Illus. in Honour, xviii.

134. Honour, 10–11.

135. Ibid., 36, figure 45.

136. *Encountering the New World, 1493–1800.* Catalogue of an exhibition by Susan Danforth; introductory essay by William H. McNeill (Providence, RI: John Carter Brown Library, 1991). I thank Katy Emck for her research and conversation on this topic (whence came the phrase)—p.7, fig. 7.

137. Adrian Johnson, *America Explored* (New York: Viking Press, 1974), 164.

138. See R. V. Tooley, *The Mapping of America* (London: Holland Press, 1985); Meursius, plate 43 no. 36; Schenck, plate 52 no. 67; Aa, plate 54 no. 71.

139. Gillian Hill, *Cartographical Curiosities* (London: British Museum Publications, 1978), 39.

140. *Ibid.*, 50.

141. Martyr, 138.

142. *Ibid.*

143. Gonzalo Fernández de Oviedo, *História general y natural de las Indias,* trans. J. H. Parry and R. G. Keith, 5 vols. *New Iberian World* (New York: Times Books, 1984), vol. 1: 13.

144. *Ibid.*

145. *Ibid.*

146. *Ibid.*

147. *Ibid.*

148. For a perceptive and full exploration of this question concerning cannibalism, see Anthony Pagden, *The Fall of Natural Man: The American Indian and the Origins of Comparative Ethnology* (Cambridge: Cambridge University Press, 1982), esp. 80–84. See also Peter Hulme, *Colonial Encounters* (London: Methuen, 1986) for a strong general account of Amazons and cannibals in the Caribbean.

149. Sedgwick, *Between Men.* See Amerigo Vespucci, *Letter to Piero Soderini, Gonfaloniere,* trans. and ed. G. T. Northrup (Princeton: Princeton University Press, 1916), 7–10.

150. Oviedo, 13.

151. *Ibid.*, 13–14.

152. *Ibid.*, 14.

153. *Ibid.*

154. *Ibid.*

155. Michele de Cuneo, "Letter on the Second Voyage," October 28, 1495, in *Journals and Other Documents in the Life and Voyages of Christopher Columbus,* trans. and ed. S. E. Morison (New York: The Heritage Press, 1963), 212. See this collection for more instances.

156. Bartolomé de Las Casas, *Historia de las Indias,* 3 vols. (Mexico City: Fondo de Cultura Economica, 1951), vol. 3, ch. 23, 517. My paraphrase. For a translation of this passage, see *1492: Discovery, Invasion, Encounter: Sources and Interpretations,* ed. Marvin Lunenfeld (Lexington: D. C. Heath, 1991), 285. A few years after I began this study, I started to use this useful book in class as a supplement to full primary sources in the coloniza-

tion of the America. It has influenced this part of a later draft of this chapter, especially by calling attention to this passage in Las Casas. So I, like my students, have benefited from Lunenfeld's book. For another view of Oviedo and sodomy, see Richard Trexler, *Sex and Conquest,* esp. 90–91. I came to Trexler's work long after I had begun my own and have found his discussion of berdaches, or permanently tranvested and sexually passive male, useful in Native American contexts (see esp. 6–9). For earlier work, see also E. Blackwood, "Sexuality and Gender in Certain Native American Tribes: the Case of Cross-Gender Females," *Signs* 10 (1984): 27–42; Walter L. Williams, *The Spirit and the Flesh: Sexual Diversity in American Indian Culture* (Boston: Beacon Press, 1986) and Irene Marsha Silverblatt, *Moon, Sun, and Devil: Inca and Colonial Transformations of Andean Gender Relations* (Princeton: Princeton University Press, 1987).

157. Las Casas, *Historia,* 518.

158. J. M. Cohen, "Introduction, " *The Conquest of New Spain,* ed. and trans. J. M. Cohen (Harmondsworth: Penguin, 1963, rpt. 1983), 7.

159. Díaz, Cohen ed. 19, see 18; " tenían muchos ídolos de barro, unos como caras de demonios, y otros como de mujeres, y otros de ostras malas figuras, de manera que al parecer estaban haciendo sodomías los unos indios con los otros " [Cabañas ed., vol. 1, capitulo 3, 47]); see Bernal Díaz del Castillo, *Historia Verdadera de la Conquista de La Nueva España,* Quinta edición, ed. Joaquin Ramirez Cabañas, Tomo 1, Tomo 2 (Mexico City: Editorial Porrua, 1960).

160. Léry, History, 153. See André Thevet, *La Cosmographie Vniverselle D' André Thevet Cosmographe dv Roy . . .* (Paris, 1575) in *Les Français en Amérique pendant la deuxième moitié du XVIe Siècle: Le Brésil et les Brésiliens,* ed. Charles-André Julien, with notes by Suzanne Lussagnet (2 vols., Paris, 1953). See Janet Whatley 250n4 in Léry, *History.*

161. Díaz describes idols performing sodomy in a temple: the riches and gold of the temples became fair game for the Spaniards because, in their view, they were full of images of barbarity or effeminacy, of human sacrifices and homoeroticism, and most certainly of paganism. See Bernal Díaz del Castillo, *La Conquista de La Nueva España.* 4 vols. (Paris and Buenos Aires: Sociedad de Ediciones Louis-Michaud, n.d.).

Chapter 5

1. James Axtell, *The Invasion Within: The Contest of Cultures in Colonial North America* (Oxford: Oxford University Press, 1985), 302.

2. Wilcomb E. Washburn, "History of Indian-White Relations," in Bruce Trigger, ed., *Handbook of North American Indians* (Washington: Smithsonian Institution Press, 1978), vol. 4; Robert Royal, *1492 and All That: Political Manipulations of History* (Washington: Ethics and Policy Center, 1992); James Axtell, *Beyond 1492: Encounters in Colonial North America* (New York: Oxford University Press, 1992). In these sixteenth-century writers we find suggestions on cultural practices that propose an alternative to stereotyping that Ross Chambers discusses in a modern setting. He suggests that the ideological othering of mediators is not inevitable. For Chambers, communities owe their meaning and existence to negotiation (Chambers, "No Montagues Without Capulets: Some Thoughts on 'Cultural Identity,'" in Jonathan Hart and Richard Bauman, ed., *Explorations in Difference: Law, Culture and Politics* [Toronto: University of Toronto Press, 1995]). Whether this desire in postmodern discourse theory to transform mediation into a politics of invitation and community works in an early modern setting and takes into account enough the material dimension of the historical record is something I want to examine.

3. As some of the narrative and rhetorical techniques of postmodern discourse have their beginnings in those of the early modern, can we find in the relation between Natives and Europeans then a way to understand those relations in a multicultural, multinational world? This chapter offers a few concrete examples of mediators, which form the basis of

inductive work toward a theoretical and practical mediation in order to provide a context for the manuscript work needed to introduce new Native and European perspectives to the topic of mediation in the encounter. The mediators discussed here may be forerunners to those writers and historical figures like Garciolaso, part Spaniard and part Incan, in the sixteenth century and Louis Riel, part Cree and part French, in the nineteenth. The work of theorists, like Michel Serres and Ross Chambers, becomes particularly useful when asking about some of the implications that mediation raised then and how might they apply now.

4. This combination of mimesis with a critique of it is something, along with Ross Chambers' subtle theory of mediation, that provides an opportunity to combine narrative theory with a social dimension of groups that were repressed or scapegoated as the Natives were and are. Looking at Las Casas' view of the oppression of the Natives in the late fifteenth and early sixteenth centuries in relation to Chambers' analysis of oppositionality and scapegoating in Western culture during the nineteenth and twentieth centuries will allow me to observe certain morphologies and estrangements. For an earlier and different version of this research, see Jonathan Hart, "Mediation in the Exchange Between Europeans and Native Americans in the Early Modern Period," special issue, *Canadian Review of Comparative Literature/Revue Canadienne de Littérature Comparée [CRCL/RCLC]* 22 (1995): 319–43.

5. My adaptation of some of the ideas of mediation in Ross Chambers' and Michel Serres' work should help make this translation between the past and present more effective. Chambers' theory counters the flattening out of different groups into others. He also suggests that we analyze the ways mediators are made into scapegoats and, adapting Serres, looks at how the mediator can become an "excluded third" in any cultural negotiation; see Chambers, *Room for Maneuver: Reading (the) Oppositional (in) Narrative* (Chicago: University of Chicago Press, 1991); Chambers, "No Montagues"; see Michel Serres, *Hermes III: La Traduction* (Paris: Minuit, 1974) and *The Parasite*, trans. Lawrence R. Schehr (Baltimore: Johns Hopkins University Press, 1982); René Girard, *Le Bouc emissaire* (Paris: Grasset, 1982); Jean-Luc Nancy, *The Inoperative Community*, trans. Peter Connor (Minneapolis: University of Minnesota Press, 1991); Michel de Certeau, *Heterologies: Discourse on the Other*, trans. Brian Massumi (Minneapolis: University of Minnesota Press, 1986), ch. 5. This one theoretical insight helps to characterize one of the difficulties Squanto and some of the other mediators in early America find themselves in. The temptation is to scapegoat the mediator and to deny any possibility of coexisting with a different cultural group. But, as Las Casas and Montaigne knew, the consequences of such polarization are disastrous. See also de Certeau's "Travel Narratives of the French to Brazil: Sixteenth to Eighteenth Centuries," *Representations* 33 (1991): 221–26.

6. See Chambers, *Room for Maneuver* and "No Montagues"; see Serres, *Hermes III;* Girard, *Le Bouc emissaire;* Nancy, *The Inoperative Community;* de Certeau, *Heterologies,* ch. 5. See also Tzvetan Todorov, *La Conquête de l'Amérique* (Paris: Editions du Seuil, 1982) and *The Conquest of America: The Question of the Other*, trans. Richard Howard (New York: Harper & Row, 1984); Deborah Root, "The Imperial Signifier: Todorov and the Conquest of Mexico," *Cultural Critique* 9 (1988): 197–219.

7. For an important earlier discussion of disease in this relation between European and Native, see Alfred W. Crosby, *The Columbian Exchange: Biological and Writers and Cultural Consequences of 1492* (Westport, Conn.: Greenwood, 1972).

8. Chambers, "No Montagues." For works that discuss writing and rewriting in this period, see Margaret W. Ferguson *et al. Rewriting the Renaissance* (Chicago: University of Chicago Press, 1986) and Wayne Franklin, *Discoverers, Explorers, Settlers: The Diligent of Early America* (Chicago: University of Chicago Press, 1979).

9. James Lockhart, *The Nahuas After the Conquest: A Social and Cultural History of the Indians of Central Mexico, Sixteenth Through Eighteenth Centuries* (Stanford: Stanford Univer-

sity Press, 1992), 330. See also Hernán Cortés, *Letters from Mexico,* trans. and ed. Anthony Pagden (New Haven: Yale University Press, 1986) and David J. Weber, *The Spanish Frontier in North America* (New Haven: Yale University Press, 1992).

10. Jr. Vine Deloria, "Afterword," *America in 1492: The World of the Indian Peoples Before the Arrival of Columbus,* ed. Alvin M. Josephy, Jr. (1991. New York: Random House, 1993), 429–43, 429–30.

11. Gordon Brotherston, *Image of the New World: The American Continent Portrayed in Native Texts* (London: Thames and Hudson, 1979), 15. See also Fernando Alvarado Tezozomoc, *Crónica Mexicáyotl,* trans. Adrián León (México D.F.: UNAM, 1975) and *Crónica Mexicana.* (México D.F.: Porrúa, 1975); *Les Figures de l'indien,* ed. Gilles Therien (Montréal: Université du Québec à Montréal, 1988); Ronald Wright, *Stolen Continents: The "New World" Through Indian Eyes* (Boston and New York: Houghton Mifflin, 1992).

12. Brotherston, 21.

13. Deloria, 432–35.

14. Pagden, 119.

15. Brotherston, 28–32, 48–53, see Jonathan Hart, "Images of the Native in Renaissance Encounter Narratives," *ARIEL* 25 (1994): 55–76.

16. Ray Gonzalez, "Preface," *Without Discovery: A Native Response to Columbus,* ed. R. Gonzalez (Seattle: Broken Moon, 1992).

17. See Hart, "Images" (1994).

18. See de Alva xii–xxi.

19. Miguel Leon-Portilla, ed. *The Broken Spears: The Aztec Account of the Conquest of Mexico* (1959; Boston: Beacon Press, 1992), 56–57.

20. Peter Martyr (Petrus Martyr Anglerius), *De Orbe Novo. The Eight Decades of Peter Martyr D'Anghera,* trans. F. A. MacNutt (New York: G. P. Putnam's Sons, 1912), 176.

21. *The Chronicles of Michoacán,* trans. and ed. Eugene R. Craine and Reginald C. Reindorp (Norman: University of Oklahoma Press, 1970), 57.

22. Bernardino de Sahagún, *Florentine Codex: General History of the Things of New Spain,* trans. A. J. O. Anderson and C. E. Dibble (Salt Lake City: School of American Research and University of Utah, 1950–82), 44–66. On the Aztec more generally, see Charles Gibson, *The Aztecs Under Spanish Rule: A History of the Indians of the Valley of Mexico, 1519–1810* (Stanford: Stanford University Press, 1964).

23. (10). The original reads:

    Y luego que legué á las Indias, en la primera isla que hallé tomé por fuerça algunos d'ellos, para que deprendiesen y me diesen noticia de lo que avía en aquellas partes, é así fué que luego entendieron, y nos á ellos, quando por lengua ó señas; y estos han aprovechado mucho. (11)

24. Gonzalo Fernández de Oviedo, *Historia general y natural de las Indias,* 5 vols (Madrid, 1959), 4:325–330, trans. in David B Quinn, ed., with Alsion M. Quinn and Susan Hillier, *New American World: A Documentary History of North America to 1612,* 5 vols. (New York: Arno Press and Hector Bye, 1979), 1: 261.

25. *Ibid.*

26. *Ibid.*

27. See Bruce C. Trigger, *Natives and Newcomers: Canada's 'Heroic Age' Reconsidered* (Kingston and Montreal: McGill-Queen's University Press, 1985, rpt. 1989), 125. This Chicora seems to have been the same person that Peter Martyr reports having dinner with and who told him about making recipes to produce giants; see Martyr (Macnutt trans.), 258–68 and Olive Dickason, *The Myth of the Savage and the Beginnings of French Colonialism in the Americas* (Edmonton: University of Alberta Press, 1984, rpt. 1997), 207. Chicora's name appears here as Francisco Chicorana.

28. *Archivio di Stato Modena, Dispacci della Spagna,* October 17, 1501, in Quinn 1979, 1: 149.

29. *Pasqualigo to the Signory of Venice, 19 October 1501,* in Quinn 1979, 1: 150.

30. *Ibid.,* 1:151.

31. *Great Chronicle of London,* ed. A. H. Thomas and I. D. Thornley (London: G.W. Jones, 1939), 320, in Quinn 1979: 1:110.

32. Gonneville, 38. See Jonathan Hart, *Representing the New World* (New York and London: Palgrave, 2001), 30–1.

33. Here is a helpful note from Julien and his co-editors. Of Essomericq, they write: "Ses descendants se virent réclamer, en 1658, des taxes d'aubaine en tant qu'issus d'étranger. Ils protestèrent que leur aïeul n'était pas venu demeurer en France de son plein gré, mais qu'il avait eu l'intention de regagner son pays après un court séjour, ce qu'il ne put faire, en dépit des promesses qu'il avait reçues, pour des raisons de force majeure. En conséquence, ils dénièrent aux traitants le droit de leur réclamer des taxes et présentèrent, à l'appui de leurs affirmations, le rapport établis par Gonneville à son retour, dont le tribunal fit vérifier l'authentcité par le grossoyement d'une expédition régulière. Les traitants furent déboutés de leur demande" (25).

34. Ramusio, *Navigationi et Viaggi* (Venetia, 1550), III, 423 verso, cited in Biggar, Introduction, *The Precursors,* xxii. See also Charles-André Julien, *Histoire de l'expansion et de la colonization françaises* (Paris, 1948), I, 336; Carl Ortwin Sauer, *Sixteenth-Century North America: The Land and the People as Seen by Europeans* (Berkeley: University of California Press, 1971), 51–2; Eugène Guénin, *Ango et ses pilotes, d'après des documents inédits, tirés de archives de France, Portugal et d'Espagne* (Paris, 1901). See also Raymonde Litalien, *Les explorateurs de l'Amérique du Nord 1492–1795* (Sillery, QC: Septentrion, 1993).

35. Cartier. For a discussion of this kidnapping that is sensitive to the Native point of view, see Dickason, *Myth,* 164–70. On Cartier's earlier experience in the New World, see Marcel Trudel, "Cartier, Jacques," *Dictionary of Canadian Biography* (Toronto: University of Toronto Press, 1966), 165–72; Trigger, *Natives,* 129.

36. Cartier; see Dickason, *Myth,* 167 and Trigger, *Natives,* 130.

37. Marcel Trudel, *Histoire de la Nouvelle France* (Montréal: Fides, 1963), 1: 113 and Trigger, *Natives,* 133.

38. Dickason does not think Cartier left the French boys as a symbol of an alliance (*Myth,* 168).

39. H. P. Biggar, ed., *A Collection of Documents Relating to Jacques Cartier and Sieur de Roberval* (Ottawa: Publications of the Public Archives of Ottawa, 1930), 362–63; Trigger, *Natives,* 133–34.

40. Jean de Léry, *History of a Voyage to the Land of Brazil,* trans. Janet Whatley (Berkeley: University of California Press, 1990), 42.

41. Michel de Montaigne, *Essais* (Paris: Garnier Freres, 1962). *The Essays of Montaigne.* E. J. Treichmann, trans. (London: Oxford University Press, 1953),180.

42. Francis Parkman, *France and England in North America* (New York: Literary Classics of the United States, 1983), 131.

43. J. H. Elliott, *The Old World and the New 1492–1650* (Cambridge: Cambridge University Press, 1970, rpt. 1992); *Spain and Its World 1500–1700* (New Haven: Yale University Press, 1989); Anthony Pagden, *The Fall of Natural Man: The American Indian and the Origins of Comparative Ethnography* (Cambridge: Cambridge University Press, 1982, rev. 1986); *Spanish Imperialism and the Political Imagination* (New Haven: Yale University Press, 1990); *European Encounters with the New World: From Renaissance to Romanticism* (New Haven: Yale University Press, 1993); Cornelius Jaenen, "Characteristics of French-Amerindian Contact in New France" in Stanley H. Palmer, ed. *Essays on the History of North American Discovery and Exploration* (College Station: Texas A & M University Press, 1988), 79–102.

44. See R. A. Gutiérrez, *When Jesus Came, the Corn Mothers Went Away: Marriage, Sexuality, and Power in New Mexico, 1500–1846* (Stanford: Stanford University Press, 1991), 48. Octavio Paz considers La Malinche to be a figure that plays out the conflict and contradictions in the Mexican past: she is to be embraced and scorned at the same time. See his *El labertino de la soledad* (Mexico: Fondo de Cultura Economica, 1959), esp. 78–79.

45. Leon-Portilla, 3; Díaz, 86–7, see below. For a suggestive and influential discussion of go-betweens in the context of Herodotus, Díaz and Montaigne, see Stephen Greenblatt, *Marvelous Possessions: The Wonder of the New World* (Chicago: University of Chicago Press, 1991), 119–51.

46. Leon-Portilla, 125. See Bernardino de Sahagún, *Florentine Codex: General History of the Things of New Spain Book 12,* trans. Arthur J. O. Anderson and Charles E. Dibble (Santa Fe, NM: The School of American Research and University of Utah, 1975).

47. Díaz, 58–59.

48. *Ibid.,* 61.

49. *Ibid.,* 65. Y desque Cortés le oyó, dió muchas gracias á Dios por todo, y le dijo que, mediante Dios, que d'él sería bien mirado y gratificado. Y le preguntó por la tierra é pueblos. (I 106)

50. *Ibid.,* 65–6. For an interesting account of the mixing of religions as opposed to a polarized idea of colonial religions in a specific time and locale, see Kenneth Mills, *Idolatry and Its Enemies: Colonial Andean Religion and Extirpation, 1640–1750* (Princeton: Princeton University Press, 1997), esp. 3–5.

51. 65. Y luego le preguntó por el Gonzalo Guerrero, é dijo que estaba casado y tenía tres hijos, y que tenía labrada la cara é horadadas las orejas y el bezo de abajo, y que era hombre de la mar, natural de Palos, y que los indios le tienen por esforzado; y que había poco más de un año que cuando vinieron á la Punta de Cotoche una capitanía con tres navíos (parece ser que fueron cuando venimos los de Francisco Hernández de Córdoba), que él fué inventor que nos diesen la guerra que nos dieron, y que vino él allí por capitán, juntamente con un cacique de un gran pueblo, según ya he dicho en lo de Francisco Hernández de Córdoba. É cuando Cortés lo oyó dijo: "En verdad que le querría haber á las manos, porque jamás será bueno dejársele. (I 106)

52. Axtell, *Invasion,* 302–5, see Inga Clendinnen, *Ambivalent Conquests: Maya and Spaniard in Yucatan, 1517–1570* (New York: Cambridge University Press, 1987); Cornelius Jaenen, *Friend and Foe: Aspects of French-Amerindian Cultural Contact in the Sixteenth and Seventeenth Centuries* (New York: Columbia University Press, 1976), "Charactersitics"; Wright, 17–18.

53. Donald Chipman, "Isabel Moctezuma: Pioneer of *Mestizaje,*" in D. Sweet and G. Nash, ed. *Struggle and Survival in Colonial America* (Berkeley: University of California Press, 1981), 214–27, 216.

54. Whatley, "Introduction," Léry, *History,* xix.

55. Editions in 1578, 1580, 1585, 1594, 1599–1600, 1611.

56. Léry, 55.

57. *Ibid.,* 43.

58. *Ibid.*

59. *Ibid.*

60. *Ibid.,* 153.

61. *Ibid.*

62. *Ibid.,* 128.

63. *Ibid.*

64. *Ibid.,* 132, see 246n14.

65. *Ibid.,* 132.

66. *Ibid.,* 133.

67. *Ibid.*, 7.
68. *Ibid.*, 140.
69. *Ibid.*
70. *Ibid.*, 141.
71. *Ibid.*, 140.
72. Léry, (1585 ed.), 280–81, qtd. in Léry, 248n14.
73. Léry (1580 ed.), 141.
74. *Ibid.*
75. *Ibid.*
76. *Ibid.*
77. *Ibid.*, 142.
78. *Ibid.*, 144, see 142.
79. *Ibid.*, 144.
80. *Ibid.*, 145.
81. *Ibid.*
82. *Ibid.*, 161.
83. *Ibid.*, 162.
84. *Ibid.*
85. *Ibid.*, 163.
86. *Ibid.*, 74–75.
87. *Ibid.*, 75–77.
88. *Ibid.*, 163.
89. *Ibid.*
90. *Ibid.*
91. *Ibid.*
92. *Ibid.*, 163–64.
93. *Ibid.*, 164.
94. *Ibid.*, 170.
95. *Ibid.*
96. *Ibid.*
97. *Ibid.*
98. *Ibid.*, 171.
99. *Ibid.*
100. *Ibid.*
101. *Ibid.*
102. *Ibid.*
103. Samuel de Champlain, *Works*, ed. H. P. Biggar, vols 1–6 (Toronto: Champlain Society, 1922–36). See Peter Hulme, *Colonial Encounters: Europe and the Native Caribbean 1492–1797* (1986. London: Routledge, 1992); Jaenen, *Friend and Foe.*
104. Champlain, 188, see IV: 138: The original reads: "Aussi ie vis mon garçon qui vint habillé à la sauuage, qui se loua du traictement des sauuages, selon leurs pays, & me fit entendre tout ce qu'il auoit veu en son yuernement, & ce qu'il auoit apris desdicts sauuages" (II 187–8, see IV: 138).
105. *Ibid.*, IV: 118.
106. *Ibid.* IV: 247.
107. *Ibid.* III: 213: The original is "tant pour passer son temps, que pour voir le pays, & apprendre leur langue & façon de viure" (III: 213).
108. *Ibid.*, 213–26.
109. *Ibid.*, III: 221–2. The original reads: "s'il n'estoit pas de la nation des François qui leur faisoient la guerre: sur ce il leur fist responce qu'il estoit d'vne autre natiõ meilleure, qui ne desiroient que d'auoir leur cognoissance, & amitié, ce qu'ils ne voulurēt croire, ains se

jetterent sur luy, & luy arracherent les ongles auec les dents, le bruslerēt auec des tisōs ardens, & luy arracherēt la barbe poil à poil, neātmoins cōtre la volōté du chef" (III 221–2).

110. *Ibid.*, V: 97, see III 213.

111. *Ibid.*, V: 132; the original is: "Le truchement Bruslé à qui l'on donnoit cent pistolles par an, pour inciter les sauuages à venir à la traitte, ce qui estoit de tres-mauuais exēple, d'enuoyer ainsi des persōnes si malviuãs, que l'on eust deub chastier seueremēt, car l'on recognoissoit cet homme pour estre fort vicieux, & adonné aux femmes; mais que ne fait faire l'esperance du gain, qui passe par dessus toutes considerations" (V: 132).

112. *Ibid.*, VI: 99; the original is: "où ie vy Estienne Bruslé truchement des Hurons, qui s'estoient mis au service de l'Anglois, & Marsolet, ausquels ie fis vne remonstrance touchant leur infidelité, tant enuers le Roy qu'à leur patrie, ils me dirent qu'ils auoient esté pris par force, c'est ce qui n'est pas croyable, car en ces choses prendre vn homme par force ce seroit plustot esperer deseruice qu'vne fidelité" (VI: 99).

113. *Ibid.*, VI: 99–100; the original reads: "encore vous qui auez esté esleuvez petits garçons en ce lieux, vendant maintenant ceux qui vous ont mis le pain à la main" (VI: 99–100).

114. *Ibid.*, VI: 101.

115. *Ibid.*, VI: 102.

116. Neil Salisbury, "Squanto: Last of the Patuxets, " in D. Sweet and G. Nash, ed. *Struggle and Survival in Colonial America* (Berkeley: University of California Press, 1981), 228–46, 241–2.

117. William Bradford, *Of Plymouth Plantation 1620–1647,* ed. Samuel Eliot Morison (New York: Alfred A. Knopf, 1952, rpt. 1991), 81.

118. See Hart, "Images," 1994.

119. Bradford, 81.

120. See *ibid.*, 81n.2.

121. *Ibid.*, 82.

122. *Ibid.*, 81n.3, 83 n.8–9.

123. *Ibid.*, 83, see *Purchas His Pilgrimes* IV: 1778.

124. Bradford 83.

125. *Ibid.*, 84, see 83.

126. *Ibid.*, 85.

127. *Ibid.*, 87.

128. *Ibid.*, 114.

129. Reuben Thwaites, *The Jesuit Relations and Allied Documents: Travels and Explorations of the Jesuit Missionaries in New France* (Cleveland: Burrows, 1896–1901), 73 vols, vol. 14: 17–21; George M. Wrong, *The Rise and Fall of New France* (New York: Macmillan, 1939), 134; Trigger, *Natives and Newcomers,* 194–96.

130. Bernal Díaz, *The Conquest of New Spain,* trans. J. M. Cohen (Harmondsworth: Penguin, 1963, rpt. 1983), 65.

131. *Ibid.*, 73.

132. *Ibid.*, 81.

133. Clendinnen, 18. See Gonzalo Fernández de Oviedo y Valdés, *Historia general y natural de las Indias (1535–1547)* (Madrid, 1959), 32:3, 6; Bernal Díaz del Castillo, *La Conquista de La Nueva España.* 4 vols. (Paris and Buenos Aires: Sociedad de Ediciones Louis-Michaud, n.d.), ch. 29; Diego de Landa, *Landa's Relación de las cosas de Yucatán,* trans. and ed. Alfred M. Tozzer (Cambridge, MA: Peabody Museum, Harvard University, 1941), 8 n.38. For other discussions of White Indians, see Jaenen, *Friend and Foe,* "Characteristics"; Wright, 17–18.

134. Francis Parkman, *The Parkman Reader,* ed. Samuel Eliot Morison (Boston: Little, Brown and Company, 1955, rpt. 1970), 339–40. Parkman gives another example of a Frenchman buying an English woman from the Natives during Queen Anne's War (1703–1713), but this time her husband ransomed her; see ibid., 368.

135. Pierre de Charlevoix, *Journal of a Voyage to North America* (Chicago: The Caxton Club, 1923), trans. Loiuse Phelps Kellog, 2 vols, vol. 2: 108; Hector de Crèvecoeur, *Letters from an American Farmer* (Gloucester, MA: P. Smith, 1968), 215.

136. Benjamin Franklin to Peter Collinson, May 9, 1753, in Leonard W. Labaree, ed., *Papers of Benjamin Franklin* (New Haven: Yale University Press, 1959), 36 vols, vol. 4: 481–2. The work of James Axtell has called this and other eighteenth-century instances of the White Indian to my attention; see his "The White Indians," (1985), 302–27. See also, for instance, Erwin H. Ackerknecht, "White Indians: Psychological and Physiological Peculiarities of White Children Abducted and Reared by North American Indians," *Bulletin of the History of Medicine* 15 (1944), 15–36; J. Norman Heard, *White into Red: A Study of the Assimilation of White Persons Captured by Indians* (Metuchen, NJ: Scarecrow Press, 1973); Gary B. Nash, *Red, White, and Black: The Peoples of Early America.* 2nd. ed. (Englewood Cliffs, NJ.: Prentice-Hall 1982).

137. Thomas Flanagan, *Louis 'David' Riel: 'Prophet of the New World* (Toronto: University of Toronto Press, 1979), 8, see 5–6.

138. Natalie Zemon Davis, *Fiction in the Archives: Pardon Tales and Their Tellers in Sixteenth-century France* (Stanford: Stanford University Press, 1987).

Chapter 6

1. All citations and quotations from *The Tempest* are from William Shakespeare, *The Tempest,* ed. Frank Kermode (1954. London: Methuen, 1958). For a discussion of earlier criticism of the play, see Kermode, Introduction, *The Tempest,* lxxxi. See August Wilhelm Schlegel, *Course of Lectures on Dramatic Art and Literature,* trans. John Black, 2nd ed., 2 vols (London: J. Templeton; J. R. Smith, 1840), 2: 184-87; *Literary Criticism of James Russell Lowell,* ed. Herbert F. Smith (Lincoln: University of Nebraska Press, 1969), 214. I thank Jean-Marie Maguin, Angela Maguin and Charles Whitworth for their invitation to give an earlier version of this chapter as a seminar at their Centre D'Études Et De Recherches Élisabéthaines, Université Paul Valéry (Montpellier III) in March 1994; for an earlier and different version of this research, see "Redeeming *The Tempest:* Romance and Politics," *Cahiers Élisabéthains* 49 (1996): 23–38. Since then, books have appeared on this topic as well as on Shakespeare's *The Tempest.* For different views of the postcolonial, see, for example, *Post-Colonial Shakespeares,* ed. Ania Loomba and Martin Orkin (New York: Routledge, 1998) and Imtiaz H. Habib, *Shakespeare and Race: Postcolonial Praxis in the Early Modern Period* (Lanham, MD: University Press of America, 2000). For a reader that places *The Tempest* in the context of later works like Daniel Dafoe's *Robinson Crusoe,* Charlotte Brontë's *Jane Eyre,* Joseph Conrad's *Heart of Darkness,* Rudyard Kipling's *Kim,* James Joyce's *Ulysses,* E. M Forster's *A Passage to India* and Salman Rushdie's *The Satanic Verses,* see *Post-colonial Theory and English Literature: A Reader,* ed. Peter Childs (Edinburgh: Edinburgh University Press, 1999); on *The Tempest,* see *Critical Essays on Shakespeare's "The Tempest,"* ed. Virginia Mason Vaughan and Alden T. Vaughan (New York: G. K. Hall, 1998); H. R. Coursen, *"The Tempest": A Guide to the Play* (Westport, CT: Greenwood Press, 2000); *"The Tempest" and Its Travels,* ed. Peter Hulme and William H. Sherman (London: Reaktion Books; Philadelphia: University of Pennsylvania Press, 2000).

2. Aimé Cesaire, *Une Tempête: D'Après "la Tempête" de Shakespeare—Adaptation pour un théâtre nègre* (Paris: Éditions du Seuil, 1961). See Thomas A. Hale, "Sur Une tempête d'Aimé Cesaire," *Études Littéraires* 6 (1973): 21–34. For early debates of imperialism and Shakespeare, see Daniel Wilson, *Caliban: the Missing Link* (London: Macmillan, 1873) and W. T. Stead, "First Impressions of the Theatre," *Review of Reviews* 30 (October 1904): 360–67. For discussions of this postcolonial use of Shakespeare, Charlotte H. Bruner, "The Meaning of Caliban in Black Literature Today," *Comparative Literature Studies.* 13 (1976): 240–53; Trevor R. Griffiths, "'This Island's Mine:' Caliban and Colonialism," *Yearbook of English Studies* 13 (1983): 159–80; Diana Brydon, "Re-writing The Tempest,"

World Literature Written in English [*WLWE*] 23 (1984): 75–88; Peter Hulme, "Prospero and Caliban," *Colonial Encounters: Europe and the Native Caribbean 1492–1797* (London; Routledge, 1986), 89–134; Rob Nixon, "Caribbean and African Appropriations of *The Tempest,*" *Critical Inquiry* 13.3 (1987): 557–78; Laura Donaldson, "The Miranda Complex: Colonialism and Question of Feminist Reading," *Diacritics* (1988): 65–77; Jonathan Hart, "Traces, Resistances and Contradictions: Canadian and International Perspectives on Post-Colonial Theories," ARACHNE 1.1 (1994): 68–93.

3. See also Frantz Fanon, *Peau noire, masques blancs* (Paris: Seuil, 1952); George Lamming, *The Pleasures of Exile* (London: M. Joseph, 1960); C. L. R. James, *The Black Jacobins: Toussaint Louverture and the San Domingo Revolution* (New York: Vintage, 1963); Dominique O. Mannoni, *Prospero and Caliban: The Psychology of Colonization,* trans. Pamela Powesland (New York: Praeger, 1964); Edward Braithwaite, *Islands* (Oxford: Oxford University Press, 1969); Lemuel Johnson, *Highlife for Caliban* (Ann Arbor: Ardis, 1973); Roberto Fernandez Retamar, "Caliban: Notes Toward a Discussion of Culture in Our America," *Massachusetts Review* 15 (1974): 7–72.

4. Lemuel Johnson, *Highlife for Caliban* (1973; Trenton, NJ: Africa World Press, 1995), 39.

5. See Anthony Pagden, *Spanish Imperialism and the Political Imagination* (New Haven: Yale University Press, 1990), 10–11.

6. This is a question that has long since interested me; see, for instance, Jonathan Hart and Terry Goldie, "Postcolonial Theory," *Encyclopedia of Contemporary Literary Theory* (Toronto: University of Toronto Press, 1993), 155–8 and my "Translating and Resisting Empire: Cultural Appropriation and Post-colonial Studies" in *Borrowed Power: Essays in Cultural Appropriation,* ed. Bruce Ziff and Pratima Rao (New Brunswick, NJ: Rutgers University Press, 1997), 137–68.

7. *Ibid.,* xviii–xix.

8. *Ibid.,* xix.

9. *Ibid.,* xxi. See also Leslie Hotson, *I, William Shakespeare* (New York: Oxford University Press, 1938), 225–6.

10. Kermode, lvi.

11. Northrop Frye, Foreword to George M. Logan and Gordon Teskey, ed, *Unfolded Tales: Essays in Renaissance Romance* (Ithaca, NY: Cornell University Press, 1989), ix.

12. Geoffrey H. Hartman, *The Fate of Reading And Other Essays* (Chicago: University of Chicago Press, 1975); Northrop Frye, *A Natural Perspective: The Development of Shakespearian Comedy* (New York: Harcourt, Brace & World, 1965), 88; see A. Kent Hieatt, "*Cymbeline* and the Intrusion of Lyric into Romance Narrative: *Sonnets,* 'A Lover's Complaint', Spenser's *Ruins of Rome,*" 117–18 and Patricia Parker, "Romance and Empire: Anachronistic *Cymbeline,*" 189–208 both in G. Logan and G. Teskey, ed., *Unfolded Tales* (Ithaca: Cornell University Press, 1989), 191–207.

13. For a few examples of interesting work over the past decade or so, see Paul N. Siegel, "Historical Ironies in *The Tempest,*" *Shakespeare Jahrbuch* 119 (1983): 104–11; Paul Brown, "This thing of darkness . . ." in *Political Shakespeare,* eds. Jonathan Dollimore and Alan Sinfield (Ithaca and London: Cornell University Press, 1985), 48–71; Thomas Cartelli, "Prospero in Africa: *The Tempest* as Colonialist Text and Pretext," *Shakespeare Reproduced: The Text in History and Ideology,* ed. Jean Howard and Marion O' Connor (London: Methuen, 1987), 99–115; Allen Carey-Webb, *Making Subject(s): Literature and the Emergence of National Identity* (New York and London: Garland, 1998), 57–93.

14. See Jonathan Hart, "Introduction: Narrative, Narrative Theory, Drama: the Renaissance." Special Issue/ Numéro Spécial. *Renaissance Narrative and Drama/ Récit et Théâtre à la Renaissance,* ed. Jonathan Hart, *Canadian Review of Comparative Literature/ Revue Canadienne de Littérature Comparée* 18 2/3 (1991): 117–18, 145–65.

15. Here I use the word "direct" advisedly. There is other evidence of the "American" dimension of this play. If at one time, too little emphasis was placed on the New World in *The Tempest,* in recent years this dimension has eclipsed all other aspects. What I have been

suggesting is a balance between the aesthetic and political elements. In arguing for that intricate relation, it may seem that I am playing down the utopian or New World thematics, but such a position is only apparent because elsewhere I have recognized the importance of the play for colonialism and post-colonialism. Now, in response to so much discussion of this dimension, I am saying that we should look at as many views of *The Tempest,* as possible (see Hart, "Perspectives" *Arachne* 1 [1994]: 78, Griffiths, "'This Island's Mine,'" *Yearbook of English Studies* 13 [1983]: 159–80). In his recent Oxford edition of the play, Stephen Orgel provides a useful reminder that it is too easy to underestimate utopia and the New World in this drama which Malone first called attention to in 1808 (Stephen Orgel, Introduction, William Shakespeare. *The Tempest* [1987. Oxford: Oxford University Press, 1994], 31–6). For instance, in the body of this essay, I mention Gonzalo's utopian speech (II.i.145–62). Both Kermode and Orgel remind us that this speech is taken almost verbatim from Florio's translation of Montaigne's "Of the Cannibals" and echoes Renaissance thought about the relation of Europe to the New World. Shakespeare uses Strachey's account of Bermuda. The playwright associated with members of the Virginia Company like Southampton, Pembroke, Christopher Brooke, Dudley Digges and others. Other allusions to the New World exist besides "the still-vexed Bermudas," as E. E. Stoll argued in 1927 (Orgel 31–2; Charles Mills Gayley, *Shakespeare and the Founders of Liberty in America* [New York: Macmillan, 1917]; Leslie Hotson *I, William Shakespeare, Do Appoint Thomas Russell, Esquire* [London: Cape, 1937], 203–36; E. E. Stoll, "Certain Fallacies and Irrelevancies in the Literary Scholarship of the Day." *Studies in Philology* 24 [1927], 487). Charles Frey, as Orgel notes, suggests that travel narratives gave Shakespeare models of behavior in the exchange between European and Native (Orgel 33; Charles Frey, " *The Tempest* and the New World, " *Shakespeare Quarterly* 30 (1979): 34; Philip Brockbank, "The Tempest: Conventions of Art and Empire," *Later Shakespeare,* ed. J. R. Brown and B. Harris (London: Arnold, 1966), 183–201. From the time of Columbus into the seventeenth century, free love, utopia and cannibalism recur in the New World narratives in word and iconography. As reading Thomas Harriot shows, there is a typology between Old World savages, such as the ancient Britons, and New World Natives (Orgel 34, Thomas Harriot, *A Briefe and True Report of the New Found Land of Virginia* [London, 1590] sig Er). A tension exists in Shakespeare's play between notions of the Natives as predatory (Purchas, John Smith) and the ideas that the Europeans are thus (Montaigne) (see Orgel, 35–6, Stephen Greenblatt, "Learning to Curse," *First Images of America,* ed. Fredi Chiapelli [Berkeley: University of California Press, 1976], vol. 2: 561–80).

16. L. C. Green and Olive P. Dickason, *The Law of Nations and the New World* (Edmonton: University of Alberta Press, 1989), 221, 235, see 87; Neal Salisbury, "Squanto: Last of the Patuxets," David G. Sweet and Gary B. Nash ed. *Struggle and Survival in Colonial America* (Berkeley: University of California Press, 1981), 239–40.

17. See Sidney Lee, "The American Indian in Elizabethan England," *Scribners* 42 (1907): 313–30.

18. Kermode, xl.

19. See Kermode, xxxii, 141.

20. See Kermode, 145–47.

21. This practice of kidnapping the aboriginal peoples of the New World begins with Columbus and, for the English, appears to have occurred earlier than Kermode (62) says. For instance, in *Sixteenth Century North America: The Land and the People as Seen by the Europeans* (Berkeley: University of California Press, 1971), Carl Ortwin Sauer notes the practice among the Portuguese: The two ships of Gaspar and Miguel Vaz Corte Real, returning from the coast of Newfoundland, "brought back to Lisbon several score of natives, male and female, described in attentive detail. They were Indians, no Eskimos, and are thought to have been Beothuks, inhabitants of Newfoundland"

(13). Sauer talks about voyages from Bristol to north of Newfoundland. In March 1501 Henry VII gave letters patent to six men of Bristol, three of whom being originally from the Azores, including John Fernandes, to explore any seas yet unknown to Christians. Two voyages occurred, the ships of second "returning with three savages, presumably Eskimos" (15).

22. See Kermode, 122.

23. Kermode, xxxvii, 66; see Cawley, "Shakespeare's Use of the Voyagers," *PMLA* 41 (1926): 688–726.

24. *The Four Voyages of Columbus: A History in Eight Documents, Including Five By Christopher Columbus, In The Original Spanish, With English Translations* Cecil Jane trans. and ed. (1930, 1933. New York: Dover, 1988), 8–10. See Jonathan Hart, "Images of the Native in Renaissance Encounter Narratives," *ARIEL* 25 (October 1994): 55–76. Other related papers that I gave at Cambridge, Warwick, Deakin and Melbourne from April to mid-July 1994 provide other points of view of the European and Native encounters as well as earlier work noted in earlier chapters. For instance, I gave a talk, "Representing the New World," for the Comparative American Studies at University of Warwick, May 4, 1994. My thanks to John King and Anthony Macfarlane. For a wide context, see Stephen Greenblatt, "Learning to Curse," Vol. 2: 561–80. Jeffrey Knapp, *An Empire Nowhere: England, America, and Literature From Utopia to The Tempest* (Berkeley: University of California Press, 1992).

25. See Northrop Frye, *Natural Perspective* (1965): 87.

26. See Kermode, xxxii, 88.

27. I discuss Morgann briefly in *Theater and World,* 129, 230.

28. E. K. Chambers, *William Shakespeare: A Study of Facts and Problems* (Oxford: Clarendon Press, 1930) vol. 1. 94, cited in Kermode, xxxviii.

Chapter 7

1. Terry Eagleton, "In the Gaudy Supermarket," *London Review of Books* (May 13, 1999): 3. He is reviewing Gayatri Chakravorty Spivak, *A Critique of Post-Colonial Reason: Toward a History of the Vanishing Present* (Cambridge, MA: Harvard University Press, 1999). Often the most interesting critics and theorists, like artists and writers, have many dimensions to their work and this is true of postcolonial theorists. For instance, just to note one of many other aspects of three leading scholars in postcolonial studies, Edward Said has a strong interest in music; Gayatri Spivak in translation; and Homi K. Bhabha in art. I have discussed Said's and Spivak's work in some detail elsewhere and I would like to call attention to Bhabha's work in art in addition to his subtle and suggestive contributions in understanding the ambiguities of colonial and "post-colonial" attitudes and cultures. See, for example, Bhabha's essays in *Negotiating Rapture: The Power of Art to Transform Lives,* ed. Richard Francis (Chicago: Museum of Contemporary Art, 1996) and Anish Kapoor, *Anish Kapoor: With Essays by Homi K. Bhabha and Pier Luigi Tazzi* (London: Hayward Gallery; Berkeley: University of California Press, 1998).

2. Frank Kermode, *The Sense of an Ending: Studies in the Theory of Fiction* (New York: Oxford University Press, 1967).

3. Some of the many recent books on the postcolonial that should give an idea of the variety in the field are Françoise Lionnet, *Postcolonial Representations: Women, Literature, Identity* (Ithaca, NY: Cornell University Press, 1995); *The Post-Colonial Literature of Lusophone Africa,* ed. Patrick Chabal, Moema Parente Augel, et al. (London: Hurst, 1996); *Postcolonial African Philosophy: A Critical Reader,* ed. Emmanuel Chukwudi Eze (Oxford: Blackwell, 1997*); The Politics of Multiculturalism in the New Europe: Racism, Identity, and Community,* ed. Tariq Modood and Pnina Werbner (London: Zed Books,

1997); *Postcolonialisme: décentrement, déplacement, dissémination,* ed. Abdelwahab Meddeb (Paris: Maisonneuve & Larose, 1997); Abraham Itty, *The Making of the Indian Atomic Bomb: Science, Secrecy and the Postcolonial State* (London: Zed Books, 1998); Sankaran Krishna, *Postcolonial Insecurities: India, Sri Lanka, and the Question of Nationhood* (Minneapolis: University of Minnesota Press, 1999); *Postcolonial Perspectives on the Cultures of Latin America and Lusophone Africa,* ed. Robin Fiddian (Liverpool: Liverpool University Press, 2000); *Postcolonial and Queer Theories: Intersections and Essays,* ed. John C. Hawley (Westport, Conn.: Greenwood Press, 2001). For one of my earlier views on postcolonialism, see (with Terry Goldie) "Postcolonial Theory," *Encyclopedia of Contemporary Literary Theory* (Toronto: University of Toronto Press, 1993), 155–8.

4. My thanks to Bruce Ziff and Pratima Rao for including in their collection an earlier version of this chapter and, more generally, for their help and encouragement: Jonathan Hart, "Translating and Resisting Empire: Cultural Appropriation and Post-colonial Studies," in *Borrowed Power: Essays in Cultural Appropriation,* ed. Bruce Ziff and Pratima Rao (New Brunswick, NJ: Rutgers University Press, 1997), 137–68. I also thank Jane Moore, Catherine Belsey, Christopher Norris, Terence Hawkes and others at the Centre for Critical and Cultural Theory (Cardiff) for their invitation and comments on my talk "Some Theoretical Difficulties in Postcolonial Studies" (January 1994) and Ken Ruthven and his colleagues at Melbourne (July 1994) for their invitation to give the paper "Colonialism and Postcolonialism," and for their questions. These two talks contained different versions of earlier material on the topic, some of which appears in a revised form in this chapter.

5. "Ventriloquy" is speaking for others, often while being unaware of doing so or pretending not to. It can also be a displacement of one voice on to another. Ventriloquy occurs as much in writing as in political speech. I had used this term for well over a decade before I began to think in the specific terms of cultural appropriation. I came to realize that voice appropriation was a kind of ventriloquy.

6. The Young-Rowell exchange I outline in this note is an example of what I am talking about in the text. James O. Young outlines three arguments against voice appropriation. First, members of one cultural group misrepresent other members of another cultural group and thereby harm them. Second, when a majority culture misrepresents a minority culture, it limits the audience the minority can reach in representing themselves. Third, when other cultural groups misrepresent cultures they steal the religious and cultural meaning of their stories and pictures. Young sets out to refute all three arguments, even the first, which he claims is the strongest, by means of finding exceptions or counter-arguments. Rather than rehearse Young's counter-arguments, I wish to stress only that he maintains that the representations by outsiders are not all harmful distortions. Taking up R. G. Collingwood's view in *The Principles of Art* (London, New York: Oxford University Press, 1958), he thinks that the artist should steal with both hands (similar to T.S. Eliot's view of great artists). Young argues that artists should take care in representing other cultures but should not give up artistic freedom. Artists should aim for aesthetic success, which precludes insensitive representations of minority cultures. John Rowell opposes Young's views and says that he would wish Eric Clapton well commercially if he were singing the blues but would not fund him if he applied for a government grant. In his rebuttal to Young, Rowell says that Young obscures the real issue, which is when a member of a dominant culture uses the material of a minority culture and even sometimes pretends to be from that group. Rowell does not see transcultural borrowing as the actual subject of the controversy. He argues that funding agencies should adopt a relativism that recognizes cultural difference.

7. Sally Kilmister, for instance, discusses music in terms of the relation to translation, gender and androgyny: she picks up on Carl Dahlhaus' topos of unsayability (related to the

classical topos, or rhetorical strategy, of inexpressibility) and its link with Theodor Adorno's view of music as a fetish and of listening as regression. Kilmister also connects unsayability (that which is unutterable) with Virginia Woolf's "Impressions of Bayreuth," an ambivalent critique of this unsayable nineteenth-century music because this essay represents "the difficulties inherent in either an appropriation or a repudiation of music's seductive lure." Sally Kilmister, "Aesthetic and Music: The Appropriation of the Other," *Women: A Cultural Review* 3 (1) 1992: 31.

8. *The Compact Oxford English Dictionary,* 2nd ed. (Oxford 1991), 1493.
9. Harold G. Fox, *The Canadian Law of Copyright and Industrial Designs* (2nd ed.) (Toronto: Carswell Co., 1967), 18.
10. Rosemary J. Coombe, "The Properties of Culture and the Politics of Possessing Identity: Native Claims in the Cultural Appropriation Controversy," *Canadian Journal of Law and Jurisprudence* 6 (2) (1993): 251–52, 259.
11. Coombe, "The Properties of Culture and the Politics of Possessing Identity," 253.
12. *Ibid.,* 254–55.
13. *Ibid.,* 270–72.
14. Loretta Todd, "Notes on Appropriation," *Parallelogramme* 16 (Summer 1990): 32, quoted in Coombe, "The Properties of Culture and the Politics of Possessing Identity," 285.
15. Coombe, "The Properties of Culture and the Politics of Possessing Identity," 285.
16. Amanda Pask, "Cultural Appropriation and the Law: An Analysis of the Legal Regime Concerning Culture," *Intellectual Property Journal* 8 (1993): 86.
17. Pask, "Cultural Appropriation and the Law," 86.
18. See Leslie C. Green and Olive Dickason, *The Law of Nations and the New World* (Edmonton: University of Alberta Press, 1989).
19. See Tim Rowse, *After Mabo: Interpreting Indigenous Traditions* (Carlton, Vic.: Melbourne University Press, 1993). The case of New Zealand is interesting. Two of New Zealand's early governors had experience that might have prevented conflict and war in the settlement. For instance, Robert Fitzroy was a captain of the *Beagle* and had seen the wasting of the Yahgan in Tierra del Fuego; George Grey had become an ethnologist while serving in Australia. See Jean E. Rosenfeld, *The Island Broken in Two Halves: Land and Renewal Movements Among the Maori of New* Zealand (University Park: Pennsylvania State University Press, 1999), 125; Rosenfeld's study brings together religion, anthropology and history; see also Keith Sinclair, *The Origins of the Maori Wars* (Wellington: New Zealand University Press, 1957) and *A History of New Zealand* (Auckland: Penguin Books, 1988); John Williams, *Politics of the New Zealand Maori: Protest and Cooperation, 1891–1909* (Auckland: Oxford University Press, 1969).
20. Rowse, 8, see 4–9. See Brian Keon-Cohen, "Case note on 'Eddie Mabo and Ors vs. the State of Queensland,'" *Aboriginal Law Bulletin* 2 (1992): 22–3.
21. Rowse, 21.
22. See Janice Hladki, "Problematizing the Issue of Cultural Appropriation," *Alternate Routes* 11 (1994): 95–119, esp. 95–96; and Francis Barker, Peter Hulme, Margaret Iversen, eds., *Colonial Discourse/Postcolonial Theory* (Manchester: Manchester University Press, 1994), 4.
23. See Hart, "Traces" (1994).
24. Anthony Pagden, *The Fall of Natural Man: The American Indian and the Origins of Comparative Ethnography* (Cambridge: Cambridge University Press, 1982, rev. 1986), esp. 14–26.
25. See my other studies in the field, especially "Opposition from Within," a chapter in *Comparing Empires* (New York: Palgrave, forthcoming).
26. For a more extensive discussion of this case, see Jonathan Hart, *Representing the New World: The English and French Uses of the Example of Spain* (New York and London: Palgrave, 2001), ch. 2.

27. Pagden, *The Fall of Natural Man*, 15. The following discussion draws on *ibid.*, 15–26.
28. *Ibid.*, 16.
29. Aristotle, *De mirabilibus auscultationibus* 836a: 10–15, cited in Pagden, *Fall,* 16.
30. Aristotle, *Politics* 1338b: 19 and *Nichomachean Ethics* 1148b: 19ff., cited in Pagden, *Fall,* 18.
31. Pagden, *Fall,* 19.
32. In some of my other work, like *Representing the New World,* I have discussed more of these examples. In *Comparing Empires* I devote a chapter, "Opposition from Within," to internal otherness and another, "Promoting Empire," to promotion.
33. Ernst Breisach, *Historiography: Ancient, Medieval & Modern* (Chicago: University of Chicago Press, 1983), 178–79. Breisach's various references to examples of *translatio imperii* have been important for my framing of this myth.
34. Pagden, *Fall,* 10 for this and the discussion below. For Oviedo, see *Comparing Empires.*
35. Thomas B. Macaulay, "History," in *The Complete Writings,* 10 vols. (Boston and New York, 1901), vol. I: 276, quoted in Breisach, 251. For my preceding discussion, see Breisach, pp. 213, 243, 245.
36. The case of Canada is appropriate here. D. M. R. Bentley begins his article on pre-Confederation English poetry in *The Canadian Encyclopedia* with J. MacKay's interrogative address to the poets of the classical and European tradition in *Quebec Hill* (1797): "Ye who, in stanzas, celebrate the Po,/ Or teach the Tyber in your strains to flow,/ How would you toil for numbers to proclaim/ The liquid grandeur of St Laurence' Stream?" Quoted in D. M. R. Bentley, "Poetry in English," *The Canadian Encyclopedia* (Edmonton: Hurtig Publishers, 1985), 3: 1431. In 1797 MacKay is still looking to European models and wonders how the poets of the European tradition could translate themselves from Italy and Rome to represent the great St. Lawrence in Canada. This problem of translating tradition, of seeing and of recognition, is as much a difficulty for the poet as for the historian and literary theorist. We do not have John Cabot's narrative about Canada, but from Jacques Cartier onward we have responses to a new and strange land, and from the seventeenth-century accounts of Canada as a French and British colony. The problems the Spanish had with seeing the New World as new, the French and the English had read about. But they made some of the same mistakes.

    And in postcolonial Canada some of the disjunctions continue between European and Amerindian, between Western ways and other ways of seeing. I want to concentrate on the way the precolonial and colonial haunt the present and make it difficult to speak about the postcolonial in Canada. There are tensions between French and English on the one hand and the various Amerindian nations on the other. This old conflict has been complicated in this period by vast movements of other Europeans to Canada, especially in the twentieth century, and in the past twenty years of Asian and Caribbean cultures. Since about 1968 the Canadian government has pursued a policy of multiculturalism, something I argued in the 1980s that needed to be recognized in the study of Canadian literature. The work of writers as successful as Michael Ondaatje, the co-winner of the Booker Prize for *The English Patient,* illustrates my point. Ondaatje came from Sri Lanka to Canada and went to Canadian universities. His own relation to the empire and the relation he found in Canada complicate the notion of postcolonialism in Canadian culture. The question of identity haunts postcolonialism even when postmodernism declares that we fashion our own subjectivities.
37. Trinh T. Minh-ha, *Woman, Native, Other: Writing Postcoloniality and Feminism* (Bloomington: Indiana University Press, 1988), 63–65.
38. Bartolomé de Las Casas, "Synopsis," *A Short Account of the Destruction of the Indies* (1542, pub. 1552) trans. Nigel Griffin, intro. Anthony Pagden (London: Penguin Books, 1992), 3.
39. Anthony Pagden, *European Encounters in the New World* (New Haven, CT: Yale University Press, 1993), 1–15; Ross Chambers, "No Montagues Without Capulets: Some

Thoughts on 'Cultural Identity'," ed. Jonathan Hart and Richard W. Bauman, *Exploration in Difference: Law, Culture, and Politics* (Toronto: University of Toronto Press, 1996), 25–66.

40. See Jonathan Hart, "Images of the Native in Renaissance Encounter Narratives," 55–76. For more on Montaigne, see my *Comparing Empires* (forthcoming).

41. Michel de Montaigne, *On Cannibals,* trans. and ed. J. M. Cohen (Harmondsworth: Penguin, 1963), 119.

42. See Trinh T. Minha-ha, *Woman, Native, Other: Writing Postcoloniality and Feminism;* Edward Said, "Representing the Colonized: Anthropology's Interlocutors," *Critical Inquiry* 15 (Winter 1989): 205–25.

43. This opposition from within is something I discuss in *Comparing Empires.*

44. This point relates to some discussions in this study and, mostly particularly, to the chapter "Opposition from Within" in *Comparing Empires.*

45. Montaigne, *On Cannibals,* 108–09.

46. See Ross Chambers, *Room for Maneuvre: Reading (the) Oppositional (in) Narrative* (Chicago, 1991); Chambers, "No Montagues Without Capulets," 1995; Stephen Greenblatt, *Marvelous Possessions: The Wonder of the New World* (Chicago: University of Chicago Press, 1991), 119–51.

47. See Ramón A. Gutiérrez, *When Jesus Came, the Corn Mothers Went Away: Marriage, Sexuality and Power in New Mexico* (Stanford: Stanford University Press, 1991), 48.

48. Miguel Leon-Portilla ed. *The Broken Spears: The Aztec Account of the Conquest of Mexico* (1959) (Boston: Beacon Press, 1993), 3; Bernal Díaz, *The Conquest of New Spain,* ed. and trans. J. M. Cohen (Harmondworth: Penguin Books, 1963, reprinted 1983), 86–87.

49. This is the matter of chapter 5.

50. Vine Deloria, Jr., "Afterword," *America in 1492: The World of the Indian Peoples Before the Arrival of Columbus,* ed. Alvin M. Joseph, Jr., (New York: Vintage Books, 1993) 429–30; Gordon Brotherston, *Image of the New World: The American Continent Portrayed in Native Texts* (London: Thames and Hudson, 1979), 15, 21; see Jonathan Hart, "Mediation in the Exchange Between Europeans and Native Americans in the Early Modern Period," special issue, *CRCL/RCLC* 22 (1995): 319–43.

51. See Tzvetan Todorov, *La Conquête de l'Amérique* (Paris: Seuil, 1982); Johannes Fabian, *Language and Colonial Power: The Appropriation of Swahili in the Former Belgian Congo 1880–1938* (Berkeley: University of California Press, 1986).

52. J. Jorge Klor de Alva, "Nahua Colonial Discourse and the Appropriation of the (European) Other," *Archives de Science Sociales des Religion* 77 (1992): 16.

53. *Ibid.,* 17.

54. *Ibid.,* 32.

55. See Chambers, *Room for Maneuvre* (1991): 245.

56. See Hart, "Images," 55–76.

57. Chambers, *Room for Maneuvre* (1991): 219.

58. Chambers, "No Montagues Without Capulets" (1995): 25–66.

59. Benita Parry, "Resistance Theory/Theorising Resistance or Two Cheers for Nativism," *Colonial Discourse/Postcolonial Theory,* ed. Francis Barker, Peter Hulme, Margaret Iversen, 193, see esp. 172–73.

60. Anne McClintock, "The Angel of Progress: Pitfalls of the Term 'Postcolonialism,'" *Colonial Discourse/Postcolonial Theory,* ed. Francis Barker, Peter Hulme, Margaret Iversen, 253–266; and, see Jonathan Hart, "Response to Shaffer and Brydon," *Arachnē* 1 (1994): 113–119, esp. 119.

61. Eagleton's discussion concentrates on the period from the eighteenth century onward, whereas Frye is talking about classical antecedents. See Terry Eagleton, *The Ideology of the Aesthetic* (Oxford: Blackwell, 1990) and Northrop Frye, *Anatomy of Criticism: Four Essays* (Princeton, NJ: Princeton University Press, 1957), 66–7.

62. Linda Alcoff, "The Problem of Speaking for Others," *Cultural Critique* 19–20 (Winter 1991–92): 5–32 at 9.

63. See *ibid.*, 22–23.

64. *Ibid.*, 24–27.

65. Homi Bhabha, *The Location of Culture* (London: Routledge, 1994), 1–6. On hybridity, see *ibid.*, 4, 207–09 and Bhabha, ed. *Nation and Narration* (London: Routledge, 1990), 4.

66. Quoted in Peter Wollen, "Tourism, Language, and Art," *New Formations* 12 (1990): 57.

67. Annie E. Coombes, "The Recalcitrant Object: Cultural Contact and the Question of Hybridity," *Colonial Discourse/Postcolonial Theory*, ed. Francis Barker, Peter Hulme, Margaret Iversen (Manchester: Manchester University Press, 1994), 89–90; see also Benita Parry, "Resistance Theory / Theorising Resistance or Two Cheers for Nativism," in same volume, 172–196, and Stuart Hall, "Cultural Identity and Diaspora," in *Identity, Community, Culture, Difference,* ed. Jonathan Rutherford (London: Lawrence & Wishart, 1990), 222–224.

68. Annie Coombes, "The Recalcitrant Object," 90.

69. *Ibid.*, 111.

70. Gareth Griffiths, "Imitation, Abrogation and Appropriation: The Production of the Post-Colonial Text," *Kunapipi* 9 (1987): 20.

71. See Jonathan Hart, "Traces, Resistances, and Contradictions: Canadian and International Perspectives on Postcolonial Theories," *Arachnē* 1 (1994): 68–93.

72. See Hart, "Traces, Resistances, and Contradictions," 84–87; Patrick Chamoiseau and Raphael Confiant, *Lettres créoles: Traces antillaises et continentales de la littérature: Haiti, Guadeloupe, Martinique, Guyane: 1635–1975* (Paris: Hatier, 1991); and George Lang, "Kribich, 'Cribiche', ou ecrevisse: l'avenir de l'eloge de la Creolite," ed. Danielle Deltel, *Convergences et divergences dans les littératures francophones* (Paris: L'Harmattan, 1992), 170–81.

73. Françoise Lionnet, "'Logiques Métisses': Cultural Appropriation and Postcolonial Representations," *College Literature* (10) 1992: 101.

74. See Aimé Césaire, *Une Tempête: D'apres la Tempête de Shakespeare—Adaptation pour un théâtre nègre* (Paris: Seuil, 1961); Frantz Fanon, *Peau noire, masques blancs* (Paris: Seuil, 1952); and Édouard Glissant, *Le Discours antillais* (Paris: Seuil, 1981).

75. Lionnet, "'Logiques Métisses,'" 105, 116.

76. See Hart, "Traces, Resistances, and Contradictions," 86–7.

77. See *ibid.*, 68–93.

78. See Linda Hutcheon, "'Circling the Downspout of Empire,'" *ARIEL* 20:4 (1989), esp. 150; Simon During, "Waiting for the Post: Some Relations Between Modernity, Colonization, and Writing," *Past the Last Post: Theorizing Colonialism and Post-Modernism,* ed. Ian Adam and Helen Tiffin (Calgary: University of Calgary Press, 1990), 23–45; Jonathan Hart, "Traces, Resistances, and Contradictions," 83–84, 87–88.

79. Jonathan Hart and Richard Bauman, eds., *Explorations in Difference: Law, Culture, and Politics.*

80. Arun P. Mukherjee, "Whose Post-colonialism and Whose Postmodernism?" *WLWE* 30 (1990): 1–9, esp. 2.

81. See Jonathan Hart, "The Book of Judges: Views Among the Critics," *Canadian Review of Comparative Literature (CRCL/RCLC)* 17 (1990): 115.

82. Edward W. Said, *Orientalism* (New York: Pantheon Books, 1978) and *Culture and Imperialism* (London and New York: Knopf, 1993). See, for instance, Said, "Orientalism Reconsidered," *Cultural Critique* 1 (1985); Rana Kabbani, *Europe's Myths of the Orient* (Bloomington: Indiana University Press, 1986); Nasrin Rahimieh, "Orientalism Revised," *CRCL* 16 (1989): 154–60; George Lang, "Through a Prism Darkly: 'Orientalism' in European-language African Writing," *Faces of Islam in African Literature*, ed. Kenneth

W. Harrow (Portsmouth, NH: Heinemann, 1991), 299–311; Lisa Lowe, *Critical Terrains: French and British Orientalisms* (Ithaca: Cornell University Press, 1991).

83. Said often returns to Conrad in his works as in his teaching. The passage I have in mind here is the one that Said uses as an epigraph to *Culture and Imperialism, ibid.*

84. See John A. Hobson, *Imperialism, A Study,* rev. ed. (London: A. Constable, 1905); Raymond Schwab, *La Renaissance Orientale* (Paris: Payot, 1950); he also cites William H. McNeill, *The Pursuit of Power: Technology, Armed Forces and Society Since 1000 A.D.* (Chicago: University of Chicago Press, 1983).

85. As Chomsky suggests in his comments on *Culture and Imperialism,* "Said helps us to understand who we are and what we must do if we aspire to be moral agents not servants of power." See, Edward W. Said, *Culture and Imperialism,* iii.

86. Said, *Culture and Imperialism,* xxii.

87. *Ibid.,* xxiii.

88. *Ibid.,* xxxi; Jonathan Hart, *Northrop Frye: The Theoretical Imagination* (London: Routledge, 1994) 164–190; Northrop Frye, *On Education* (Don Mills, ON: Fitzhenry & Whiteside, 1988).

89. See also Said, *Culture and Imperialism,* xxviii, and Anthony Pagden, *The Fall of Natural Man: The American Indian and the Origins of Comparative Ethnography,* esp. pp. 14–26.

90. See Hart, *Representing the New World,* especially 1–13.

91. Simon During, "Postmodernism or Postcolonialism?" *Landfall* 39 (1985): 366–80; "Postmodernism or Postcolonialism To-Day," *Textual Practice* 1 (1987): 32–47; and, "Waiting for the Post," 23–45, esp. p. 30. See also, Northop Frye, *The Bush Garden: Essays on the Canadian Imagination* (Toronto: Anansi, 1971).

92. A good summary of Riel's life and his role in the rebellions can be found in George F. G. Stanley, "Riel, Louis," *The Canadian Encyclopedia,* 1584–5. For a discussion of Riel's religion, see Thomas Flanagan, *Louis 'David' Riel: Prophet of the New World* (Toronto: University of Toronto Press, 1979).

93. Flanagan, *ibid.,* 8, see 5–6.

94. See Patrick Chamoiseau and Raphael Confiant, *Lettres créoles: Traces antillaises et continentales de la littérature: Haïti, Guadeloupe, Martinique, Guyane: 1635–1975* (Paris: Hatier, 1991); *Convergences et divergences dans les littératures francophones,* ed. Danielle Deltel.

Index